ALL IS CHANGE

Also by Lawrence Sutin

Divine Invasion: A Life of Philip K. Dick
Jack and Rochelle: A Holocaust Story of Love and Resistance
A Postcard Memoir
Do What Thou Wilt: A Life of Aleister Crowley

ALL IS CHANGE

THE TWO-THOUSAND-YEAR JOURNEY

OF BUDDHISM TO THE WEST

Lawrence Sutin

LITTLE, BROWN AND COMPANY

New York Boston London

Little, Brown and Company
Hachette Book Group USA
1271 Avenue of the Americas, New York, NY 10020
Visit our Web site at www.HachetteBookGroupUSA.com

First Edition: August 2006

Library of Congress Cataloging-in-Publication Data
Sutin, Lawrence.
   All is change : the two-thousand-year journey of Buddhism to the West / Lawrence
Sutin — 1st ed.
      p. cm.
   Includes bibliographical reference and index.
   ISBN-10: 0-316-74156-6
   ISBN-13: 978-0-316-74156-9
   1. Buddhism — Western countries — History 2. Buddhism — Relations.
3. Buddhism — Influence. I. Title.

BQ702.S88 2006
294.309182'1 — dc22   2006040824

10 9 8 7 6 5 4 3 2 1
Q-MART
Book design by Bernard Klein
Printed in the United States of America

For Mab and Sarah, the lights by which I write

The West is passing through a new Renaissance due to the sudden entry into its consciousness of a whole new world of ideas, shapes and fancies. Even as its consciousness was enlarged in the period of the Renaissance by the revelation of the classical culture of Greece and Rome, there is a sudden growth of the spirit to-day effected by the new inheritance of Asia with which India is linked up. For the first time in the history of mankind, the consciousness of the unity of the world has dawned on us. Whether we like it or not, East and West have come together and can no more part.

Sarvepalli Radhakrishnan, Eastern Religions and Western Thought *(1940)*

CONTENTS

❖

A BRIEF PREFACE

❖

It would hardly seem necessary to argue for the need to examine the history of relations between Buddhism and the West with great care. After all, it is a matter of reasonably broad consensus that Buddhism, in its many forms, offers the West remarkable teachings and practices that can be of vital use in the spheres of religion, philosophy, psychology, neurology and related cognitive sciences, and even politics.

How we came to know of Buddhism, the difficulties of that knowing, the means by which we continue to overcome those difficulties — these are the essential subjects of this book. I am indebted — as my notes and bibliography indicate — to the many excellent writers and scholars who have preceded me in these fields. What I have tried to do is to weave together, in a single narrative, an account more equally detailed in all of its parts than has yet appeared.

The majority of prior writings on this subject have been written either by Christians or Buddhists. I am neither. Indeed, I am not a formal, practicing religionist of any sort. I was raised in a secular Jewish family, and I believe in the value of all of the world's great religions — and many of the smaller ones as well. Good people can be found in all religions, and they tend to resemble one another regardless of doctrinal differences. As relations between Christianity and Buddhism, in particular, are frequently alluded to in the text, I can only say, to allay any undue suspicions, that I am "rooting" for neither side, but rather for a world in which multifold religious perspectives are not only tolerated but also deemed essential for human well-being.

There have been many obstacles to the understanding of Buddhism in the West — language, geographical distance, religious and cultural differences, colonial and postcolonial politics. These are all examined herein, and I believe that all of them play an ongoing part in the difficulties that the West is continuing to experience in coming to terms with Buddhism. For all that Buddhism is here among us, its roots are yet shallow, and the development of a fully indigenous Western Buddhism is still a work in progress, to which I hope this book can contribute.

Readers are always astute at discerning for themselves the biases they believe a writer to possess. I accept the modern critique of metahistorians that absolute historical "objectivity" is impossible — that is, all historians create a narrative of their own, based on their own assessments and "emplotment" strategies. I do, however, continue to believe that a historian can and must exercise integrity. Let the reader judge if I have done so.

Just a few comments on language usage. I do not believe in the actual existence of monolithic separate entities that can be designated as "East" and "West." I use those terms because they are necessary shorthands, employed commonly by authors around the world, for certain vast cultural realms that have gradually come into ever greater contact. The term "Buddhism" is a relatively recent Western construct to refer to what had been known for more than two millennia in Asia as the teachings of the Buddha. It is well to remember that the filters of Western understanding of Buddhism are pervasive. I have found no consistent usage pattern, even among Buddhist writers, for "dharma" and "Dharma," and have chosen the latter out of a sense of respect and its parallel function to my use of "Gospel." The term "Sri Lanka" is employed rather than "Ceylon" except when the British colony and its functionaries are under specific discussion.

I have undertaken to provide a broad historical overview, based on the conviction that such an overview is badly needed. Length considerations have made it impossible for all of the developments of the present era — which themselves have been addressed in dozens of recent books — to be examined in the closing chapters. Further, although some background is given for the Buddhist teachings discussed herein, this book should not be regarded as an introduction to Buddhist thought and practice. I am not competent to teach the Dharma, and fortunately many good books with that intent already exist. I have written a history, not a spiritual guide. And history is quite difficult enough.

1

BUDDHIST INDIA AND THE CLASSICAL AND EARLY CHRISTIAN WEST

❖

According to the Pali Canon — a body of writings that includes most of the earliest recorded teachings of the Buddha — the presence of a very different Western world was well-known even to an isolated Indian sage such as the Buddha, whose life span is often approximated as 563 to 483 BCE. In the *Assalayana Sutta,* written in the form of a philosophic dialogue, the Buddha is challenged by a bright young Brahman student steeped in Vedic learning who has been urged by his priestly elders — who deemed themselves the sole earthly descendants of the creator god Brahma — to defend their privileged caste status by defeating, in a public debate, the newly arisen challenger who taught that distinctions such as caste were empty of meaning.

The student, Assalayana, knows from the outset that his task will be a vain one, for "the recluse Gotama [Buddha] is one who speaks the Dhamma." The Dhamma (Pali; in Sanskrit, Dharma) is truth as it pertains to all aspects of existence — the truth that is the awareness of an awakened one. In this avowedly Buddhist text, the Vedic Brahman is tacitly acknowledging that his is a lesser understanding. Still, he endeavors as best he can, but a key point is scored against him by the Buddha as follows:

"What do you think, Assalayana? Have you heard that in Yona and Kamboja and in other outland countries there are only two castes, masters and slaves, and that masters become slaves and slaves masters?"

"So I have heard, sir."

"Then on the strength of what argument or with the support of what authority do the brahmins in this case say thus: 'Brahmins are the highest caste . . . heirs of Brahma'?"

"Yona" was the Pali equivalent of the Sanskrit "Yavana" and the Greek "Ionian" — the name given, as a group, to the large number of Greeks who had, since the eighth century BCE, colonized Ionia (the west coast and coastal islands of modern Turkey). Their identification with the politics and culture of mainland Greece remained avid. Indeed, several of the renowned pre-Socratic philosophers were Ionians — Thales and his pupil Anaximander lived in Miletus, and the great Pythagoras came from Samos.

It is as common knowledge, and not as a matter of dispute, that the Buddha asserted the existence of a relatively fluid political and economic life in the West. A closely similar statement may be found in one of the carved Rock Edict Dharma declarations of the third-century BCE Indian Buddhist king Ashoka. In a tone of regret, in the context of his teaching on the pervasiveness of human suffering, Ashoka wrote: "Except among the Greeks, there is no land where the religious orders of brahmans and *sramanas* [wanderers] are not to be found, and there is no land anywhere where men do not support one sect or another."

The *Assalayana Sutta* is not an active call to revolution against the Brahmanic caste system. Were it such, it would have to be deemed a signal failure, for the strength of the castes was waxing, not waning, in the centuries following the death of the Buddha and the creation of the Pali Canon. The Buddha was certainly no supporter of castes, but his teaching included tolerance for all religious orders. In the Pali Canon suttas, which often feature dialogues between the Buddha and various Brahman interlocutors, the tone on both sides is markedly respectful. The key practical aim of the *Assalayana Sutta* was to establish respect for the premise on which the Buddhist *sangha* (community) was based — the human equality of all of its members. It is true that the orders of Buddhist nuns did not enjoy equal practical status within the *sangha* at that time — nor would they for twenty-five hundred years to come. Changing social customs and power structures, consistent alone in their misogyny, overrode the strict principles of the Dharma. The point remains that Buddhist teaching went remarkably far for that time in declaring women — and all others — as equals in their capacity to realize the truth of their own nature. There was, to this extent, a similarity of spirit between the democracies of the Ionian city-states and of the Indian Buddhist *sanghas*. The statements attributed to the Buddha and to Ashoka testify to this.

The Ionians were always vulnerable to attack from the Persian Empire, and at last, in 545 BCE, Cyrus the Great annexed all of the Ionian cities, as well as Bactria (roughly modern Afghanistan) to the east. The expanded Persian hegemony created an open route from Ionia down through the Hindu Kush into the fertile Indus Valley of northwestern India, to which many Ionians made their way as merchants, craftspersons, physicians, and even administrators of the Persian Empire; they also served as mercenaries in its armies. During this era of Persian conquest, a well-traveled Phrygian slave named Aesop brought folktales back to the Greeks, certain of which contained monkeys, crocodiles, and other creatures more familiar to India than to the Hellenic world. Parallels to these tales can be found in famous Indian compendia such as the *Pancatantra* and the Buddhist *Jataka* stories that recount the prior incarnations (often in animal form) of Gotama Shakyamuni before he became the Buddha.

At least one Ionian seems to have ventured deep into the Indian subcontinent. In 517 BCE, the Persian emperor Darius I chose a Greek sea captain, Scylax, to track the course of the Indus River. Scylax wrote a book on what he saw — the first written Western account of India — but it is lost; mentions of it survive in other Greek sources, including Herodotus and Aristotle. Herodotus credited Scylax with having sailed to the mouth of the Indus and then on to the Isthmus of Suez. Just as Ionians had been swept up in the expansion of the Persian Empire, so now were the peoples of northwestern India. Herodotus noted that Indian troops served in the army of the Persian ruler Xerxes I in two critical Western battles in which Greece fought to defend its very existence — Thermopylae (480 BCE) and Plataea (479 BCE).

Aristotle, in his famous fourth-century BCE treatise the *Politics,* relied on the writing of Scylax to make a point — the identical point, as it happens, made by the Buddha and later by Ashoka as concerned the greater political freedom enjoyed by the Greeks. Aristotle argued that the justification for such freedom is the essential equality of rulers and ruled:

Now, if some men excelled others in the same degree in which gods and heroes are supposed to excel mankind in general [. . .] it would clearly be better that once for all the one class should rule and the others serve. But since this is unattainable, and kings have no marked superiority over their subjects, such as Scylax affirms to be found amongst the Indians, it is obviously necessary on many grounds that all the citizens alike should take their turn of governing and being governed.

Nor was this an isolated instance of an awareness of the East in Aristotle's writings. As the German classical scholar Werner Jaeger observed, "We find in the fragments of Aristotle's lost dialogues, which were mostly written during his earlier period, a surprising interest in certain features of oriental religion." In one of those early dialogues, there is mention of the visit of an Indian personage to Athens.

The Indian philosopher and scholar (and onetime vice president of the Republic of India) Sarvepalli Radhakrishnan argued that the "importance of Indian influence on Greek thought is not to be judged by the amount of information about it which has survived." Radhakrishnan illustrated his point — that the early East-West dialogue may have been more vital than is commonly supposed — by citing the fourth-century CE Greek Christian historian Eusebius. Eusebius related that Aristoxenus, a fourth-century BCE student of Aristotle, "tells the following story about the Indians. One of these men met Socrates at Athens, and asked him what was the scope of his philosophy. 'An inquiry into human phenomena,' replied Socrates. At this the Indian burst out laughing. 'How can we inquire into human phenomena,' he exclaimed, 'when we are ignorant of divine ones.'"

The reply of Socrates, if he replied, has not been preserved. But there is posed the possibility that Socrates knew of Indian philosophy. Even if the account is regarded as no more than a tantalizing legend, it is striking that Socrates, the master Greek dialectician, is portrayed, in a legend conveyed by a Christian historian who was also a student of Greek philosophy, as having been tacitly bested by Indian wisdom.

The Japanese Buddhist abbot Seiyu Kiriyama, in a recent book addressing the parallels between Greek and Buddhist philosophy, argued that Socrates and his student Plato were aspiring toward Buddhist nirvana without knowing of it. In the *Phaedo,* Kiriyama observed, Socrates held that perfect realization of truth can come only when the philosophically purified soul is released from the body and its distracting desires at the point of death. One of the key aims of philosophy, Socrates insisted, was to instill such wisdom that the soul might face death calmly. "Unfortunately, however," Kiriyama wrote, "Plato says one can only get there through death, whereas the Buddha was able to reach nirvana while still alive, after his practice of spiritual austerities."

The dichotomy between Plato and the Buddha on this issue was perhaps not so sharp as Kiriyama suggested. A potentially everlasting transmigration of souls, each new birth reflecting the wrongful or righteous awareness attained through previous lives, is described by Plato in the apologue of his *Republic* — by way of the tale told by a warrior, Er, the Pamphylian, a tale of which Socrates told his listeners, "it will save us if we believe it, and we shall safely cross the River of Lethe, and keep our soul unspotted from the world." Er related his near-death experiences during a twelve-day period when he was mistakenly deemed slain in battle. His fellow warriors had already set his body on a pyre for immolation when his sudden recovery occurred. In the interim, Er viewed the immortal souls of the dead as they were accorded their next incarnations by the three Fates, the daughters of Necessity, whose choices reflected the justice described in the penultimate lines of the *Republic:* "We shall hold ever to the upward way and pursue righteousness with wisdom always and ever, that we may be dear to ourselves and to the gods both during our sojourn here and when we receive our reward, as the victors in the games go about to gather in theirs." The view that transmigration rewarded virtuous souls with favorable rebirths was also held by the Pythagoreans and the Orphics; the Greek tragedian Sophocles, in a surviving fragment of his play *Triptolemus,* echoed the Orphics by declaring that simply to have experienced the cultic mysteries ensured benefit in the next lifetime.

Plato was familiar with the teachings of Pythagoras, and it is likely that the tale of Er in the *Republic* was influenced at least to a degree by those teachings. As to where Pythagoras came by them, the renowned Viennese classical scholar Theodor Gomperz speculated that Pythagoras had somehow learned of certain doctrines of India, that in many respects — a rigorous ascetic life with a vegetarian diet, a belief in the ultimate purification of the multilived soul — harmonized with his own views. Gomperz posed the possibility with admirable moderation:

> It is true that no account would be acceptable which would require Pythagoras to have sat at the feet of Indian priests or to have been even indirectly influenced by the newly hatched Buddhistic religion. But we may dispense alike with both of these wild assumptions. The Indian doctrine of metempsychosis is older than the Buddhists, and it is not too much to assume that the curious Greek who was the contemporary of Buddha, and it may have been of Zarathustra too, would have acquired a more or less exact knowledge of the religious speculations of the East, in that age of intellectual fermentation, through the medium of Persia.

But it remains that no direct evidence exists of an interchange between Pythagoras — or any other Greek thinker — and the sages, Brahman or Buddhist, of India. Even so, the writings of the Greek philosopher Heraclitus, another rough contemporary of the Buddha, bear some similarities to Buddhist thought, such as the sense of pervasive impermanence as expressed in Heraclitus's famous dictum: "It is not possible to step twice into the same river." Where evidence of direct influence is lacking, mere conviction sometimes prevails. In 1910, an ardent Western Buddhist, Edmund J. Mills, argued that, as the similarities between Heraclitus and the Buddha were so great, and the likelihood of their meeting so small, the most likely explanation was that the Buddha had acted as a "telepathic missionary," transmitting his Dharma across western Asia into the mind of the Greek, whose comprehension was not entirely accurate because he had "received the message on a tarnished instrument, and gathered uncertain signals." The passion to find a link between the pre-Socratics and the Buddhists continues to this day. In the modern scholarly literature, the common verdict is "unlikely" — though it would be more truthful to deem it "unknown."

❖

The contacts between Greek and Indian thought become far less hypothetical some seventy years after the death of Socrates. A precocious student of Aristotle, Alexander the Great, having established his firm rule of the Hellenic world, embarked in 327 BCE on a campaign to conquer India, the geographical extent of which was not known to him. Along with the conqueror's troops came philosophers — including one Kallisthenes, the nephew of Aristotle. There is a signal irony recorded in several of the early histories of Alexander's conquests. Whether legend or fact, these historians have it that after Alexander had crossed the Hindu Kush and led his forces into India, the first town he encountered was Nysa, named after the birthplace of Dionysus. The town was populated by descendants of Ionian Greeks, who greeted Alexander as a conquering hero and held a Bacchanalian festival in his honor. In this setting arose a much-storied encounter between Alexander and a certain number of Indian gymnosophists, or naked philosophers, whose precise religious affiliations, if any, are unknown; scholars speculate that they were Jains or Brahmans.

The earliest version of the tale is found in a manuscript ascribed to the Kallisthenes who journeyed with Alexander, but the author is now identified by scholars as "pseudo-Kallisthenes," the unknown writer (circa first century CE) of an imaginative account of Alexander's eastern conquests. Pseudo-Kallisthenes sets the stage by noting that, as Alexander was readying his eastern campaign, Aristotle requested that his onetime student send back to Greece, as part of the booty of conquest, an Indian gymnosophist with whom Aristotle could discourse. That request went unfulfilled. But pseudo-Kallisthenes, and other classical authors such as Arrian and Plutarch, did chronicle Alexander's own encounter with the gymnosophists. In all of these versions, the gymnosophists decisively rejected the worldly ambitions of the man the West declared "Great."

Alexander did at least attempt to supply a gymnosophist for Aristotle, or so the classical historians tell us. Kalanos was the naked philosopher persuaded, by unspecified means, to accompany Alexander back to Greece. The possibility of coercion exists, particularly if Plutarch was correct that, when initially approached for questioning by the Greek philosopher Onesicritus (who, like Kallisthenes, had accompanied Alexander), Kalanos "very arrogantly and roughly commanded him to strip himself and hear what he said naked, otherwise he would not speak a word to him, though he came from Jupiter himself." An older and more patient gymnosophist, Mandanis, intervened at this point, explaining that the greatest philosophy was that which liberated the mind from all passions, pleasant and painful alike, and hence could bring peace and harmony. Did the Greeks possess similar teachings? Mandanis inquired. Onesicritus replied that his own mentor Diogenes held like ideas, as did Socrates and Pythagoras. But Mandanis (according to the first-century CE Roman geographer Strabo) faulted these Greek thinkers for placing too much importance on social convention — "for otherwise they would not be ashamed to go naked like himself and to subsist on frugal fare — for that was the best house which required least repairs."

A hypothetical rejoinder for Onesicritus here would have been that Diogenes, of all Greeks, most disdained custom and convention. Although he wore a coarse robe, Diogenes performed all of his bodily functions in public and relished living as freely and shamelessly as a dog. (The term "Cynic" stems from the Greek for "doglike.") Indeed, Diogenes, according to tradition, possessed — as did the gymnosophists — the temerity to defy the ruler of the known world, Alexander. In Corinth, the Macedonian king had once encountered the Cynic sage sunning himself as he lay on the ground. Alexander offered to bestow any gifts or honors that Diogenes wished; the latter asked only that Alexander not block the sun. Alexander later declared, "If I were not Alexander, I should wish to be Diogenes." But the dialogue between the Greek philosophers of Alexander and the Indian gymnosophists was not nearly so eloquent. One problem was the sheer difficulty of communication. Mandanis, as recorded by Strabo, tersely posed the dilemma that has beset East-West dialogue to the present day: "It is impossible to explain philosophical doctrines through the medium of three interpreters who understand nothing we say any more than the vulgar; it is like asking water to flow pure through mud."

At last, by whatever means, the recalcitrant gymnosophist Kalanos was prevailed upon to join Alexander's imperial return to the West. Shackled in body, Kalanos perhaps resolved to find escape in spirit. In the Persian city of Susa, Kalanos (who suffered from a bowel disease) realized that his time had come and requested that a funeral pyre be constructed, which he calmly mounted after bidding farewell to the Macedonians and informing Alexander that he was certain that they would meet again in Babylon. This gnomic remark takes on striking meaning (as Plutarch, who recorded it some three hundred years later, was surely aware) when one considers that Alexander died young, in 323 BCE in Babylon.

Kalanos then lay down on the pyre, covered his face, and "stirred not when the fire came near him, but continued still in the same posture as at first, and so sacrificed himself, as it was the ancient custom of the philosophers in those countries to do." Such was the end of the first concerted effort at East-West philosophical dialogue.

❖

Among the holdings of Alexander's empire — which was slowly dismembered and separately ruled by his successors — were portions of modern-day northwestern India, northern Pakistan, and southern Afghanistan, then collectively known as Bactria. It was in Bactria that the first historically verifiable contacts between Greeks and Buddhists took place.

The Seleucids, who ruled Bactria for some two centuries, traced their lineage to Seleucus I Nicator ("Conqueror"), one of the ablest of Alexander's generals. After Alexander's death, Seleucus succeeded in wresting power for himself and his son, Antiochus I, in a region stretching from Bactria to Ionia. The mid-twentieth-century British historian W. W. Tarn described the total holdings:

> The Seleucid empire was nothing organic, in the sense that the Roman state, up to a point, was organic. The latter resembled a vertebrate animal; it expanded outward from a solid core, the city of Rome. The Seleucid empire resembled rather a crustacean, not growing from any solid core but encased in an outer shell; the empire was a framework which covered a multitude of peoples and languages and cities.

One key means of strengthening the shell, Tarn argued, was the importation of substantial numbers of Greco-Macedonian laborers and soldiers who were particularly loyal to the Seleucid rulers, who stood as guarantors of Greek enterprise and culture in the region. Tarn's contemporary, the Indian historian A. K. Narain, dissented from this view, arguing that the Seleucids drew their principal support not from any massive immigration, but rather from a Bactrian Greek population that had already been in place for centuries. To govern this population effectively, Narain argued, the Seleucids drew on Greek cultural and economic values that could serve as effective wedges into the popular support enjoyed by the ruling Brahmans. One such value was the easing of restrictions on land ownership, so as to grant hereditary serfs of the lowly Sudra caste the opportunity to become peasant farmers.

The Indian scholar Abbay Kumar Singh argued perceptively that the Indo-Greeks "were the *first* people in the era of foreign invasions (beginning *circa* 3rd century B.C.), who themselves initiated their assimilation into the Indian society by posing a remarkable attitude of understanding, sympathy and appreciation towards India and everything Indian. Such attitude is rarely found in invaders." The Indo-Greek attitude toward intermarriage was utterly permissive. As Singh noted, "History testifies that the Indo-Greek population mixed inseparably and indistinguishably in the native Indians." All of this was heartily disapproved of by later Roman historians such as Livy and Tacitus. It was also disapproved of by the Indians themselves, who during this era regarded the northwest of their land as "un-Aryan."

The social and religious divisions between the dominant Brahmans and the disempowered Buddhists were bound to be of interest to the Seleucids, who, as foreign invaders, were identified with the Kshatriya, or warrior, caste, while the Brahmans formed the priestly caste. Because the Buddha, Gotama Shakyamuni, had been born a prince of a royal family that wielded military power, Buddhists were classified socially in the same manner as Greeks — as Kshatriyas. This was not as anachronistic a linkage as may first appear. The Buddhism of this period exercised an appeal not only for monastics but also for certain of the warrior chiefs of the Kshatriya caste, who found in Buddhism an alternative to the religious teachings of their Brahman political rivals. From the third century BCE through the third century CE, Indian Buddhist monasteries received far greater sums in donations than did Brahman temples. The lay Buddhist *sangha* included not only aristocrats but also merchants, who found in Buddhism relief from the caste restrictions that plagued them in the marketplace.

❖

Seleucus appointed, as his ambassador to the court of Chandragupta — the powerful Indian king who founded the Maurya empire — a Greek diplomat, Megasthenes (circa 350–290 BCE). In his account of his time in the East, *Indika,* Megasthenes ranged broadly in subject matter, assisted in his researches by Indian translators. Megasthenes has long been accused of unseemly credulity, but recent scholarship has vindicated his acumen to a degree. Although his chief interest was politics, he did note of the philosophers of India that "in many points their teaching agrees with that of the Greeks." Modest as this observation may seem, it bears noting that Megasthenes was the first of a long series of Western observers who noticed such similarities.

The royal court that Megasthenes chronicled must have been remarkable, given the flamboyance of its monarch. There are legends that Chandragupta, while still an uncrowned, ambitious young warrior, arranged a meeting with Alexander the Great to encourage him to take advantage of popular unrest in India and move boldly against the reigning Nanda king. Such boldness would also have served the interests of Chandragupta, known in Greek and Roman histories as "Sandracottus" or "Androcottus." But Chandragupta offended Alexander by failing to show proper obeisance in their face-to-face meeting and was sent away. To the end of his life, it is said, Chandragupta would insist that Alexander had squandered an opportunity upon which Chandragupta himself had made good. Chandragupta died circa 297 BCE, having reigned for some twenty-five years, during which he drove from India the Seleucid successors of Alexander.

The British writer George Woodcock raised the remote yet real possibility that Chandragupta's grandson, the great Indian Buddhist king Ashoka, was of partial Greek ancestry. Woodcock noted that a treaty struck between Seleucus I and Chandragupta called for Seleucus, as part of a settlement ceding his holdings in northwest India, to join one of his daughters to the house of Chandragupta through marriage. (Dissenting scholars have argued that only the provision of a Greek princess-bride — not necessarily the daughter of Seleucus — was specified.) Woodcock posited that the suitable husband of so royal a daughter would have been Chandragupta himself, or else his son and successor, Bindusara, who was the father of Ashoka. We know that Seleucus and Chandragupta were on frank terms with each other, as evidenced by the fact that, in one of the lavish gift exchanges common to neighboring monarchs, Chandragupta sent Seleucus aphrodisiac potions. As for Bindusara, his fascination with the Greeks seems to have been pronounced. He once made a request — reminiscent of that made by Aristotle to Alexander — that Seleucus's son and successor, Antiochus I, send him raisins, wine, and a Greek

Sophist. Antiochus I was forced to decline on the grounds that "in Greece it is not done to trade in philosophers." Amid the speculations, there is one point of clarity. If Ashoka was in part of Greek ancestry, there is no evidence that he placed any importance on it. Intermarriage between Greeks and Indians — royals or not — was commonplace during this period.

Ashoka first achieved his throne through bloody ruthlessness. In roughly 269 BCE, upon the death of his father, Bindusara, he waged a four-year fratricidal war on his many half brothers (their legendary number is 101, by Bindusara's many consorts), all of whom had their own legitimate claims to the throne. Ashoka earned the name Candashoka, or Ashoka the Wicked, through outsize atrocities — the slaughter of five hundred opposing ministers, the immolation of five hundred ladies of the royal court, the ready use of torture. Even if the numbers are questioned — as they are by most scholars — the fact of considerable killing is uncontested.

In a reign that extended some thirty-seven years, Ashoka came to rule nearly all of the Indian subcontinent. Early on, he kept publicly to the Brahmanical rites favored by his late father. But he gradually began to request that teachers from the various Indian religions come to his court, so that he might assess their views. Ultimately, it was Buddhism that most drew him, and in homage to its teachings, Ashoka undertook to excavate — from their eight scattered burial mounds — the bodily relics of the Buddha. He then constructed a great number of stupas (tradition records the number as 84,000) to house them. His famous edicts, frequently on matters of the Dharma, were inscribed both on large rock surfaces and on specially constructed pillars. In the Gandhara region of northwest India, certain of these inscriptions are in Greek. In his edicts, Ashoka claimed to have spread the teachings of the Buddha, by way of Buddhist missionary embassies, to the lands of five contemporary Hellenistic kings — Antiochus II, Ptolemy II Philadelphus, Antigonus Gonatas, Magas of Cyrene, and Alexander of Corinth (or perhaps Epirus).

The skilled carvings found in many of the Ashoka stone pillars mark a departure in Indian sculpture, in which, prior to the reign of Ashoka, wood had been used as a medium. It is likely that some of the Greek artisans who lived in the region came to be employed by the proselytizing emperor to enhance the impact of his Rock Edicts. Both the fifth and the ninth Rock Edicts declared that Yavanas, or Greeks, were numbered among the subjects of Ashoka who showed devotion to the Dharma. Two Pali texts from the centuries just following Ashoka, the *Dipavansa* and the *Mahavansa,* provide the Indianized names of Greeks who took up life as Buddhist monastics and preached the Dharma to tens of thousands of people.

Through the teachings of the edicts, a new name came to be attached to the once brutal king — Dharmashoka, or Ashoka the Wise. But Ashoka remained a tenacious ruler, waging a fierce war to annex the southern territory of Kalinga. According to Ashoka's thirteenth Rock Edict, one hundred thousand people were killed and "many times that number perished." Remorse ensued because "when an independent country is conquered the slaughter, death and deportation of the people is extremely grievous to the Beloved of the Gods [one of Ashoka's royal epithets], and weighs heavily on his mind." The king came to realize that a ruler should pursue the path of Dharmavijaya, conquest through wisdom. Admirers of Ashoka often view him as a monarch who came to embrace pacifism, but that is a considerable overstatement. While Ashoka ceased his wars of conquest, he retained the option of violence as a means of maintaining power. In the same edict in which he spoke of repentance, Ashoka also issued a bloodcurdling ultimatum:

> The Beloved of the Gods believes that one who does wrong should be forgiven as far as it is possible to forgive him. And the Beloved of the Gods conciliates the forest tribes of his empire, but he warns them that he has power even in his remorse, and he asks them to repent, lest they be killed. For the Beloved of the Gods wishes that all beings should be unharmed, self-controlled, calm in mind, and gentle.

Ashoka's efforts to balance Buddhist teachings with the practicalities of empire have led some scholars to disbelieve the sincerity of his conversion to Dharmavijaya. The Indian historian Romila Thapar speculated that Ashoka abandoned violent conquest "not because he completely forsook the idea of war as a means to an end, though he claims to have done so, but because with the conquest of Kalinga the consolidation of the empire was complete." As evidence of Ashoka's sensitivity to political considerations, Thapar noted that the thirteenth Rock Edict, with its expressions of grief over the Kalinga war, was not proclaimed in Kalinga itself.

It is possible, indeed reasonable, to speculate in this way, but the collateral damage is considerable. The Ashoka beloved of legend and history has all but vanished. It was of this Ashoka that the Nobel Laureate Rabindranath Tagore wrote: "He gave up a life of insatiable hedonism and embraced a life of timeless service. [. . .] This was the endless bounty of the spirit of altruism, which suddenly made the sovereign its vehicle, putting at once into shade the splendour of royalty and bringing the entire human society into the limelight." H. G. Wells, in his *Outline of History,* declared that "amidst the tens of thousands of names of monarchs that crowd the columns of history [. . .] the name of Ashoka shines, and shines almost alone, a star." Whether his abstention from aggressive war was partial or whole, earnest or felicitously timed, its influence has been lasting. Within India, that influence bore fruit in the politics of satyagraha, or nonviolent truth-force, espoused by Mahatma Gandhi.

Ashoka died circa 228 BCE. There stems from his final years a disheartening story as to the difficulties of living by the Dharma even within the confines of a royal palace. The aged Ashoka had taken to holding great feasts in the vicinity of the Sambodhi, or Bodhi Tree, under which the Buddha achieved his awakening. The elaborate preparations that so occupied Ashoka aroused the ire of his chief consort, Tisyaraksita, who either destroyed or attempted to destroy (the testimonies vary) the venerated tree. For this and other misdeeds, Ashoka condemned her to death not long before his own passing.

Ashoka's earnest desire to disseminate wisdom has not been questioned. But whether the Dharma preached by Ashoka was a specifically Buddhist Dharma has been called into doubt by a scholarly minority whose arguments bear some weight. During his reign, Ashoka extended financial support not only to Buddhists but also to righteous followers of other paths, including Brahmans and Jains. By the testimony of his own edicts, his primary aim was to secure not Buddhist converts, but peaceful relations between the various religions of his empire. This catholicity of outlook may have brought about an outcome quite unforeseen and unwished for by a Buddhist monarch. As the Japanese scholar Hajime Nakamura observed, "Ashoka's policy of tolerance had the effect of harmonizing and blending various religions of India, so that his reign gave impetus to the growth of Hinduism." Indeed, with the fall of the Maurya dynasty, the post-Vedic Brahmanism that became known as Hinduism arose in what some Western historians have viewed as a kind of Indian Counter-Reformation.

The seeming irony of this outcome stems from the assumption that Ashoka wished to promulgate Buddhism. But it is possible to see in the Rock Edicts a body of teachings that are not distinctly Buddhist, but rather common to the Indian religions of Ashoka's time. The Pali term "Dhamma," which occurs in so many of the edicts, can be found in Brahmanic texts that long predate Buddhism. Romila Thapar argued that "to narrow the meaning of Ashokan *dhamma* to the teachings of a single religious sect is perhaps to do an injustice both to Ashoka and to the concept of *dhamma* as it prevailed at that time." As with the issue of Ashoka's pacifism, there is with the question of his ultimate religious aims the risk of cutting deeply against the venerated legends of the great Buddhist king. But there are grounds for upholding the gist of the legend. Ashoka did support Buddhist missionary efforts to all parts of his empire, including the five Greek kingdoms to the northwest, and boasted of his successes in his edicts. These efforts were intensified after the Third Buddhist Council, convened by Ashoka at Pataliputra in the seventeenth year of his reign. Ashoka's own son, Mahendra, served as a Buddhist missionary to Sri Lanka during this period.

Whether Ashoka earnestly wished that his neighboring western kingdoms convert to Buddhism and whether he achieved any real success in this endeavor are matters subject to debate — a debate that has sometimes been reduced to distressing cultural partisanship. One of the preeminent Victorian scholars of Buddhism, T. W. Rhys Davids, adjudged that Ashoka's boasts in the thirteenth Rock Edict of converting Greek monarchs were vainglorious:

It is difficult to say how much of this is mere royal rhodomontade. It is quite likely that the Greek kings are only thrown in by way of makeweight, as it were; and that no emissary had actually been sent there at all. Even had they been sent, there is little reason to believe that the Greek self-complacency would have been much disturbed. Ashoka's estimation of the results obtained is better evidence of his own vanity than it is of

Greek docility. We may imagine the Greek amusement at the absurd idea of a "barbarian" teaching them their duty; but we can scarcely imagine their discarding their gods and their superstitions at the bidding of an alien king.

The tone of Rhys Davids aggrieved several generations of Indian scholars. The most concerted rebuttal, launched by D. R. Bhandarkar in 1923, chided Rhys Davids for failing to consider the ongoing contacts between Ashoka and the Greeks for philanthropic as well as religious reasons. Would Rhys Davids or his successors dare to claim that Ashoka lied in his Rock Edicts not only as to his missionary efforts but also as to proffered medical assistance to the western Greek kingdoms? "This would be charging him with downright fabrications, — a conclusion that no sane person will accept." Bhandarkar noted that historical records of the period confirmed the existence of Indo-Greeks who joined Buddhist monastic orders and even served as missionaries to their fellow Yavanas, and for whom great successes were claimed. He further argued that evidence of the fruits of Ashoka's missionary work could be found in the obvious borrowings from Buddhism in Christianity — "confessions, fasting, celibacy of the priesthood, and even rosaries. And, above all, there was Mara the tempter, who was to Buddha what Satan was to Christ." Bhandarkar was careful to stress that the influence of Buddhism did not deprive Christianity "of its claim to originality, beauty and truth." But his assertion of that influence as a historical certainty is unfounded. The debate over the impact of Ashoka's missionary endeavors came full circle when Thapar, the leading modern Indian scholar on Ashoka, noted that the thirteenth Rock Edict "includes the Greek kingdoms of Syria, Egypt, Cyrene, Macedonia, and Epirus as having been conquered by *Dhamma,* whereas in fact all that may have happened was a cordial exchange of embassies or missions or merely the sending of one of these by Asoka to the Greek kings mentioned." The tone here resembles that of Rhys Davids's "royal rhodomontade."

There was, in nineteenth-century Norway, a highly implausible theory conceived as to the ultimate reach of Ashoka's missionary efforts. As the theory evidences the fascination exerted by Ashoka even in the West, it shall have its say here. According to the Norwegian scholar Christopher Andreas Holmboe, in his *Traces of Buddhism in Norway Prior to the Introduction of Christianity* (1857), the Buddhist missionaries went far beyond the realms of the Indo-Greeks into the Caucasus and Baltic regions, where dwelled the ancestors of the Scandinavians. The missionaries received a gracious welcome and were encouraged to travel still farther into the present-day Scandinavian lands. By faulty etymology, Holmboe derived the name of the Norse god Odin from the Sanskrit root *budh* (to know) found in the Buddha's name. Harriet Murray-Aynsley, a Victorian British folklorist who lived many years in the Himalayan regions of northern India, was not a supporter of Holmboe's theory. She did, however, demonstrate that the theory was no mere academic flight but rather had actual life among the Norwegian people. While visiting Christiania (Oslo) in 1883, Murray-Aynsley remarked on the resemblance between Norwegian horses and the Yarkandis breed of central Asia; this evoked the response by a resident that "the people in my part of Norway say that Odin brought horses from the Himalayas."

The lasting influence of Ashoka on Asian Buddhism came by way of legendary tales disseminated by the Mahayana schools in China and Tibet. These legends took the form of *avadanas* (comparable to the Catholic *vitae sanctorum,* or lives of the saints), which, though originally written in Sanskrit, became far more popular in the lands north of India. In these legends, Ashoka is portrayed as having evolved from the bloodiest of conquerors into the compassionate benefactor and transmitter of the Dharma. It was through these legends, not by way of his edicts, that Ashoka was primarily remembered, even in India, for nearly two millennia. A pointed irony of the British colonial reign in India was that it facilitated the work of a British scholar, James Prinsep, who in 1837 deciphered the Brahmi script in which most of the edicts had been inscribed, and thus prepared the way for their modern-day fame.

❖

The later rulers of the Seleucid empire — whose power base lay to the west, in Babylonia and the Mesopotamian Fertile Crescent — found it difficult to retain control over the eastern Bactrian Greeks. As the Maurya empire weakened, Diodotus I (circa 230 BCE) led a breakaway Bactrian military campaign that briefly established an independent kingdom in northwest India. Some twenty years later, the Seleucids regained control. Bactria remained wracked by civil wars until, in 145 BCE, Menander again consolidated power and expanded the kingdom more deeply into India than had Alexander himself. At his apex, Menander reigned from the Kabul Valley in the west to the Ravi Valley in the east, and from the northern Swat Valley to Arachosia in the south.

The argument has often been made, on the basis of certain of the coinage designs of his reign, that Menander was either a Buddhist or strongly in sympathy with Buddhist ideals. The principal example is the presence on some coins of an eight-spoked wheel — which, by the time of Menander, was a widespread symbol of the Dharma. But it is equally plausible that the wheel represents a sun disk, a symbol of the Chakravartin — the great king who conquers both by force and through wisdom. Further, the wheel symbol appears in Jain and Brahman, as well as Buddhist, art.

Although the facts do not permit certainty, there are stout partisans for the view that the greatest of the Indo-Greek kings came to accept the Dharma. In the most recent edition of *The Oxford Classical Dictionary,* the brief entry on Menander asserts that he "embraced Buddhism," which perhaps reflects the view of many historians that so strong a legend must contain some truth. Heinrich Zimmer, the German Indologist, summed up the matter adroitly: "If the Greek king was not himself actually a member of the Buddhist Order, he was at least so great a benefactor that the community looked upon him as one of their own."

Then, too, there were allegations — the accuracy of which historians debate — that Pushyamitra, the Sunga king against whom Menander fought for control of northern India, had persecuted and killed Buddhists. The legend that emerged over time was that whereas Ashoka had constructed 84,000 stupas (in accordance with the belief that the human body — and thus the Buddha's human remains — consisted of 84,000 atoms, each of which required reverence), Pushyamitra had resolved to destroy 84,000 stupas. Both numbers are apocryphal, but they illustrate that Buddhists of the region viewed Menander not as an alien conqueror, but as a welcome counterforce, just as those Buddhists were viewed by Menander.

According to Plutarch, the first-century BCE Greek historian, Menander died as a warrior should — in a military camp, while campaigning in defense of the eastern borders of his kingdom. Plutarch further recorded that several stupas were raised over deposits of Menander's ashes.

If this is fact and not legend, the stupas may be seen as evidence of a Buddhist affiliation, or as memorials suited to a Chakravartin, or both. But then it was as a legend that Menander left his greatest legacy to India. As a military conqueror, he enjoyed successes, though hardly on the scale of an Alexander or an Ashoka. Yet he became the most heralded Greek in classical Indian literature. (By contrast, Alexander receives no mention whatsoever.) Stories originally ascribed to the Buddha or to Ashoka became, in later variants, the deeds of Menander.

Under the name "Milinda," the Greek king emerged as the featured protagonist of a Buddhist sacred text, the *Milindapanha,* or *Questions of King Milinda,* written roughly a century after the historical Menander's death. King Milinda — in response to the eloquent arguments on behalf of the Dharma by his teacher Nagasena, who now and then scores his points in the manner of a Buddhist Socrates — gives up his reign to pursue a life of contemplation, therein contradicting the little firm information there is about Menander's life. But his presence in a Buddhist text testifies to the degree to which Buddhists embraced his overtures toward their way of life. In a Thai Buddhist account, Menander even attains high enlightenment as an Arhat.

The legend of Menander endured, but his Bactrian kingdom did not. By the second century BCE, the Seleucid empire had crumbled. As for the Greco-Macedonian homeland from which Alexander had set forth, it was now conquered, in its turn, by the Romans.

❖

There is a possibility, and merely that, that the Greek presence in northwest India had some influence on the emergence of Mahayana Buddhism. It is a remarkable claim — that something of the spirit of classical Greece entered into what became the dominant school of Buddhism. Scholars poke and scratch at the question, lacking definite evidence; those who support the theory surmise from facts that can be summarized as follows.

The principal goal of the Third Buddhist Council convened by Ashoka was to unify the various codes of conduct employed by the Buddhist monastic orders. But the opposite result occurred — a deeply felt schism arose, leaving two doctrinally opposed Buddhist schools. The Theravadins (Elders) believed themselves to be the heirs to the true teachings of the Buddha, a venerable human teacher whose enlightenment could be emulated only through complete monastic renunciation of the world. The Mahasanghikas (Great Assembly) argued that lay followers could also attain enlightenment by way of devotion to the ideal of the compassionate Buddha, who, in a spiritual sense, was more than human because of the universal truth of his teachings.

In the aftermath of the schism, some eighteen different Buddhist sects emerged over the next three centuries from the twin branches of the Theravada and Mahasanghika schools. One of these was the Sarvastivadins, whose monasteries stretched across northern India from Mathura to Kashmir. The impact of Sarvastivadin teachings extended outside India proper. Through Sarvastivadin contacts with central Asian peoples, Buddhist teachings reached China. In Afghanistan, a Sarvastivada monastery in Nagarahara (now Jalalabad), which housed a skull and other relics of the Buddha, attracted pilgrims.

The name Sarvastivada stems from the Sanskrit for "everything exists" (*sarvam asti*), an encapsulation of the principal doctrine of the Sarvastivadins that "everything exists everywhere at all times and in every way." In terms of Buddhist practice, this means that one's past karma influences but does not control one's present choices. The Sarvastivadin doctrine of transferred merit offered particular hope to lay Buddhists. It held that the wise karmic choices of one's lifetime could lead to ultimate nirvanic attainment in subsequent rebirths. Wise choices included compassionate practices, such as giving alms to support the *sangha,* but also worshipful veneration of the relics of the Buddha. These were housed in stupas, which became centers of devotion for both monastic and lay followers.

But what of the nature of nirvana itself? Once attained, what remained? In the Theravadin writings, emphasis was placed on the bliss of release from attachment as one realized the Dharma of the benevolent Buddha. But in the writings of the Sarvastivadins, a new vision of enlightenment arose — one that proved vital in the emergence of the Mahayana teachings. This was the ideal of the bodhisattva.

At root, the ideal is simple — a matter of emphasis rather than radical change. The Buddha had shown the compassion to teach others after his own attainment of nirvana. Should not his true followers do the same? Bodhisattvas, whose enlightenment was complete, put off their own release from suffering until they fulfilled their vows to liberate all fellow beings. The conception of the bodhisattva thus emerged from its minor role in Theravadin teachings — where it referred to the nature of the man Gotama before he became the Buddha — to form the center of Mahayana practice.

It is not known precisely when and how Mahayana Buddhism arose. Scholars place the time as the first or second century BCE and the locale as northern India. The cultural interplay between the Sarvastivadins and the Greeks in Gandhara — in modern terms, northwest India, northern Pakistan, and eastern Afghanistan — could perhaps have influenced Mahayana teachings, but the surmises of the scholars are merely that. The verdict of the Indian Buddhist scholar G. C. Pande still stands — that the proposed influence of the Bactrian Greeks on the emergence of the Mahayana school "remains a speculative hypothesis so far."

❖

It was in the region of Gandhara that the Sarvastivadins encountered the culture of the Hellenistic Greeks, the Yavanas, with their worship of images and statues of the Greek gods and goddesses. In great cities such as Taxila and Mathura, there emerged, in the first through fourth centuries CE, the earliest known sculpted figures of the Buddha in a meditative human form. In these sculptures, with their unmistakable Greco-Roman motifs, a bodhisattva's head may bear a striking resemblance to a smiling Apollo, albeit with a stylishly twirled Indian mustache. As the British art historian Christopher Tadgell observed, the impulse to give worshipful human form to the Buddha stemmed both from Western influence and from the cultic practices of the people of the Gandhara region: "The venerable symbols of the Buddha were supplemented, then supplanted, by shrines sheltering worshipful images of the Buddha and *bodhisattvas* formed after the example set by native *yaksha* [personified tree-spirit] cults and under the inspiration of Hellenistic anthropomorphic pantheism." In the Bactrian capital of Taxila — designed in a grid pattern in accordance with Hellenistic practice — lie the remains of the earliest shrines featuring the Buddha's human form.

But the artistic influences and merits of the Gandhara style have been subject to sharp debate, with colonial and postcolonial politics figuring prominently in the rhetoric. The verdict of Ananda Coomaraswamy, one of the great twentieth-century art historians (born in Sri Lanka of a

Tamil father and a British mother and raised, after age two, in England), was that the Jain religion of India had long portrayed human meditators as devotional figures, and hence Jain rather than Greek iconography could have influenced Gandhara Buddhist art. He did allow that "it seems probable that the actual Gandhara sculptures are mainly the work of western craftsmen employed by the Gandhara kings to interpret Buddhist ideas, rather than Indian workmen under western guidance; and if some of the workmen were Indian by birth, they nevertheless did not give expression to Indian feeling." But given the absence of any meditative figures in the Greco-Roman iconographic tradition, Coomaraswamy complained with justice of "how great an exaggeration is involved in speaking of the 'Greek Origin of *the* Image of Buddha.'"

The debate over the origins of the human Buddha image can readily be framed within the broader context of colonialist culture wars. As the scholar Stanley K. Abe observed, "It was not until 1852, soon after the British annexation of the Punjab in 1849, that examples of sculpture from Gandhara were described as exhibiting Greek attributes." But John Ruskin and other Victorian critics vulgarly condemned the entirety of Indian art, with which they were barely familiar, on the basis of its failure sufficiently to attain to the standards of Greek classicism. There did, over time, emerge Western scholars with broader perspectives. Consider, for example, this comparative insight by the British art historian Benjamin Rowland:

> In Gandhara the translation of Buddhist iconography into ready-made foreign patterns is essentially the same process that took place in the formation of Early Christian art, so that it is not surprising in the earliest Gandhara Buddhas to find Sakyamuni with the head of a Greek Apollo, and arrayed in a pallium or toga. In exactly the same way the earliest representations of Christ show him with the head of a Greek sun god, and dressed in the garb of the teachers of the ancient world.

The simple fact underlying Rowland's analysis is that cultural confluences are pervasive. And, one might add, they also are mutual — Apollo becoming Buddha is as much a "defeat" as a "victory" for the West, if one cared to keep score. Nor was the blending of Apollo and Buddha a unique case in Gandhara sculpture. Zeus, the king of the Greek gods, became

Indra, the king of the Vedic gods, while Heracles became Vajrapani, the thunder-bearing protector of the Buddhist Dharma. In neither case did the Greek theology survive along with the borrowed Greek god forms.

❖

The absorption of the Indo-Greeks into Indian culture was final by the first century CE, at which point Buddhism still reigned as the dominant Indian religion. There also came about at this time the first vital renewal of commercial and cultural exchanges between India and the Mediterranean world since the time of Alexander. The emperor Augustus had extended Roman rule into Parthia and Bactria on India's northwestern frontiers. A sea trade route between East and West was established by the subsequent Roman conquest of Aden and the Red Sea. Between the first and third centuries CE, the frequency of contact between the Roman and Indian worlds was such that all manner of spiritual and philosophical interchanges can be posited or imagined.

The later Roman writers — perhaps due to the fact that Egypt had by then been integrated into the empire and hence grown familiar — began to place the locus of the earliest and highest esoteric wisdom in India. Pythagoras, according to his third-century CE biographer Philostratus, traveled first to Egypt and then to India in search of truth. The philosopher Porphyry recorded that Plotinus (205–270 CE), the great founder of the Neoplatonic school, tried unsuccessfully to make the same journey by enlisting, at age thirty-eight, in the campaign of the Roman emperor Gordian III against Persia. That campaign ended in the death of that monarch and the failure of Plotinus's hopes. Nonetheless, it has been held by a minority of Western scholars that Indian wisdom plays a decisive role in the mystical Platonism put forward by Plotinus in his *Enneads*. As the German scholar Wilhelm Halbfass — not himself among that minority — observed:

It has been suggested that Plotinus' teacher, the Alexandrian Ammonius Sakkas, might have been a transmitter of Indian ideas and thus responsible for his disciple's interest in India and the East in general, and that the epithet "sakkas" itself ought to be derived from the Sanskrit word *sakya*, "(follower of) the Buddha," instead of meaning "sack-carrier." This would, therefore, indicate a Buddhist affiliation. We need not dismiss this suggestion, but we should always remember that it is nothing more than a hypothesis. What we know about Ammonius' teachings is vague and uncertain and does not contain any recognizable Indian elements.

❖

There have been abundant unsubstantiated theories linking Gnostic, Christian, and Jewish beliefs to Buddhist teachings.

The Gnostic cosmology of the eastern Mediterranean first appeared in Greek Orphism and in Jewish apocalyptic and pseudepigraphic writings of the final two centuries BCE. It flourished in the centuries following Christ, taking tantalizingly diverse forms — as in early Jewish kabbalah, in Hermetic tractates drawing from the esoteric traditions of Alexandrian Egypt, in the teachings of Mani, and in certain early Christian writings.

There are key divergences between the various Gnostic schools, and the term "gnosis" has proven so fluid in application that an international conference of scholars reached agreement only on the broadest of definitions — "knowledge of the divine mysteries reserved for an elite." The genuine members of this "elite" are chosen — or choose themselves by the exercise of their free will — solely by means of intuitive awareness of the spiritual realities behind material existence, coupled with dedicated practice. By the fourth century, the alliance of Christianity with Constantine led to widespread suppression of Gnostic teachings (and destruction of Gnostic writings) throughout the West.

The third-century Church Father Hippolytus was sufficiently familiar with Indian thought to declare as heretical the teachings of the Brahmans, whom he viewed as akin to the Gnostics: "They say that God is light, not like the light one sees, nor like the sun nor fire, but to them God is discourse, not that which finds expression in articulate sounds, but that of knowledge (*gnosis*) through which the secret mysteries of nature are perceived by the wise." While the teaching condemned here is Brahmanism, the ideas are equally to be found in Buddhist texts. The first direct reference to Buddhism in the patristic writings comes in the *Stromata* of the second-century Church Father Clement of Alexandria, who briefly noted that "some, too, of the Indians obey the precepts of Buddha; whom, on account of his extraordinary sanctity, they have raised to divine honours." It is not known whether Clement personally encountered Indian Buddhists who had — as was possible at the time —

voyaged to the busy trading port of Alexandria. Clement did describe certain "Sarmanae" (a Greek transcription of the Sanskrit *sramana,* or "wanderers") who "neither inhabit cities, nor have roofs over them, but are clothed in the bark of trees, feed on nuts, and drink water in their hands." But scholars cannot agree as to whether Clement was writing from his own observations or merely borrowing from Megasthenes or other prior sources; nor can they decide whether the "Sarmanae" were Brahmans, Jains, gymnosophists, or Buddhists.

But then Clement himself had no clear idea as to the differences between Buddhists and other Indian ascetics. Thus he wrote in his *Stromata* that "the Indians who are called Holy Men go naked throughout their entire life. They seek for the truth, and predict the future, and reverence a certain pyramid beneath which, they think, lie the bones of a certain god." The "pyramid" could be a reference to a stupa, but Buddhists did not go about naked and did not, at least not commonly, prognosticate the future, insisting instead on the consequences of karma. But Clement did know of the Buddha as a human teacher upon whom had been bestowed "divine honours" — correct enough, as both the Theravada and Mahayana schools offered prayers to the Enlightened One.

The ascetic teachings of the Essenes, which warned against the vanities and illusions of the world (the Roman writer Pliny the Elder described the Essenes as "without women, sex, or money"), were frequently viewed by late-nineteenth-century scholars as showing the distinct influence of Buddhism. This was by no means a minor argument; as it was and is deemed possible that Jesus knew of the Essenes, a Buddhist element in Christian thought could in this manner be hypothesized. The British writer Arthur Lillie, for example, argued roughly a century ago that "it was through the Jewish sect of the Essenes that Buddhist influences reached Palestine, and were passed on to Christianity." The Christian historian T. Sterling Berry complained, in his *Christianity and Buddhism* (1890), of the prominence of the view that the Essenes had been "Buddhist Jews." The discovery of the Dead Sea Scrolls and accompanying archaeological finds have transformed modern knowledge of the Essenes, and the "Buddhist Jews" are no more, or rather, appear much later — in the twentieth-century West.

But there are kindred speculations that have continued up to the present day. Certain scholars speculate that Jesus might have encountered traveling Buddhist teachers in Alexandria or even in Galilee. A prominent supporter of this view was the Swiss psychologist Carl Gustav Jung, who once observed:

> The theologians and the historians of the Christian conviction always try to make us believe that Christianity fell from heaven. But it grew very naturally through the course of centuries. Everything was well prepared. We spoke of the Persian origin of Christianity, but a great deal came also from Egypt, something from India even, because already in the second century B.C. there were Buddhistic monasteries in Persia, so through Persia the Buddhistic ideas probably crept into the formation of Christianity.

Less scholarly hypotheses contend that during the years unaccounted for in the Gospels, Jesus traveled to India and there gleaned from Buddhist teachings on selfless compassion, which appear in transformed guise in his parables. As to such speculations, the judgment of the Christian scholar Marcus Borg seems astute: "The similarities are not of the kind that suggest cultural borrowing. They are not at the level of specific images or language. [. . .] The similarities of their wisdom teaching flow out of the similarity of their religious experience, not from cultural borrowing."

❖

It is clear, at least, that Buddhist missionaries preached the Dharma in Alexandria in the same period as the Gnostics flourished. The possibilities of an interchange were explored by an obscure scholar, J. Kennedy, in a stylish essay titled "Buddhist Gnosticism, the System of Basilides." It was published in 1902 in the recondite *Journal of the Royal Asiatic Society of Great Britain and Ireland* and has since enjoyed a surprisingly long-lived influence. Kennedy contended that Basilides, a renowned Christian Gnostic who taught in second-century CE Alexandria, had incorporated Buddhist teachings on the universality of suffering and the truth of rebirth into his writings. Basilides argued that only the elect — those who experienced intuitively and directly the truth of the Gospel — were saved. This Kennedy viewed as akin to Buddhist teachings on the difficulty of attaining enlightenment: "The office of Jesus is the office of the

Buddha; the elect alone are saved, and the mass of mankind remains content to be born again." Nonetheless, Kennedy insisted that Basilides remained a sincere Christian: "He adopts the Buddhist philosophy, but not the Buddhist religion; the Buddhist faith is nothing to him. And it is as a metaphysic, not as a religion, that Buddhism first penetrated to the West."

Kennedy's belief in a Buddhist influence on Basilides is by no means a majority opinion among scholars. He does, however, have significant supporters, including Radhakrishnan. And there is a striking doctrinal bridge between Basilides and Buddhism, for Basilides argued for a spiritual path based on a potentially everlasting transmigration of souls — each new birth reflecting the sinful or righteous awareness attained in the previous life. As we have seen, a similar viewpoint was set forth by Plato in the apologue of his *Republic.* The spiritual practices of the elect included compassion and detachment from the material world, beliefs that correspond to Buddhist teachings. Clement quoted Basilides as holding that the first precept of God's will (and hence the will of the attained elect) is "to love everything, for everything is interrelated; and the second is not to desire anything; the third is not to hate anything." It was the centrality of his belief in rebirth that confirmed Basilides as a heretic in the minds of the majority of the early Church Fathers, who felt that belief to be an ignoble evasion of the significance of this one life as leading to eternal blessedness or damnation. Basilides, however, found scriptural confirmation of the truth of rebirth in Romans 7:9 — "I was once alive apart from the law" — meaning, according to Basilides, that "before I came into this body, I lived in a sort of body that did not come under the law, the body of a beast or bird."

Basilides was not alone among Gnostic — or even Christian — thinkers of the era in his belief in reincarnation. Among the Church Fathers, influential figures such as Origen, Justin Martyr, Clement of Alexandria, and Tertullian also voiced their assent, using both Jewish and Christian texts in support of the doctrine. Origen, whose teachings prompted the most controversy from among this group, nonetheless participated in the attacks on Basilides. The concern of Origen was that Basilides had "deprived men of a salutary fear by teaching that transmigrations are the only punishments after death." The eternal flux of transmigrations required, for Origen, greater ongoing elements of loss or gain. Hence, in Origen's writings, it is held that although originally all living spirits are created alike, free will enables them to choose sanctity or sin, and hence to incarnate in angelic, human, or demonic hell-bound forms. But damnation is not eternal in the system propounded by Origen. Ultimately — by means of a final Apocatastasis — all angels, all humans, all demons, even Satan himself will be vouchsafed salvation.

As Origen lived and taught in Alexandria, it is not surprising that he knew of the existence of Buddhist teachings. There is, in his writings, one brief but highly perplexing reference to Buddhism. In assessing the potential value of missionary efforts to Britain, Origen argued that its people would be predisposed to Christianity, as they had already been exposed to "the doctrines of the Druids and the Buddhists, who had already inculcated the unity of the Godhead." Origen was mistaken in his belief in British-based Buddhists. But his sense of an affinity between Buddhism and Christianity — a shared vision of an underlying spiritual unity to existence — was astute and indicates a degree of knowledge of Buddhist teachings. There is, however, no evidence whatsoever that those teachings exercised a substantive influence on him.

The views of Origen provoked severe attacks from the emerging Church hierarchy. In particular, his belief in a final Apocatastasis was held to diminish the salvific power of Christian ritual. At last, in 543, the Byzantine emperor Justinian issued a decree, approved by the Church, that anathematized and excommunicated the long-dead Origen. Ten years later, in what became known as the Second Council of Constantinople, Origen and those who accepted his writings were again condemned. In particular, belief in reincarnation was anathematized, as it ran contrary to two intertwined Christian orthodox tenets — the indivisible unity of body and soul, and the physical as well as spiritual resurrection of the dead at the Last Judgment.

The doctrine of the soul's transmigrations, a persistent visionary element in Western thought in the works of Pythagoras, Empedocles, Plato, and Origen, to name but a few, had now become heresy — or so, at least, has been the ecclesiastical perception of the matter. But there is a minority viewpoint, expressed by certain Catholic scholars, that as the Second Council of Constantinople was composed almost exclusively of bishops from the Eastern as opposed to the Western Church; as the

Western pope Vigilius did not, for political reasons, attend the Second Council; and, finally, as the proceeding was "extra-conciliary" rather than "an actual ecumenical council," Origen and his teachings were never anathematized. Skillful as the argument may be, it exists in a vacuum outside the history of Christianity to date. Perhaps it will have cause to be reborn in the future if the intertwining of Buddhist and Christian thought progresses.

❖

The quest for demonstrable Buddhist influence on any single Gnostic or Christian thinker is still only a quest. But there remains the ongoing appeal of a related argument — that the multifold parallels between Buddhist and Gnostic teachings strongly suggest a broad, if unspecified, mutual influence. The first influential formulation of this theory was published in 1828 by Isaac Jacob Schmidt, a German writer residing in Russia who had become familiar with the Vajrayana Buddhism of Tibet and Mongolia. Schmidt's thesis commended itself to his contemporary, the philosopher Arthur Schopenhauer, who championed it in his own writings. In the twentieth century, the British historian Steven Runciman took up the cause, deeming it "certain" that Buddhist legends "were absorbed into Gnostic scripture."

But it was Edward Conze, an esteemed modern German scholar of Buddhism, who put forward the most compelling formulation of this argument, noting a number of fundamental resemblances between Gnosticism and Buddhism, including the teaching of salvation or release stemming from direct spiritual insight — gnosis (Greek) or jnana (Sanskrit) — rather than faith; a rejection of rule-based ethics as opposed to an awareness of the subjectivity of all human codes of conduct; an emphasis on a mystical reunion with an ultimate One, which, whether conceived of as a remote Godhead or an inconceivable nirvana, displays none of the involvement with human affairs of a theistic creator god; and a tendency to stress, even relish, the unattainability of their teachings, which the masses could never be expected to comprehend. Conze allowed that corroborative facts were lacking, and further that Gnostic writings made reference to Jewish, Babylonian, and Egyptian sacred texts, but not to Buddhist sources. The sole and unique exception was to be found in the teachings of Manichaeism, a Gnostic creed that, when preached in central Asia, used Buddhist terminology to enhance its appeal to indigenous Buddhists.

The most prominent modern American scholar of Gnosticism, Elaine Pagels, argued on behalf of Conze's direct-influence hypothesis, stressing a possibility to which Conze had only briefly alluded — the known contact between Buddhists and the so-called Thomas Christians (or Malabar Christians) of southern India. This community, which remained separate from the Roman Church until the sixteenth century, and for which the Gnostic *Gospel of Thomas* served as a sacred text, claimed to have been founded by Saint Thomas the apostle. According to a third-century apocryphal text, the *Acts of Saint Thomas,* Jesus sold Thomas as a slave to a merchant in Jerusalem seeking to acquire a skilled carpenter for the Indo-Parthian king of Taxila, Gondophernes; Jesus struck the bargain so that Thomas might preach the Gospel in India. Thomas was said to have succeeded in converting many in Taxila to Christianity. Upon venturing farther south into India, however, he was martyred in the kingdom of Mazdai as a direct result of having too successfully preached the Christian doctrine of chastity, making believers even of the king's own wife and son, much to the displeasure of the king himself. Imprisonment was ordered, but the doors of the cell of Saint Thomas flew open on their own. At last he was taken to a mountain and there executed by four spearmen. But the murderous king was himself converted to Christianity after his son, suffering from demonic possession, was healed by dust from the grave of Saint Thomas. The enduring belief in the healing properties of the dust of this holy grave was attested to some twelve centuries later by Marco Polo.

The *Acts of Saint Thomas* is attributed to Bardesanes of Edessa (in southern Turkey), a third-century Christian Gnostic who was also a student of Indian religion, on which he wrote a book that has survived only in fragments. Such as they are, those fragments confirm that Bardesanes knew that the rulers of the Kushan empire of India venerated Buddhist sages, supported their temples, and relied on their prayers for maintenance of peace. The Kushan rulers — the most famous of whom, Kanishka, was deemed a "second Ashoka" — strongly supported Buddhist missionary efforts along the Silk Road. Indeed, their Manichaean competitors deemed Buddhism the "state religion" of India. The knowledge possessed by Bardesanes suggests, of course, that an interchange between Buddhists and Gnostics could have occurred during this period.

In the same city of Edessa, roughly one century later, there dwelled Saint Ephrem, a Syrian-born theologian and poet who reviled Bardesanes (Ephrem wrote of him that he died "with the Lord in his mouth and demons in his heart") but accepted the truth of his *Acts of Saint Thomas.* Ephrem composed Syriac hymns of praise for the triumphs achieved by Saint Thomas:

> *The sunburnt India thou hast made fair . . .*
> *   a tainted land of dark people thou hast purified.*
> *More than snow and white linen*
> *the dark bride of India thou hast made fair . . .*
> *the crown of light has obliterated India's darkened shades.*

We may date the linkage between racist preconceptions and Christian conversion efforts in India to as early as the fourth century. Ephrem's view of the taint of darkness was embraced by later missionaries from both the Eastern and Western churches.

There is general agreement among both scholars and believers that had Saint Thomas wished to journey to India, he could have done so, either by land through the mountain passes of central Asia or by sea along the Persian Gulf and Indian Ocean. There were established trade routes between the Roman Empire, central Asia, and India by this time. And there are records of the existence of an established Syriac Christian church in Kerala, on the southwest Indian coast, by the fourth century. But the earliest evidence of a distinct group of Thomas Christians comes only in the sixth century, through the writings of an Alexandrian merchant turned Christian monk named Cosmas Indicopleustes ("Cosmas the Indian navigator"), who, despite his boastful name, is now believed unlikely ever to have sailed so far as India. Nonetheless, it is with Cosmas that the history of the Thomas Christians — who remained allied with the Syriac, as opposed to the Roman, church until the late sixteenth century — is deemed by scholars to have begun. But scholarly insistence on written evidence is often offensive to present-day Thomas Christians, whose belief in the teachings of their tradition is firm. Their fervor is reflected in a 1955 Saint Thomas Day speech by the president of India,

Rajenda Prasad: "Remember, St. Thomas came to India when many of the countries of Europe had not yet become Christian, and so, those Indians who trace their Christianity to him have a longer history and a higher ancestry than that of Christians of many of the European countries. And it is really a matter of pride to us that it so happened."

Given the hard-fought battles over the origins of the Thomas Christians, it seems still more perilous to ask if they enjoyed a dialogue with Indian Buddhists. As recounted above, the *Acts of Saint Thomas* claims considerable successes for Thomas in India. The traditions of the Thomas Christians hold that some indigenous temples were converted by Thomas into Christian churches. But there is scant evidence of any subsequent missionary work by the small community, which was estimated, as late as the sixteenth century (when Portuguese mariners "discovered" the Thomas Christians), to number only thirty thousand.

A major Gnostic text (dated variously as first or second century CE by scholars) was attributed to this same apostle, leading Pagels to ask, "Could the title of the *Gospel of Thomas* — named for the disciple who, tradition tells us, went to India — suggest the influence of Indian tradition?" More recently, Pagels posed the question of influence in a context bearing directly upon Buddhist-Christian relations of the present day. In her introduction to *Living Buddha, Living Christ* (1995) by Thich Nhat Hanh, she wrote:

> Does Thich Nhat Hanh know the *Gospel of Thomas* and other gnostic sources or did he choose the term "living Christ" — a term more characteristic of gnostic texts than of the New Testament — by a kind of spiritual intuition? In either case, those who are more familiar than I am with Buddhist tradition, and especially those more experienced in meditation and contemplation, will surely notice in these ancient Christian sources many more resonances than I can mention here. Comparative study of Buddhism and early (gnostic) Christianity has barely begun.

Explicit in the arguments of Pagels, and implicit in the arguments of others who have posed a potential link between Buddhism and Gnosticism, is the belief that Gnosticism preserved — while Christianity rejected — vital spiritual teachings that lie at the heart of the Buddhist tradition. These teachings include, most notably, a stance of respectful equality with all religious traditions that reflect basic spiritual truths; an emphasis on direct experiential knowledge as opposed to passive faith; and an insistence that all human beings partake of Buddha-nature, or, alternatively, that the kingdom of God is innate within each of us, regardless of the nature or even the existence of our theological convictions. In short, certain of the teachings viewed as cursed heresies by the early Church are, in the present day, being put forward again by Buddhists in the ecumenical West.

Far more interest has been shown in Buddhist influence on Christianity than the reverse. But there is evidence of possible Christian influence as well. Hajime Nakamura noted that a "Buddhist counterpart" to Christ's parable of the prodigal son is found in the *Lotus Sutra,* a highly influential early Mahayana text (first or second century CE). More expansively, the American Christian scholar Kenneth S. Latourette, the D. Willis James Professor of Missions and Oriental History at Yale University in the mid-twentieth century, took note of a "most alluring" but unproven theory that Mahayana Buddhist thought, as disseminated in China, was "in many respects Christianity in disguise." A good disguise it was, as there is no record of Christian travelers or missionaries to China ever recognizing it as such.

But there remain stronger theoretical possibilities of Gnostic, if not Christian, influence on Buddhism. In Bactria, ongoing commerce with the West endured for centuries after the fall of the Indo-Greek kingdom. Mircea Eliade, perhaps the preeminent twentieth-century historian of religion, speculated that Gnostic thought and practices (which included ascetic and sacred-sex techniques) could have reached India by way of Iran and Afghanistan, and hence could have affected the development of Tantrism — meditation, visualization, and sexual practices that became vital elements both of Hinduism and of the Vajrayana Buddhism of Tibet and central Asia. As Eliade argued, "More than one curious parallel can be noted between tantrism and the great Western mysterio-sophic current that, at the beginning of the Christian era, arose from the confluence of Gnosticism, Hermetism, Greco-Egyptian alchemy, and the tradition of the Mysteries."

Eliade noted the emphasis, both in Gnosticism and in Tantrism, on teachings that could not be set to writing but rather depended on oral transmission from a proven master to a suitably developed adept. This personal and private mode of teaching helps to explain both the provisional state of our knowledge of Gnosticism and the particular difficulty that the West encountered in making sense of Vajrayana Buddhism. If the speculations of Eliade are correct, the resulting irony is remarkable. The Buddhism of Tibet, romanticized by Westerners as the pure and remote wisdom of the East, would then be rooted, in some small measure, in Western spiritual practices from the classical and Christian eras. Then again, it was a scholarly protégé of Eliade, Ioan Couliano, who warned against the ceaseless search for direct historical influence between religions with similar beliefs. If Couliano's point is taken, the resemblances between Gnosticism and Buddhist Tantrism stem simply from the same sorts of questions being asked by divergent human groups fascinated with human spiritual capacities.

That such groups existed in the East and the West, and had opportunity for discourse in the centuries preceding and following the founding of Christianity, is sufficiently plain. As to what was communicated and when, therein lies the enduring mystery.

2

SYNCRETISM ALONG THE SILK ROAD

❖

Nestorius, a fifth-century bishop of Constantinople, played a signal role in ensuring a faint but ongoing contact between Christians and Buddhists in the one thousand years from the fall of the Roman Empire to the formation of the Jesuits. For his part, Nestorius almost certainly possessed no such ambition. He lost his bishopric when his writings were deemed heretical for positing that Jesus Christ had contained within himself two distinct persons, Jesus the human and Christ the God. The orthodox view, as expressed in the same period by Pope Leo I, held that the incarnate Christ was one person, but with two natures, human and divine. The primary importance of the difference to the Church had to do with the salvific power of Christ; for if he were deemed only half-human, his sacrifice could be viewed as unfittingly redemptive of wholly human sinners. There was also the factor of the rising devotional popularity of Mary, the Virgin Mother of God, whom the Greek Fathers called *Theotokos* — God-Bearer. If Mary bore only a human Jesus guided by a separate spiritual Christ, she was *Theotokos* no more.

Nestorius intended none of this furor. When first named bishop, he took power with a pledge to rid Constantinople of its heretics. But he became a victim of the battle for power between the Greek and Roman churches of the West and the Syriac, Persian, and Mesopotamian churches of the East, in which his teachings on the dual personage of Christ were widely accepted. In 430, his writings were condemned by Pope Celestine. In 436, the Eastern Roman emperor Theodosius II banished him to

Upper Egypt, where he died some fifteen years later, all the while insisting that his views reflected those of the Church. Here, as a recondite example of early Christological debate, the matter might have rested, but it
did not. For the bishops of western Asia would not concur with the con-
demnation of Nestorius. Gradually, they created an autonomous Nestorian
Church, which, as its missionary opportunities in the Mediterranean region were blocked, preached its faith across the breadth of central Asia,
as well as in southern India, where it wielded ecclesiastical authority
over the Thomas (or Malabar) Christians.

The Nestorians were not the first or the only Christians to reach central Asia. In the late second century, Bardesanes of Edessa — the same
Bardesanes to whom the *Acts of Saint Thomas* is attributed — wrote of a
Christian community living in Bactria that its women (he did not mention men on this score) refrained from "any intercourse with strangers."
By the fourth century, Christians, as well as Indian Buddhists, had established centers in the oasis city of Marv in eastern Persia, from which
both launched missionary efforts to China. But it was the Nestorian
missions, commencing in the sixth century, that spurred the first sustained contacts between Buddhists and Christians.

The principal route for all of these travels was the famed Silk Road,
which extended from Persia to China, skirting the Himalayas to the
south and the Gobi Desert to the north. The Nestorian missionaries, as
well as the Buddhist and Manichaean monks, made their way along the
same roads the merchants traveled and congregated in the same oases. As
the scholars Ian Gillman and Hans-Joachim Klimkeit observed, "One
could almost speak of a Christian-Buddhist dialogue being conducted
in Central Asia 1000 years ago, Christians and Buddhists not only living
together, but being in constant interaction." If there is an "almost" to
speaking of such a "dialogue," it stems not from real uncertainty as
to whether it occurred — people in "constant interaction" do tend to
communicate as to the central beliefs of their lives, and there were Buddhist and Christian missionaries aplenty, who could scarcely have
avoided comparative discussions of some sort — but rather from the
scanty surviving evidence as to the matters discussed and the resulting
influences. But evidence there is, and it has intrigued religionists and re-
searchers alike for centuries.

In Dunhuang, the westernmost city of the Chinese empire and a stop along the Silk Road, a massive repository of manuscripts and art was, in the eleventh century, hidden and sealed in a cave. That cave was discovered in the early twentieth century. Contained therein, among other treasures, were substantial collections of Buddhist, Manichaean, and Nestorian writings. Included were some early attempts at translation of Nestorian scriptures into Chinese by A-lo-pen, a seventh-century Persian Nestorian priest. One of these, *The Jesus Messiah Sutra,* reflects the awkwardness of the earliest effort to bring Christian teachings into a new linguistic universe. For instance, to convey the concept of God, A-lo-pen used the term "Buddha." He also explained the Ten Commandments in terms drawn from Buddhist and Confucian thought.

❖

Buddhism, like Nestorianism, was a foreign religion in the T'ang court. From its position of favored support in the Kushan empire of northwest India, Buddhism had expanded as far as China by the first century CE, and on into Korea and Japan by the fourth and fifth centuries, respectively. Sogdians and Parthians from central Asia served as pioneer translators of Indian Buddhist texts into Chinese. By the time of the Nestorian arrival, Buddhism had firmly established its presence in China, not least through the creation of a Chinese Buddhist idiom that had won the stylistic, if not the spiritual, approval of the cultured and meticulously literate Confucian ruling elite.

China produced distinct and lasting varieties of Buddhism. Both the Chan (Zen) and the Ching-t'u (Pure Land) schools came of age during the T'ang dynasty. Bodhidharma, a fifth-century Indian Buddhist monk who journeyed for three years by sea and land to teach the Dharma in China, founded the Chan approach. Legend has him cutting off his eyelids so that sleep would not erode his meditative concentration; where his eyelids touched the ground, tea bushes sprang forth. In one of his talks, he explained the essence of his Chan teachings:

In India, the twenty-seven patriarchs only transmitted the imprint of the mind. And the only reason I've come to China is to transmit the instantaneous teaching of the Mahayana: *This mind is the buddha.* I don't talk about precepts, devotions or ascetic practices such as immersing yourself in water or fire, treading a wheel of knives, eating one meal a day, or never lying down. These are fanatical, provisional teachings. Once you recognize your moving, miraculously aware nature, yours is the mind of all buddhas.

He attracted only two devoted disciples in his lifetime, but his approach spread in the two centuries following his death, until Chan, which pollinated nicely with Chinese Daoist thought, became a cultural force both in China and Japan. Bodhidharma was also revered as the founder of the martial art of kung fu, which he used for the training of monks at the Shaolin temple in Honan.

The roots of the Pure Land school lay in Buddhist teachings of the Gandhara region of northwest India. There, in the first century CE, from out of the welter of past and future Buddhas that had emerged in popular Indian belief, came a dominant new presence — Buddha Amitabha. This future Buddha of Immeasurable Light presided over the Sukhavati realm, into which the worthy could (through meditation, ritual observance, and virtuous deeds) be reborn, thus evading regression into baser incarnations. The blissful conditions for ongoing practice in the Sukhavati realm would lead assuredly, at long last, to perfect enlightenment. The Pure Land school gained in strength in China from the fifth century onward and, like the Chan school, spread to Japan as well. By the eighth century, Japanese monks traveled regularly to train under Chinese masters of both schools and to learn to translate Chinese Buddhist texts into Japanese.

❖

The Nestorian priest A-lo-pen also learned Chinese, so as to win for his Christian texts the same respect in which Buddhist teachings were held. A-lo-pen made little headway with the broader Chinese population, but he did win the esteem of the T'ang court, whose expansive tolerance in religious matters is attested to in this decree issued by the emperor T'ai-tsung in 638:

The Persian monk A-lo-pen bringing scriptures and teaching from far has come to offer them at Shang-ching. The meaning of the teaching has been carefully examined: it is mysterious, wonderful, calm; it fixes the essentials of life and perfection; it is the salvation of living beings, it is the wealth of man. It is right that it should spread through the empire.

The Nestorian creed became known in China as the "Luminous Religion." It has been argued by some scholars that Nestorians, or perhaps itinerant Gnostics, might have influenced the early development of Pure Land Buddhism. The similarities in outlook include, most vividly, the encompassing devotional focus on Buddha Amitabha, who in Pure Land Buddhism is a savior deity akin in compassionate power to Jesus Christ. But parallels are not evidence, and evidence is lacking.

The most prominent record of the Nestorian presence in China is the Sian-fu monument, an inscribed stone tablet created in 781. In the upper arch of the tablet is carved a lotus from which a cross emerges, with a flame arising on its uppermost point. This blending of Christian and Buddhist iconography, with the lotus of realized wisdom supporting the cross of redemption, captures the spirit of the author of the carved text — a Nestorian priest from Persia named Adam, who became known in China as Ching-Ching. On this monument, Adam provided a concise history of the Nestorian presence in China from the time of A-lo-pen, some 150 years earlier. Adam charged that during the seventh century, Buddhists used lies and violence to halt the spread of the Nestorian faith. But Adam was astute enough to borrow from the strengths of his Buddhist rivals. In one of his texts, *The Ta-ch'in Luminous Religious Sutra on the Origin of Origins,* he offered this admonition: "Let you who hold the Law of God attain the utmost pure Emptiness." Here the Buddhist term "Emptiness" (the essential impermanence and interdependence of all being) is used instead of the Christian term "Grace."

The Sian-fu monument was not the only work undertaken by Adam. While in China, he also collaborated with a Persian Buddhist monk named Prajna on the translation of the *Satparamita Sutra* from *hu* (a western Asian language the precise identity of which remains uncertain) into Chinese. In 800, the Chinese Buddhist Yuan-chao wrote a stinging account of the outcome of the collaboration, which reveals that religious dialogue had its parameters even within the T'ang court:

> Since at that time Prajna (Pan-jo) was unfamiliar with the *hu* language and did not yet understand the speech of T'ang, and Ching-Ching did not know Sanskrit nor understand Buddhist doctrine, though they professed to have made a translation they had not caught half the gems. They were seeking for vain glory with no thought of doing good. [. . .] Ching-Ching

must preach the teaching of Messiah (Mi-shih-he) and the Buddhist monk (sha-men) make known the *sutra* of Buddha. We wish to have religious teaching well defined that men may have no uncertainty. Truth and error are not the same; the Ching and the Wei [rivers] are not alike.

Buddhism, according to Yuan-chao, was represented by the clear-flowing Ching River, while Christianity was comparable to the murky waters of the Wei.

For all this partisan rivalry, the mutual interplay of these two religions was, in this period, altogether exceptional — not to be equaled again, in its depth and freedom, until the twentieth century. One of the discoveries in the Dunhuang cave was of a painting on silk, damaged in part, which portrays a Christian devotional figure — there is disagreement as to whether it is Jesus or a saint. What is clear is that the painting shows the influence of the Buddhist iconography of central Asia. The right hand of the devotional figure is raised in the *vitarka mudra* (sacred gesture) of instruction also used in Buddhist depictions of compassionate bodhisattvas. The ongoing spread of traditional Christian symbols by Nestorian monks has been established by the discovery of eighth-century rock carvings of Nestorian crosses in western Tibet. The nineteenth-century British scholar Sabine Baring-Gould enthused — perhaps overmuch, given the scant evidence — that the Nestorian Church

faced Buddhism and wrestled with it for the religious supremacy in Tibet; it established churches in Persia and in Bokhara; it penetrated India; it formed colonies in Ceylon, in Siam, and in Sumatra; so that the Catholicos or Pope of Bagdad exercised sway more extensive than that ever obtained by the successor of St. Peter. The number of Christians belonging to that communion probably exceeded that of the members of the true Catholic Church in East and West.

❖

There is from this era one enduring Buddhist influence on Christendom that, tacit as it was, is undeniable. As the Indian scholar Gauranga Nath Banerjee wrote, "The most curious thing borrowed by the Roman and Greek churches, is [. . .] the quasi-worship of Gautama Buddha himself (in so far as a Romanist worships his Saints)." The root of this "quasi-worship" is the legend of Barlaam and Josaphat, two saints of the Catholic Church, whose piety was particularly venerated in the Middle Ages.

Although there have been many Christianized versions of the Barlaam and Josaphat tale, the basic recurrent narrative is as follows: Josaphat (a Westernized corruption of "Bodhisattva") is the son of an Indian king, Abeneer, who persecutes Christians and is displeased at the prophecy, issued during Josaphat's infancy, that the boy would someday convert to Christianity. To prevent this, his father places him in a lavish palace isolated from all of life's woes. But Josaphat escapes from his palace one day and encounters four people who personify four aspects of the truth of the world's suffering — an aged man, a leper, a corpse, and a mendicant Christian monk named Barlaam. The latter, in the disguise of a wealthy jewel merchant, promises to reveal to the young man an especially precious stone, which proves to be a metaphor for the precious saving grace of Christ. Not only is the prophecy of Josaphat's youth fulfilled, but the newly baptized son succeeds in converting his father the king, after which Josaphat departs for a life of ascetic seclusion in the forest.

It was in the mid-nineteenth century that scholars first concurred that the origins of the Barlaam and Josaphat legend lay in the traditional life story of the Buddha, who as a young man left the palace in which he had been shielded from the sufferings of the world. This discovery prompted Israel Zangwill, a British Jewish writer, to pen these lines of bemusement:

> *Was Barlaam truly Josaphat,*
> *And Buddha truly each?*
> *What better parallel than that*
> *The unity to preach —*
>
> *The simple brotherhood of souls*

The legend comes from traditional Indian written lives of the Buddha, but no single text can be cited as its origin. Rather, the story has appeared in multiple cultures and religious environments. Its first great transformation came when it was adapted into a Manichaean holy tale in central Asia. Mani, born in Babylonia (modern Iraq) in the third century, was the religious prophet and hybridizing genius who created a world religion, Manichaeism, out of Gnostic dualist doctrines as to the cosmic opposition between good and evil, spirit and matter. At its height, Manichaeism extended as far as Egypt, Rome, and Carthage in the West (Saint Augustine was, prior to his conversion to Christianity, an ardent Manichaeist, and it is often said that dualist tendencies persist even in his Christian writings) and as far as Mongolia and China in the East. Because Manichaeism was ousted from the Christianized Roman Empire in the sixth century, Mani and his doctrines remain little known in the West, although Manichaeism survived in China into the seventeenth century.

The breadth of appeal of Manichaeism was due in considerable measure to the dedicated assimilationist approach of Mani himself. Having been raised in a Jewish-Christian sect with traditions extending back to the Qumran Jews of the Dead Sea Scrolls, Mani — once he had experienced his own prophetic revelations from "the Living Paraclete" at age twenty-four — found it quite natural to extend his universal teachings in the varying doctrinal guises of competing, or rather subsumed, paths, for Mani saw himself as the prophetic successor to Noah, Zoroaster, the Buddha, and Christ. In one Turkish Manichaean text, Jesus is referred to as "the Messiah-Buddha," the first known instance of a deliberate merging and blurring of these two great teachers. In other texts, Mani was identified with Maitreya, the future Buddha, and also with the Christian Paraclete and the messianic son of Zoroaster.

The Manichaean version of the story of Prince Gotama and his first encounters with suffering traveled westward through Sogdian, Arabic, and other versions, becoming both a Muslim holy tale and the Christianized Barlaam and Josaphat legend. It was in the Georgian language that the Barlaam and Josaphat story was first written as a Christian devotional text. The translation from Georgian to Greek by the tenth-century monk Saint Euthymius led to the spread of the tale throughout Europe in pious, heretical, and literary forms. The heretical use stemmed from the fact, as the British scholar D. M. Lang noted, that the legend's "advocacy of the ascetic way of life and renunciation of the world inspired the mediaeval Albigensian heretics, to such an extent that the work has sometimes been taken to be a Cathar document." The heresies of the

Albigensians and Cathars (the names are used interchangeably) are widely regarded as late-surviving forms of Gnosticism. So, at any rate, did the Church regard them, and thus it ordered the mass murder of the Cathars of Languedoc in the thirteenth century.

It cannot be demonstrated that any distinct Buddhist teaching had survived in the oft-mutated Barlaam and Josaphat legend. Extremes of ascetic passion are common to all religious paths. Nonetheless, it has been argued by certain Western esotericists that there is a spiritual lineage between the doctrines of Buddhism and the world-shunning views of the Cathars. Steven Runciman, who rejected any such theory, also posed the most striking resemblance between the two creeds. The Cathars, he wrote, held that "Christ taught by His example; He showed the Way — like a Buddha rather than the Christ of Orthodox Christianity."

In the sixteenth century, Saint Barlaam and Saint Josaphat were added to the Roman martyrology. Their joint feast day is observed on November 27, a date that has been ignored by present-day Western Buddhists but might well serve as a time for celebration of longtime affinities between the two paths.

❖

As compared to the Manichaeans, who drew freely from Buddhist and other religious terminology, the Nestorians borrowed little from Buddhism, or at least evidence to that effect is limited and faint. The legend of Saint George is recounted in one Sogdian text, but here, instead of a dragon, his adversary is a Mahakala (wrathful deity) of the Tibetan Buddhist tradition. In another Nestorian text, a translation from Syriac into Uighur, the story of the Magi is told, and the titles they bestow on the Christ child include that of "Physician," which, as the scholars Gillman and Klimkeit observed, is "both a Christian and a Buddhist epithet of the Saviour."

Did Buddhists borrow in turn from the Christian teachings of this era? Certainly, there was extensive contact between Buddhists and Christians, even instances of intermarriage. There was also, in certain central Asian Buddhist texts, the emergence of an idea that also appears (with reference to Christ) in apocryphal Christian and Gnostic texts — that the Buddha came to offer his life as a "ransom" for the benefit of all who would receive the teachings. Gillman and Klimkeit argued for the influence of two key Gnostic scriptures, the *Gospel of Philip* and the *Gospel of Thomas,* on the emerging Mahayana vision: "Thus the idea, already conceived in India, that the 'Buddha-Nature' pervades everything in the world, even the smallest speck of dust, an idea that was to become central for certain East Asian schools of Buddhism, was apparently accentuated under the catalytic influence of early Christian and Gnostic notions about the ubiquitous Saviour."

❖

In the eighth century, China was engaged in a struggle with expanding Islamic forces for control of its western frontiers. It was the hope of the T'ang emperor Hsuan Tsung that an appreciative reception of Nestorian missionaries might gain for China a useful alliance with Christians against a common Muslim enemy. But after Chinese forces were decisively defeated in 751 at the Talas River (in modern Kazakhstan), the T'ang court concluded that a Western alliance was no longer of value. As the T'ang rulers declined in power, so did the status of the Nestorians. But the expulsion edict of Emperor Wu-tsung, issued in 845, applied to all foreign religionists, Buddhist and Christian alike — a joint punishment for having sought, as one Chinese text from the period put it, "to confound the customs of China."

During the persecutions of the late T'ang dynasty, it was the Buddhists, with the strongest presence among the foreign-based religionists, who suffered the greatest destruction. Some 4,600 Buddhist monasteries were razed or converted to different uses. This was accompanied by the forced secularization — and return to tax-paying status — of roughly 260,000 nuns and monks. The slaves owned by the Buddhist monasteries — some 150,000 — were freed and accepted into the Chinese population. The other foreign religions suffered their horrors as well. In the Cantonese city of Khanfu, in the late ninth century, some 6,000 Christians, Jews, Muslims, and Zoroastrians were murdered. By the time of the Sung dynasty (960–1279), the onetime Christian presence in China — dominantly Nestorian, but also including Roman Catholics and Monophysites (a western Asian creed that held Christ to be solely divine and not at all human in nature) — was extinct.

❖

In the seventh century and after, the dual expansion of Indian Buddhism from the south and Chinese and central Asian Buddhism from the north brought about the conversion of Tibet to a largely Buddhist nation. Indian Buddhism was without question the most powerful influence on Tibet, particularly the Tantric teachings that had emerged in northern Indian Buddhist (as well as Hindu) ritual practice. These esoteric Tantric teachings — known as Vajrayana Buddhism and primarily conveyed in Indian texts of instruction known as tantras — were translated widely into Tibetan and conveyed privately by lamas to suitable monks. By the eighth century, Vajrayana teachings had also made their way by sea from India to Japan, where they took the form of Shingon Buddhism. But in India itself, Hinduism had emerged as the dominant religion by the ninth century. In this same period, Muslim conquests in the West drove Buddhist Tantric practitioners to eastern India, where they found favor under the Pala and Sena dynasties.

Buddhist monasteries flourished under these dynasties by allying themselves with feudal overlords, for whom they administered sizable landholdings and from whom they received financial support and military protection. The importance of the Tantric work — artistic, philosophic, and ritual — being done at monasteries such as Nalanda and Vikramashila was recognized at the time by the Buddhist communities of the world. (Among the seminal teachings produced during this period was the *Kalachakra Tantra,* a rite currently favored by the Fourteenth Dalai Lama, who conducted the first Kalachakra initiation in the West in Madison, Wisconsin, in 1981.) Buddhist merchants and pilgrims alike made their way to eastern India from Tibet, Nepal, China, the Mongolian steppes, Burma, and Indonesia. Some of the Tibetan pilgrims went on, after their return to their homeland, to become founding figures of Tibetan Buddhism. The most famous example is Marpa (1012–1097), who made many difficult trips to a remote teaching center established by the great Tantric yogi Naropa (956–1040), after whom the first Buddhist-affiliated university in the West — founded by Chögyam Trungpa in Colorado — was named nearly a millennium after his death. Marpa became the most renowned Tibetan translator of Buddhist teachings; he was also guru to Milarepa, the most famous of all Tibetan masters.

Vikramashila, built to the architectural plan of a cosmic mandala, was the most revered of the many Buddhist temples destroyed from the eleventh through the early thirteenth century by the conquering Muslim forces, which had at last overcome the Pala kings. The special status of Vikramashila was known to the conquerors, for the physical remains of the monastery were handled with a ritual care that bespeaks both fear and respect. Its foundation stone was dropped into the Ganges, while its bricks and stones were employed in the construction of a new mosque. The carnage of the conquest included wholesale slaughter of Buddhist believers and the burning of Buddhist texts. Islamic chroniclers showed little interest in the religious beliefs of the lands that fell under Muslim dominion. The most detailed account of Buddhism by a medieval Islamic writer is that of Rashid al-Din, a physician of Jewish and Persian descent, who in the early fourteenth century compiled a history of relations between the Mongols and the Muslim lands of western Asia since the time of Jenghiz Khan. It included an account of the beliefs of the Buddhists of the region, as well as *Jataka*-style tales of the Buddha's incarnations prior to his enlightenment. Beyond this, the interchange between the two religions was minimal.

Nepal, Tibet, and Java were the primary destinations of Buddhists who managed to evade the Muslim conquests. Java was the least hospitable to Buddhism, due to the more pervasive inroads of both Islam and Hinduism. In India, the land of its founder, Buddhism as a visible living creed had all but vanished.

❧

The return of both a Christian and a Buddhist presence in China was due to the expansive conquests and religious tolerance of the Mongol Empire, founded by the famed thirteenth-century warlord Jenghiz Khan. The Mongol policy was to slaughter the enemy until control was assured, and thereafter to permit their subjects to practice whatever religion they wished. Thus in Marv, a major Nestorian center, the initial Mongol conquest occasioned the mass murder of roughly one million people in the city and surrounding areas. How many victims were Christian is unknown, but the Nestorian Church was thereafter allowed to reestablish itself, not only in Marv but throughout the Mongol Empire, which, by its stabilizing rule, enabled travel and commerce across all of Asia.

Jenghiz, like many of his fellow Mongol chieftains (some of whom were Nestorians), numbered among his wives Nestorian women from the

Turkish Uighur and Karait tribes in western Asia. Sorghaghtani Begi, a Nestorian, became the mother of the most storied Mongol khan — Khubilai, the protagonist of Coleridge's famed uncompleted poem and the founder of the Chinese Yuan dynasty, which ended the culturally isolated reign of the Sung emperors.

Under the reign of Ögödei, the successor to Jenghiz as Great Khan, the Mongols extended their military dominance through western Russia and on into Poland, Hungary, Bohemia, and Moravia. The fear they inspired was such that many Christians believed they were in allegiance with Gog and Magog, the satanic harbingers of the end of the world. The death of Ögödei in 1241 led to a withdrawal of Mongol forces that Europeans deemed a miracle bestowed by the Christian God. The earthly cause was a convening of the Mongol leaders in their capital, Karakorum, to elect a new khan — Güyük, who died after seven years of rule and was succeeded by Möngke, who in turn was succeeded by Khubilai in 1259.

Khubilai restored the expansive religious tolerance of the early T'ang dynasty rulers. As a matter of personal affinity, Khubilai's closest leanings were toward the teachings of the Tibetan Buddhists. But he also supported the indigenous Confucian teachings and welcomed Christian, Jewish, Muslim, Manichaean, and Zoroastrian emissaries as well. Nestorians understandably thrived under an emperor whose own mother was of their creed. In 1275, Khubilai approved the establishment of a Nestorian archbishopric in the new Mongol capital of Khanbaliq (modern Beijing).

❖

In the twelfth century, word reached Europe of a great Christian king in Asia — Nestorian in outlook, and with a shared enmity toward the Muslim warriors with whom the Roman Catholics of Europe were doing battle in the Crusades for the Holy Land. Letters purportedly written by Prester (or Priest) John to the Holy See and to various European monarchs began to circulate widely. In one such letter, addressed to the emperor of Constantinople, Prester John (or, as he named himself in the letter, "John, Priest by the almighty power of God and the might of our Lord Jesus Christ") boasted of his victories in Asia: "In the three Indies our Magnificence rules, and our land extends beyond India, where rests the body of the holy apostle Thomas. [. . .] The Amazons and Brahmins are subject to us. The palace in which our Supereminency resides is built after the pattern of the castle built by the apostle Thomas for the Indian king Gundoforus [Gondopharnes]." The hope for a mighty ally from the East was alluring enough that, in 1177, Pope Alexander III addressed a diplomatic missive to the "Indorum Regi, Sacerdotum Sanctissimo" (the King of the Indies, the Most Holy Priest), whom some historians have held to be Prester John. Others have argued for known personages, such as the king of Abyssinia or the Chinese prince Gor Khan, under whom many Nestorians lived. Nonetheless, popular belief in Prester John persisted for centuries. The Portuguese explorer Vasco da Gama, when commencing his 1497 voyage around the Cape of Good Hope to India, carried a letter addressed to the great king and holy priest.

❖

As the legend of Prester John indicates, European ignorance of Mongol politics and military capability was all but complete. So it was that popes and other Western rulers dispatched a number of missions to the Mongol court. At a minimum, useful information might be obtained, and at best, the Mongols might be induced to join with Christian Europe in a two-front campaign against the expanding power of the Muslims. Such was the goal of King Louis IX of France, who, in the mid-thirteenth century, sent as envoys both a Dominican monk, André de Longjumeau, and a Franciscan monk, William of Rubruck, in an effort to secure an alliance between the Mongols and his own troops in the Holy Land. During this same period, Pope Innocent IV dispatched the Franciscan monk John of Piano Carpini with a letter to Güyük Khan requesting that the Mongols cease "from the persecution of Christians" — a reference to the military defeats Christian Europe had suffered at the hands of Güyük's predecessor, Ögödei. Skepticism as to the desirability of treaties with Mongol, or any other, heathens is evidenced by a letter from the bishop of Winchester to the English king Henry III: "Let these dogs destroy one another and be utterly exterminated and then we shall see the universal Catholic Church founded on their ruins and there will be one fold and one shepherd." No alliances were struck; instead, what resulted was a gradual conversion of the Mongol rulers of western Asia to Islam.

The Western emissary efforts did produce the first recorded dialogues, of a kind, between Roman Catholicism and Buddhism. The aforementioned William of Rubruck left a detailed record of his travels, called the *Itinerarium,* which is full of vivid incidents and yet failed in its own day, and has failed ever since, to find readers. Consider this encounter with central Asian Buddhist priests in a temple William visited. Having confirmed through translators that the priests did not believe that God had ever incarnated in human form, William questioned why they made so many human figures for purposes of worship. The historical figure of the Buddha and the deities of the central Asian Buddhist traditions were unknown to William, and he seems not to have been interested in gathering such information. The Buddhists replied that the statues had been commissioned in memory of wealthy deceased donors. William wrote:

> To these words, I answered, "Then you do these things for no other reason than to flatter men." "Not so," they said. "We do it in their memory." Then they asked me, as if jeering at me, "Where is God?" In return I asked, "Where is your soul?" They said, "In our body." Whereupon I said, "Is it not everywhere in your body? Does it not rule the whole and yet it is not seen? Similarly God is everywhere and governs all things; nevertheless He is invisible, for He is intellect and wisdom." Then when I wanted to argue more points with them, my interpreter, tired and unable to express the words, forced me to silence.

William encountered a crowd when he presented himself to offer his religious views to Möngke Khan. Also in attendance at the court were Nestorians, Muslims, and Buddhists. In 1254, on the Vigil of Pentecost, as William noted, he engaged with members of these three paths in a religious debate staged for the benefit of the khan and his court. It was agreed that the Muslim emissaries were to be left out of the opening round, as they, like the Christians, believed in one God. The first focus was to be on Christian versus Buddhist teachings. But William, much to his displeasure, was being grouped together with Nestorian missionaries. Confident in his Franciscan training in theology, rhetoric, and logic, William staged a mock debate with the Nestorians, taking the part of a Buddhist against them and besting them, thus winning the right to make the opening statement.

The need for respect and decorum throughout the proceedings had been suitably emphasized by an advance decree of Möngke to all participants: insults, abusive language, or interference with opponents would result in death. William, by his own account, won his portion of the debate decisively by forcing his Buddhist opponent to admit that there were, from the Buddhist perspective, no omnipotent gods. The Muslims in the audience burst out in derisive laughter at this point. But William was denied further success because his Nestorian peers refused to keep silent any longer and demanded to debate the Muslims, who refused the challenge, because the teachings of Islam included affirmation of the truth of the Gospels. According to William, the Muslims admitted "that in all their prayers they beseech God to grant that they may die a Christian death." This was, perhaps, a confusion through translation of the Muslim acceptance of Jesus as one of the prophets of Islam. But the aftermath of the debate, also described by William, is clear enough: "When this was finished the Nestorians and Saracens [Muslims] alike sang loudly while the *tuins* [Buddhists] kept silence, and afterwards they all drank their fill." All of the religions involved in the debate were of a universalist missionary persuasion. All seemingly had before them a plum opportunity — special favor from Möngke Khan — and all failed. The preference of Möngke remained for tolerance, in accordance with the shamanistic beliefs of the Mongol people, which held that all religions stood upon an equal footing.

❖

Political alliances and religious conversions aside, there were Western merchants whose principal concern with the Mongol Empire was to make a profit from the ardors of reaching it. In 1260 or perhaps 1261, two brothers and fellow Venetian merchants, Niccolò and Maffeo Polo, departed from Constantinople for Khubilai's new capital, Khanbaliq. They arrived after some four years of travel, won favor in the court of Khubilai, and returned in triumph to Rome in 1269, carrying a letter from the Great Khan to the pope requesting one hundred Catholic missionaries to instruct his court, as well as a quantity of the oil used for the lamp that burned before the Holy Sepulchre in Jerusalem.

When Niccolò Polo came home at last to Venice, he laid eyes for the first time on his son Marco, whose mother — pregnant when Niccolò had departed some seventeen years before — had died shortly after Marco was born. To avoid another such parting, and also because young Marco shared the family taste for extended travel, it was agreed that Marco would accompany the brothers on their return trip to China in 1271.

Their first port of call was Palestine, where the Polos made their way to Jerusalem to obtain the requested holy oil. They then traveled to Acre, where they won support for their journey from the legate apostolic there — who shortly thereafter became Pope Gregory X. The new pope promptly provided the Polo brothers with two Dominican monks, William of Tripoli and Nicolas de Vicenza, in meager but earnest answer to the Great Khan's request for missionaries. But en route through Armenia, when the five travelers found themselves in the midst of an invasion launched by Egyptian troops, the two monks called an end to their mission.

At last, in 1275, the Polos arrived at the summer palace of the Great Khan at Chandu — which would be termed "Xanadu" by Coleridge. That poet, who dreamed more than five centuries later of the splendor of the Mongol court, first learned of its existence from the writings of Marco Polo. Twenty years later, in 1295, the Polos made their return to their native city of Venice. Three years after that, Marco was taken prisoner during a war between Venice and Genoa. During his months of captivity, he dictated the story of his travels, which he titled *The Description of the World,* to a cellmate, Rustichello of Pisa. Rustichello translated the tales into French as the *Livre des merveilles du monde,* although the work became better known among Italian readers as *Il Milione* — in mocking homage to the "millions" of lies that "Messer Marco Milione" was alleged to have told in his book. One of the obvious howlers, to Marco's contemporaries, was his account of black rocks that the Chinese set aflame for fuel. (Coal was as yet unknown in Europe.) Marco was undaunted. At his death, he is supposed to have said, "I have not told the half of what I saw."

Most modern scholars concur that, although *The Description of the World* contains its share of factual inaccuracies and outright fabrications for the sake of a tale well told, Marco was a trustworthy observer of the China of Khubilai Khan. He certainly possessed ample opportunity to observe, for in his twenty years of service as a trusted administrator for Khubilai, he attained a greater intimacy with Chinese affairs of state than any Western personage has since enjoyed.

Marco's style is unadorned but vividly detailed. Although he personally cared little for religion, he embodied the biases of his European culture and described the practitioners of Chinese religions as "idolators" or worse. As a government minister, Marco traveled throughout southern China and on into Tibet. As for Tibetan magical practices — whether of the Buddhist or indigenous Bon variety is not clear — he offered a tersely breathless account: "Among these people you find the most skilled wizards, who by their diabolic art perform the most extraordinary marvels that were ever seen or heard. They cause tempests to arise, accompanied with flashes of lightning and thunderbolts, and many other miraculous effects."

Marco Polo does not lack for fame, but he has never been recognized for one rather signal achievement — the first popular telling in the West of the life story of the Buddha. On his seaward return journey to Italy, Marco disembarked in Sri Lanka, where he visited a tomb that local Buddhists regarded as that of "Sagamoni Borcan," as Marco transcribed the name Shakyamuni Buddha. Marco recorded what was told him of Borcan — circumscribed as it is, it conveys something of the echo of a remarkable teacher:

> The son of a king of the island, he devoted himself to a holy life, refusing to accept kingdoms or any other worldly possessions, although his father endeavored, by tempting him with women and every other imaginable gratification, to divert him from his resolve. Every attempt to dissuade him was in vain and the young man fled secretly to this lofty mountain where, observing chastity and strict abstinence, he at length died.

Marco further revealed that the grieving father erected a statue of his son, bedecked with gems, which all were to worship as a god. This was in accord with local Buddhist belief, as described by Marco, which held that the Buddha "has died eighty-four times; that he died first as a man and came to life again as an ox, that he then died as an ox and came to life as a horse, and so on; and every time he became some sort of animal. But when he died the eighty-fourth time they say he became a god." Marco here chaotically condenses recognizable elements from the Pali *Jataka* tales that recount Shakyamuni Buddha's prior incarnations.

It is doubtful that Marco Polo understood that the "Sagamoni Borcan" of Sri Lanka was the same person as "Sakyamuni-Burkhan," whom Marco cited as the most prominent figure of worship of the Buddhist "idolators" of China. But it should come as no surprise that a European newcomer to Asia would be unaware that among the creeds that thrived there, one had achieved the breadth and catholicity of Christianity itself. Indeed, in Marco's mind, the entity that the West now calls "Buddhism" did not yet exist.

In writing of Khubilai, Marco emphasized the ruler's strong interest in Christian teachings. When the oil from the Church of the Holy Sepulchre was presented by the Polos, the pleasure of the Great Khan was manifest. Marco further observed that Khubilai held magnificent feasts on Christmas and Easter, at which times visiting Christians were especially welcome at his court. But then, as Marco also noted, the same sumptuous feasts were held for Jewish, Muslim, and Buddhist holy days.

There is no reason to suspect the sincerity of Khubilai's ecumenism, but the evidence is also clear that the Great Khan's close relationship with Phagpa, a Tibetan lama in residence at the Mongol court, lent a favored status to Buddhist teachers — a status that only grew stronger with Khubilai's Yuan dynasty successors through the fourteenth century. Phagpa had the benefit of prior family contacts with the Mongol rulers. His uncle Kunga Gyaltsen, known also as Sakya Pandita, had earned a place of favor in the Mongol court even prior to the election of Khubilai. The Mongol prince Godan, the grandson of Jenghiz, launched in 1240 an invasion into Tibet that resulted, early on, in the destruction of two Buddhist monasteries and the murder of some five hundred Tibetan monks and laypeople. Having established his formidable presence, Prince Godan issued in 1244 a letter of honeyed ultimatum to Sakya Pandita to come to his court and instruct him in Buddhist wisdom. The letter read in part:

The Lord Buddha gave his life for all living beings. Would you not, therefore, be denying your faith if you tried to avoid this duty of yours? It would, of course, be easy for me to send a large body of troops to bring you here; but in so doing, harm and unhappiness might be brought to many innocent living beings. In the interest of the Buddhist faith and the welfare of all living creatures, I suggest that you come to us immediately.

As a favor to you, I shall be very kind to those monks who are now living on the west side of the sun.

It is a delicate irony that, in this letter, which established roughly a century of close relations between Mongol rulers and Tibetan Buddhist lamas, the reference to the Buddha's having given "his life for all living beings" bespeaks a Nestorian influence in the Mongol court. Sakya Pandita assented to the royal request, explaining his reasons to his fellow Tibetans in a subsequent letter:

> The Prince has told me that if we Tibetans help the Mongols in matters of religion, they in turn will support us in temporal matters. In this way, we will be able to spread our religion far and wide. [. . .] I have been preaching constantly to his descendants and to his ministers, and now I am getting old and will not live much longer. Have no fear on this account, for I have taught everything that I know to my nephew, Phagpa.

❖

Sakya Pandita not only preserved Tibet from further military onslaughts, but he also wrested a degree of political autonomy for his nation by virtue of his being appointed, by Prince Godan, the de facto governor of the provinces of central Tibet that had fallen within the Mongol ambit. After his death in 1251, his nephew Phagpa, though still in his teens, continued the dual task of ensuring Tibetan security and spreading Tibetan Buddhist teachings within the broader Mongol Empire. After Prince Godan died, the Mongol prince Khubilai, who became Khubilai Khan in 1259, asked Phagpa to become his spiritual teacher. But the conditions set by Phagpa were severely in conflict with the etiquette of the Mongol court. Phagpa demanded, in accordance with Tibetan Buddhist tradition, that Khubilai prostrate himself on each occasion that they met, and that on journeys together Phagpa should be seated in higher state. Khubilai negotiated a compromise by which prostrations and like deferences should take place only in private. But Khubilai did agree to consult with Phagpa prior to making any governing decisions concerning Tibet.

Phagpa was ultimately granted the title "imperial preceptor" and was given practical political control over all of Tibet. Phagpa thus became the first lama to rule Tibet. Successor lamas of his Sakyapa sect reigned through the mid-fourteenth century. Nearly three centuries passed until the Fifth Dalai Lama (1617–1662) achieved a like merging of political and spiritual rule. In a letter of investiture for Phagpa in 1254, Khubilai declared,

> As a true believer in the Great Lord Buddha, the all-merciful and invincible ruler of the world, whose presence, like the sun, lights up every dark place, I have always shown special favor to the monks and monasteries of your country. [. . .] We Mongols shall not respect you, if your monks do not conscientiously carry out the teachings of the Buddha. Do not think the Mongols incapable of learning your religion. We learn it gradually.

The power attained by Phagpa — a favored status for Buddhism in the Mongol Empire — was still being rued seven centuries later by the Catholic missionary Abbé Huc, who nonetheless questioned whether Khubilai was a genuine Buddhist: "History informs us that the adoption of a new worship was with Kublai an affair of policy rather than of conviction; and indeed, one must know very little of the Chinese, amongst whom Kublai had been educated, to suppose that conviction had usually had anything to do with the religious systems accepted by their princes."

Phagpa died in 1280, having returned to Tibet four years earlier. He had for years weathered criticism from certain of his fellow lamas that he had betrayed his country and his religion by ingratiating himself so completely with the Mongol khan. Phagpa's death was likely due to poison administered by a member of his own inner circle, in which there was uneasy contention for status with Khubilai and his court. Khubilai died fifteen years after his teacher, in 1295. Under his successors, the Karmapa sect of Tibetan Buddhism gained ascendancy in the Yuan dynasty.

For his part, Marco Polo remained convinced that Khubilai retained a special sympathy with Christianity. But when Niccolò and Maffeo Polo broached the subject of conversion on their first visit to the Great Khan, they were given what, as recorded by Marco, reads as an extraordinarily frank statement by an absolute ruler content to weigh religions on their proofs. It may also be read as a challenge to Christianity to match the magical elements of Tibetan Buddhism:

> But return to your Pope, and request him in my name to send hither a hundred persons learned in your law, who, being confronted with the idolators, shall have power to counter them and show that they themselves are endowed with similar art, but refrain from exercising it because it is derived from evil spirits, and thus shall compel them to give up such practices in their presence. When I witness this, I shall ban them and their religion, and shall allow myself to be baptized. All my nobles will then also receive baptism, and this will be imitated by my subjects in general. In the end the Christians of these parts will exceed those in your own country.

❖

A very few Mongol travelers decided to return the favor and journey to Rome to witness the exotic wonders of the West. One such was Rabban Sauma, a Nestorian of Turkish heritage born in Khanbaliq and deeply versed in Syriac sacred literature. Sauma arrived in Rome in 1287 and, describing himself as an emissary of the khan, dared to pray — with the pope and the college of cardinals in attendance — in the heretical Syriac liturgy of the Nestorian Church. But Sauma's aim was to ease political, rather than religious, tensions, and he proposed the old plan of a joint alliance against the Muslims. As in the past, interest was faint. Whether Sauma was genuinely acting on behalf of the Mongol court is unclear, but his proposal was soon rendered moot. As the Christian scholar John W. Witek observed, "The Egyptian capture of Acre on May 18, 1291 turned the tide so that the Mongol leader of Persia, Oljeitu, son of Argun, who had been baptized as Nicholas in honor of Pope Nicholas IV, became a Muslim. Not long afterwards the Mongols in Persia also became Islamic converts." The Church was thus all but isolated from China.

There were exceptions to the isolation, however, the most prominent of whom was the Franciscan papal envoy Giovanni da Montecorvino, who journeyed to China in 1290 and remained there until his death in 1338. Giovanni became the archbishop of Khanbaliq in 1307 and translated the New Testament into the Uighur language used widely by central Asian Mongols. During his time as archbishop, the Blessed Friar Odoric of Pordenone arrived in the Mongol capital in 1321. Odoric was an Italian Franciscan monk whose travels were spurred by his own strong inclination to reach "the countries of the unbelievers in order to win some harvest of souls." During a visit to Cansay (modern Hangzhou), he was invited to tour the monastery of the "idolators," or Buddhists, where he was assured he would witness "something worth seeing." A monk filled two large buckets with table scraps, went outdoors, and beat a gong. Down from a hill, Odoric wrote, came "a multitude of animals of divers kinds [. . .] such as apes, monkeys, and many other animals having faces like men, to the number of some three thousand." All were fed from the two large buckets in an orderly manner and then returned to the hill when the monk beat the gong once more. "So I, laughing heartily, began to say: 'Tell me, prithee, what this meaneth?' And he answered: 'These animals be the souls of gentlemen, which we feed in this fashion for the love of God.'" The monk further explained that those who led noble lives were reborn as nobler animals, with the reverse being true as well. "And say what I list against it," Odoric noted, "nought else would he believe." Given that Catholic theology denied souls to animals, the bewilderment of Odoric at interchanging human and animal incarnations is understandable.

Whether Odoric did, as he claimed, travel as far as Tibet has been disputed. But as his brief account is the earliest Christian response to that country and its Buddhism, it is worth examining in any event. The people of Tibet, Odoric observed, possessed as "great plenty of bread and wine as anywhere in the world." Its "chief and royal city," then as now Lhasa,

> is all built with walls of black and white, and all its streets are very well paved. In this city no one shall dare to shed the blood of any, whether man or beast, for the reverence they bear a certain idol which is there worshipped. In that city dwelleth the *Abassi,* i.e., in their tongue the Pope, who is the head of all the idolators, and who has the disposal of all their benefices such as they are after their manner.

"Abassi" cannot refer to the Dalai Lama, for the first of the Dalai Lamas did not emerge until the early fifteenth century. The most prominent lama during the period of Odoric's visit was Danyi Zangpo Pal (1262–1322) of the Sakyapa lineage, which held a fragile dominance in Tibet. Nonetheless, Odoric was the first, though not the last, Western observer to note parallels between the lamas of Lhasa and the papal court.

Two factors led to the disappearance of Christianity in central Asia by the end of the fourteenth century. The first was a widespread pestilence — it earned the famous sobriquet "Black Death" — that spread across Asia and Europe in the thirteenth and fourteenth centuries. The second was the gradual conversion of the rulers of the western reaches of the Mongol Empire to Islam. By 1295, when Mongol Persia declared its independence from the Mongol khans of China, the unified empire that had controlled the breadth of Asia had come to an end. In the fourteenth century came the conquests of the Mongol warlord Timur the Lame (the subject of Christopher Marlowe's Elizabethan play *Tamburlaine the Great*), a Muslim who defeated the remaining Christian rulers in the Caucasus and merged secular rule with Islamic law.

The obstacles facing would-be Western missionaries now seemed insurmountable. As Islamic power in the region grew, the politics of enmity stemming from the Crusades — an enmity held as deeply in Christian Europe as in Muslim lands — made passage for all Christians a matter of tenacious difficulty. The Chinese portion of the former Mongol Empire was now governed by the Ming dynasty (1368–1644), which had come to power as a violent reaction against outside influences. All foreigners were expelled by the Chinese-born Ming rulers, who despised the Tibetan Buddhist advisers to the alien Mongols as much as they did Christian missionaries.

It would take time — not more missionaries — for the reaction against foreign religionists to subside and even reverse. For nearly two centuries, the activities of Chinese Buddhists were restricted, and there was no sign of a Christian presence in China.

3

THE JESUIT ENCOUNTER
WITH BUDDHISM

❖

It has been said that only Saint Paul stands as a greater figure in the history of Christian missions than does Francis Xavier (1506–1552). Xavier was, in capacity and deed, far and away the most remarkable of the early Jesuit followers of Ignatius Loyola. It was Xavier, not Paul, who undertook the greater missionary challenge: not Paul's Romanized domain of Europe and Asia Minor, but the vastness of a little-known southern Asia and an utterly blurry eastern Asia, with all the racial, cultural, and linguistic divides that should have made conveyance of a European faith impossible.

Ignatius Loyola, the creator of the Jesuits, was a Spanish noble who had fought with honor and been wounded in the leg in the Battle of Pamplona in 1521. He was sent home, a failing invalid, to Loyola, where he received last rites — and four days later rallied. During his recuperation, Ignatius asked for some reading material. His preference was for adventurous tales of knight chivalry, the popular Spanish genre that Cervantes adored and lampooned. As these were unobtainable, devotional lives of the saints were provided instead, and Ignatius found these adventures even more to his liking. That summer of 1521, he resolved to imitate those saintly lives, as indeed he did, receiving his canonization in 1622, a prompt seventy years after his death, in recognition of two intertwining aspects of his genius — as an inspirational mystic and as an organizational leader.

In 1529, Ignatius was merely a late-blooming undergraduate at the

University of Paris, the greatest of all medieval European universities. (Its past students and teachers included Thomas Becket and Thomas Aquinas.) Xavier, a professor of philosophy, first encountered Ignatius at this time — during which Ignatius composed the *Spiritual Exercises,* the purpose of which was "seeking and discovering the divine will regarding one's life orientation for the health of one's soul." It is not altogether usual for a professor to allow his life to be transformed by the ideas of a student, albeit one fifteen years older than himself. Xavier, born in Pamplona of a noble family, had established himself as a brilliant academic, with prospects of obtaining a canonical benefice from the cathedral of Pamplona. There was much to lose in joining an order such as Ignatius came to propose. In his twenty-third *Exercise,* Ignatius set a credo for all Jesuit labors, and, in particular, for missionary work in far-off lands:

> Man is created to praise, make reverence, and serve God our Lord and by these means to save his soul. All other things on the face of the earth are created for man to help him in the pursuit of the goal for which he is created. From this it follows that man is to use these things as much as they will help him attain his end. Likewise, he must rid himself of them as much as they prevent him from attaining it. Therefore, we must make ourselves indifferent to all created things, in so far as it is left to the choice of our free will and is not forbidden; in such manner we should not prefer health to sickness, riches to poverty, honor to dishonor, a long life to a short one, and so in all things; we should desire and choose only those things which will best help us attain the end for which we are created.

The Society of Jesus, or Jesuits, would not be formally established until 1540, when it received papal approval. But its foundational moment came in a Montmartre chapel on the Feast of the Assumption in August 1534. Ignatius created vows by which he, along with five fellow students and one professor — Xavier, then twenty-eight — formed an apostolic society committed to lives of holy poverty and chastity and, if humanly possible, a pilgrimage to Jerusalem, then a Muslim city. If that were impossible, the Jesuits would serve however the pope willed.

Xavier was the only one of the six acolytes recruited by Ignatius who had not yet passed through the one-month spiritual course set forth in the *Exercises.* That was remedied in September 1534, and the outcome of Xavier's month of largely solitary practice was an enflaming love and devotion to Christ, whom Xavier would henceforth serve in life and in death, with the *Exercises* as a manual of practice to ensure that his ardor did not wane. Thereafter, Xavier referred to Ignatius as the "father of his soul" and "only father in the love of Christ."

Risk and ardor in the spread of the Gospel lay at the heart of the early Jesuit vision. Ignatius and Xavier both had Jerusalem in mind, but the obtaining of approval from the Holy See for yet another Christian order — some in the Vatican felt there were already enough — required a stance of abject obedience. The September 1540 papal bull creating the Society of Jesus declared that all Jesuits bound themselves to travel according to papal dictates, "whether they should send us to the Turks, or to any other unbelievers, even in the parts which they call the Indies, or to any heretics whatever or schismatics, or to any of the faithful."

Those papal dictates as to where to deploy the few but dedicated Jesuits had everything to do with the geopolitical situation as viewed by the Vatican. For an articulation of this view, we may look ahead eighty-three years, to the text of the bull of 1622 that canonized Ignatius. Here is recalled vividly the world of 1540, in which

> the pious Kings of Portugal had paved a way for extending the Lord's vineyard in the distant Indies and remotest islands, and when the Catholic Kings of Castille had done no less in the New World discovered in the West; while on the other hand, in the northern regions, Luther, that abominable monster, and other detestable pests were attempting to corrupt and deprave the Old Faith, its holiness and teaching regarding a more perfect life, and to overthrow the authority of the Apostolic See.

The Jesuits grew with impressive rapidity and became the leading force of the Counter-Reformation. Their chief strengths were extraordinary dedication and an unparalleled ability to couple the teaching of the faith with a curriculum that firmly grounded students in mathematics, the sciences, and logic. First and foremost, in Europe, the Jesuits owed their prominence to their skill as educators, and this skill would serve them in Asia as well, where demonstrable Western technological advances, such as the sextant, could leaven the acceptance of Western theology. What became known to Western historians as the "Age of Discovery" was under way, with the Portuguese and the Spaniards in the early lead in colonizing and establishing trade within southern and eastern Asia. The monarchs of Portugal and Spain were willing to fund and promote Jesuit missionary efforts in exchange for papal privileges such as the Treaty of Tordesillas, effected in 1494 by Pope Alexander VI, which divided the newly discovered lands of eastern Asia, North America, and South America evenly between Spain and Portugal down a line of demarcation measured 370 leagues due west of the Cape Verde Islands.

This was the onset of Western colonialism in the East, with its backdrop of Eurocentrism, racism, and Christian triumphalism. (There were cognate racist responses in both China and Japan, which regarded Europeans as barbarians at best and foreign devils at worst.) The Portuguese, within whose colonial territories Xavier labored, imposed exploitative terms of trade, as well as restrictions on the practice of indigenous religions, all the while tolerating licentious and avaricious behavior by Portuguese settlers taking full advantage of their distance from their Christian homeland. Military conquest of large landholdings was not the Portuguese colonizing method. Rather, they occupied the territories of scattered vassal lands and established small base colonies, the most prominent of which was Goa, an island off the west coast of India, seized by the Portuguese in 1510. Goa became the center for Portuguese-sponsored missionary work. The Diocese of Goa, the largest in the world, was created in 1534 by Pope Paul III and stretched from the Cape of Good Hope to Japan. It remained only for missionaries to journey forth in their new spiritual holdings. But willing and able missionaries were few and the difficulties great. Thus the Portuguese king John III was willing to entrust the task to the new Jesuit order.

The challenges were formidable from the outset. In Sri Lanka, the Buddhist king Bhuvaneka Bahu VII — who had need of good relations with the Portuguese, which had established a colony on Sri Lankan territory in Kotte — declared to the Jesuit missionary Frei João de Vila do Conde his potential willingness to convert to Christianity were the truth of the religion made plain to him. In 1543, Frei João urged upon the king the idea of a debate, to be staged before the royal court, in which seven questions would be disputed between Buddhist and Hindu monks and Frei João himself on behalf of Christianity. These questions, a basic

menu of Christian theological concerns, pertained to the respective natures of God, heaven, virtue, angels, saints, the Devil, sin, and vice. Vice
was a particularly pointed topic because, Frei João believed, the king
himself had been corrupted to unnatural vices with the encouragement
of the Buddhist monks. The outcome of the debate, according to Frei
João, was rampant confusion among his opponents and embarrassment
for the king and his court.

For his part, after fifteen days of disputation, Bhuvaneka Nahu suspended the debate, after declining an offer by Frei João to face — along
with his Buddhist and Hindu opponents — the ordeal of a burning pyre
or, alternatively, immersion in a lake teeming with crocodiles. When
Frei João continued to press, on behalf of God and the king of Portugal, for a decision, Bhuvaneka Bahu at last issued this reply, which nicely
blended political defiance, cultural pride, and perhaps a personal distaste
for the debating tactics of all religionists:

Neither for the present king of Portugal nor for two more like him will
I abandon the law in which I was born, nourished, and educated; and I
assure you that I shall never accept the law of the Christians and profess
it. And if anyone would force me to do so, I would rather lose my kingdom and my country than be baptized. You and your friars can offer your
law to my subjects. If any wish to accept it, this will be agreeable with
me; and I shall prevent no one from joining you. But if they do not wish
to do so, no one will be able to blame me for it.

The Jesuit missionaries did not view themselves as separate from the
Portuguese authorities. As the Christian historian W. L. A. Don Peter
observed,

The missionaries were not only teachers of Christianity, but also, as the
need arose, political agents of the king, and promoted his interests. We
see them engaged in persuading local rulers to become vassals of Portugal
or bequeath their kingdoms to the Portuguese crown; functioning as go-
betweens or emissaries of the Portuguese authorities in their dealings with
local kings and princes; and not only serving as military chaplains but
even taking up arms as occasion demanded.

Our knowledge of the activities of the Jesuits in Asia rests almost exclusively on their letters, or on books based on their experiences that were subsequently published in Europe. Extant Asian accounts are scanty, perhaps because the Jesuits were regarded as of limited importance.

The distinction between Jesuit letters and books is not as significant as one might expect, for Jesuit missionaries were trained to regard their letters as public records. If anything said in them was deemed impolitic — including, for example, too detailed an account of the teachings of Japanese religions — they were censored by Jesuit authorities in Europe. In a letter of June 1549, Xavier set forth the tone required for all correspondence: "Let the letters be about things of edification, and take care not to write about matters which are not of edification. Remember that many people will read these letters, so let them be written in such wise that no one may be disedified." The practical outcome of this approach was described by the modern-day Jesuit historian Michael Cooper:

> What may be conceded without argument is the unctuous tone of many of their published letters. Right invariably triumphs over wrong, good over evil; virtue is repaid, wickedness receives its just desserts; Christians are generally good and fervent people, pagans often leave much to be desired[. . . .] There is a general note of optimism, not to say triumphalism, in many of the published letters, and the credulous reader may well be forgiven for supposing that everything in the Japanese mission garden was lovely.

This policy of selective disclosure was particularly effective in blocking out any information about Buddhism that might have stimulated the interest of European readers. As the American scholar Donald F. Lach observed, "It is obvious from what we know now that the Jesuits had a much clearer idea of the doctrines and strength of the Japanese religions than they were willing to admit during the sixteenth century. [. . .] European censors seem to have been determined not to let the European public know too much of Shinto and Buddhism and of their hold upon the Japanese." Already, then, by the sixteenth century, the Church was loath to see the importation of competing Eastern creeds, even as it keenly pursued a hearing for its teachings in Eastern lands. Elaborate care was exercised in all aspects of potential information exchange. When early members of the *Kirishitan* daimyo — Christian converts from the Japanese nobility — visited Europe on invitation of the Church, they learned nothing of the Reformation, nor of any historical accounts that might conflict with the missionary teaching that unbroken peace had reigned in Christendom for more than one thousand years.

The nineteenth-century British historian Andrew Steinmetz, astutely in advance of recent scholarly critiques of Western Orientalism, described a pattern of deliberate exoticism in Jesuit accounts, designed to win interest for their missionary efforts while veiling the reality of the cultures being missionized. Steinmetz wrote in 1848:

> Very early they formed the design; followed out the scheme with great perseverance; and, in process of time, a wonderful "development" was given to their missionary lore in their famous "Edifying and Curious Letters, concerning Asia, Africa and America" [popular reading texts for Catholics of the time]. From first to last, it is an Arabian Night's Entertainment — the story of Noureddin Ali and Bedreddin Hassan forever.

But even Steinmetz allowed that Xavier had achieved remarkable results in his missionary efforts. The devotion accorded to Saint Francis Xavier by centuries of Catholics draws not only from the elaborate trappings of the Xavier legend but also from the manifest faith that enabled Xavier to endure the hardships and isolation of his travels to India and Japan, to name only the chief locales of his two decades of voyaging in the East. Not that Xavier lacked for what comforts could be afforded by the Portuguese empire. During the two and a half years he spent in Japan — the years that chiefly concern us here — Xavier received as alms from the Portuguese king the generous sum of 1,000 crusados. Although Xavier himself lived austerely, he bestowed fine gifts when he paid calls to the ruling daimyo nobility of Japan, and he drew from readily available sums to establish Jesuit missions and schools as he saw fit. For the first time, a competition for souls between Christianity and Buddhism was formally — and formidably — under way.

❖

Buddhism entered Japan by way of sixth-century Japanese contacts with Korea. One important factor in its early advances was the appeal of

Buddhist magical rituals, which were viewed by the various Japanese aristocratic clans as a means to extend their power in a disunified land. By the eighth century, Buddhism was designated by the daimyo as an approved religion of Japan, with the proviso that such rituals were to be conducted for two purposes only — the maintenance of peace and the protection of the daimyo. Dreams of dominance aside, Buddhism also took hold among the broader Japanese population, with Zen, Shingon, and other schools gaining in support.

At the time Xavier arrived in Japan, the emperor was a nominal figure, with true power resting in the hands of the warring daimyo, who held territories in the manner of Western dukes. The pace of political unification of Japan, achieved by the late sixteenth century, was hastened by the introduction of a European invention — the smoothbore musket. The introduction was accidental, but the Japanese made the most of it. In 1542, a Portuguese ship bound for China was wrecked along the Kyushu coast. The muskets the Japanese found on board, used by the Portuguese crew in their piratical raids along the Chinese coast, were swiftly and accurately copied. One of the surviving crewmen, Fernão Mendes Pinto (1509–1563), who had little knowledge of the Japanese politics of the period, ascribed the rapidity with which firearms were adapted to the intense martial spirit of the Japanese people. Mendes Pinto and his fellow pirates were the first Europeans to set foot in Japan. Years later, inspired by the sanctity of Xavier, Mendes Pinto not only donated a large sum to support the Jesuit mission in Japan but also became a Jesuit lay brother.

Mendes Pinto soon left the order for reasons that, according to the British scholar Charles David Ley, had to do with the dismissive Jesuit attitude toward Asian culture and religion. Ley's theory is borne out, to a degree, in the *Peregrination,* a voluminous work composed by Mendes Pinto after his return to Portugal in 1558. This book described his Asian travels, including a journey into China in the 1540s (prior to his meeting with Xavier) for purposes of plundering tombs constructed lavishly in accordance with the Confucian reverence for ancestors. Avarice aside, Mendes Pinto came to view Buddhism with an admiration that could perhaps have clashed with the Jesuit outlook. For example, he described the Buddhist monks of Nanking as "very austere in their manner of living, such as the Capuchins are, and verily if they were Christians, one might hope for great matters from them in regard of their marvellous abstinence and sincerity."

Particularly remarkable is his account of a sermon given by a Buddhist lama, whom Mendes Pinto described as a "*talapicor* [monk] of Lechuna [Lan-chow], which is their pope." It is tempting to see in this an inexact reference to the Dalai Lama of Tibet, but such cannot be the case, as the Second Dalai Lama, Gedun Gyatso, died in Tibet in 1542, just prior to the adventures recounted by Mendes Pinto. Nonetheless, a lama of the Tibetan Buddhist tradition based in Lan-chow would have enjoyed a strong degree of political prestige, for Lan-chow was the capital of the Chinese province of Kansu, located on the northeastern border of Tibet. It was in Lan-chow, in 1251, that Sakya Pandita, the Tibetan Buddhist who held such eminence in the Chinese Mongol court, passed away. Lan-chow was also visited in the late 1570s by Sonam Gyatso, the Third Dalai Lama, who preached to the people in Tibetan and was provided Chinese translators by the governor of Kansu. Such was likely the case as well for the sermon heard by Mendes Pinto, who understood Chinese but not Tibetan. The sermon, transcribed by Mendes Pinto in a style strongly influenced by Christian spiritual usage, is nonetheless far more sympathetic in tone and profound in content than any Buddhist discourse recorded by the Jesuits who followed him. Indeed, in its fidelity to the Buddhist ideal of the compassionate bodhisattva, by whose acts suffering is alleviated and peace established, it stands well above and beyond any other European writing on Buddhism for some three centuries to come. Here is an excerpt from a seventeenth-century English translation of Mendes Pinto's text:

I do advise and enjoin you all, since you have ears to hear me, that you do that which the law of the Lord obligeth you to do, which is, that you give of that whereof you have too much to the poor, who have not wherewith to feed themselves, to the end God may not be wanting to you when you shall be at the last gasp of your life. Go to, then, let this charity be so remarkable and universal in you, that the very fowls of the air may taste of your liberality. And this you ought to do to keep the poor, having need of what you possess in excess, from being forced by their necessity to rob other men of their goods, whereof you would be no less blameable than if you killed an infant in the cradle.

Mendes Pinto noted that the lama went on at some length and included "a world of extravagancies and fooleries" in his talk. Nonetheless, the Chinese audience manifested "extreme devotion" and repeatedly responded *"Taiximida,"* that is, "So we believe." But then Mendes Pinto went on to describe something altogether strange — the reaction of one of his fellow Portuguese, one Vicente Morosa, who was entirely carried away by the lama's talk and

> hearing the auditors so often use the word *"Taiximida,"* said in imitation of them, "Such may thy life be"; and that with such a grace and so settled a countenance, not seeming any way to jeer him, that not one in the assembly could forbear laughing. He in the meanwhile continued still firm, and more and more confirmed, seeming even to weep out of an excess of devotion. [. . .] When the sermon was ended the *talapicor* returned to the pagoda where he lodged, [. . .] all the way as he went he ceased not to commend the devotion of the Portugals. "Look," said he, "there is not so much as these people, who live like beasts, and without the knowledge of our truth, but see well enough that there is nothing but what is godly in that I have preached"; whereunto all answered that it was as he said.

Mendes Pinto had no idea that he and his enraptured Portuguese companion were listening to what we would term "Buddhist" teachings. Mendes Pinto knew it only as "the religion of these gentiles," but apparently his companion received it in a manner that made do without classification. Vicente Morosa is the first Westerner on record to respond wholeheartedly to the words of a lama of the Tibetan Buddhist tradition. This is not to say that Morosa became a Buddhist. Indeed, we know little of what became of him thereafter, as Mendes Pinto had other adventures to tell and left only this brief sketch. Brief as it is, note that it includes as well the first recorded perspective of a Tibetan Buddhist lama on the West — albeit as represented by eight straggling Portuguese travelers — as a lesser culture lacking in Buddhist wisdom.

Mendes Pinto was not the only contemporary of Xavier to display a fascination with the Buddhism of Asia. Guillaume de Postel (1510–1581) was the first Western Christian ever to reach the still controversial conclusion that Buddha and Christ were teachers of equal spiritual stature. The manner in which Postel reached it constitutes remarkable fantasy. In his *Des merveilles du monde* (1532), Postel argued that the Japanese people had received, by means of astrological transmission, a revelation of Christ and redemption that was entirely independent of the New Testament accounts. The result was that "Xaca [Buddha] is there worshipped as Jesus Christ crucified." Xaca would eventually be superseded by the Jesus of the West, but by means of a natural merging rather than a competition, for the teachings of the two creeds were essentially one.

Postel was a young and impoverished student at the University of Paris during the time when both Ignatius and Xavier lived in the city. He possessed an extraordinary gift for languages, mastering Greek, Latin, Hebrew, and Arabic and ultimately translating a number of works from the latter two languages into Latin, including the Jewish kabbalistic text *Sefer Yetzirah*. In 1535, Postel served as a French diplomat to the sultan of Constantinople and shortly thereafter became a professor of Oriental languages at his alma mater. He was accepted into the Jesuit order in March 1544 — subsequent to Xavier's departure for the East — but was dismissed from that order in December 1545 "because of his illusions," as the Jesuit scholar Georg Schurhammer put it in his biography of Xavier. Schurhammer further clarified that "in 1544 he [Postel] joined the Society of Jesus in Rome but was dismissed the following year because of signs of mental illness. [. . .] From 1564 on he was interned in the monastery of Saint-Martin-des-Champs, where he died in 1581, after publishing a series of works full of oriental learning and phantastic tales."

One of the prominent "signs" of his alleged mental illness was the publication, also in 1544, of Postel's treatise *De orbis terrae concordia* (*Concerning the Harmony of the Earth*), in which he argued for the essential spiritual unity of Catholicism, Protestantism, Judaism, Islam, Buddhism, and indeed all major world religions. Postel further declared that no one religion could claim exclusive spiritual truth — a claim as to which only God, and not his earthly worshippers, could render ultimate judgment. Postel's declaration that Buddhism was "the most wonderful religion in the world" was, however, based on scant knowledge of its teachings and practices, coupled with a fervent conviction that the Buddha and Christ were one in essential outlook. Postel's signal aim was to achieve a world harmony of grace and love based on a merging of all world religions into the Christian vision, with the practical management of government left to the king of France.

Subsequent works of Postel were placed on the Inquisition Index of Forbidden Books. The central inspiration for Postel's later writings was a nun in her middle years, Mother Jeanne, whose teachings are reflected in Postel's impassioned charge against European Christendom: "Observe [. . .] how religion is understood by the majority of Christians; it is only as an ignorant and persecuting partiality, a superstitious and stupid stubbornness, and fear — base fear — above all. Why is this? Because those who profess it have not the woman-heart, because they are foreign to the divine enthusiasms of that mother-love which explains all religion." Postel served as spiritual adviser and, at last, as confessor to Mother Jeanne upon her death, at which time she assured him that she would yet return to guide him. As Postel recounted, Mother Jeanne made good on her promise: "Two years after her ascent into heaven her spiritual body and substance descended into me and permeated sensibly my whole body, so that it is she rather than myself who lives in me." Thereafter, Postel took the name Postellus Restitutes, or "Postel Arisen." During his final years of confinement, he peaceably retracted all heresies attributed to him.

Having quoted the Jesuit perspective on Postel's mental capacity, I shall quote also the eulogy offered by a fellow heretical French Catholic priest who lived some three centuries later, the celebrated occultist Eliphas Levi, who wrote of Postel:

Mad because he believed in reason and justice on earth. Well, well, they spoke truly; poor Postel was mad. The proof of his madness is that he wrote [. . .] to the Fathers of the Council of Trent [convened by Pope Paul III in 1545 to condemn the errors of Martin Luther], entreating them to bless the whole world and to launch anathemas against no one. As another example, he tried to convert the Jesuits and cause them to preach universal concord among men — peace between sovereigns, reason among priests, and goodness among the princes of the world. In fine, as a last and supreme madness, he neglected the benefits of this world and the favour of the great, lived always humbly and in poverty, possessed nothing but his knowledge and his books, and desired nothing but truth and justice. May God give peace to the soul of poor Guillaume Postel.

Some have speculated as to the degree of influence that Postel, with his scholarly enthusiasm for Asia, might have exercised on Xavier while they were contemporaries at the University of Paris. But there is no evidence that Xavier shared any of the views expressed in Postel's writings, which were without European parallel in their own era and remain so to this day.

❖

Xavier's career as a missionary began with his departure from Portugal to India on his thirty-fifth birthday, April 7, 1541. The title granted to him by Pope Paul III was "Apostolic Nuncio to the East." He arrived in Goa in May 1542. In October, he sailed to the Fishery Coast of India, and there concentrated his efforts for the next three years. In August 1545, Xavier ventured still farther east in the vast Asian diocese of which he was the Jesuit superior — voyaging some 1,500 miles, first to Malacca and then, in January 1546, to the Moluccas, or Spice Islands.

Malacca, to which Xavier returned in December 1547, lay on the southern tip of the Malay Peninsula and was the center of the Portuguese spice trade in the southern Pacific. Xavier encountered there a Japanese man named Anjiro, who had, with a servant, undertaken the long voyage from Japan to Malacca expressly to receive Christian teaching from Xavier. Anjiro came from a respected samurai family and was a member of a Shingon Buddhist temple. In his early manhood, he committed a homicide under circumstances unknown to us. Anjiro fled his native province of Satsuma, seeking a means of cleansing his wrongs. Portuguese merchants in Japan told him of a saintly Jesuit priest in Malacca. Anjiro's contact with those merchants had given him a working knowledge of Portuguese, by which he and Xavier could communicate. At Xavier's urging, Anjiro sailed to Goa to study Christian teachings while improving his Portuguese. There, in May 1548, he was baptized and received the name Paul of the Holy Faith.

During the same period as Xavier's encounter with Anjiro, the Jesuit Jorge Alvares, a fellow missionary who had already arrived in Japan, prepared a written report on that land for Xavier. The report contained a detailed portrait of Japanese Buddhist temple life, most likely of the Zen sect. It is worth quoting, as it demonstrates not only the race-dominated projections of early European observers but also the relative sophistication of the advance intelligence upon which Xavier could draw:

> They read in the manner of the Chinese and have many writings of the Chinese. They ring a bell about midnight, at Matins, Vespers, and Compline, and when it becomes night. They have bells shaped like leathern bags made of copper and iron, which they beat, and drums like the Chinese. I believe that this type of order came from China, for I saw the same in China. When they ring the bells, all who are in the house come together to pray. The eldest begins and the others answer, having their books in their hands; and they also pray with rosaries like the laity. They are forbidden to have wives, and they are put to death if it is found out. They engage in sodomy with boys whom they instruct. As a rule they are not reproached for this. [. . .] Their idols are gilded, and the head of their god is like that of a Kaffir. Its ears are pierced like those of Malabar idols, and they have diadems. [. . .] They are a people very eager to learn what we worship, and they are delighted with our pictures and place them upon their heads. They are also anxious to see our country. [. . .] They also have women of this same order, and these have houses for themselves. They have no sexual relations with men; and if they fail in this respect, they also are punished. They go dressed and shaved like the *frades* [male monks], and the daughters and wives of the most prominent men enter into this order.

As one example of how such intelligence was used, Xavier resolved, while in Japan, to abstain from all meat and fish so as to cause no offense either to Buddhist priests or to their devoted laity. Cultural tensions would be avoided but for issues of ultimate significance with respect to conversion.

In April 1549, Xavier embarked for Japan in the company of Anjiro, who, as a bilingual Christian convert and former Buddhist, would prove invaluable to Xavier during his early months in Japan. For Xavier, Japan was an exciting prospect because of qualities he perceived in Anjiro and attributed, by extension, to the Japanese people as a whole — literacy, propriety, discipline, and reasoned wisdom. After his arrival, in a November 1549 letter, Xavier declared that Japan offered the greatest hope for Christian conversion in all of Asia:

> First of all, the people with whom we have thus far conversed are the best that we have yet discovered; and it seems to me that, among pagan nations, there will not be another to surpass the Japanese. They are a race of very fine manners and generally good and not malicious, a people of an astonishingly great sense of honor, who prize honor more than any other thing; they are in general a poor people; and the poverty that exists among *fidalgos* [the samurai class] and those who are not, is not considered to be a reproach.

The perceived similarities between Europe and Japan were the basis for the Jesuit strategies of conversion. A later Jesuit missionary to Japan, Alessandro Valignano (1539–1606), expressed this viewpoint in terms of the highest compliment a European could pay, that of racial equality: "The people are all white, courteous, and highly civilized, so much so that they surpass all the other known races of the world."

Certain scholars have argued that Xavier was so taken with Japanese culture that he studied it as an "Orientalist" would; that is, with an interest in that culture for its own sake and value — a resurgence, in a new setting, of the interests of Xavier the onetime academic. Xavier was respectful of certain Japanese values and regarded the Japanese as the most advanced race in Asia. But there is no evidence whatsoever that he sought to learn anything of Japan that did not pertain directly to his missionary work. In this regard, it is well to recall the admonition in the *Exercises* of Ignatius, quoted earlier: "Man is created to praise, make reverence, and serve God our Lord and by these means to save his soul. All other things on the face of the earth are created for man to help him in the pursuit of the goal for which he is created." Such was the dedication of Xavier to this creed that he may well have viewed the label "Orientalist" as an insult to his faith.

Indeed, in the manner of a conscious strategist, Xavier outlined, in one letter to his Jesuit superiors, what he felt to be the bases of the social and cultural power of the prevailing Buddhist monasteries — their economic austerity, their vegetarianism, and their ability "to relate some accounts, or better to tell some tales about the things in which they believe." The rooted differences between Christian and Buddhist teachings would, Xavier believed, lead to Buddhist resistance that would place the entire Jesuit mission at risk: "It will not take much for us to be persecuted by them, and more than in words, because of the contrary opinions which we and they have about the perception of God and how the nations are to be saved. [. . .] It seems to me that the laity will not contradict or persecute us on their part were it not for the great importunities of the *bonzos* [monks]." For Xavier, the prospect of his own martyrdom, for which he had wished long before coming to Japan, was in accord with a life in Christ's service: "The evil which comes to us from them [Buddhists] is a favor which our Lord will grant us, if, for His love and service and through zeal for souls, we should shorten the days of our life, since they are the means through which this continuous death in which we live will come to an end, and our desires will be accomplished in a short time when we go to reign forever with Christ."

Xavier and Anjiro arrived in Kagoshima on August 15, 1549 — fifteen years to the day since the Montmartre vows that had formed the Jesuits. Anjiro became Xavier's interpreter and guide in Japan. As Xavier wrote, shortly after their arrival, "Paul [Anjiro] is in such a haste with many of his relatives and friends, preaching to them by day and night, that he has been the reason why his mother, wife and daughter, and many of his relatives and friends, both men and women, have become Christians." Xavier sought permission to preach Christianity from the local daimyo, Shimazu Takahisa, whose broad religious outlook was a blending of Confucian ruling principles with Buddhist and Shinto ritual and practice. The first meeting with Takahisa on behalf of the Jesuits was conducted by Anjiro, who answered Takahisa's questions on the military and economic strength of the Portuguese. Anjiro then showed the daimyo a wooden altarpiece painting of a Madonna with child that Xavier had brought with him to Japan. Takahisa knelt before the image with great reverence and ordered his retinue to do the same. According to Schurhammer, the most meticulous of Xavier's biographers, the likely cause of Takahisa's worshipful response was that he "probably mistook the painting for a representation of Kannon, the Buddhist goddess of mercy, who is often represented as holding a child in her arms and is difficult to distinguish from a Christian representation of the Mother of God." Schurhammer went on to note the regret of later Protestant missionaries that, as one such wrote, "the first step in the conversion of Japan was marred by a worship of Mary."

Xavier also met with Buddhist monks from the various Kagoshima monasteries, including Fukusho-ji. Xavier now developed a friendship with Ninshitsu, the chief abbot of Fukusho-ji, who at age eighty was nearly twice Xavier's age. With Anjiro acting as interpreter, the two men engaged in a friendly spiritual dialogue. That Ninshitsu was capable of candor and humor is confirmed by his response to the puzzlement of Xavier as the Jesuit viewed the monks in the *zendo* (meditation hall) during an intensive *zazen* (Zen meditation) session. When Xavier asked what they were doing, Ninshitsu replied: "Some of them are counting up how much they received during the past months from their faithful; others are thinking about where they can obtain better clothes and treatment for their persons; others are thinking about their recreations and their amusements; in short, none of them are thinking about anything that has any meaning at all."

The most striking exchange arose when Xavier asked Ninshitsu whether he preferred old age or youth. Ninshitsu chose youth because of the body's freedom from infirmities. Xavier then asked, "If you saw a ship sailing from a harbor which has to arrive at another harbor, when should the passengers be happier: when they are still in the midst of the open sea, exposed to the winds, the waves, and the storms, or when they see that they are already near the harbor and begin to pass through the bar in order to rest there from the past storms and shipwrecks?" Ninshitsu answered, "Father, I understand you very well. I know for sure that the sight of the harbor is naturally more pleasant and delightful for those who are to enter it. But since I am still uncertain and have not as yet decided which is the better harbor, I do not know how or where I must land."

Certainly, Xavier meant the ship's voyage to serve as a metaphor of the passage through life; a similar use of this device can be found in the writings of Saint Ambrose and Saint Augustine. But there is a further possible intricacy, for Xavier had previously recorded his conclusion, based on his conversations with Ninshitsu and other monks, that nirvana was "a 'Nothing,' the impersonal Absolute, without form, without attributes, and that man was only a wave in the sea of this Absolute which came and went without leaving a trace behind." Xavier could therefore have been turning the familiar Christian trope to a new use — that of limiting the teachings of Buddhism to the seas of earthly suffering and of posthumous disappearance, without the safe Christian harbor of heaven. Ninshitsu's response may then be read as acknowledging the comfort provided by Xavier's faith, while yet subtly affirming the bodhisattva vow of ongoing service through repeated incarnations.

Ninshitsu died in 1556. Subsequent Jesuit chroniclers claimed that the elderly monk had been persuaded of the truth of Christianity by Xavier but would not convert because he dared not risk his position as superior of Fukusho-ji. Luis Frois, one of those chroniclers, wrote of Ninshitsu with undisguised contempt: "This old man lived on [after Xavier's departure] for some years; but, so as not to lose the position that he had and the credit and reputation which he had with the people and the revenues which he possessed, he haplessly and wretchedly preferred to land in hell."

❖

Instructive as is the friendship of Ninshitsu and Xavier, it was the latter's subsequent impact on two other Buddhist monks of Fukusho-ji, Shunka and Unshu, that is the more remarkable.

In 1562, long after the deaths of both Xavier and Ninshitsu, Unshu had succeeded the latter as chief abbot of Fukusho-ji, while Shunka served as chief abbot at the nearby Nanrin-ji monastery, which was subject to the rule of Fukusho-ji. At Fukusho-ji that year, Unshu and Shunka jointly received a visiting Jesuit missionary, Brother Almeida, who had brought with him a translator. According to the later account of Brother Almeida, Unshu remembered Xavier well and burst forth with a rush of questions to which he had long wanted answers from the Christian teachings — questions on the survival of the soul and the nature of God. The answers Brother Almeida provided evidently satisfied Unshu, who then declared "that he would tread upon all of Shaka's and Amida's books, and promised that from then on he would pray only to the true God." "Shaka" is Shakyamuni Buddha, "Amida" is the Buddha Amitabha of the Japanese Shin, or Pure Land, sect. Shunka in turn said that "he had read more than seven thousand books printed in China on the teaching of Shaka that had been composed by scholars of Tenjiku (India), China, and Korea; but what he had once heard from Father Master

Francis [. . .] convinced him that his teaching contained the essentials of truth." Both Unshu and Shunka requested "with hands upraised" that Brother Almeida secretly baptize them. Shunka confided to Brother Almeida his plan to instruct the Japanese nobility in "the elements of Zen meditation in order to lead them afterwards to a knowledge of the Christian faith." Both Unshu and Shunka allowed, however, "that if the prince or a prominent lord died, they would have to conduct his funeral and during it read prayers from their sacred Buddhist books." Brother Almeida demanded that they openly acknowledge Christianity and resign their monastic positions. The two agreed to this, but then, according to Brother Almeida, his required departure the next day made their baptism impossible. Another priest was to be sent, but Unshu died in November 1562.

Nine years later, the daimyo Takahisa died. His successor, Yoshihisa, sent a formal request to the Jesuits to resume their missionary work in Kagoshima. The aim here was to obtain gunpowder and naval support from the Portuguese to ward off a threat from Bungo to the north. In 1577, Brother Miguel Vaz arrived in Kagoshima and visited the aged Shunka. According to Vaz, he preached the Gospel to Shunka for some days until at last Shunka requested baptism. But again the request was unfulfilled, and again for the same strange cause: Vaz had at once to depart. He promised to return but did not. Shunka died in 1582.

If we accept the accounts of Brother Almeida and Brother Vaz, we face the puzzlement of why dedicated Jesuits would have let slip away the chance to convert two such prominent Buddhists. That the same narrative device should appear in two letters written fifteen years apart — Almeida's in 1562, Vaz's in 1577 — suggests either remarkable coincidence or a degree of hyperbole with respect to the desire for baptism of the two Zen abbots. As for the proposal of Shunka to teach Zen meditation so as to deepen understanding of the Christian faith, roughly four hundred years later, a small number of Western Christians, the foremost of whom was Thomas Merton, proposed precisely the same thing. It is possible that Shunka, like Merton, possessed a remarkable ecumenical vision.

❖

In July 1551, in Yamaguchi, Xavier won an audience with the daimyo Yoshitaka, at which were also present some Shingon priests. Yoshitaka was a supporter of Shingon, as well as Tendai and Rinzai Zen, monasteries. Having learned from prior encounters that modest priestly dress did not impress the Japanese nobility, Xavier appeared in the full regalia of an ambassador of the Portuguese governor of India. He also bestowed elegant gifts on the daimyo, the pièce de résistance being a musical clock that emulated the thirteen stringed tones of the Japanese koto. Yoshitaka responded by granting Xavier's request for permission to preach in Yamaguchi and even provided the Jesuits with an abandoned Buddhist monastery.

Xavier also attempted to forge an ecumenical bond with Shingon Buddhism, the sect with which Anjiro had been affiliated. Shingon was and is, in rough terms, the Japanese correlate to the Vajrayana Buddhism of Tibet, insofar as Shingon employs Tantric practices that originated in northern India. These teachings were brought to Japan in the ninth century through the dual efforts of two revered teachers who had journeyed to China, where such practices flourished. Each, upon their return to Japan, recast the teachings into a distinct form — Saicho as the founder of Tendai Buddhism, and Kukai as the founder of Shingon. Both sects stressed Tantric practice — termed *Mikkyo* in Japanese. For Kukai, *Mikkyo* alone — without need for sutras, precepts, or meditation — was sufficient for ultimate realization. Kukai died in 835; in 921 the Japanese emperor granted him the title of Kobo Daishi, or Dharma-Spreading Great Master, a title by which he is known in Japan to this day.

The contemporary Japanese scholar and Shingon abbot Taiko Yamasaki described the principal deity of the Shingon sect, Dainichi Nyorai, "as a personification of the Dharma Body, [. . .] further seen to unite the wisdoms and qualities represented separately in the many deities of esoteric Buddhism." Dainichi is the Japanese translation of the Sanskrit god name Mahavairocana, or Great Sun, with the sun serving, in Shingon teaching, "as a metaphor to explain the deity that brings light and cuts through darkness." Such helpful explanations as are quoted here were not, of course, available to Xavier. Shingon Buddhism, as an esoteric sect, had since its founding transmitted the most important of its teachings by way of private spoken instructions. Anjiro, though once a member of a Shingon temple, was, by his own admission, unacquainted with its more esoteric practices. His postconversion account to his teacher Xavier was

that "the Japanese worshipped only one God, a personal God who rewarded the good and punished the evil, the Creator of all things, to
whom even Shaka [Buddha] had ordered worship. [. . .] The name of
this god was Dainichi but, represented with three heads, he was at times
also called Cogi. Dainichi and Cogi however were one, as God and the
Trinity are in the Christian faith." Anjiro offered these explanations in
1549, in the context of translating a Christian catechism that Xavier
had composed. On Anjiro's suggestion, Xavier employed "Dainichi"
for "God."

During the July 1551 royal audience before Yoshitaka, one of the
Shingon priests asked Xavier if his God had color or shape. Xavier
replied that God was not subject to mere material accidents of color or
shape but was rather "Pure Substance" and the "Creator" of all things.
The conclusion of the Shingon priests was that the God of Xavier was
in essence the same as Dainichi. Xavier was invited to visit a Shingon
temple in Yamaguchi, where he was received with ceremonial ado, as it
was the hope of the Shingon priests to use Xavier and his fellow Jesuit
missionaries to promote Shingon teachings. Xavier was sufficiently impressed by their enthusiasm, as well as by similarities of worship — such
as rosaries, prayer choirs, vestments, signs of the cross, and three-headed
representations of Dainichi — to reflect on the legend that Saint Thomas
had brought Christianity not only to India but also to China. Were that
legend true, Xavier reasoned, it could account for the possibility that
Christian teachings thereafter reached Japan as well in the form of Shingon practice. Xavier began to question Shingon priests about their
knowledge of the Holy Trinity and the Incarnation. Not only were these
conceptions unknown, but they also provoked laughter among certain
of the respondents.

A somewhat perplexed Xavier turned to some of his new Japanese
converts to ascertain the meaning of "Dainichi." This was no small
matter, as Xavier had for some time been calling people to the Lord, in
the streets of Yamaguchi, with the cry "Pray to Dainichi!" Xavier was
now informed that contrary to the understanding of Anjiro, Dainichi
was not a personal God, but rather an underlying reality similar to what
Christian Scholastics termed the *"materia prima."* Still worse, the name
"Dainichi" — that of a Tantric deity — possessed what Xavier regarded,
in the words of his biographer Schurhammer, as

an obscene meaning, since it referred to the center of the human body and its powers of procreation. Xavier now clearly recognized the trick of the devil. He immediately ordered Brother Fernandez to cry out upon the streets: "Dainichi na ogami asso!" ("Do not worship Dainichi!") and to preach that he should not be honored as God and that the Shingon sect, like all the others, was a fraudulent law and an invention of the devil. From then on, in order to avoid any misunderstanding, Xavier used only the Latin word *Deus* for God, which was pronounced by the Japanese as *Deusu*.

The religious differences raised by Xavier went beyond theological terminology. In Shingon and other Japanese Buddhist monasteries, sexual relations were commonplace between male monks and the young boys left to monastic teaching and care. Ignatius Loyola had discovered similar practices in Catholic monasteries in Barcelona. But Xavier regarded Japanese morals as particularly base in this regard:

> We frequently tell the *bonzos* [monks] that they should not commit such shameful sins; and everything that we tell them amuses them since they laugh about it and have no shame when they are reproached about so vile a sin. These *bonzos* have many boys in their monasteries, sons of *hidalgos* [nobility], whom they teach how to read and write, and they commit their corruptions with them; and this sin is so common that, even though it seems an evil to them all, they are not upset by it.

The observations of Xavier as to widespread homosexuality in Buddhist monasteries accords with known history. The climate was one of broad tolerance, tempered by prohibitions against immodest clothing and undue proximity of living quarters. There was, however, an edict against pederasty issued in 1303 by the shogun Hojo Sadatoki to the Zen Engakuji monastery in Kamakura. But within Japanese Shingon practice, and Japanese culture generally, there was an ease of spiritual and psychological acceptance of homosexuality that baffled Xavier, who could not account for the absence of a sense of sin in this domain.

Kukai, or Kobo Daishi, the ninth-century founder of Shingon, was accounted as the first to have brought homosexual love to Japan. There was a Tantric aspect to this love, as evidenced in *Kobo Daishi's Book*

(1598), a text of instruction attributed to Kukai and summarized here by the American scholar Paul Gordon Schalow:

The preface of the brief work describes how a layman goes into seclusion to pray to Kobo Daishi for instruction in "the mysteries of loving boys in Japan" (*nihon shudo no gokui*). On the seventeenth day of the man's austerities, Kobo Daishi appears and agrees to present him with a one-volume book explaining the love of boys, the basics of which "even monkeys in the hills and fields can comprehend." The text speaks of the "mysteries" of loving boys, implying a connection with the esoteric mysteries of True Word [Shingon] Buddhism. The fact that the preface identifies the book as personally transmitted by Kobo Daishi substantiates the primary importance of the relationship between master and pupil in True Word Buddhism and, in a sense, legitimizes the book's contents.

Not that homosexual practices were limited in Japan to the Shingon school, or to the confines of Buddhist monasteries. Ihara Saikaku, the seventeenth-century Japanese fiction writer, published a volume of forty stories, *The Great Mirror of Male Love* (1687), which included not only the homoerotic legends associated with Kukai but also tales of elegant dalliances between boys and adult samurai warriors — a form of sexual mentoring then much favored by Japanese society.

Xavier attacked not only Shingon but also the founders of Buddhism, including Shakyamuni, who "had not been men but were pure inventions of the devil, demons and not gods, since according to them Shaka had come eight thousand times into the world." In turn, the Buddhist monks of Yamaguchi described Xavier and his fellow Jesuits as eaters of human flesh and worshippers not of *Deusu* but rather of *Daiuso*, Japanese for "the Great Lie."

Anjiro has been taken to task for having, in the words of one twentieth-century Christian historian, "proved indeed to be a broken reed: he had very little knowledge of his own country; he was not a highly educated man; his efforts at the translation of Christian terms into Japanese was to lead the missionaries into errors [. . .] in particular of the harm wrought by his choice of the wholly inappropriate Buddhist term *Dainichi* to represent 'God.'" But Xavier's letters establish his deep feelings of indebtedness to Anjiro. And by entrusting him with the leadership of the newly founded Kagoshima Christian community in 1550, Xavier showed considerable confidence in him.

By 1552, however, Anjiro abandoned that post. In the Jesuit chronicles of the period, there are two different versions of what occurred. According to the first, Anjiro fled the city after persecution by Buddhist and Shinto priests, voyaged to China for reasons unknown, and was there killed by robbers. An alternate speculation came from Father Luis Frois, who wrote of Anjiro:

> Some later said of him that he was like the star which led the Magi from the East, but which, in spite of this, did not approach the crib of Bethlehem with them. For, after he had advised his wife, his children, relatives, and friends to become Christians, which they did, he chose another way a few years later (although it is not known that he ever gave up the faith or ceased to be a Christian). The kingdom of Satsuma is very mountainous and thus of its nature poor and in need of imported food. To alleviate this want, men have for many years engaged in an activity called *bafan,* that is, they go on expeditions of theft and plunder to the coastal towns and regions of China; and each one equips a ship for himself for this according to his means, even if it is not large. It now seems that Paulo [Anjiro], driven by poverty or prompted by the profit and gains which his countrymen were accustomed to obtain there, sailed in a ship of these pirates to China and was there, as it is said, slain. He perhaps had sorrow for his sins and died well. But we are not certain of this, and we do not know anything else about his end.

Whatever his fate, his plight as the first supporter of a new faith in his native land must have been extreme.

❖

In 1551, a Portuguese ship arrived in Yamaguchi harbor with a request from the daimyo of Bungo that Xavier visit his province as well. Xavier accepted. During his two months in Bungo, Xavier met with its young daimyo, Otomo Yoshishige, a Zen Buddhist who was favorably impressed with Xavier and consented to the establishment of a Japanese-language training center for new Jesuit arrivals in Funai, the Bungo capital.

In 1578, well after Xavier's death, Yoshishige converted to the Catholic faith and took the name Francisco. By that time, Jesuits estimated that there had been some two thousand conversions in Bungo, although most of these had taken place with dying patients in the Jesuit hospital in Funai. With the conversion of Yoshishige and the replacement of his anti-Christian wife (called "Jezebel" by the Jesuits, who held her marriage to Otomo to have been invalid under Catholic teaching) with a recently baptized Christian bride, the Jesuits seemed to have established a formidable base of operations in Japan. In October 1578, Yoshishige gathered some sixty thousand troops and invaded the nearby Hyuga province, inviting a small group of Jesuit missionaries to accompany his forces. Early victories came easily, and on Yoshishige's order, several Buddhist temples in Hyuga were carefully taken down so that the Jesuits might use the timber to construct new churches. In early December, however, Yoshishige and his forces were routed in a counteroffensive and forced to retreat back to Bungo, where popular feeling arose against what was seen as the baleful influence of the Jesuits on the aging daimyo. Many of Yoshishige's troops attributed their defeat to the just punishment imposed by offended Buddhist deities whose temples had been dismantled. According to the Jesuit historian Michael Cooper, the situation grew so severe "that for several months the missionaries at Funai were prepared to die at the hands of the anti-Christian mob." Violence was averted, but for many Japanese the memory of Yoshishige's defeat lingered as evidence of the consequences of Christian teachings.

❖

Xavier departed Japan after about two and a half years. His results were unimpressive in terms of total converts. Three small Christian communities had been established, of which one Christian historian opined, "How much they understood of the Gospel is questionable — they probably imagined themselves to have accepted a new and superior kind of Buddhism." This seems more patronizing than factual. Whatever hybrid of the Christian spirit emerged in Xavier's inadequate Japanese translations of the Gospel teachings, the impact was distinct enough that, with Jesuit tilling, the numbers of Christian converts in Japan grew slowly but steadily through the seventeenth century.

Xavier died of a feverish illness in December 1552 on the tiny island of Sancian, some twenty leagues from Canton, the chief harbor on the Chinese mainland. Foreigners were denied access to China during this period, and the interference of Christian "foreign devils" — as the Portuguese and other European outsiders were known — with traditional Chinese religions would have been particularly unwelcome. During his time in Japan, Xavier had recognized that the source of ultimate cultural influence in Asia was China. In the months before his death, he plotted incessantly but futilely to convince Chinese and Portuguese merchants alike to smuggle him ashore. For the Chinese merchants, the punishment for such aiding and abetting would have been death, for the Portuguese, lengthy imprisonment. After final medical treatment on a Portuguese merchant vessel, Xavier died on the Sancian shore in the company of his Chinese servant, Antonio de Santa Fé, a convert to the Christian faith. His final words, as related by Antonio, were "In Thee, O Lord, have I hoped; let me never be confounded."

❖

Alessandro Valignano, who arrived in Japan in 1579, had been appointed the Jesuit visitor-general of the eastern regions of the globe. In 1582, he reported to Rome that 200 churches had been established in Japan and estimated the total number of Christians at 150,000. Valignano was in a position to insist on policies, the most controversial of which was to allow Japanese converts to enter the priesthood. To this end, Valignano established a seminary, which, by 1593, had attracted some ninety Japanese students. The bishop of Japan, Luis de Cerquiera, conducted the first ordinations of Japanese priests in September 1601. One of these would die as a Christian martyr twenty-one years later during the persecutions of the Tokugawa dynasty.

❖

The Japanese-born Fabian Fucan affords the most dramatic individual story resulting from the encounter of Christian teachings with Japanese culture. The facts of his early life are unclear, except for his background as a Buddhist monk, perhaps of the Zen sect, and his decision, in 1586, to join the Society of Jesus.

In his subsequent anti-Buddhist work, *Myotei Mondo* (1605), Fabian argued — in the form of a dialogue between two Japanese ladies of wealth and leisure — that, as opposed to the blessings of salvation offered by Christianity, Buddhism

> preaches the absolute void, and considers good and evil undifferentiated, perniciousness and righteousness the same. How can the claim that our mind is of void and that there is no master over punishment or bliss be construed into a basis of peace! Quite the contrary: here is the origin of revolt and perturbation. [...] At any rate, unless all of Japan turns Kirishitan, it cannot be perfectly put to order.

Fifteen years later, in *Hai Daiusu* (*Deus Destroyed*) (1620), Fabian denounced Christendom, making him an apostate of both Buddhism and Christianity. Fabian explained that he had become a Christian

> at an early age; diligently, I studied its teachings and pursued its practices. Due to my stupidity, however, I was long unable to realize that this was a perverse and cursed faith. Thus fruitlessly I spent twenty years and more! Then one day I clearly perceived that the words of the adherents of Deus were very clever and appeared almost reasonable — but in their teaching there was little truth. So I left their company.

It is debatable whether Fabian's attacks on Christianity signaled a full return to the doctrinal Buddhism of his youth. Although he described himself in his preface to *Deus Destroyed* as "a Zen recluse in my hermitage," the values and beliefs he defended were syncretistically drawn from Buddhism, Daoism, and even Confucianism. It is noteworthy, however, that the essential charge he raised against Christianity was the same one he had made against Buddhism — the absence of a teaching of sufficient compassion for the needs and wants of human beings. In this vein, Fabian took Christians to task for the doctrine of the Immaculate Conception: "Their religion expounds at length Deus' special assistance to *Santa Maria* (who is the mother of *Jesus Christus*), who was thereby rendered immaculate of even one sin. If he is the self-sufficing Deus, then why did he not bestow upon all sentient beings the same special assistance he granted to *Santa Maria*?"

❖

The political situation for the Jesuits in Japan grew more tenuous. Toyotomi Hideyoshi, who seized control of a consolidated Japan in 1582, five years later issued an edict expelling all Christian monks from the country. Out of deference to Portugal, this edict was not fully enforced. Hideyoshi informed the Jesuits that although he wanted expanded trade with the Portuguese, he opposed the preaching of Christianity because of its corrosive impact on the feudal structures of Japanese society, upon which his power depended.

As a personal matter, Hideyoshi was fascinated with European culture, now and then dressing in Portuguese garb and accessories, including a rosary. In this, he exemplified a trend in Japanese taste for Christian accoutrements and bric-a-brac that prefigured the boom — in later centuries, including our own — of Western trade in Buddhist artifacts and trinkets. By 1594, one Jesuit missionary described non-Christian Japanese daimyo who

> wear rosaries of driftwood on their breasts, hang a crucifix from their shoulder or waist, and sometimes even a handkerchief. Some, who are especially kindly disposed, have memorized the Our Father and the Hail Mary, and recite them as they walk in the streets. This is done not in ridicule of the Christians, but simply to show off their familiarity with the latest fashion, or because they think it good and effective in bringing success in daily life. This has led them to spend no small sums in ordering oval earrings bearing the likeness of Our Lord and the Holy Mother.

Interest in the foreign faith was mounting in terms of personal conviction as well. By 1596, the Jesuits estimated that there were 300,000 Japanese converts.

For their part, the Jesuits were required to pay heed to the shifting realities of both Japanese and world politics. There was, for example, the question of whether the pope should encourage other missionaries — Spanish as well as Portuguese, Franciscan, and Dominican as well as Jesuit — to come to Japan, as in fact they did from the late sixteenth century on. They were joined, in the early seventeenth century, by Protestant missionaries from Great Britain and the Netherlands. The Portuguese Jesuits opposed all such enlargements, their principal grounds being that a unified Christian front was necessary in Japan, where dissatisfaction with the welter of Buddhist sects was an effective point of entry for Christian teaching. It would not do for the Japanese to witness Christian bickering.

It was not religious bickering, however, but colonial ambition that undermined the Christian cause in Japan. On February 5, 1597, in Nagasaki, twenty-six Christians — including twenty Japanese converts, four Spaniards, one Indo-Portuguese, and one Mexican — were, by order of Hideyoshi, roped and clamped to crosses and then killed by lances. Three were Jesuits; twenty-three were Franciscans. In the aftermath, recriminations flew between the Portuguese and Spanish missionaries in Japan, each side blaming the other for political blunders that had enraged Hideyoshi sufficiently to murder not only his own people but Westerners as well — a first for any Japanese ruler. Historians still wrestle over the precise causes, while concurring that Spanish aims in Japan played a role. Hideyoshi was aware that the Spanish had used mission work as a tactic of control in its colonization of the Philippines, and in a letter to the Spanish governor of the Philippines, written the same year as the martyrdom in Nagasaki, Hideyoshi asked, "If Japanese were to go to your kingdom, preaching Shinto and upsetting the people, would you rejoice?"

Hideyoshi died in 1598. The daimyo Tokugawa Ieyasu — who founded the Tokugawa shogunate, which reigned through the mid-nineteenth century — assumed control of Japan in 1600. Ieyasu and his successors were equally hostile to foreign Christian influence. Hidetada, who took power in 1616, executed some seven hundred Christians during his eight-year reign. During the subsequent reign of Iemitsu, the death toll increased exponentially. The Tokugawa persecutions sought to win back — or, in Christian terms, to apostasize — the converts to the foreign religion. The tortures carried out rivaled those of the Inquisition in Europe in ferocity, although the victims were fewer in number in Japan. As the twentieth-century British missionary and historian Stephen Neill wrote,

As usual, legend has greatly exaggerated the numbers of the martyrs. Careful calculation has shown that the number of those put to death was about 1,900 in twenty-four years [1617–1641], of whom sixty-two were

European missionaries. To these must be added the far larger number of those who died from the hardships of imprisonment and malnutrition. There were, no doubt, cases of timidity and too ready repudiation of the faith. But the great Japanese persecution has added a memorable chapter to the long record of Christian endurance and faithfulness unto death.

❖

Christovão Ferreira came to Japan as a thirty-year-old Portuguese Jesuit priest in 1610. For nearly two decades, despite the stringent measures taken by the Tokugawa shogunate against foreign missionaries who defied its expulsion order, Ferreira continued covertly to work for his cause — rising to become the Jesuit vice provincial in Japan, undergoing personal dangers, and smuggling out written reports to Jesuit superiors in Macao of the struggles and martyrdoms of the remaining Catholic believers, European and Japanese alike. At last, in 1633, Ferreira was arrested. For those captured Christians who would not abandon their faith by means of verbal persuasion, a physical means, the *anatsurushi,* was designed. It was, as the American scholar George Elison observed, "a consummate torture." The victim was tightly bound so as to impede blood flow to the brain, then hung head down in a narrow pit filled with excrement, the fumes of which afforded a mild anesthetic effect that allowed the ordeal to be prolonged. To this same end, slits were made in the temples to prevent too swift a death from a cerebral hemorrhage. As Elison explained, "The inquisitors wanted the victim to hang in the balance between overpowering pain and release-bringing death; and the *anatsurushi* enabled them to utilize that most minute of intervals. The only salvation for the victim was, as he felt himself bursting, to signal his apostasy."

Ferreira was subjected to the *anatsurushi* along with seven other lower-ranking priests and novices, one of whom endured for nine days before dying. Ferreira became an apostate after five hours. In the remaining seventeen years of his life, he took the name Sawano Chuan, lived and wrote as a convert to Zen Buddhism — the first European ever to do so — and served the Tokugawa regime in the interrogation and torture of captured Christians by means including the *anatsurushi.* Following his death in 1650, the Jesuits circulated stories that Ferreira had, in his last days, returned to the faith, dying — in a recasting of history that Ferreira himself might have fantasized — as a martyr after three days of the *anatsurushi*.

After 1660, only an underground practice of Christianity remained in Japan. More than two centuries later, when Japan was again opened to foreigners in 1858, Europeans encountered Japanese families who had preserved the faith.

❖

Two months before Francis Xavier died just off the coast of China, Matteo Ricci (1552–1610) was born. Ricci is far and away the most chronicled and revered of all the Jesuit missionaries to China. His achievements warrant his fame, for he was the first Western figure since Marco Polo to win a position of respect within the highest Chinese ruling circles.

Ricci was born in Macerata, on the Adriatic, to a noble Italian family. While still in his teens, he discovered his vocation to become a Jesuit missionary to the East. He went on to attend the Jesuit College in Rome, where his novice master was Alessandro Valignano, who would, in 1573, assume leadership of all Jesuit missionary efforts in the East Indies. Ricci would have learned of Francis Xavier and his work at some stage in his schooling. Although it is tempting to impute Xavier as an inspirational role model, there is no direct evidence of this. Indeed, Ricci was completely ignorant of past Christian missionary efforts in China, from the Nestorians of the sixth century to the Franciscans and Dominicans of the thirteenth — a strange state of affairs when one considers that the Holy See might have drawn upon its past efforts in forging new ones.

Ricci achieved, at age twenty-five, an audience with the elderly Pope Gregory XIII, who granted his request for a missionary assignment in Asia. In 1578, he was sent, in the company of a fellow Jesuit, Michele Ruggieri, to Goa, where Ricci studied theology and taught the local children Greek and Latin. But life in a fortified Portuguese colony was not to Ricci's taste. The subsequent order of Valignano to bring him to China was far more to his liking. With Ruggieri, Ricci established a mission in Zhaoqing on the Xi River in the southern province of Guangdong.

There had been other Jesuits — as well as Dominicans, Franciscans, and Augustinians — who had attempted to found mission houses in China. But none had established a real foothold, given the barriers of language, culture, and government restrictions on preachers of foreign religions. There was, in addition, the considerable factor that the Portuguese — the Europeans the Chinese knew best, as Chinese trade with Japan and other Asian nations was shipped (on rapacious terms) by means of Portuguese vessels — often conducted themselves in the plundering manner of pirates. Corresponding reports of Spanish brutalities in the Philippines inspired no greater confidence. The Chinese knew well — their own history was replete with such examples — that foreign political and religious incursions were intertwined.

To counter such suspicions, Ricci brought with him texts and implements of European civilization — intricate mechanical clocks, finely polished prisms, oil paintings, and magnificently bound and illustrated volumes on architecture, mathematics, and technology — by which to win the respect of the Chinese. In 1602, he adapted a European map of the world into a larger form with his own Chinese annotations. The Ricci map, which was widely copied, included the first cartographic portrayal of the Americas to appear in China. Many of his Chinese designations of world place names have been retained to the present day. Ricci won further admiration from the Chinese for his prodigious feats of memory — such as the word-for-word recital of Chinese texts after only one reading. These feats were made possible by his construction of "memory palaces" of the mind (a mnemonic technique first devised by the Greeks and Romans) in which myriad recollections could, with discipline and practice, be placed to allow for ready retrieval.

Nonetheless, the five years that Ricci and Ruggieri spent in Zhaoqing were humbling. Valignano's approach to conversion efforts was based on a policy of "cultural accommodation" with respect to both Japan and China. Ricci also came to realize that an accommodation of Chinese culture was necessary. Christian missionaries in the New World, Africa, and southern Asia saw themselves as both converting and civilizing (Europeanizing) the peoples of those lands. The Chinese, however, outnumbered the entire populace of Europe and were the inheritors of a civilization that extended farther back in time than the Athens of Pericles. Ricci would become a master of the cultural accommodation approach, but in the face of cultural hostility toward barbarous Europeans and legal sanctions against the preaching of the foreign Christian cult, he was compelled to make his way as a missionary slowly. Even so, the situation was, for all its frustrations, eminently to his liking. In none of the voluminous letters that he produced during his twenty-seven years in China — the final twenty-seven years of his life — did he manifest any homesickness for Europe.

Although the policy of cultural accommodation was elastic enough to condone civil and political practices that differed from those of Christian Europe, it was by no means intended as an argument for religious tolerance. On the contrary, Valignano detested Buddhism and, in particular, viewed the beliefs of the Pure Land sect as akin to the teachings of Martin Luther, "since the Evil One even gave both of them their doctrine, unchanged save for the name of the person in whom they believe and hope." The "doctrine" referred to is salvation through faith alone, and Valignano's contempt for it is shown in his diminutive use of "person" for both Buddha Amitabha and the Protestant Jesus Christ. Cultural accommodation did suggest, however, that Jesuit missionaries, to present themselves as holy men to the Chinese, take on the cropped hair, beardless faces, and austere robes of Buddhist monks. It was by order of Valignano, who knew firsthand of the esteem in which Buddhist monks were held in Japan, that Ricci at first adopted a Buddhist appearance. But the mandarins of China held scant regard for Buddhist monks. Eventually, Ricci and his fellow Jesuits adopted the long beards and purple silk robes of the mandarins, to show the Chinese — as Ricci explained in a letter to Europe — "that we are not priests as vile as their own."

Nonetheless, by 1595, there were fewer than one hundred Christian converts in China. Having been forced, due to mandarin opposition, to abandon his original base in Zhaoqing, Ricci continued his efforts in Shaozhou and Nanking. Even with the lure of Western mathematics and science, Ricci realized that winning souls would require a style and subtlety in the Chinese language equal to that of the Confucians, Daoists, and Buddhists. He ultimately achieved, as writer and speaker, a fluency that won the admiration of the mandarins, who were at once civil administrators and tastemakers. Indeed, his knowledge of Chinese thought, politics, manners, and religious beliefs was plainly superior to that of any European, not only of his time, but for some two centuries following his death. Ricci translated into Chinese the *Elements* of Euclid, as well as numerous Western scientific texts and selections from the Bible. He also composed his own short treatises on friendship and morality in the accepted mandarin style known as "The Twenty-five Words," in which a virtuous theme was elucidated in twenty-five short chapters. Ricci went on to publish a book of Christian apologetics, *The True Doctrine of God,* which drew quotations from the Five Classics attributed to Confucius in support of Christ's teachings. *The True Doctrine* included an attack on Buddhist teachings on rebirth, emphasizing — by contrast — the clarity of the Christian view of salvation.

Li Chih, a mandarin of independent outlook who met Ricci in Nanking in the 1590s, attested both to Ricci's attainments and to the caution he employed in pursuit of his missionary aims:

> Now he has perfectly mastered the art of speaking in our language, and of writing with our script, comporting himself according to our rules of behavior. He is an extraordinarily impressive person. His mind is lucid and his appearance is simple. [. . .] Amongst all the men I have seen, none can compare to him. All who are either too arrogant or too anxious to please, who either display their own cleverness or are too ignorant and dull, are inferior to him. But I do not know how it is that he came here. I have already been with him three times, and still do not know why he has come here. It would be more than foolish if it were perhaps his wish to alter our doctrine of the Duke of Chou and of Confucius on the basis of his doctrine.

Li Chih mistakenly concluded that such was not Ricci's purpose. But Li Chih was perhaps reaching his judgment based not on his reading of Ricci's true desires, but rather on the practical impossibility of their attainment, which the mandarin expected the Jesuit to recognize. The greatness of Ricci as a missionary was that he recognized no such thing.

After years of imperial refusal, Ricci persisted and at last attained permission to reside in the capital city of Beijing. Here, in the nine years from 1601 to 1610, Ricci transformed what would have been the noble failure of his Chinese mission into a successful establishment of Christian influence within the imperial court. In so doing, Ricci survived frequent efforts by Buddhist priests and ministers to link his religious views

with the colonial aims of the European powers. These attacks failed sig-
nally. Upon Ricci's death, a lavish tomb was constructed for him upon a
plot donated by Emperor Wanli.

There is a sharp irony to this bestowal of Confucian-style posthumous
remembrance. For it was Ricci's conviction that Confucian and Christian teachings could be, to a degree, interwoven so as to hasten the conversion of China. Ricci recognized that the broad religious tolerance of
the Chinese — blending with ease Buddhist, Daoist, and Confucian
rites and practices — posed a problem for a Christian religion that
claimed spiritual supremacy. Ricci, however, was heartened by the ethical quality of Confucian writings and believed that the Chinese "could
certainly become Christians, since the essence of their doctrine contains
nothing contrary to the essence of the Catholic faith, nor would the
Catholic faith hinder them in any way, but would indeed aid in that attainment of the quiet and peace of the republic which their books claim
as their goal." Several Chinese Confucian writers contemporary with
Ricci found unconvincing the parallels he drew between Christian and
Confucian belief. But in Ricci's understanding of the Chinese tradition,
Confucius occupied a role akin to the Greek philosophers in the European tradition. If Thomas Aquinas had melded Aristotle and Christ, the
same could surely be done with Confucius and Christ.

But a like accommodation with Buddhism was out of the question for
Ricci, who viewed it solely as a false pagan creed that contained within
itself "a Babylon of doctrines so intricate that no one can understand it
properly, or describe it." The tone of Ricci's attacks here resembles, as
the American scholar Jonathan D. Spence noted, that of the Protestants
of Europe in deeming the Roman Catholic Church a corrupt "whore
of Babylon." Spence wrote:

> It was inevitable that the Jesuits and their converts would spend much —
> perhaps most — of their energies attacking Buddhism in China, since
> Buddhism was their central rival in its claim to ethical good and in perfor-
> mance of acts of charity. Buddhist charitable organizations often involved
> themselves in projects to improve the lot of the poor through endowing
> hospitals and homes for the aged, giving food or low-interest loans in
> times of trouble, establishing bath houses, planting trees, and mending
> bridges; while Ricci was living in Peking there were institutions to give

food and medicine to the poor and to provide coffins for those who died indigent.

The declaration by Ricci that no one could understand or describe Buddhism was not applied to himself, as is evidenced in an epistolatory exchange between Ricci and Yu Chunxi, a Chinese scholar who had written in response to Ricci's publication, in 1608, of *Ten Discourses by a Paradoxical Man*. Ricci had argued therein that the Buddhist monastic practice of dietary abstention from all animal products was based on false doctrines. The irony of this attack was that Ricci himself kept to a Buddhist diet on Christian fast days so as to retain his religious standing in Chinese society. But Ricci insisted that while Christian fasting and dietary abstentions were justified as penitence for sins, the Buddhist viewpoint — that animal products were forbidden because humans and animals intertwined in ceaseless transmigrating lives, and so one might be eating one's own mother or other kindly beings — was patently absurd in practice. Why, Ricci argued, did such a doctrine not prohibit marriage, as one could never know whether one's spouse was also one's deceased family member? And why was the extraction of labor from domestic servants and animals permitted, given who they might once have been?

In his response, Yu took Ricci to task for condemning Buddhist teachings without giving them adequate study, while in the process denigrating the many generations of Chinese who had either been Buddhist or been influenced by Buddhist doctrine. Yu enclosed a basic Buddhist reading list for Ricci's edification.

Ricci did not like to be thus upbraided. In certain prior cases when Chinese scholars had sought to circulate attacks on Ricci, a Chinese examiner sympathetic to the Jesuit had stepped in, as Ricci recounted, to censor the attacks "by changing a few words, so that all the criticisms that had been directed against us were made to fall on the idols of the other religions." But Ricci's position in the Beijing court was secure enough, in the last years of his life, that he could respond to Yu "in such a way that I don't think he'll reply to me in that fashion again, and we are planning to print both the letters, because by doing so we will be able to explain many aspects of our faith." In Ricci's lengthy response, he argued, among other points, that Buddhism flatly violated the first of the ten commandments and had further failed, in its long years as a dominant religion, to uplift Chinese morality.

Yu sent both his own and Ricci's letter to Zhuhong, a leading Buddhist teacher of the period under whom Yu had once studied. The recommendation of Zhuhong was that Ricci's arguments were unworthy of response:

> Marriages between men and women, the use of carts and horses, as well as the employment of servants are all ordinary things in the world. They can never be compared to the cruelty of taking the lives of animals. That is why the sutra says that one should not kill any sentient being, but does not say that one should not get married or employ domestic animals. The kind of sophistry [used by Ricci] is a clever play on words. How can it harm the clear teaching of the Great Truth?

The context of Ricci's efforts must be kept in mind. He was seeking conversions, not ecumenical understandings. What he was conducting was a kind of spiritual war on Buddhism, as he tacitly recognized by applying the term "battle prizes" to the occasional fine examples of Buddhist devotional art provided him by Chinese converts to Christianity who no longer wanted pagan statues in their homes — these treasures Ricci sent on to the Portuguese colony of Macao for preservation. In the majority of such cases, however, the converts were urged by Ricci simply to melt down their bronze Buddhist statues and to burn all Chinese religious, alchemical, and divinatory prints and texts in their possession.

This militance is exemplified in Ricci's response to the death, in 1603, of Zhenke, an esteemed and pious elder Buddhist monk and writer, who was a victim of violent intrigues conducted by Emperor Wanli and the eunuch nobles of his court. Zhenke perished as a result of a public beating administered for his alleged authorship of a pamphlet slandering the emperor's consort. Ricci wrote that Zhenke had disgraced himself by his inability to endure torture, for although "he was wont to boast of caring nothing for the things pertaining to his body, afterward, while being beaten, he cried out like any other profane mortal."

By 1608, two years before Ricci's passing, there were Jesuit mission houses in five cities and some two thousand Christian converts in China — not a great figure, but a definite start, with the converts including a goodly percentage of mandarins with some degree of political and cultural influence. Ricci had further succeeded, within the imperial court, in establishing Christianity as a respected competitor to Daoist and Buddhist religious views.

❖

Ricci argued vigorously that Chinese converts ought to be allowed to perform Confucian rites — and thus maintain their essential identities within Chinese culture — without taint of heresy or apostasy. But this argument was not obvious to all of his fellow Christian missionaries. Nicolo Longobardi, who worked under Ricci and later succeeded him as head of the Jesuit mission in China, never embraced Ricci's view. Throughout the seventeenth century, the dispute known as the "Rites Controversy" quite literally raged within the Church, with the predominant Jesuit view being that China could be won only through cultural accommodation, while the Dominicans and Franciscans argued that conversions achieved in this way were valueless.

By the close of the seventeenth century, there were some 250,000 Chinese Christians, although estimates vary widely in this regard. They formed an insignificant portion of the total Chinese population, and despite the best efforts of the Jesuits, their numbers were drawn principally from the poor. The mandarins tolerated but did not embrace Christianity, and none of the missionaries who followed Ricci — Franciscan and Dominican as well as Jesuit — could equal his successes in the imperial court.

Tolerance of the foreign creed was drastically reduced by the Church's resolution of the Rites Controversy. Pope Clement XI forbade performance by converts of Confucian rituals in 1704 and again in 1715. Pope Benedict XIV affirmed their heretical status in 1742. It is a historical commonplace to argue that these decisions wrecked whatever hope existed for substantial conversions in China. In this case, the commonplace view seems quite accurate, given the clarity of the Chinese response. In the personal writings of the Manchu emperor K'ang-hsi (1654–1722), a tolerant supporter of the Ricci perspective toward Confucianism, the maneuvers of one early-eighteenth-century papal emissary, Bishop Maigrot, are recorded. According to the emperor, Maigrot commenced telling me that Heaven is a material thing and should not be worshiped, and that one should invoke only the name "Lord of Heaven" to show the proper reverence. Maigrot wasn't merely ignorant of Chinese literature, he couldn't even recognize the simplest Chinese characters; yet he chose to discuss the falsity of the Chinese moral system. [. . .] He talked for days, with his perverse reason, his poorly concealed anger, and fled the country when he could not get his way, a sinner against the Catholic teaching and a rebel to China.

Plainly, the eighteenth century was a period of decline for Christianity in China. Missionary work was not forbidden outright, but individual missionaries were widely subject to arrest and deportation. Martyrdoms were less common but hardly rare. Then, in 1773, the Society of Jesus was abolished by order of Pope Clement XIV — due to objections to their power by various Catholic European monarchs — thus severing the most attuned and effective of the Catholic missionary orders in China. The Church tallied only 150,000 converts in China in 1798, down by 25 percent or more from the estimates of 1700. The Jesuits were reinstated in 1814, but the damage had been done.

At last, in 1939, authorization for Catholics to take part in traditional Chinese rites honoring Confucius, the Chinese emperor, and one's ancestors was issued by Pope Pius XII. It is tempting to see in this evolution of doctrine the possibility that, perhaps centuries from now, the Holy See will find itself in a position of increased accommodation with Buddhist thought and practice. But that time has not yet come.

❖

Tibet, more written of than witnessed by prior Western travelers, became in the seventeenth and early eighteenth centuries a keenly desired destination for a series of Jesuit explorers. A Portuguese Jesuit, Bento de Goes, skirted western Tibet in 1602–1604 as part of a journey from India to China that included crossings of the Hindu Kush and the Gobi Desert. Two decades later, Antonio de Andrade, another Portuguese Jesuit, endured blizzards and mountain sickness to reach far into the Himalayas to the summit of Mana Pass. He became the first European to view Tibet from its heights rather than its western plains. His hope had been to locate fellow Christians in southern China, for the rumor had been circulating in India that there were Christian remnants to the north as a result of long-forgotten evangelization efforts. Theoretically, this could have been the case, but it was not. Andrade's own account of the Mana Pass vista reflected the bitter difficulties of his journey: "It was all one dazzling whiteness to our eyes, which had been weakened by snow blindness, and we could see no indication of the road to follow." The Lisbon publication, in 1626, of Andrade's *Nuevo descubrimiento del gran Cathayo, o reynos de Tibet* marked the first Western geographic account of Tibet.

The first Europeans to reach Lhasa, in 1661, were two Jesuits from Austria and Belgium, Johannes Grueber and Albert d'Orville, whose principal aim had been to find a serviceable land route from China to India. They stayed in the city for one month while they tried to locate a new caravan to take them on to Kathmandu in Nepal. Grueber, a gifted amateur artist, made the first sketches by a Westerner of both the Tibetan Buddhist prayer wheel and the Potala (which Grueber transcribed as "Pietala"), the palatial residence of the Dalai Lama overlooking Lhasa. This drawing was first transmitted to Europe in *China Monumentis* (1667), one of many diverse works, issued with sumptuous illustrations, by Athanasius Kircher, a Jesuit priest and one of the great polymath scholars of late Renaissance Europe, whose studies encompassed mathematics, medicine, archaeology, earth sciences, comparative religion, and philology.

Kircher had volunteered for missionary service in China but was rejected. In his preface to *China Monumentis,* he paid tribute to the great labor and risk endured by Grueber and other Jesuit missionaries upon whose researches he drew. One of the images of China included in Kircher's book, titled "Idol of 'Pussa,'" portrays a robed woman with her face encircled by a solar nimbus as she sits serenely on a lotus blossom rising from a harbor. Three European-style sailing ships are approaching the harbor. Beside the woman is a slender vase from which a blossom emerges. Below her, on a smaller lotus blossom, a young man sits in rapt attendance upon her. Kircher believed that the woman represented the Great Mother worshipped in Egypt as Isis, while the lotus was the "humid principle" essential to life. It is tempting, as the American scholar Joscelyn Godwin suggested, to see in the lotus rising from the water a "confused image of Buddhist iconography."

My own opinion is that the image is indeed a Buddhist one, but not so confused that a reasonable surmise cannot be made. Kircher perhaps transmitted unwittingly to Europe its first vision of Kuanyin, the Chinese Buddhist goddess of compassion, who is frequently portrayed in robes and with a shining crown, seated or standing upon a lotus blossom that sometimes arises from the sea. Kuanyin is often attended by a handsome youth named Shan Ts'ai, who, when he first approached the goddess, proved his devotion to her by diving off a cliff into the sea to protect her from pirates of her own magical devising. Shan Ts'ai died in this effort but was restored to life by the goddess, who reigned, as the twentieth-century English Buddhist John Blofeld observed, over a "seagirt paradise," the island of Potala.

Although the vase in Kircher's illustration, with its unidentified blossom, rests beside — and not in the hands of — the female figure, both fit strikingly within Blofeld's account of Kuanyin's "principal emblems": "a precious vase held in one hand and a willow spray held in the other, symbolizing respectively 'sweet dew' (also known as *amrta*) meaning the nectar of wisdom and compassion, and secondly her willingness to sprinkle it upon the heads of all who invoke her aid." It is even possible that Kircher's surmise as to the "humid principle" embodied by the lotus (a widespread Buddhist symbol of compassion and wisdom) was a confused reference to the "sweet dew" of Kuanyin. The three ships pose the least clear attribution, but it is helpful to recall that Kuanyin was a special figure of devotion to sailors, who invoked her compassionate powers at times of danger at sea.

Kircher's interest in Chinese and Tibetan Buddhism was relatively limited. He assessed their doctrines solely within the framework of Christian theology. In *China Monumentis,* he declared that the Devil was responsible for transferring veneration rightly due the pope to a grand lama of Lhasa: "From him, as from a certain Fountain, floweth the whole form and mode of their Religion, or rather mad and brain-sick idolatry." Chief among the idols was "Manipe," to whom, Kircher reported, "this foolish People commence their sacred Rites, with many unwonted Gesticulations and Dances, often repeating of these words: *O Manipe Mi*

Hum, O Manipe Mi Hum, that is, *O Manipe save us;* and these sottish People are wont to set many sorts of viands and meats before the Idol for the propitiating or appeasing of the Deity." Kircher's garbled transliteration of the Tibetan Buddhist mantra *Om Mani Padme Hum;* his ignorance of the mantric function of the syllables *Om* and *Hum,* as well as of the literal, much less spiritual, meanings of *Padme Hum,* the Jewel in the Lotus; and his lack of knowledge of the exercise of compassion that lies at the heart of ritual offerings — all combined to form a most unfortunate European introduction to Tibetan Buddhism.

Kircher's was the first in an increasing salvo of attacks on Tibetan religion — often called Lamaism — by Catholic writers as the eighteenth century proceeded. The principal aim was to distance the Church from what were viewed as disconcerting resemblances between Lhasa and Rome in terms of structure and ritual, if not in spiritual doctrine. The disturbing irony confronting the Church was that the negative accounts provided by the Jesuits began to be used against Rome by Protestant critics, who pointed to the striking similarities between Catholicism and Lamaism in terms of grand ecclesiastical wardrobes, elaborate ritual, the prominent use of rosary beads, and the centrality of the pope and grand lama, respectively.

◈

All the while, Christian missionaries were, by their own accounts, welcomed without restraint into Tibet. It was not until 1760, when Tibet expelled the Capuchins (or so it is stated in Catholic histories; the Tibetan account is that the Capuchins themselves abandoned their efforts in 1745), that sanctions against foreign travelers were created and the Western stereotype of a jealously forbidden Tibet arose.

Far and away the most remarkable of the early Christian travelers to Tibet was the Jesuit Ippolito Desideri, who not only made his way to Lhasa in 1716 but who also won the interest and support of the Mongol ruler of Tibet, Lhazang Khan. Desideri remained in Tibet for five years, living for extended periods in two great monastic centers of Tibetan Buddhism. He learned the Tibetan language sufficiently to be able to study Tibetan Buddhist texts — an attainment unduplicated by a European until the mid-nineteenth century. Desideri recorded his researches in a book that was, for its time, a landmark of Western understanding of Tibet. He suffers from uncommonly unjust historical neglect, however, because of the merest accidents of fate. His manuscript, completed shortly before his death at age forty-eight on Easter 1733, was entirely lost to common knowledge until its rediscovery in 1876 in his hometown of Pistoia, Italy. It was subsequently published in 1904, to little notice, by the Italian Geographical Society, with a title bestowed by its editor: *Il Tibet (Geografia, Storia, Religione, Costumi); secondo la Relazione del Viaggio di Ippolito Desideri 1715–1721.* The book was translated into English but drew little notice, given the more recent writings by Western travelers that seemed to eclipse Desideri's work. Nonetheless, he has had his admirers, including the twentieth-century Swedish explorer Sven Hedin, who eulogized, "the general merit of his narrative, the absence of fantastical speculation, the quiet matter-of-fact way in which he gives his observations, and nobody will call it an exaggeration if I regard Ippolito Desideri as one of the most brilliant travellers who ever visited Tibet."

Desideri's arrival in Lhasa in 1716 was preceded by an eighteen-month trek across the western Tibetan steppes. The prior determined efforts of Jesuit and other Christian missionaries to Tibet had yet to result in substantial conversions. But Desideri — who was granted by Lhazang Khan the signal honor, for a foreigner, of being permitted to purchase, not rent, a house in the center of Lhasa — felt that he might succeed where others had failed. A basis for this hope had been extended by Lhazang Khan, who encouraged Desideri to learn Tibetan so that he and the khan might converse on religious and other matters without an interpreter. The motivation here need not have been solely religious zeal. Lhazang Khan, as a blood relation of the Chinese emperor, knew of the frequent visits of Christian missionaries to China and was not averse to forging his own contacts with Europe. Desideri recorded that the khan promised "to listen to what I had to say, and if, after mature discussion and examination of what I had to propose he should be convinced of having hitherto lived in error, he, his whole family, his Court, and all his people would become followers of the word of Jesus Christ."

Desideri was skeptic enough to ponder if all of this were but a mere dance of courtly diplomacy, but he resolved to seize the opportunity. "I made it a rule," he wrote, "to study from early morning till sundown, and for nearly six years took nothing during the day save *cia* [tea] to drink, except on solemn feast days, or any extraordinary occasion." Nine months after his first royal audience, Desideri produced a treatise in Tibetan on Christian teaching for Lhazang Khan to review. According to Desideri, after a ceremonial reception of and reading from a part of the treatise, the khan declared that he was gratified by the gift, which he intended to "finish at his leisure and even read over again." Some months later, the khan summoned Desideri again and informed him that not only he had read the book carefully but so had several learned lamas. "Their opinion," Desideri duly noted, "was that the maxims and principles contained therein were well set forth and seemed to be well reasoned, but were entirely opposed to their dogmas and opinions."

This stalemate could only be resolved by a debate before the royal court between Desideri and selected Buddhist lamas. To ensure that the debate would be meaningful, Desideri would need considerable time to prepare, for Lhazang Khan insisted that the Jesuit undertake further studies of Tibetan translations of Indian Buddhist sutras and commentaries, and also live among Tibetan monks and teachers. Two monasteries, Ramoche and Sera, were deemed suitable for Desideri's unhindered studies. At Sera, Desideri conducted mass in a small oratory space allotted to him.

Lhazang Khan was deposed and murdered in December 1717, and Mongol rule over Tibet was ended altogether in 1720 by Chinese forces of the Manchu dynasty, which restored the rule of the Seventh Dalai Lama — with a Manchu military governor and some two thousand troops installed in Lhasa. Desideri's preparations for the great debate were over, but his studies and writings did not slacken. His removal from Tibet in 1721 was due not to political upheavals, but to the maneuvering of Capuchin missionaries, who convinced Rome that Tibet was theirs to till for souls and that the Jesuit Desideri should be expelled.

In his book, Desideri explains plainly and repeatedly that he studied Buddhist texts so as better to prevail against their false pagan teachings. But even as he systematically deprecated Buddhism, Desideri grappled deeply with Buddhist teachings, without altogether trivializing, demonizing, or falsely contextualizing them — as so many other Christian missionaries to Asia did, and would do, in their writings. Compare, for example, his discussion of Tibetan funerary practices with that of the

Franciscan Odoric more than three centuries earlier. Whereas Odoric fulminated about the practice of leaving corpses to be devoured by raptors and beasts, Desideri explained the practice as a posthumous gift of oneself as food to other living creatures: "This the Thibettans regard as an act of compassion and a step toward arriving, after many transmigrations, at the supreme heroism of giving their living flesh, and therefore their life, out of compassion to living creatures. This is the foundation and the real origin of this usage in Thibet."

The Buddhist teaching with which Desideri wrestled most fiercely has often been translated into English as "emptiness" or "voidness." Desideri wrote:

Above all I applied myself to study and really attempt to understand those most abstruse, subtle, and intricate treatises called Tongba-gni [Sanskrit, *shunyata*] or Vacuum, which are not to be taken in a material or philosophic, but in a mystical and intellectual sense; their real aim being to exclude and absolutely deny the existence of any uncreated and independent Being and thus effectually to do away with any conception of God.

The stakes were high. If Desideri was to convince Tibetans of the truth of Christ, he would have to overcome Tibetan belief in the doctrine of emptiness. Desideri wrote that when he began to study the treatises on that subject,

the Doctor who had been appointed my Master declared that he could not explain them or make me understand them. Thinking this was only a pretext to prevent my gaining any real knowledge of such matters, I repeatedly entreated him to explain what I did not understand without help. Seeing that I was by no means convinced that he was so incapable and that, as he said, only some of the chief and most learned Lamas would be able to instruct me, he offered to bring other Doctors, declaring that he would be well pleased if I found any one who could throw light on these intricate and abstruse questions. In fact we both applied to several of the most esteemed Masters and Doctors and all gave me the same answer.

Desideri harbored early suspicions that all these responses were a mere "pretext" to deflect a Christian missionary seeking to study the Dharma only to undermine it. Whether he at last discarded these suspicions, Desideri did not say. But given the fulsome regard expressed in his book for the Tibetan Buddhists with whom he studied and lived, it is at least clear that he was treated for the most part with the deepest respect. Consider his account of the Tibetan monastics who observed his Christian worship in their midst:

> I was often persuaded by their persistent prayers to allow them to attend the Holy Sacrifice of Mass, and it was touching to see how they kneeled down with hands clasped in prayer and listened devoutly. Sometimes they brought incense and begged that it might be burnt in the chapel. This was very much owing to the esteem in which they held European Missionaries. They look upon them as Lamas, that is to say not only monks who have renounced the world and doctors who have studied science, but as masters and spiritual directors who have dedicated themselves to this ministry and to all the hardships it entails solely in order to save others from error and evil ways and lead them to eternal felicity.

The responses on emptiness provided to Desideri by his Tibetan teachers could be read as plain and respectful communications indicating that the doctrine was, at root, an experiential truth beyond mere verbal formulae. Indeed, to resolve his dilemma of comprehension, Desideri pursued just such an experiential path within his own Christian tradition:

> Seeing that human aid was of no avail, I prayed to God, the Father of Light, for whose glory alone I had undertaken this work, and again applied myself to solitary study. [. . .] I read, re-read and studied until, thanks be to God, I not only understood, but completely mastered (all Glory being to God) all the subtle, sophisticated, and abstruse matter which was so necessary and important for me to know.

Desideri then declared the significance of his breakthrough: "Having by my aforesaid diligence discovered the site of the enemy's camp, the quality of their arms and their artifices, and provided myself with arms and ammunition, towards the end of November [1717] I resolved to challenge them and begin war." One of his weapons was a book that he composed in Tibetan — *Questions on the Views of Rebirth and Emptiness, Offered by the White-Headed Lama Called Ippolito to the Scholars of Tibet*. The manuscript survives in the Jesuit archives in Rome; what readership it found among Tibetans is not known.

It is idle to speculate as to the depths of Desideri's experiential attainment of Buddhist emptiness. What is clear, from his later discussion of the basic teachings of the Buddha — whom Desideri called the "Legislator" — is that Desideri intellectually grasped the Buddhist view that "nothing exists because nothing has any essence by itself." This much corresponds with the Buddhist view of dependent origination — the absence of innately separate selves or entities of any sort. But what Desideri missed is the sense of interdependence that Buddhist teachers insist must emerge from such a realization — expressed, in recent times, by the Vietnamese Zen master Thich Nhat Hanh as "interbeing." In Desideri's interpretation, the absence of essences means that human beings are to be regarded as "independent of any cause, and having no connection with any other thing." This would render unenlightened beings free of the causal laws of karma, as well as helpless to benefit from the path of compassionate practice, neither of which are Buddhist views.

Desideri's summation of the strengths and flaws of the Tibetan Buddhist creed is a remarkable blend of ecumenism, reflexive contempt, and strained self-reassurance as to the justness of Christian theology when applied to persons raised outside the Christian tradition:

> Although I believe the articles of [Buddhist] Faith to be absolutely wrong and pestiferous, yet the rules and directions imposed on the will are not alien to the principles of sound reason; they seem to me worthy of admiration as they not only prescribe hatred of vice, inculcate battling against passions, but, what is more remarkable, lead man toward sublime and heroic perfection. God has bestowed so much intelligence, even on uncivilized man, that it ought to be sufficient to guard him against evil and incline him to love virtue. Even these blind pagans, abandoned as some think by God, are intelligent enough to follow the instructions of teachers, and if they cannot use the one talent given them by God, He

is justified in not granting them the supernatural light of Faith, and, angered by their sloth and infidelity, to cast them off and condemn them to suffering and punishment.

It is an odd note to charge sloth against a creed that he had praised two sentences before for its aim of "sublime and heroic perfection." It is equally odd to raise a charge of Tibetan "infidelity" to the "intelligence" granted by God after having already conceded that Buddhist doctrine is "not alien" to reason. But to note inconsistencies in Desideri's argument is not to argue that he was insincere. He genuinely admired and reviled at the same time, and it is his openness on this score that makes him such a valuable register of this first extended dialogue between Christianity and Tibetan Buddhism.

4

THE "CHINA CRAZE" AND THE RISE
OF THE EUROPEAN ORIENTALISTS

❖

Jesuit accounts had convinced Europeans that China was the most peaceful and efficient nation in the world. Literacy and scholarship were venerated there, while its imperial government — which came to be praised in Europe as an exemplar of "enlightened despotism" — had seemingly prevailed since time immemorial, for there was as yet in the West no clear conception of the beginnings of Chinese civilization.

The Jesuit writings had as a principal agenda the promotion of tolerance for Confucianism among European Catholics, so as to strengthen the Jesuit position regarding the Rites Controversy. Their accounts, meticulously edited prior to publication, did not frankly address issues of ministerial injustices and widespread poverty. Nor were adequate descriptions provided of the upheaval that accompanied the defeat of the Ming dynasty in 1644 — after nearly three centuries of rule — by invaders from Manchuria. But even as the Jesuits lauded the stability of China, within China itself they came increasingly to be viewed as would-be disrupters, due to papal refusal to countenance the practice of Confucian rites by Chinese Christian converts.

A further irony here is that the Jesuit writings spurred widespread acclaim in Christian Europe for the founder of those very rites. In the eighteenth century, Confucius received the type of intellectual veneration — as the "great representative" of Eastern thought — now frequently accorded by Western thinkers to the Buddha. For example, the German mathematician and philosopher Christian Wolff (1679–1754) gave a lecture at the University of Halle in 1721, "De Sinarum philosophia practica," in which he placed Confucius alongside Christ as a prophet of morality for all humankind. This fulsome praise led to calumnious charges by Protestant theologians (who were less enamored of Confucianism than the Catholic Jesuits) that Wolff was an atheist — charges that led to the temporary loss of his professorship. The stakes involved in extolling foreign creeds were high, even in a post-Inquisition Europe. But Confucius, as the Jesuits had presented him — in comfortable secular accord with Western moral values — offered precisely the counterpoise to biblical revealed religion for which deists of the European Enlightenment had been searching. The deists, who argued for a natural religion of calm reason and practical morality, saw in Confucianism the political success for which they longed — establishment as a state religion that did without clergy, miracles, or divinely inspired scriptures.

The European "China craze" of that time — which, beyond philosophy, displayed itself in a fervid taste for chinoiseries, such as porcelain "china," silk fabrics, painted screens, and lacquer furniture — is relevant to our narrative because it so plainly illustrates tendencies that would emerge again, quite intact but in a mirror-opposite mode, in the deprecatory nineteenth-century Western view of Buddhism as the worship of "nothingness." First and foremost, there was the overweening arrogance that gave European thinkers the sense that they could pass judgment on the whole of an Asian spiritual tradition while knowing precious little of its history, doctrine, and practice. There was also the tendency to use discussions of Asian religion and philosophy as surreptitious blinds, by means of which the controversial and far more pressing issues of Western society could be addressed. It is striking how strongly the fantasy of an ideal China — one grasped secondhand from Church sources often objected to by Enlightenment thinkers in other contexts — figured in the writings of some of the greatest philosophers of the era, including the Frenchmen Pierre Bayle (1647–1706), Malebranche (1638–1715), and Montesquieu (1689–1755).

The most passionate of the early paeans to China came from the pen of Baron Gottfried Wilhelm von Leibniz (1646–1716), the German philosopher, theologian, mathematician, statesman, and diplomat whose achievements include the discovery, alongside Sir Isaac Newton, of calculus, and authorship of the *Discourse on Metaphysics*. The famous opening postulate of that work — that God is perfect and so the world he created must be the best of all possible worlds — was lampooned by Voltaire. Even so, the viewpoint of Leibniz still underlies many Western approaches to consolation in the face of the bitterness life has to offer.

Leibniz was a Protestant with an ecumenical outlook who sought to reduce doctrinal tensions between Protestants and Catholics at a time, in Reformation Europe, when they badly needed reducing. His approach was essentially the same in the case of China. He was prepared to offer respect, if not full equality, to the essential moral reasonableness — the "natural theology" — of Confucianism, which Leibniz had studied by means of Jesuit accounts. In his *Novissima Sinica historiam nostri temporis illustratura* (1697), Leibniz went so far as to concede superiority in temporal, if not eternal, wisdom to China:

> Our circumstances seem to me to have sunk to such a level, particularly with regard to the monstrous and increasing breakdown of morality, that one could almost think it necessary for the Chinese to send missionaries to us to teach us the purpose and use of natural theology, in the same way as we send missionaries to them to instruct us in revealed theology. And I believe that if a wise man were set up to judge not the beauty of goddesses but the excellence of nations, we would give the golden apple to the Chinese, were it not that we excel them in one single but superhuman quality, the divine gift of the Christian religion.

It is from Leibniz that Europe received the first grand statement of an ultimate harmonious unity to be formed between East and West — a dream still held with conviction by many. Leibniz argued from a combined perspective of practical geopolitics and, in a tone unusual for the period, pervasive tolerance. Such tolerance, Leibniz believed, reflected the world order envisioned by the Christian God:

> It is in my view a unique disposition of fate which has placed the highest civilisations the human race has achieved as it were at the two extremes of our continent, that is in Europe and in China, which adorns the opposite end of the earth as a kind of oriental Europe. And the highest providence is also at work in the fortunate circumstance that while the nations which are most highly developed and at the same time the furthest

separated, reach out their arms to one another, everything that lies between them is gradually brought to a higher way of life.

❖

Notwithstanding this faith in divinely inspired diversity, Leibniz was also a strong proponent of launching Protestant missions in China to follow up on the efforts of the Jesuits, who, Leibniz believed, had faltered in their task since the death of Matteo Ricci. Indeed, in 1716, roughly a century after Ricci's passing, Leibniz composed, in response to a French correspondent, a *Discours sur la théologie naturelle des Chinois,* in which he argued on behalf of the Ricci stance of accommodating Confucian ritual. As his biographer E. J. Aiton observed, "A favorite device adopted by Leibniz in the *Discourse* was to show that some aspect of ancient Chinese thought was compatible with his own philosophy. Then it followed that, as his own philosophy was comparable with Christianity, so was that particular aspect of Chinese natural theology." The most surprising line of compatibility pursued by Leibniz (based on what proved to be inaccurate findings provided to him by a member of the Jesuit mission in China) was that the key to interpreting the hexagrams of the *I Ching* lay in the binary arithmetic created by Leibniz himself. Given his respect for Chinese culture, it is saddening to see Leibniz lay claim so readily to that which he scarcely knew.

Such claims continued apace, as Western thinkers ambitiously expanded their theories to take in the newly revealed East. The French philosopher Pierre Bayle, in his *Dictionnaire historique et critique* (1697), sought to encapsulate the essential doctrines of all the world religions. His entry on "Brahman" (into which category he confusedly grouped both Hindu and Buddhist beliefs) was based on classical Greek writings as well as more recent Jesuit reports, from which Bayle concluded that there was a Brahmanic sect in China that worshipped the divinity Fo — the Chinese name for the Buddha. In his entry on "Japan," Bayle found similarities between Zen thought and the pantheistic teachings of Spinoza, who "taught, like these Japanese priests, that the first principle of all things, and all beings that make up the universe, are of one and the same substance, that all things are God, and God all things." Bayle imported a conception of God into Zen Buddhism that does not belong there, but perhaps that error aided him in comprehending that the "noth-

ingness" of Buddhism did not denote nihilism. Rather, Bayle explained —
in a manner that captured some sense of its paradoxical fullness —
"they meant roughly by this word what the moderns mean by the word
'space.'" Bayle further offered a summary of Zen meditation practice
that was overstated — ritual practice and language disciplines were not
excluded from Zen — but astute for its time: "They neglect the externals, apply themselves exclusively to meditation, reject any discipline
that has to do with words, and apply themselves only to the exercise
they call *Soquxin Soquent* [J(apanese). *sokushin sokubutsu,* "This very mind
is the Buddha"] that is to say, the *heart.*"

Rifely inaccurate as was Bayle's conflation of Hinduism and Buddhism,
he was cribbed wholesale in this regard by Denis Diderot in the *Ency-
clopédie,* one of the seminal compilations of the Enlightenment era.
Diderot, in his entry "Bramines," described his hybridized Buddhists and
Brahmans as alike asserting that

> the world is nothing but an illusion, a dream, a magic spell, and that the
> bodies, in order to be truly existent, have to cease existing in themselves,
> and to merge into nothingness, which due to its simplicity amounts to
> the perfection of all beings. They claim that saintliness consists in willing
> nothing, thinking nothing, feeling nothing. . . . This state is so much like
> a dream that it seems that a few grains of opium would sanctify a brah-
> min more surely than all his efforts.

Diderot's touch of originality here was to add the parallel between Indian religion and opium intoxication. Some fifty years later, Hegel borrowed from this for his own description of Indian mystics who "could
only attain a dream-world and the happiness of insanity through opium."
From Hegel, the usage passed on to Karl Marx, who expanded it to a
global description of religion as the "opiate of the masses." In this manner, what began as an ignorant condescension of Eastern thought became
one of the most famous Western quotations on the subject of religion.

❖

In *Candide,* the radical skeptic Voltaire (1694–1778) pitilessly scalded the
view of Leibniz that this was the best of all possible worlds. Believe
nothing that contradicts the lessons of reason and experience, Voltaire's

satire teaches. But when it came to his handling of the Jesuit accounts of China, Voltaire proved as credulous as Leibniz — although the myths promulgated by the antireligious Frenchman had a markedly different agenda than Leibniz's pious accommodations to Christian supremacy.

For example, in his short story "An Indian Adventure," Voltaire portrayed the early Greek philosopher Pythagoras journeying to India, reflecting Voltaire's fascination with the possibility of Pythagorean influence on Indian thought. Voltaire's Pythagoras preaches tolerance, only to be met with the absurdity of an Indian public throng gathering to burn a man "for having said that the substance of Xaca [Shakyamuni] is not the substance of Brahma." While Voltaire was here satirizing, in Indian garb, the Inquisition in Europe, it is also clear that he viewed Asian and Western religions as equally foolish.

It was Confucianism — as portrayed by the Jesuits, whom he otherwise opposed — that held Voltaire's fascination. He regarded Confucian teachings as historical proof that the conclusions of natural religion were independent of particular national customs. In his "Chinese Catechism," his fictional Prince Koo of the Chinese imperial court asserts that "the God Fo does not impress me either, although his father was a white elephant and he promises an immortal life. What displeases me most of all is that such fantasies are commonly preached by bonzes [monks] who beguile the people in order to govern them." When Prince Koo complains of the difficulties such intransigent ignorance poses even for just rulers, the response of Ku-Su, a Confucian who serves as a mouthpiece for Voltaire, is that "natural law permits everyone to believe what he pleases, just as he can eat as he pleases. [. . .] A prince has no right to have those of his subjects hanged who do not think like him; but he has the right to prevent disturbances; and if he is wise it will be very easy for him to uproot superstitions." Voltaire overstated the power of the Buddhist bonzes, who were dependent on the reigning nobility. But then, his primary concern, albeit in a narrative set in Chinese costume, was with Christian "superstition" and with European monarchs.

The aim of many of the prominent Enlightenment thinkers was the peaceful but decisive overthrow of Christian dominance in the public life of Europe. This overthrow was to leave Christian morality intact, as that morality was viewed as identical to the tolerant tenets of natural law writ large in the hearts of men. But the Christian theology that pitted itself against all who would not submit to it — that was to be cast aside as a barbarous remnant. Voltaire had this answer to those who wondered what adequate bulwark of societal goodness might be established in place of the Church: "What! A ferocious animal has sucked the blood of my family; I tell you to get rid of that beast, and you ask me, What shall we put in its place!" The true Christianity, according to Voltaire, a believer in God in his own fashion, was a view that ethically transcended all of established Christendom: "May this great God who is listening to me, this God who surely cannot have been born of a virgin, or have died on the gallows, or be eaten in a piece of dough, or have inspired these books filled with contradictions, madness, and horror — may this God, creator of all the worlds, have pity on this sect of Christians who blaspheme him!" Similarly, Diderot rejoiced, in 1768, that "it was raining bombs in the house of the Lord" — that is, that Christianity seemed to be losing its hold on the public in France, due in no small measure to attacks such as those made by Diderot himself — and that "the great prostitute of Babylon" — not only the Catholic Church, but Christianity itself — might at last fall, thus clearing the way to the "reign of Anti-Christ" — with whom Diderot here both mockingly and proudly linked the entire Enlightenment movement.

❖

The onset of the French Revolution in 1789 put an end to ideals of enlightened secular monarchies of any sort, and fascination with Chinese politics thereafter ebbed throughout Europe. With the Jesuit order disbanded during this era and resistance to all forms of Western presence increasing in China itself, the onetime praises of the Jesuits were replaced by disgruntled reports from European merchants and missionaries.

The fantasy of an ideal China became an utterly transparent falsehood by the mid-nineteenth century, when the Manchu dynasty, lacking in military power, fell victim to colonial incursions and became, in effect, a vassal state to Europe. Western interest in learning from the Chinese model of rule vanished, being replaced instead by the broad consensus that China was a land of inherited customs that were outmoded at best and barbarous at worst. The decline and fall of imperial China deprived

Confucianism of its status, in much the same manner as the collapse of the Soviet Union and the economic transformation of China have deprived Marxism of its status as a serious alternative to capitalism. In matters of so-called intellectual judgment, the cachet of political power often plays a shaping role.

❖

David Hume (1711–1776) never shared the fascination of his fellow Enlightenment thinkers with Confucian thought. But similarities between the philosophy of Hume and prevalent Buddhist views on the nature of mind have been noted, most famously by the British mathematician and philosopher Alfred North Whitehead. These similarities are certainly not based on any knowledge that Hume possessed as to the subtleties of Buddhist thought. Adequate translations and studies were simply not available to him. It is further clear from his two fleeting references to Buddhism in *The Natural History of Religion* (1757) — a work in which Hume argued that all religions arose to serve the universal human needs for solace and certainty — that he had little regard for Buddhism and only a cursory knowledge of its practices based on Jesuit accounts. Thus Hume wrote, perhaps of Buddhism and Confucianism alike, that "the Chinese, when their prayers are not answered, beat their idols." The second reference, in passing, is to "the excessive penances of the Brachmans and Talapoins," the latter being an English transliteration of the southern Asian Pegu term (*talapicor*) for a Buddhist monk.

The few limited English-language sources potentially available to Hume — whether he read them or not is unknown — would have included the writings of British merchant seamen who visited southern Asian lands in which Buddhism was practiced, such as Ralph Fitch and Robert Knox, in the sixteenth and seventeenth centuries, respectively. Fitch left some sparse descriptions of Burmese Theravada monks, from which Richard Hakluyt drew for his famous compendium, *The Principal Navigations, Voyages, Traffiques and Discoveries of the English Nation* (1599). Knox, who in 1659 was shipwrecked on Sri Lanka and thereafter was condemned, due to his refusal to enter the service of the Sri Lankan monarch, to more than a decade of enslavement and degradation, at last escaped and thereafter published, in London in 1681, *An Historical Relation of the Island of Ceylon,* which offered readers both a good adventure story and a vengeful portrayal of the island's king. The book sold briskly and influenced Defoe's *Robinson Crusoe* (1719).

Knox included accounts of Sri Lankan "idolatry" that far exceeded in detail anything previously published in English on Buddhist practice. "There is," Knox wrote, "another great God, whom they call Buddou, unto whom the Salvation of Souls belongs. Him they believe once to have come upon the Earth. And when he was here, that he did usually sit under a large shady Tree, called Bogahah." Knox told of elaborate pagodas and of Buddhist priests who practiced chastity, nonviolence, and charity. The Buddhist doctrine of rebirth was related by Knox in terms that, perhaps unintentionally, echoed Christian teachings: "These people do firmly believe in a resurrection of the body, and the Immortality of Souls and a future State. [. . .] They hold that every man's good or bad Fortune was predetermined by God, before he was born, according to an usual Proverb they have, *Ollua cottaula tiana,* It is written in the head." This last sentence represents perhaps the first Western effort to explicate the doctrine of karma, with "God" inserted by Knox as a force of predestination, as opposed to the Buddhist view of ongoing causal impacts from prior lifetimes.

Such were the beginnings of British knowledge concerning Buddhist belief. They could never have provided Hume with inspiration for his singular speculations on causation and the self. The writings of the Frenchman Pierre Bayle, whom Hume read and admired, contained little on the specifics of Buddhist thought. Nonetheless, Hume, of all the eighteenth-century European thinkers, held to a radical skepticism on matters of religion that parallels Buddhist caution on metaphysical questions. The similarities — and differences — between the philosophy of Hume and the tenets of Buddhism reveal the nature of the gulf between West and East in the Enlightenment era.

In his posthumously published *Dialogues Concerning Natural Religion* (1779), Hume posed a tentative conclusion as to what a reasonable person might claim to know of the creation of the world (the italics are Hume's): *"That the cause or causes of order in the universe probably bear some remote analogy to human intelligence."* He then added an elegiac coda, as if Hume — in the persona of "Philo," the skeptic in the *Dialogues* — recognized that such a conclusion must disappoint anyone seeking solace for life's sorrows:

If this proposition be not capable of extension, variation, or particular explication, if it affords no inference that affects human life, or can be the source of any action or forbearance, and if the analogy, imperfect as it is, can be carried no further than to the human intelligence, and cannot be transferred, with any appearance of probability, to the other qualities of the mind, if this really be the case, what can the most inquisitive, contemplative, and religious man do more than give a plain, philosophical assent to the proposition, as often it occurs, and believe that the arguments on which it is established exceed the objections which lie against it?

Consider how strange it is that Hume so readily conceded that his "proposition" was a barren one — neither capable of "extension" nor of offering an "inference that affects human life." In our current era of virtual intelligence and communication, certain practical applications of universe-like minds do come rather easily to mind. But leaving aside technologies of which Hume could have had no idea, what remains striking in his concession is that he does not discuss possibilities for inner reflection based on his own speculations. "Contemplative," in Hume's usage, included no sense that a means of disciplined meditation could exist whereby the workings of a universe that seemed to resemble a mind might be further explored, with the source of that universe ultimately being traced back to the minds of human meditators. Such, in summary form, is the aim of a great deal of Buddhist meditational practice, of which, of course, Hume had no knowledge. There is, however, a clear hint given in his *Enquiry Concerning the Principles of Morals* (1751) as to the low regard in which Hume held Christian contemplatives, and from this we may surmise how he would have regarded Buddhist ascetics:

Celibacy, fasting, penance, mortification, self-denial, humility, silence, solitude, and the whole train of monkish virtues; for what reason are they everywhere rejected by men of sense, but because they serve to no manner of purpose; neither advance a man's fortune in the world, nor render him a more valuable member of society; neither qualify him for the entertainment of company, nor increase his power of self-enjoyment?

The point here is not to suggest that Hume was in need of Buddhist wisdom, but rather to establish the degree to which, in the late eighteenth century, central themes of Buddhist thought were absent from Western culture, and hence from the outlook of a philosophical giant of the West who had nonetheless approached, altogether independently, the Buddhist viewpoint that the universe resembles the workings of a mind. Where Hume and Buddhism part company is that Hume believed that the "remote analogy to human intelligence" of a universal mind, if indeed it existed, could not be known with certainty. Buddhism, by identifying such a mind with human Buddha-nature, held that enlightenment was the achievement of just such knowledge.

There is a second striking similarity between Hume's philosophy and Buddhist thought — one that pertains to the tenuous nature of reality and of selfhoods. Hume argued, in his *Treatise of Human Nature* (1739), that our beliefs as to the reality of material objects and human selves were fallacious because they depended on an erroneous belief in causation. Hume established, by a logical demonstration that still prevails in analytical philosophy, that the fact that B follows A cannot ever mean, as a matter of pure reason, that A *caused* B. Experience and memory may lead us to the overpowering conviction that A can and will cause B, but we cannot prove that A *must* cause B. Reality is — as a purely theoretical matter — subject to random change. There is no logical contradiction in saying that the sun will not rise tomorrow. Applying this to the question of a human self, a belief in causation would lead one to put forth the platitude that each person is the sum of his or her past experiences. Hume's response, unconvincing to his Western philosophical successors — though it follows readily enough from his widely accepted argument on causation — is that no such entity as a consistent human personality really exists. Rather, we patch together our ever-shifting notions of our selves from the unreliable data of our overwhelmed senses and memories.

As to the illusion of personhood, Hume wrote:

I may venture to affirm of the rest of mankind that they are nothing but a bundle or collection of different perceptions, which succeed each other with an inconceivable rapidity, and are in a perpetual flux and movement. Our eyes cannot turn in their sockets without varying our perceptions. Our thought is still more variable than our sight; and all our other senses and faculties contribute to this change; nor is there any single power of the soul, which remains unalterably the same, perhaps for one moment. The mind is a kind of theatre, where several perceptions successively make their appearance; pass, repass, glide away and mingle in an infinite variety of postures and situations.

This language strongly resembles accounts commonly found in Buddhist texts about the nature of the illusory transitory self that is clung to out of ignorance.

The conscious dialogue between Western philosophy and Buddhism began not with Hume, but two generations later, in the early nineteenth century, with the German thinker Arthur Schopenhauer. Let us reserve discussion of Schopenhauer's thought for the moment, but for the obvious point that its profound pessimism as to human affairs — a pessimism as to which Schopenhauer found in Buddhism what he believed to be a welcome parallel — contrasts sharply with the more genial and tolerant skepticism of Hume, who delighted in social contacts and political debate. If the translations available in Schopenhauer's time had been known to Hume, the early philosophical reception of Buddhism in the West — through the calm, rational lens of Hume — would surely have differed from that fostered by the dark mirror of Schopenhauer.

Bertrand Russell wrote of the profound difference in outlook between the two thinkers, separated by so little time but by so profound a gulf in terms of method:

Hume's philosophy, whether true or false, represents the bankruptcy of eighteenth-century reasonableness. He starts out, like Locke, with the intention of being sensible and empirical, taking nothing on trust, but seeking whatever instruction is to be obtained from experience and observation. But [. . .] he arrives at the disastrous conclusion that from experience and observation nothing is to be learned. [. . .] Subsequent British empiricists rejected his skepticism without refuting it.

Russell argued that the only philosophies immune to Hume's arguments are those rooted in overt irrationality, such as the philosophies propounded by Schopenhauer and Nietzsche: "The growth of unreason throughout the nineteenth century and what has passed of the twentieth is a natural sequel to Hume's destruction of empiricism." As we shall later examine, the Buddhism extolled by Schopenhauer — and thereafter imbibed by European readers — drew foremost upon the First Noble Truth of the Buddha, that of the inescapability of life's woes.

❖

The term "Orientalism," which has become a pejorative term in our era — connoting a manipulative exoticizing and romanticizing of Eastern cultures, all the better to justify their colonial exploitation by the West — held no such meaning in the late eighteenth century, when it arose as a name for a field of study conducted by Europeans, predominantly male, who wished better to understand the Asian lands that had indeed been colonized by the European powers. The Orientalists of that era possessed a swaggering sense of racial and cultural superiority, and their work is plainly tainted by it. The enduring value of some of their work is equally plain and has been attested to by Eastern and Western scholars alike. Given that all humans who think and write are subject to severe biases and limitations, and that all of us who think and write today will seem foolishly embedded in outdated rhetoric and beliefs to the readers of tomorrow, let us examine as best we can what the Orientalists sought to accomplish and where, often enough, they faltered.

Certainly, in their initial attempts to determine the origin and nature of the strange figure of the Buddha, they faltered mightily. One widespread body of opinion had it that the deity known as the Buddha was related — through distant shared origins vague enough to accommodate any surmise — to the Hermes of Greece and the Thoth of Egypt. This theory was posed by one of the earliest Orientalists, the French writer La Loubere, in his widely read work *On the Kingdom of Siam* (1691): "Mercury, who was the God of the sciences, seems to have been adored by the whole earth; because knowledge is undoubtedly one of the attributes of the true God." Elaborate theological and even astrological justifications of this surmise were put forth by subsequent Western theorists, such as the British author Edward Upham, who, in his *History and Doctrine of Buddhism* (1829), opined without benefit of factual evidence that "the followers of Brahma honored the planet Mercury as the star of Buddha." The popularity of this speculative — one might say fantasized — comparison was perhaps based on the pride of place it gave to Christianity as the culmination of all religions.

The Englishman who became the leader of the European boom in Orientalist studies was Sir William Jones (1746–1794), whose staunch efforts earned him the nickname "Asiatic" Jones. Without question, Jones was a brilliant polymath. Educated at Harrow and Oxford, he had by his early twenties a thorough knowledge of Hebrew, Greek, Latin, Arabic, Persian, and Turkish, as well as contemporary French, German, Italian, Spanish, and Portuguese — in short, the primary languages of the world from western Asia to western Europe. By age twenty-four, Jones had published his first translation — a Persian historical work on Nader Shah, to which Edward Gibbon acknowledged a debt in his *Decline and Fall of the Roman Empire*. Gibbon and Jones were both members of a London literary club headed by Samuel Johnson, who tolerated only the brightest of the younger generation. After publishing a Persian grammar in 1771 that was definitive for its time, Jones decided to pursue a livelihood in the law. A mere decade later, his *Essay on the Law of Bailments* appeared and became the standard work of its era. All the while, he kept up prolific translations from the Persian and Arabic, as well as private studies in astronomy, botany, zoology, music, and the history of chess.

In 1783, Jones was appointed to a post he very much desired, as it promised to merge his two intellectual passions of law and Orientalia — a judgeship in the Supreme Court of Judicature in Calcutta, the ruling judicial body of colonial India. That same year, Jones was knighted. Setting out for India in August 1783, he could not have more firmly embodied an emissary of the ruling British nation and race.

Promptly upon his arrival, he became the chief founder of the Asiatic Society, later the Asiatic Society of Bengal. This was not the first group of its kind; Dutch scholars residing in Java had six years earlier founded a pioneering Western society devoted to Asia. But the Asiatic Society was the first to attain a dedicated readership across Europe for its journal *Asiatick Researches,* edited and largely written by Jones in its early volumes. The popularity of *Asiatick Researches* may be judged by the five pirated editions that had appeared in London by the early nineteenth century. The journal became the first prominent European source for translations from classical Indian Sanskrit texts. Granted, there had been some prior Western publications in this field. Abraham Roger, a Dutch missionary to India, had produced as early as 1651 a study on Brahmanic beliefs provocatively titled *Open Door to the Hidden Heathendom*. In 1701, Johann Ernest Hanxleden, a Jesuit missionary in southern India, became the first European to compose a Sanskrit grammar guide. But these works never attained the readership of *Asiatick Researches*.

In his inaugural address as president of the Asiatic Society in January 1784, Jones explained what had led him to leave behind his successes and comforts in England and establish himself half a world away. Certainly, there was wealth and power to be had as a nabob in India, but Jones did not speak of these. What emerged instead was his sense of rapture in approaching what he viewed as the undiscovered treasure chest of Indian wisdom:

> When I was at sea last August, on my voyage to this country, which I had long and ardently desired to visit, I found one evening [. . .] that India lay before us, and Persia on our left, whilst a breeze from Arabia blew nearly on our stern. [. . .] It gave me inexpressible pleasure to find myself in the midst of so noble an amphitheatre, almost encircled by the vast regions of Asia, which has ever been esteemed the nurse of sciences, the inventress of delightful and useful arts, the scene of glorious actions, fertile in the production of human genius, abounding in natural wonders, and infinitely diversified in the forms of religion and government, in the laws, manners, customs, and languages, as well as in the features and complexions, of men. I could not help remarking, how important and extensive a field was yet unexplored.

The riches of the Indian classical traditions were now open for plunder. Charles Wilkins, an Asiatic Society member, enjoyed considerable success with his translation of the Bhagavad Gita (1785) — the first Sanskrit work to be translated directly into a European language. His 1789 translation of the drama *Shakuntala,* by the classical Indian playwright Kalidasa, strongly influenced Goethe through a 1791 German translation of Jones's version. Goethe adapted Kalidasa's use of a convention of classical Indian drama — a prologue acted out by the supposed owners of the theater in which the play is being held — for his prologue to *Faust.* Scholarship has documented an array of faint borrowings and touches drawn from the Sanskrit translations of Jones by English Romantic and Victorian poets. The cumulative effect of the Asiatic Society translations

was the emergence of what became a commonplace phrase in Europe —
an "Oriental Renaissance" of knowledge comparable to the European
Renaissance, stimulated by translations from the Greek, five centuries
earlier.

Under Jones, the Asiatic Society was made up entirely of his fellow
colonial Englishmen, many of whom — Charles Wilkins, for example —
held high positions in the East India Company, the principal arm of
British commerce and political rule. The study of Sanskrit by Wilkins,
Jones, and others had been taken up first and foremost out of the perceived need to master Hindu religious texts so that British leaders could
formulate laws that would not unduly offend the Indian people, who
were already being denied racial equality and representative government. But Jones and his fellow Orientalists, seen within the context of
their time, represented the liberal wing of British colonial policy in
terms of respect for Indian culture. Not long after Jones's death, the
conservative wing waxed preeminent. James Mill, a follower of Jeremy
Bentham and the father of John Stuart Mill, argued in his widely read
History of British India (1818) that Jones had exceeded both fact and sense
in his praises of Hinduism and of Indian achievements in general. The
rightful task of the British Empire, Mill held, was to enable India to
free itself of a history and religious creed that had left it markedly inferior, both materially and spiritually, to the West. The empire and India
would benefit mutually by the accomplishment of this task. This utili-
tarian argument — the greatest good for the greatest number — was in
political accord with the views of British Evangelicals such as William
Wilberforce, who urged intensive Christian mission work in India as a
means of strengthening both colonial morals and imperial rule. It is with
these later outlooks that Jones's pioneering scholarship can usefully be
compared.

The accomplishments of Jones the Orientalist scholar are on a surer
footing than those of Jones the colonial jurist. He was the first clearly to
articulate the theory — one that still prevails in philology and linguistics — that there is an Indo-European "family" of languages descended
from a lost common source. His praise of Sanskrit — a sacred language
of both Hinduism and Buddhism, although Jones had no knowledge of
Buddhist Sanskrit texts — is striking in that he deemed it greater in
linguistic richness than the two sacred languages of Christendom: "The

Sanscrit language, whatever be its antiquity, is of a wonderful structure; more perfect than the Greek, more copious than the Latin, and more exquisitely refined than either, yet bearing to both of them a stronger affinity, both in the roots of verbs and in the forms of grammar, than could possibly have been produced by accident."

Jones the scholar was gifted both in broad theorizing and in fine textual examination. But his weakness, stemming from the arrogance of empire, was his avidity to play the pundit on matters of Indian culture about which he possessed not so much as basic information. Such was the case regarding his views on Buddhism, the texts of which, Sanskrit or other, Jones had not studied. Indeed, they were unknown to him, as some one thousand years of Hindu ascendancy and Islamic conquest had all but eradicated evidence of Buddhism within India, and the Brahman teachers with whom Jones studied had no interest in alleviating his ignorance.

The unfortunate writings of Jones on Buddhism were triggered by a 1788 article by Charles Wilkins in *Asiatick Researches:* "Translation of a Sanscrit Inscription, copied from a stone at Boodha-Gaya by Mr. Wilmot." Details about the British Mr. Wilmot are scarce, but the essence of the matter was that Wilmot provided Wilkins with a rubbing of a carved plaque inscription, in archaic Sanskrit, that told, as Wilkins translated it, of "Bood-dha, the Author of Happiness. . . . He who is omnipresent, and everlastingly to be contemplated, the Supreme Being, the Eternal One, the Divinity worthy to be adored by the most praiseworthy of mankind, appeared here with a portion of his divine nature." The carving had been made by a Hindu, who nonetheless revered the site of the Buddha's enlightenment, which — as is now known to us and could not have been to Wilkins — occurred in human, not divine, form.

Wilkins offered his translation to the world with little theoretical apparatus beyond a dating of the text to the tenth century CE. Based on utterly rash speculations inspired by the spate of inscriptions and carvings being unearthed by the British, Jones concluded that the same unknown race had once populated both "Ethiopia and Hindustan" and had shared and disseminated the same religious creed: "The Hindu religion spread probably over the whole earth, there are signs of it in every northern country, and in almost every system of worship; in England it is obvious: Stonehenge is evidently one of the temples of Boodh." The

Hindu sage Boodh, who was worshipped at Stonehenge, was linked by Jones with the Germanic god Odin, the Egyptian deity Sesostris, and the Ethiopian deity Sesac, hence his Indian name, Sacya. Boodh was, Jones believed, in historical fact an Ethiopian who, roughly one thousand years before the birth of Christ, had traveled to Asia to teach his wisdom, which ultimately reached as far as China and Japan. This theory somewhat resembles the "language family" speculations that form Jones's surest claim to fame, with Hinduism forming a kind of original "religious family" for all of pre-Christian polytheistic humankind. That it reads as ludicrous to us is a lesson in the perils of large learned guesses. The surmise that Buddha was a black Ethiopian was bolstered, from Jones's perspective, by what appeared to be persistent portrayals in Indian statuary of a Buddha with tightly curled hair.

But then Europeans possessed the irrepressible gift — in this early stage of encounter with Buddhism — to see whatever satisfied their theories of unknown ancient India. Thus Francis Wilford, a British lieutenant and a contributor to *Asiatick Researches,* wrote of the Buddha in 1792:

> It is completely certain that he was not of truly Indian descent: in all the images and all the statues of the Buddhas, both male and female, which can be seen in a number of places in these provinces and these two peninsulas, there is something Egyptian or Ethiopian in their appearance; and in physical characteristics as well as in dress, he differs greatly from the figures of the ancient heroes and demigods of the Hindus.

It was not until the mid-nineteenth century that the theory of the Ethiopian Buddha was generally discarded.

There were other scholars who, coming upon the trove of speculations by Jones and others in *Asiatick Researches,* launched their own equally ambitious theories. One of the most fascinating examples is Henry O'Brien (1808–1835), who, in *The Round Towers of Ireland; or, The Mysteries of Freemasonry, Sabaism, and of Buddhism, for the First Time Unveiled* (1834), opined that the eponymous round towers — hundreds of which were located throughout Ireland, with no known historical origin — had been constructed long before by a migrating Eastern population, Buddhist in belief (for Buddhism was the most ancient of the world religions), that had settled Ireland. As for the nature of the Buddhist teachings of those Asian inhabitants, O'Brien argued, based on the lingamlike shape of the towers and the fact that the Gaelic word *Budh* stands both for sun and for phallus, the Buddhists were phallic worshippers. Such were the untrammeled joys of scholarship in the absence of obtruding facts.

For all his passion for Orientalist studies, Jones always maintained firmly the theological boundaries — and supremacy — of Christianity. Indian teachings were a fascinating source of pagan wisdom, akin in value to the cultures of Greece and Rome, but where those teachings contradicted the Bible, they were in plain error. There was, however, one tantalizing exception. In a letter of the late 1780s, Jones conceded that the Hindu doctrine of reincarnation offered a superior means of promoting justice and social welfare. The emphasis is Jones's own: "I am no Hindu; but I hold the doctrine of the Hindus concerning a future state to be incomparably more rational, more pious, and more likely to deter men from vice, than the horrid opinions inculcated by Christians on punishments *without end.*" Here we see a forerunner of the favorable modern Western response to the Buddhist doctrine of rebirth.

Although the work of Jones and his fellow British Orientalists was largely slighted in Victorian England, that work stimulated the foundation of similar societies elsewhere in Britain and in France, Germany, Russia, and other European nations, as well as in India itself. The Indian scholar Suniti Kumar Chatterji, in his 1946 assessment of Jones — written near the dawn of Indian independence from Britain — was impressive both in his incisiveness and his generosity, crediting Jones with spurring native Indians to reassess their own culture:

As in the case of most great men, he [Jones] was both national and international at the same time. He thought that "reason and taste" were "the grand prerogatives of the *European* minds, while the *Asiatics* have soared to loftier heights in the sphere of imagination." With him, born and brought up in an "age of reason," there was undoubtedly a tacit feeling that reason and the intellect were superior to emotion and the imagination. [. . .] We can ignore the occasional expressions of contempt, betraying but his misunderstanding or ignorance, which he has used with regard to religions other than the one he professed: for these were but a current fashion of speech in his language and its style, saturated as they were with the spirit of orthodox Christianity, and these did not express his deepest convictions or predilections as a scholar and a sympathetic student who had imagination and culture enough not to remain unmoved by the great thoughts and ideas he found in other religions. [. . .] So that, in spite of his having belonged to a totally different world, this Christian gentleman, this cultured son of England with the best that her public schools and her universities could give, with all the hesitating steps and the mystic intuitions of the first explorer, was able to draw out some of the noblest and most abiding things in our Eastern civilization, and to inspire others from among his own countrymen, and later on, from amongst ourselves, Indians, too, to do the same.

❖

Brian Houghton Hodgson (1800–1894) was the most prominent successor to Jones in the lineage of nineteenth-century British Orientalists. He voyaged to India in 1818 in hopes of a grand career in the diplomatic service, and in 1823 he was duly named undersecretary to the British foreign office in Calcutta. But his health was damaged by the strong heat, and he was compelled to put aside his ambitions and continue his service in the remote but cooler mountain regions of Nepal, where in 1833 he became the resident of the British Empire. Hodgson promptly came into conflict with the Nepali monarchy, which he regarded as corrupt and untrustworthy. Such was his conviction on this score that he was recalled by British authorities from Nepal for his refusal to obey orders dictating greater moderation. Hodgson resigned from the diplomatic service but in 1845 returned as a private citizen to Darjeeling, where he continued to serve the British cause by proffering astute advice on the recruitment of Gurkhas as a buttress of the colonial Indian army.

Through all the personal and political upheavals, Hodgson carried on intensive studies of Indian and Nepalese philology, ethnography, natural science, and religion. He published more than three hundred scholarly essays and became not only a leading scholar of Buddhism but also the preeminent Western expert on the flora of the Himalayas. His studies were inspired in part by the practical need of a colonial empire to understand the people it ruled. Hodgson also possessed a born archivist's penchant for collecting information and preserving manuscripts. In 1824, his Nepalese sources procured for him what proved, from the Western perspective, to be a rare and remarkable trove of Buddhist writings in Sanskrit — the original texts of sutras and other teachings that had, in some cases, already reached the attention of Russian and other Western scholars through Mongolian or Chinese translations. Hodgson sent off copies of his finds first to the Asiatic Society of Bengal, then in 1835 to the Royal Asiatic Society, and finally in 1837 to the Société Asiatique of Paris. In the latter setting, due to the labors of the French scholar Eugène Burnouf, these finds bore their most important fruit.

Burnouf dedicated his 1852 translation of the *Lotus Sutra,* a prominent Mahayana Sanskrit text, to Hodgson "as the founder of the true study of Buddhism by its texts and its monuments." Consultation with living Buddhist practitioners is strikingly absent from this list of study methods. Nonetheless, it was an appropriate recognition of the labors of Hodgson, who had published a volume of essays, *Illustrations of the Literature and Religion of the Buddhists* (1841), in which he set forth historical findings on Buddhism that far exceeded what had previously been understood by Europeans. It was Hodgson who first established that the Sanskrit canon of Buddhist teachings had reached Nepal in the second century and then, roughly six centuries later, had been translated into Tibetan to form the *Kangyur,* or basic body of teachings of the Tibetan Buddhist tradition. Hodgson further recognized that both Nepalese and Tibetan Buddhism had been deeply influenced by the emergence, centuries before, of esoteric Tantric practice by Hindus and Buddhists in northern India:

> It is clear that the Baudda religion, as cultivated in Nepal, is far from being so simple and philosophical a matter as has sometimes been imagined. The objects of worship are far from being limited to a few persons of mortal origin, elevated by superior sanctity to divine honours, but embrace a variety of domifications and degrees more numerous and complicated, than even the ample Pantheon of the Brahmans.

❖

Among the early European Orientalists, there is none whose travels and sacrifices can rival those of the Hungarian Alexander Csoma de Körös (1784–1842), who remains a cultural hero of his nation. Csoma came from a poor family and rose, through sheer devotion to learning, to an ill-paid academic position in Transylvania. He abandoned this position at age thirty-six to undertake his own private, unfunded trek into central Asia to locate the linguistic origins of the Hungarian race, which Csoma believed to have descended from the Huns.

He commenced his journey on foot in 1819. His route, dictated in part by the necessity of avoiding outbreaks of the plague and cholera, extended through Turkey, Egypt, Persia, Afghanistan, and the Punjab, but with no evidence of a onetime "Greater Hungary" yet in sight. In Kashmir, in 1822, Csoma met the British veterinarian William Moorcroft, the man responsible for bringing Western attention to the excellence of Kashmir, or cashmere, shawls. Moorcroft, who gathered intelligence for the East India Company, convinced Csoma to devote himself — on a meager salary to be afforded by the British — to the all-but-unknown field of Tibetan studies, in which, Moorcroft deftly hinted, Csoma might learn something of Hungarian origins while opening the Tibetan language and culture to the West. Moorcroft's aim here was to use Csoma's linguistic talents to provide detailed knowledge that could aid the Raj in its imperial ambitions in central Asia.

For seven years, Csoma pursued his studies in monasteries in Ladakh, Zanskar, and other locales in the southwestern borderlands of Tibet, ultimately producing the first Western grammar of the Tibetan language, as well as a Tibetan-English dictionary and a translation of the *Mahavyutpatti,* a vast glossary of Buddhist terms. These works, while riddled with errors and amateurish etymologies, were nonetheless groundbreaking studies in the West. In 1830, Csoma moved to Calcutta, where for twelve years he lived in a small room provided by the Asiatic Society of Bengal, which published his works and for which he worked as a librarian in charge of Tibetan manuscripts. His furnishings were boxes for his books and a sleeping mat for himself. Csoma owned and wore only one suit; his diet remained the same through all his years of researches — Tibetan butter tea and unseasoned boiled rice.

In 1842, perhaps weary of his cell at last, he embarked again on a solitary journey to Lhasa, the holy city of Tibet, which he had never seen. His principal aim remained tracing Hungarian origins. Although he respected Tibetan Buddhism to a degree — believing it to be the closest to Christianity of the Asian religions — he held no particular regard for Buddhist teachings and had translated Christian prayers and psalms into Tibetan to aid future missionaries in their work. He died of fever in April 1842 on the outskirts of the Himalayas.

The British Buddhist historian Stephen Batchelor observed that "despite the aura of romance surrounding Csoma de Körös, his twenty years of work for the British government point to his endorsement of the link between scientific knowledge and colonial power. Csoma's dictionary and grammar served as the philological equivalents of maps." There is no question that Csoma served the interests of British imperialism. But he shunned luxury and devoted himself to studies that broadened understanding beyond the requirements of colonial administration. Even among modern-day academics who begrudge Csoma the status of a genuine scholar, he is regarded as the "Father of Tibetology." And even though Csoma never thought of himself as a Buddhist, in 1933 Taisho University in Japan designated him a bodhisattva in honor of his labors.

❖

Among the most gifted of the early French Orientalists was Michel-Jean-François Ozeray, who in 1817 published *Recherches sur Buddou ou Bouddou, Instituter religieux de l'Asie orientale,* a little book that fell into utter obscurity until it was rescued by the modern French scholar Roger-Pol Droit. Ozeray posited that the Buddha was neither a divinity related in type to Odin or Hermes nor a prophet in the biblical sense preaching a divinely inspired wisdom, but rather "a distinguished philosopher, a wise man born for the happiness of his fellow creatures and the good of humanity." It hardly seems a controversial thesis, but as Droit observed, "The statement marks a break: the move from myth to history. [. . .] The form of this Buddha-philosopher would occupy the century." A number of fellow Orientalists echoed Ozeray's judgment that the Buddha was "a wise man" and not a deity or an avatar in the Hindu sense of a divine incarnation in human form. Ozeray was well aware that even within the Buddhist tradition, deifications of the Buddha abounded. But he argued that the Buddha was a "deified man" — deified, that is, by his followers — and thus altogether distinct from the pagan gods whom Ozeray detested. "One must not confuse deified Bouddou with all those gods that are products of immorality," he wrote.

Ozeray was one of the first European scholars to adopt the term "bouddisme" — a Western abstraction without parallel in prior Asian usage, which instead referred simply to the Dharma or the teachings of the Buddha and his spiritual lineage. The term came into full vogue in the 1820s, with Brian Houghton Hodgson becoming the first to use the English term "Buddhism" in his *Sketch of Buddhism* (1828). (An analogous history accompanies the Western term "Sufism," which has no prior analogue in Persian and Arabic Sufi writing and practice, where the indication of the teaching tended often to be symbolic or veiled.) The Western invention of the category "Buddhism" — a category that has since been adopted around the globe — enabled the early Orientalists to recognize the underlying unities of Buddhist practice in lands as separate as Sri Lanka and Tibet. The real problem arose when Buddhism began to be examined within a larger Western category under which it had been filed — that of "Religion." The more the West learned of Buddhism, the less it seemed to resemble what "religion" had long been taken to be — the worship of creator deities who took regard of human affairs. The Buddhist nirvana seemed, to the early Orientalists, suspiciously like sheer nothingness, which could hardly be regarded as a religious ideal.

Droit and other scholars have observed that nineteenth-century European interpreters of Buddhism tended to project on it their own unacknowledged fears of a void, nihilistic universe — fears that were, for the most part, concealed by the positivistic philosophies and Christian Evangelicalism of the period. This is certainly true to an extent, but it is also true that every era of Western study of Buddhism will reveal its own pet preoccupations. In the early twenty-first century, for example, one might posit a Western tendency to demand of Buddhism an increasing emphasis on the healing of the worst of the neuroses of samsaric life, with a latent accompanying fear that the ultimate goal of nirvana might — for all our supposed sophisticated understanding of it — be no more than a mirage. By the standards of the famous wager of Pascal — believe in the Christian God in case there is indeed a heaven and a hell — Buddhism makes a very nice side bet, for its teachings on daily compassion and patience can ease your mind even if you retain your samsaric personal self until a death without rebirth.

❖

Eugène Burnouf (1801–1852) was the most intellectually ambitious of all the European Orientalists of the nineteenth century. His dedication to the task of understanding Buddhism whole led him to acquire textual proficiency in Sanskrit, Pali, Tibetan, Sinhalese, and Burmese. Burnouf was the first European scholar to recognize fully, through a pioneering comparison of Pali and Sanskrit texts, the distinctive developments of Theravada and Mahayana Buddhism — which he referred to as the "Southern" and "Northern" branches of Buddhism. This usage would long endure despite its misleading sense of an absolute geographic division, as opposed to a series of innovations in practice as Buddhism migrated through Asia, with Theravada teachings remaining as the accepted core of Buddhist belief. Burnouf held that the "Northern" schools had become degenerate through their worshipful fascination with divinities. The source of the pure and original Buddhism worthy of the interest of the West lay, in Burnouf's view, exclusively in the Theravada Pali texts. His denigration of "Northern" Mahayana Buddhism was accepted by Western scholars and enthusiasts alike, virtually without exception, through the early twentieth century. At that time, as we shall see, an equal and opposite reaction would occur, leaving Mahayana as the more respected Buddhism, with Theravada as its less ripened precursor — a bias that continues to endure to a degree in the West.

As for why Burnouf's preference for Theravada should have been so long and widely accepted, consider that Buddhism had been understood by European scholars in a kind of reverse chronological order, with Mongolian, Tibetan, and Chinese texts — often translations of Indian Buddhist works — having been discovered prior to the intensive work by Burnouf on Sanskrit and Pali texts. With the "originals" located at last, Western scholars — who in the decades following Burnouf showed little interest in living Buddhists Northern or Southern — were content to wield a yardstick of pristine origins by which all of contemporary Buddhism could be dismissed as a fallen creed in need of Christian supplantation.

When the Sanskrit manuscripts collected by Hodgson arrived in Paris in 1837, Burnouf knew at once that they represented a scholarly trove — venerable Buddhist teachings, as yet unknown to the West, that could cast light on the origins of this strange pan-Asian religion. Burnouf devoted the next seven years to their study, at last publishing, in 1844, his *Introduction à l'histoire du Buddhisme indien,* the first Western scholarly work to grasp and organize the basics of early Buddhist history and the beliefs of its varied Indian schools. The tone of the writing was precise and rooted in philological analysis; Burnouf was plainly fascinated with the task of assembling the pieces of so vast a puzzle. There were times when the mentality of the European conqueror took over, and Burnouf sought to impose classifications that had no relation to the Buddhist tradition of teachings, as when he distinguished broadly between "simple" and "developed" sutras, with the latter including mentions of bodhisattvas. But he was also capable of an impressive depth of understanding of Buddhist conceptions then utterly unfamiliar to the West. An example here concerns what is now commonly termed, by Western Buddhists, "dependent origination" or "dependent arising," and which Burnouf translated, from the Sanskrit *pratitya samutpada,* as "the production of the successive causes of existence." In explanation of this intricate process, Burnouf wrote with admirable clarity:

> As for the notion of existence, it is implicitly contained in its composition; it seems to me necessary to explain in a positive manner, that these successive causes, or in more general terms, these conditions which are successive and reciprocal effect and cause the one after the other, are, following the thought of the Buddhists, the unique and incessant origin of the situation of living beings in this world and the other, so much so that these beings cannot succeed in liberating themselves by the absolute science and obtaining Nirvana.

The regrettable aspect of Burnouf's legacy was his insistence on Buddhist nirvana as a kind of nihilism. Burnouf chose, as a translation of nirvana, "extinction." He defined nirvana as "a disappearance of individuality by way of absorption — into the Supreme Being or into the void (*sunyata*). . . . In any event, nirvana means a fundamental change in the condition of the individual, that would, to all appearances, be utter annihilation." For Burnouf, the perplexing question remained whether nirvanic annihilation more closely resembled "absorption" into the ultimate or rather the utter "extinction" of physical and mental being.

Burnouf's chief successor among French Orientalists was Jules Barthélemy Saint-Hilaire (1805–1895). In *The Buddha and His Religion* (1860), Saint-Hilaire inveighed against the adoption by Western thinkers (Schopenhauer is not expressly named but is plainly regarded as a principal offender) of the nihilistic vision of Buddhism, a vision that could only bring despair to the believing Christian masses of Europe:

> For some time past the doctrines of Buddhism have found favor amongst us, a favor of which they are most unworthy. We see systems arise in which metempsychosis and transmigration are lauded, and, after the manner of the Buddha, the world and mankind are explained without any reference to Providence or God; systems in which man is denied all hope of an immortal life, in which the immortality of the soul is replaced by the immortality of good works, and God is dethroned by man — the only being, it is averred, through whom the Infinite develops consciousness of itself. Sometimes it is in the name of science, sometimes in that of history or philology, or even metaphysics, that these theories are propounded — theories which are neither novel nor original, and which are calculated to be extremely harmful to any weak or vacillating mind.

Saint-Hilaire, as had Burnouf before him, held firmly that nirvana meant utter annihilation, spiritual and physical — "when all the elements of which he [man] is composed, both material and spiritual, are completely destroyed, he need no longer fear transmigration; and the blind fatality which rules all things in the universe has power over him no more." Buddha had done no more, Saint-Hilaire believed, than cobble together a derivative Brahmanism without the solace of the Vedic gods. The French scholar did concede — faced with the survival of Buddhism in Asia for some 2,400 years — that the Buddha had "displayed an ingenuous dauntlessness that will never be exceeded."

Just why no one could exceed the Buddha's "ingenuous dauntlessness" is ingenuously unclear. The sense lingers that a compliment had to be granted that would not be resented by Christian readers jealous for their own founder. Under the guise of scholarship, the cultural warfare between the Christian West and the Buddhist East was now reaching a stage of full and formal engagement. Saint-Hilaire remained to his death the most intransigent Western critic of Buddhism. In 1893, at age eighty-eight, Saint-Hilaire addressed the French Académie des Sciences Morales et Politiques. The purpose of his speech was to attack the growing fascination with Buddhist thought among fin de siècle European intellectuals who no longer accepted his thesis that Buddhism stood for nothingness. Buddhism appealed to "atheists" and "materialists," Saint-Hilaire charged. The preservation of Europe required something more:

> Regardless of the shortcomings for which our societies could justly be reproached, they would need to decline by a number of degrees to take refuge in the Buddhist nirvana. [. . .] Souls are wracked with enough pains without adding one more. Let the Buddha's character, his intentions, his entire life be admired as much as one wishes; but let us flee his deleterious teachings.

❖

The tensions between Western scholarly and missionary aspirations toward the East were vividly embodied in the life and work of Friedrich Max Müller (1823–1900), a German-born scholar and translator who, as an intellectual child prodigy, early on met with Goethe and Schopenhauer. Müller later studied under Eugène Burnouf in Paris and ultimately was named professor of comparative philology at Oxford, where, having become a naturalized British subject, he emerged as the most prominent Orientalist of imperial England. His circle of friends and acquaintances included Prime Minister William Gladstone and a host of eminent Victorians.

Müller edited, for the Oxford University Press, some fifty volumes of the Sacred Books of the East series, which appeared over the last decades of the nineteenth century and served as the first entrance into Buddhist and Hindu religious teachings for several generations of Western readers. Müller's aim was to establish a science of religion by which the origins and ultimate affinities between all of the world's religions could be decisively discerned. He possessed a profound belief in his ability to ascertain the genuine essence of both Hinduism and Buddhism, having himself translated both the *Rig Veda* and the *Dhammapada,* the perceived root texts of those traditions. In this belief, and in the good he believed he could do the world with it, Müller remained steadfast through a long and prolific life.

The irony of a British professor seeking to purify Indian religion may seem palpable now, but it never appeared to Müller as such. Over and again, in his writings, he wrung his hands over the failure of contemporary Indians to appreciate the value of their spiritual origins. In an 1869 letter to the Duke of Argyll — Müller served as explicator of the Indian religions to many of the British imperial elite — Müller argued that

if the religion of India could be brought back to that simple form which it exhibits in the *Veda,* a great reform would be achieved. Something would be lost, for some of the later metaphysical speculations on religion, and again the high and pure and almost Christian morality of Buddha, are things not to be found in the *Veda.* But, as far as the popular conceptions of the deity are concerned, the Vedic religion, though childish and crude, is free from all that is so hideous in the later Hindu Pantheon.

What was "hideous" to Müller, apparently, was an evolving Hindu polytheism with fluid theological underpinnings to accommodate diverse forms of worship. Müller did not care for religions that evolved beyond the purities of their origins, although he did tend to see those origins as intermingled in the distant past. Thus he confessed to Prime Minister Gladstone, "I cannot resist the impression that there must have been historical contact between the Christian and the Buddhist intellectual atmospheres." In this respect, he saw Christianity, Islam, and Buddhism as all fundamentally flawed by their failure to live up to their founders: "They start with a high ideal conceived by a representative man [. . .] and that high standard is hardly ever realized; it has to adapt itself to larger circles and lower levels, and can only be kept from utter degeneration by constant efforts at reform."

Müller's own religious stance was that of a Christian who denied — with a tinge of awkward regret — the doctrine of exclusive salvation through Christ. Even so, he supported the work of the Evangelicals in India, explaining that "there is this great blessing about Missions, that, however we may differ about theological questions at home, we are all united when it comes to missionary work. We should all rather have a man High, Broad, or Low Church, Roman Catholic, or Unitarian, than to have him not a Christian at all." Müller also insisted that "there is a Divine element in every one of the great religions of the world. I consider it blasphemous to call them the work of the Devil, when they are the work of God. [. . .] Holding that opinion, I do not wish to see the old religions destroyed. I want to see them reformed, reanimated, resuscitated by contact with Christianity."

Müller was a supporter of the Burnouf majority view in the ongoing Orientalist debate about whether nirvana was extinction or something more like mystical rapture. Müller correctly argued that as a matter of etymology, "nirvana" had originally meant "the blowing out," as in the case of a flame. But he did allow that perhaps the nihilistic views of the early Theravadins were not in fact shared by the historical Buddha. To make this point, Müller constructed a portrait of an ideal Buddha — ideal, that is, from the perspective of Müller, a Western Protestant student of world religions who believed them all to point to a Christian paradigm of eternal salvation:

> And finally, if we may argue from human nature, such as we find it at all times and in all countries, we confess that we cannot bring ourselves to believe that the reformer of India, the teacher of so perfect a form of morality, the young prince who gave up all he had in order to help those whom he saw afflicted in mind, body, or estate, should have cared much about speculations [as to extinction] which he knew would either be misunderstood, or not understood at all, by those whom he wished to benefit; that he should have thrown away one of the most powerful weapons in the hands of every religious teacher — the belief in a future life; and should not have seen, that if this life was sooner or later to end in nothing, it was hardly worth the trouble which he took himself, or the sacrifices which he imposed on his disciples.

Müller is often credited, by virtue of this stance, of having been one of the first Western scholars to recognize that Buddhism stood for more than mere nihilism. What seems more germane, however, is that Müller reached this viewpoint by systematically disparaging the beliefs of virtually all Buddhists, Theravada and Mahayana alike, other than the Buddha himself — a variation of sorts (though there is no evidence that Müller viewed it as such) on Nietzsche's argument against Christianity, put forth in this same period, that the only true Christian died on the cross.

Having resolved that the Buddha could not have stomached nothingness, Müller still had to confront the "riddle which no one has been able to solve" — how it was that so bleak a vision had inspired and comforted, over two thousand years, believing Buddhists, all of whom were plainly examples of the "human nature" that required, in all times and places, the promise of eternal life. The answer suggested by Müller was that the evolving religion of Buddhism seldom paid heed to the teachings of its venerable sutras: "We must distinguish, it seems, between Buddhism as a religion, and Buddhism as a philosophy. The former addressed itself to millions, the latter to a few isolated thinkers."

The futility of the debate over nirvana stemmed from the failure to comprehend the Buddhist framework within which nirvana possessed its living meaning. Within that Buddhist framework, the polarities of nihilism (*ucchedavada*) and eternalism (*sassatavada*) are both expressly identified as reductive errors in understanding — and are agreed upon as such in the Theravada, Mahayana, and Vajrayana traditions. Nirvana is always regarded as outside the realm of discursive thought. It cannot be confined, defined, or expressed by language, because it is the experiential outcome of Buddhist practice that seeks to elude the dualities of language. The Western scholars to whom the riches of Sanskrit and Pali texts were now being opened were not drawn by the inexpressible. They were engaged, rather, in what the American scholar Steven Collins termed "the attempt to produce a quasi-Buddhist account, an account which accepts Buddhist conceptual presuppositions but not the conclusions which Buddhists have drawn from them, nor respects the silences which they have preserved." Collins placed the "quasi-Buddhist" Orientalist debates over nirvana within the context of a pervasive Christian reevaluation of the conception of heaven, which had been traditionally regarded as a realm of eternal static beatitude — a "celestial lubberland," one Evangelical termed the old vision — but was now seen as a domain of vibrant service of the Lord.

For Müller, there was an obvious worldwide pattern in which the purity of the teachings of religious founders was degraded by the popular needs of subsequent generations of worshippers. In the case of Buddhism, this degradation began with the emergence of the Mahayana school and was particularly evident in the Pure Land Buddhism of China and Japan. Müller quoted with approval the verdict rendered by a British academic colleague, one Dr. Edkins, who had witnessed the chanting of the name of Buddha Amitabha by Japanese worshippers: "It appeared to us that nothing was more calculated to produce idiocy than such a perpetual repetition of a single name, and the stupid appearance of many of the priests whom we have seen seems to have been induced by some such process." For Müller, the failure of Japan to recognize the basic facts of Buddhist history and doctrine was appalling. It was his hope that from among his Japanese students learning Sanskrit at Oxford, some would return home and help to rectify matters:

> Is it not high time that the millions who live in Japan, and profess a faith in Buddha, should be told that this doctrine of Amitabha and all the Mahayana doctrine is a secondary form of Buddhism, a corruption of the pure doctrine of the Royal Prince, and that if they really mean to be Buddhists, they should return to the words of Buddha, as they are preserved to us in the old Sutras?

This professorial stance of seeking to correct the religious beliefs of an Asian continent on which he had never set foot, and of whose Buddhist residents he had never sought explanations, was utterly typical of the time. Müller's French contemporary Saint-Hilaire, on the basis of the writings of the British Wesleyan missionary Robert Spence Hardy, declared from Paris that the Buddhists of Ceylon had degraded the teachings of their founder and were unlikely — due to the lassitude of their race — to redeem themselves or to resist Christianity: "It is only by serious study and a return to the purity of the primitive faith that the Buddhist clergy would have some chance of saving their religion."

By the late nineteenth century, a new generation of European scholars — tolerant, even agnostic, in matters of religion and frankly drawn to Eastern teachings — arose to argue for the excellences of Buddhism. The most prominent of these was Thomas William Rhys Davids (1843–1922), the foremost British Buddhist scholar of the late Victorian era and the founder of the London School of Oriental Studies.

In his early twenties, Rhys Davids, after a stint of studying Sanskrit in Germany, joined the Ceylon civil service, in which he rose to the position of magistrate. In that role, he witnessed the indignities suffered by the Sinhalese and Indian populaces alike from the British policy, instituted in the aftermath of the Sepoy Mutiny, of placing Christian educators in charge of all schools and requiring the teaching of the Bible as a condition for funding by the Raj. In Ceylon, the British sought to combat the influence of Buddhism by a means — public debates between British Christian missionaries and Sinhalese Buddhists — that backfired badly. The debates did not produce the easy triumphs predicted by the British. On the contrary, the largest of these debates — held in 1873 and drawing an audience of some ten thousand Sinhalese — ended in a resounding popular victory for the Buddhist monk Gohottivatte Gunanda. The debates did succeed in spurring a revival of interest in Buddhism among the populace, as well as the restoration of a small number of Buddhist schools.

It was in this climate that Rhys Davids first encountered Buddhism. During his time in Ceylon in the 1860s, Rhys Davids learned Tamil, Sinhalese, and Pali — the last from an elderly Buddhist monk, Yatramulle Unnanse, who left a deep impression on the colonial judge: "There was a strange light in his eyes and he was constantly turning away from questions of Pali to questions of Buddhism. . . . There was an indescribable attraction, a high-mindedness that filled me with reverence."

As Rhys Davids pursued his Buddhist studies, he came to the conviction that the Orientalists who had preceded him had failed to comprehend Buddhist teachings on enlightenment because of their own world-weariness, which they falsely projected onto Buddhist believers. The etymological approach of Müller to the meaning of nirvana as extinction had failed to take into account the non-Christian cognitive framework of early Buddhism, in which enlightenment meant an awakening to reality:

The choice of this term (Nirvana) by European writers, a choice made long before any of the Buddhist canonical texts had been published or translated, has had a most unfortunate result. Those writers did not share, could not be expected to share, the exuberant optimism of the early

Buddhists. Themselves giving up this world as hopeless, and looking for salvation in the next, they naturally thought the Buddhists must do the same; and in the absence of any authentic scriptures to correct the mistake, they interpreted Nirvana, in terms of their own belief, as a state to be reached after Death. As such they supposed the "dying out" must mean the dying out of a "soul"; and endless were the discussions as to whether this meant eternal trance, or absolute annihilation, of the soul.

Rhys Davids insisted that Western understanding of Buddhism — a religion of rational wisdom — would be obscured by prior assumptions of Christian spiritual supremacy. His own personal outlook toward the Dharma was respectful, even reverent: "Buddhist or not Buddhist, I have examined every one of the great religious systems of the world, and in none of them have I found anything to surpass, in beauty and comprehensiveness, the Noble Eightfold Path of the Buddha. I am content to shape my life according to that Path." Rhys Davids was careful not to claim the title of "Buddhist." Nonetheless, he was the first Western scholar to affiliate himself openly with Buddhism. Among European thinkers of the era, only Schopenhauer preceded him in this regard.

Rhys Davids's sense of what we would today call the Eurocentrism of his culture was far more acute than that of most of his contemporaries, although he did allow that some progress had been made: "We can at least rejoice that the cultivated world is beginning to enter upon the fruits of Oriental research in Indian matters, and that the habit of Western historians of considering all things at any distance from the basin of the Mediterranean as beneath notice, is beginning to be broken through." We may now look back at Rhys Davids and see him still enmeshed in a cultural arrogance that allowed him to pair Christianity and Buddhism as the two unquestioned nonpareil religions, and to refer with ease to his own "cultivated world." But it remains that Rhys Davids was of enormous influence in clearing the way for Western studies of Buddhism that were not at the same time apologetics for Christianity.

In 1881, with his wife and fellow Buddhist scholar Caroline Rhys Davids, he founded the Pali Text Society, which published, during his lifetime, nearly one hundred volumes of translations of early Buddhist texts and continues in operation today. As the Sri Lankan Buddhist thinker Piyadassi Thera observed a century later, "Had it not been for the Pali Text Society, Theravada Buddhism would not have been so widely known, particularly in the Western world."

❖

Rhys Davids's sympathetic interpretations of Buddha struck deeply into the mind of one of his readers, who created a poem that earned a popular readership. It was through Sir Edwin Arnold that the outlook of Rhys Davids became a fixture of family reading in English and American households of the late Victorian era. *The Light of Asia* (1879), the most famous of Arnold's works, is an epic-length versification of the life of the Buddha composed by a stalwart of the British establishment.

After graduating from Oxford, Arnold served as principal of the Government Sanskrit College in Pune, in western India. But in 1860, with the death of his child and health problems plaguing his wife, Arnold returned to England, where he became editor in chief of the *London Daily Telegraph*. Arnold had tried his hand both at translations from the Sanskrit and original poems with Indian themes. But with *The Light of Asia,* a mellifluous account of the simple yet piercing goodness of the Buddha of the Theravada canon, Arnold found his theme and voice.

Twelve years later, Arnold attempted, in *The Light of the World,* to create a similarly vivid versification of the life of Christ. That work found little favor and has fallen into oblivion. Perhaps the sense of novelty was lacking, or perhaps Arnold's enthusiasm for his subject was not quite so complete, for there are those who surmise that his public Christianity was but a necessary social mask. Francis Story (Anagarika Sugatananda) (1910–1971), an Englishman who became a Theravada Buddhist at age sixteen and spent much of his life in India, Burma, and Sri Lanka, offered speculative testimony in this regard that is interesting for its depiction — based no doubt on his own experience — of the social stigma that Buddhist affinities brought upon Westerners in the colonial era:

Personally, I have no doubt Arnold was a Buddhist at heart. But many people in the West still feel that being a Buddhist does not exact any public avowal. It is not like Christianity, in which a failure to declare one's faith openly is reckoned an offense meriting punishment hereafter. And in Arnold's time, more than now, an open declaration of Buddhism by a prominent and titled man would have caused something of a scandal.

Arnold was ultimately awarded the title "Companion of the Star of India" for his efforts in making India known to its British rulers. As many critics have observed, the Buddha as portrayed by Arnold won the sympathies of Protestant readers in particular, due to a tacit similarity between the Buddha's rejection of Brahmanism and the Reformation struggle against Rome. Consider this passage, in which the Buddha denounces the extremities of Brahmanistic asceticism and in which the parallel to certain monastic practices of Catholicism is reasonably evident:

> Will ye, for love of soul, so loathe your flesh,
> So scourge and maim it, that it shall not serve
> To bear the spirit on, searching for home,
> But founder on the track before night-fall,
> Like willing steed o'er-spurred? Will ye, sad sirs!
> Dismantle and dismember this fair house,
> Where we have come to dwell by painful pasts;
> Whose windows give us light — the little light —
> Whereby we gaze about to know if dawn
> Will break, and whither winds the better road?

Plainly, there were matters in his poem, such as the cycle of reincarnation alluded to here, that were well outside accepted Christian doctrine. Arnold was aware of the difficulties. As he noted in his author's preface, Europe had only in his own generation become broadly aware of the existence of Buddhism, much less of the nature of its teachings. The necessity of sympathetic comprehension was, for Arnold, based on both the wisdom of the Buddha and the sheer number of his followers: "More than a third of mankind, therefore, owe their moral and religious ideas to this illustrious Prince, whose personality, though imperfectly revealed in the existing sources of information, can not but appear the highest, gentlest, holiest, and most beneficent, with one exception, in the history of Thought." From the Eurocentric perspective of Arnold, there could be no greater compliment. Christian supremacy having been affirmed, his readers could feel free to admire what the poem afforded of Buddhist teachings.

The success of *The Light of Asia* was based in part on the author's careful framing of Buddhism as an inferior but worthy religion. The long-term impact of the poem could not be so carefully controlled, however, and many Western and Eastern readers alike were seriously drawn by it to Buddhism. As for Arnold himself, he became devoted to the cause of worldwide religious ecumenism. How confusing this cause could become is illustrated by one of the specific reforms for which he labored.

In 1886, Arnold again visited India, this time making a pilgrimage to Bodh Gaya, the site of the Buddha's enlightenment. This site he now approached as "the land of the Light of Asia." But what Arnold found was a temple area, littered with broken Buddhist bas-reliefs and statuary, that was now being used for Hindu worship — a worship that included, as a traditional representation of Shiva, a stone lingam. It is not uncommon for a successor religion to use a sacred site for its own practice, and there was no distress over the matter in India. But Arnold was fully distraught, and after journeying on to Ceylon, he raised his objections with Buddhist priests there and put forth the suggestion that Bodh Gaya be made a protected site ruled by "a representative committee of the Buddhist nations."

As part of this rule, the Hindu practices were, of course, to cease. The Hindus in residence at Bodh Gaya were forthrightly opposed to the plan, and the British Raj cared more for the feelings of its Hindu populace than for the Buddhist cause championed by one of its own. The acrimony endured long after Arnold's death in 1904 and well into the twentieth century. By then, the role of the European Orientalists had considerably diminished. The fate of Buddhism had — both in the East and in the West — reverted to the hands of its believers.

5

FROM HERDER TO HEIDEGGER: THE EMBEDDING OF BUDDHISM IN WESTERN PHILOSOPHY

❖

For all the growing availability of Orientalist knowledge, it remained the unquestioned prerogative of European philosophers to interpret Eastern religions according to their own preconceptions and fantasies. In no country did this process take on more vivid and epochal form than in Germany, where a succession of its greatest philosophers forged the first elaborate intertwining of Eastern and Western thought.

❖

Johann Gottfried von Herder (1744–1803), a Lutheran pastor and a rhetorical writer of genius whose historical and philosophical essays spurred the rise of Romanticism not only in Germany but throughout Europe, was the first among Western thinkers to extol India — as opposed to the reigning favorite, China — as the ultimate fount of Eastern wisdom.

Herder always insisted on the intrinsic superiority of Christianity as the religion of "purest humanity." But his passion for an India he deeply admired, never visited, and altogether little understood — "childlike Indians" he termed its people — was groundbreaking and contagious. Herder was abreast of the researches of the Orientalists, but he interpreted their findings in his own impassioned voice, which merged undertones of Christian piety with a vision of a newly discovered pristine pagan wisdom: "The Hindus are the gentlest branch of humanity. They do not with pleasure offend anything that lives. [. . .] Moderation and calm, soft feeling and a silent depth of the soul characterize their work and their pleasure, their morals and mythology, their arts and even their endurance under the most extreme yoke of humanity." From this could be culled promotional copy for a present-day chic spa, if one cut the tacit mention of the onset of British colonial rule. But then, the "endurance" of the Indian people under this "most extreme yoke" only contributed to their "silent depth of the soul." Such was the India held forth by Herder for European consideration. In Germany, especially, his impact was immense.

A case in point is that of the German philosopher and Sanskritist Friedrich von Schlegel (1772–1829). Schlegel argued that as Western culture was degenerating and no longer possessed a living mythology, the West — and Germany in particular — had no choice but to draw from the rich living myths of India, which were there for the taking. Schlegel was prepared to serve as translator and guide for the new Oriental renaissance, along with his brother August Wilhelm, named by the University of Bonn as its first professor of Sanskrit.

In 1800, Schlegel declared famously that "the pinnacle of Romanticism" was to be found in the wisdom and arts of India. There was a racial affinity for Germans to draw upon here, for Schlegel believed, as had Sir William Jones, that northern Europe had long ago been populated by a wave of energetic migration from northern India. As Schlegel declared in a letter to the German Romantic writer Ludwig Tieck, "Everything, yes, everything has its origins in India." But after further study, Schlegel, in his influential Romantic work *On the Language and Wisdom of the Indians* (1808), came to reject vehemently basic aspects of Indian religion of which he had at last taken serious cognizance, such as pantheism, the workings of the law of karma, and, most abhorrent, the phallic symbolism and sexual esotericism of Shaivism. That same year, Schlegel converted to Roman Catholicism. In his later life, he theorized anew that the true beginnings of civilization lay not in India but in Mesopotamia. He also gave up the reading of Sanskrit, the mastery of which had won him such renown.

The first German thinker to attempt seriously to comprehend Indian thought — and to place it within the Western construct of a progressive "history of philosophy" — was Georg Wilhelm Friedrich Hegel (1770–1831). Hegel was steadfastly opposed to the vision of India urged upon Europe by Herder and Schlegel. Rejecting their Romantic portrayals of a pristine primal wisdom and mythology, Hegel instead argued that Indian thought belonged to a remote past to which a more evolved European humankind could never return, although its teachings still held value when viewed as an early revelation of the "World Spirit" (*Weltgeist*) in its ongoing, ineluctable movement from East to West. Hegel drew alike upon the findings of Orientalist scholars and Jesuit missionaries. Particularly in the last decade of his life, he persistently attempted to fasten hold of the essence of the newly discovered wisdoms of the East. The Indian philosopher J. L. Mehta went so far as to argue — in defiance of the standard emphasis on Schopenhauer — that "Hegel has been the only Western philosopher of rank to devote serious attention to Indian philosophical and religious ideas."

The attention paid by Hegel was indeed serious, but certainty eluded him, particularly in the case of Buddhism, regarding which Hegel wrestled with shifting conceptions. In his *Lectures on the Philosophy of Religion,* largely delivered in the 1820s, Hegel alternately termed Buddhism a "nature religion" and a "religion of being-in-itself" akin to Brahmanism. He explained Buddhistic "being-in-itself" as a pantheistic view in which God becomes the ultimate spiritual substance pervading all phenomenal reality. For Hegel, this was a relatively lowly stage on the path of religious evolution, which culminated in the self-revelation of the World Spirit known as Protestant Christianity.

Hegel struggled with the Buddhist belief — not so utterly distant from that held by Christians about their founder — that human teachers could be viewed as incarnate examples of an infinite divine wisdom:

God is grasped as nothing, as essence generally. [. . .] This essential God is nevertheless known as a specific, immediate human being, as Fo, Buddha, or Dalai Lama. This may appear to us as the most repugnant, shocking, and unbelievable tenet, that a human being with all his deficiencies could be regarded by other human beings as God, as the one who eternally creates, preserves, and produces the world. We must learn to understand this view. [. . .] But it is also pertinent for us to have insight into its defective and absurd aspect.

Hegel plainly viewed with distaste the elevation of human teachers into divine exemplars and held as quaintly ridiculous the practice of selecting toddlers as reincarnated Dalai Lamas (a practice he had learned of through the writings of the British diplomat Samuel Turner in *Asiatick Researches*). But he was also capable of being moved aesthetically by what he believed to be a standard form of Buddhist iconography:

> The image of Buddha is in the thinking posture, with feet and arms intertwined so that a toe extends into the mouth — this [is] the withdrawal into self, this absorption in oneself. Hence the character of the peoples who adhere to this religion is one of tranquility, gentleness, and obedience, a character that stands above the wildness of desire and is the cessation of desire.

As the American scholar Peter C. Hodgson noted, Hegel was here most likely confusing with the Buddha an image of the Hindu divinity Brahma Narayana that he had viewed in a German reference work of the era. And yet, as the Hindu and Buddhist traditions share many techniques of spiritual meditation, Hegel was not altogether wrong in his response, even though his Western students may have puzzled over the toe-sucking Buddha, with its strange resemblance to the Ouroboros of Western Hermetism and alchemy.

To underscore the spiritual gulf between Europe and the East, Hegel argued that the aim of Buddhistic nirvana was that "man must make himself nothing. In his being, he must act in a negative way, defend himself not against the outside but against himself." But Hegel showed a greater awareness of the dimensions of nirvana than did many of his European contemporaries, for whom nothingness and nihilism seemed, in Buddhism, to merge. Indeed, Hegel expressly rejected that reductive viewpoint:

> At first glance it must astonish us that humans think of God as nothing; that must be extremely strange. Most closely considered, however, this characterization means nothing other than that God purely and simply is nothing determinate. [. . .] When we adopt the forms that are commonplace today, i.e., "God is the infinite, the essence, the pure and simple essence, the essence of essences and only the essence," then this sort of talk is necessarily either totally or tolerably synonymous with the claim that God is nothing. That does not mean, however, that God is not, but rather that God is the empty, and that this emptiness is God.

Note how, with a casual, almost colloquial, manner of explanation, Hegel made of Buddhist nirvana something easily compatible with the German Protestant outlook of his era. There is a further parallel suggested here, although Hegel did not draw it. The thirteenth-century German mystic Meister Eckhart held that even though God and humankind were one in soul and being, it was impossible for any person to speak of God except in negative terms, for any delimiting definition could only falsify the limitless divine reality. Hegel's analysis of nirvana concurs with Eckhart's analysis of God. Consider, too, that Arthur Schopenhauer, whose views on Buddhism will next be examined, wrote that "Buddha, Eckhart and I all teach essentially the same." Roughly a century after Hegel and Schopenhauer, the Japanese Zen thinker D. T. Suzuki would make the affinities between Buddhism and Eckhart the subject of a highly influential and controversial text, *Mysticism: Christian and Buddhist* (1957), to which we shall turn in a later chapter. Suzuki did not owe his knowledge of Eckhart to Hegel or Schopenhauer, which makes the similar reading of Eckhart by all three men all the more remarkable.

❖

Arthur Schopenhauer (1788–1860) insisted that the theism shared by Judaism, Christianity, and Islam was not, as held by so many European thinkers, a necessary criterion of religion. Buddhism, then believed the most populous of the world's religions, paid no heed whatsoever to divine creators and was thus unfairly denigrated as a base heathen creed. On the contrary, Schopenhauer argued, Buddhism offered an intricate wisdom comparable to the finest insights of European philosophy.

Schopenhauer drew much of the basis for his own thought from the insights of Kant. The opening words of Schopenhauer's magnum opus, *The World as Will and Representation,* vouchsafe the Kantian separation of human consciousness from external reality. We create what we call the world based on categories insisted upon by our minds — time, space, and causation, to name the three most prominent. All we can say about the reality outside us is that it seems to exist:

"The world is my representation": this is a truth valid with reference to every living and knowing being, although man alone can bring it into reflective, abstract consciousness. If he really does so, philosophical discernment has dawned on him. It then becomes clear and certain to him that he does not know a sun and an earth, but only an eye that sees a sun, a hand that feels an earth; that the world around him is there only as representation, in other words, only in reference to another thing, namely that which represents, and this is himself.

Schopenhauer came to see this Kantian viewpoint as in complete accord with Buddhist doctrines on the nature of reality, which eschewed speculations on divine creators in favor of a focus on the workings of the grasping mind enmeshed in samsaric illusions. For Schopenhauer, obedience to the frantic dictates of the metaphysical will was the underlying source of human misery. The means of freeing oneself from this will included the exercise of reasoned detachment, compassion for one's fellow sufferers, and aesthetic contemplation — all of which reduced the hold of the world and its suffering on human consciousness.

Schopenhauer wrongly believed — whether due to the limited knowledge of Buddhism of his time or to his delight in treating Indian teachings, both Brahmanic and Buddhist, as mere precursive confirmations of his own genius — that the Kantian noumenon and the Buddhist nirvana were neatly one and the same. In truth, in the works of both Kant and Schopenhauer, there is a strong tendency to affirm the unknowable "thing-in-itself" as an enduring, albeit nonmaterial, underlying substance of the universe. The mainstream of Middle Way Buddhist thought rejects any such affirmations of enduring substances of any kind.

As several scholars have noted, the Kantian outlook that Schopenhauer shared is somewhat reflected in a minority school of Buddhist thought, the Yogacara, of which Schopenhauer was unaware. The Yogacara school arose in India in the fifth century CE and held that emptiness (*sunyata*) and suchness (*tathata*) are identical with the awakened wisdom (*prajna*) of human consciousness. More simply, ideas, feelings, and all the other antics and insights of the mind are the closest we can come to a sense of reality. The underlying mind that is reflected in individual minds draws from the inexhaustible storehouse consciousness (*alayavijnana*), which some scholars have compared to Freud's unconscious — the repository of all conceivable mental states and perceptions. With respect to Schopenhauer, the

Yogacara storehouse consciousness from which all life as we know it flows bears some limited resemblance to the metaphysical will, the dictates of which, Schopenhauer believed, nearly all of us act out unawares with every breath. As the American scholar Janice D. Willis astutely stressed, however, the founding Yogacara thinkers never intended *alayavijnana* "as a synonym for ultimate reality."

In short, the Yogacara writings provide no justification for Schopenhauer's declaration that Immanuel Kant was in outlook an orthodox Buddhist — a finding that would have startled Kant himself, who made little mention of Indian religions in his writings, but for brief and passing praise of the tolerance of the Hindus. However, in a curious footnote in his *Religion Within the Limits of Reason Alone* (1793), Kant did speculate, avidly but inaccurately, about the origins of Lamaism, which he could not have known, given the state of European knowledge of the time, to be a form of Buddhism. Kant observed that "the Mongols adhered to the Tibetan faith (of the Lamas) which agrees with Manichaenism, perhaps even arose from it, and spread it to Europe during their invasions." The limited overlapping between Manichaeism and the Buddhism of central Asia was discussed in chapter 2. Their independent initial development is clear to us now, as is the absence of missionary ambitions by the Mongol forces attacking Europe. But Kant's vision of a Mongol importation to Europe of a sharply dualistic Tibetan Buddhism, which thereafter merged among the heresies combated by the Inquisition, is a measure of the distance in knowledge of Buddhism between the generations of Kant and Schopenhauer.

By making of Kant a Buddhist in outlook, Schopenhauer was simultaneously — some would say egregiously — merging the histories of Eastern and Western philosophy into a culmination based on the work of Kant and of Schopenhauer himself. This was appropriation on a grand scale, but it was also tolerance on a grand scale — an acknowledgment that East and West had been equal contributors to the development of philosophical thought. For Schopenhauer's time, this was a daring assessment. In his *On the Fourfold Root of the Principle of Sufficient Reason,* Schopenhauer made his case blithely:

> Kant's *Critique of Pure Reason* is the most serious attack ever made on theism, and this is why the professors of philosophy have hastened to put his

Buddha in mudra, or posture of concentrated dhyana meditation, from Gandhara region circa second or third century CE. The Apollonian head and togalike garment show the influence of Hellenistic sculptural techniques. From M. A. Shakur, *Gandhara Sculpture in Pakistan* (Bangkok: SEATO, 1963).

Bodhisattva from Gandhara region, same period. From Shakur, *Gandhara Sculpture in Pakistan.*

Buddha from Gandhara region, same period. From Shakur, *Gandhara Sculpture in Pakistan.*

Yaksha, or Buddhist protective deity, that marked the boundary of the city of Mathura in Gandhara, same period. From J. Ph. Vogel, *Catalogue of the Archaeological Museum at Mathura* (Allahabad, India: Government Press, United Provinces, 1910).

A sketch by the Jesuit missionary Johannes Grueber of the Potala Palace, principal residence of the Dalai Lamas, overlooking the city of Lhasa. From Athanasius Kircher, *China Monumentis* (Amsterdam: Jacobum and Meurs, 1667).

Termed the "Idol of 'Pussa'" by the Jesuit scholar Athanasius Kircher, this image by a Jesuit artist almost certainly depicts Kwanyin, the Buddhist goddess of compassion. From Kircher, *China Monumentis*.

"A Tirinanxes or Cheif [*si*
Priest"— such was the ca[
for this illustration of a
Buddhist priest and devote
that appeared in Robert K
An Historical Relation of Ce
(1681), as the West began **t**
forge a new vocabulary to
approach an unfamiliar As:
religion.

Drawing of a
Tibetan Buddhist
meditating in
seclusion in a
cave, from Abbé
Huc, *Travels in
Tartary, Tibet, and
China During the
Years 1844–1846*
(London: Office
of the National
Library, 1852).

A photograph of Madame Blavatsky that served as the frontispiece to her first major work, *Isis Unveiled* (1877).

The Buddha as the embodiment of cosmic mystery, as he came to be seen by many cultured Europeans of the late nineteenth century. Lithograph by the French artist Odilon Redon, from his book *L'Estampe Originale* (Paris, 1895).

The explorer Sven
Hedin in Mongolian
garb. From Sven Hedin,
Central Asia and Tibet
(London: Hurst and
Blackett, 1903).

Hedin in the contrasting
guise of a European savant.
From Sir Thomas Holdich,
Tibet the Mysterious
(London: Alston Rivers,
1906).

Temple of the Three Precious Buddhas in San Francisco. From Frank S. Dobbins, *Story of the World's Worship* (Dominion Company, 1901).

Two armored Tibetan infantrymen encountered and photographed by the British invasionary force of 1903–1904 led by Sir Francis Younghusband. From L. Austine Waddell, *Lhasa and Its Mysteries* (London: John Murray, 1905).

Photograph of the entrance gate to Lhasa, a symbolic image of conquest of the Forbidden City. From Sir Francis Younghusband, *India and Tibet* (London: John Murray, 1910).

"High Mass in the Temple of Sera at Lhasa" was the caption penned by the British Anglican medical officer L. Austine Waddell for this photograph, exemplifying a tendency of Western Orientalists of the era to compare Catholicism and so-called Lamaism. From Waddell, *Lhasa and Its Mysteries*.

work on the shelf. If it had appeared in Buddhist countries, then in accordance with the above quotations one would have seen in it nothing but an edifying treatise on the more thorough refutation of its heretics, and the more salutary confirmation of the orthodox doctrine of idealism, namely that of the merely apparent existence of this world that is presented to our senses.

Of course, Kant had set out to define the limits of reason so as to carve a proper place for the moral and spiritual guidance that Christian faith could best provide. Schopenhauer departed from his master here, rejecting theism as unworthy of philosophy and insisting that reason could indeed comprehend the noumenon, the thing-in-itself, that Kant had declared as forever off-limits to mere human cognition. Schopenhauer identified the noumenon as the metaphysical will, the underlying force that drives all of existence — from inanimate matter to humankind — toward ceaseless, painful craving and change.

The resemblance between Schopenhauer's outlook and the suffering that stems from ignorance — addressed by the first two of the Buddha's Four Noble Truths — was evident to Schopenhauer himself. That Schopenhauer, like the Buddha in his Third Noble Truth, offered a means of escape from the pain of existence is also clear. But Schopenhauer was not a believing Buddhist, and admire as he did the teachings of the Dharma, the means of escape he proposed was altogether different in scope: a mere list of aesthetic and psychological coping mechanisms, including polite consideration for others; solitary philosophical reflection; immersion in great works of literature, art, and music; and ironic distancing of oneself from the futile preoccupations of humankind. These resemble Buddhism less than they do the teachings of the Greek philosopher Epicurus on virtuous restraint and appreciation of life's simpler pleasures.

Schopenhauer insisted that his philosophy was not influenced by Buddhism, but rather had proven — once he learned of Buddhist thought — to be in happy "agreement" with it. His study of Buddhism was intensive, however, as evidenced by the numerous volumes on Buddhist thought in his personal library. Schopenhauer went to great lengths to stay abreast of ongoing European developments in both Hindu and Buddhist scholarship, and he bemoaned, in the second volume of his masterwork, *The World as Will and Representation,* published in 1844, that "up till 1818, when my work appeared, there were to be found in Europe only a very few accounts of Buddhism, and those extremely incomplete and inadequate." As to the emerging work of the Orientalists, Schopenhauer took the role of active promoter, urging upon readers a list of twenty-six Buddhist studies and translations that "I can really recommend for I possess them and know them well."

Did such passionate study of Buddhism over the last forty years of his life influence his completion of and revisions to *The World as Will and Representation*? The scholar Moira Nicholls persuasively argued that Schopenhauer's later thought was indeed shaped to a degree by Buddhism, particularly with respect to his vision of fundamental reality, the Kantian noumenon or thing-in-itself. Based on his study of the writings of the Russian Orientalist Isaac Jacob Schmidt, Schopenhauer expanded his conception of the "nothingness" that follows upon escape from the tyranny of the striving metaphysical will. In the 1818 first edition of the first volume of *The World as Will and Representation,* Schopenhauer wrote of this nothingness:

> We must not even evade it, as the Indians do, by myths and meaningless words, such as reabsorption in *Brahman,* or the *Nirvana* of the Buddhists. On the contrary, we freely acknowledge that what remains after the complete abolition of the will is, for all who are still full of the will, assuredly nothing. But also conversely, to those in whom the will has turned and denied itself, this very real world of ours with all its suns and galaxies, is — nothing.

But in the 1844 second edition, Schopenhauer added a note explaining that "this [nothing] is also the Prajna-Paramita of the Buddhists, the 'beyond all knowledge,' in other words, the point where subject and object no longer exist. See I. J. Schmidt, *Ueber das Mahajana und Pradschna-Paramita* [published in 1836]."

Schopenhauer's note indicates that the teachings on nirvana of the *Prajnaparamita* writings of the Mahayana Buddhist tradition had conveyed to him a broader understanding of the state of knowing that is possible when the self is overcome. It was possible to experience a new awareness in which subject and object merged into something quite wondrously other — indescribable in language and yet capable of being pointed to, hinted at. In this regard, the account of the *Prajnaparamita* literature by Heinrich Zimmer — a twentieth-century German Indologist with an intimate knowledge of both the German philosophical tradition and Buddhist thought — is most helpful. Zimmer stressed that the central insight of the *Prajnaparamita* texts was that a knowledge beyond duality can somehow be conveyed, if not precisely communicated:

One may well marvel at the bold experiment — an effort to represent the ultimate essence of an incommunicable intuition through words and conceptions familiar to the usual philosophical and pious understanding. But, wonderful to relate, a vivid sense of the ineffable reality known in extinction (*nirvana*) is actually conveyed in this unexampled body of strange, esoteric texts. They are named *Prajna-paramita:* "The Accomplishment of Transcendental Wisdom," or "The Wisdom (*prajna*) Gone to the Other Shore (*param-ita*)."

These texts take the form of dialogues between Buddhas and bodhisattvas who

delight in declaring, time and again, that there is no such thing as Buddhism, no such thing as Enlightenment, nothing remotely resembling the extinction of nirvana, setting traps for each other and trying to trick each other into assertions that might imply — even remotely — the reality of such conceptions. Then, most artfully, they always elude the cleverly placed hazards and hidden pitfalls — and all engage in a glorious, transolympian laugh; for the merest hint of a notion of nirvana would have betrayed a trace of the vestige of the opposite attitude, samsara, and the clinging to individual existence.

Such was the world of the *Prajnaparamita* to which Schopenhauer had been exposed by the scholarly work of Schmidt, whose Buddhist translations were drawn largely from Mongolian texts. Schmidt was one of the first Europeans to write of the Mahayana and the *Prajnaparamita.* (The writings of Schmidt also encouraged Schopenhauer to believe, as discussed in chapter 1, that there had been an interchange between Buddhists and Gnostics in the early centuries CE.) The note mentioning

Schmidt and the *Prajnaparamita* was placed in a remarkable position — at the very end of the revised 1844 first volume of *The World as Will and Representation*. Plainly, Schopenhauer meant for it to matter.

In his later writings, Schopenhauer took up the cause of the Buddhist doctrine of metempsychosis, which, he believed, had been unfairly excised from the realm of Western discourse since the rise of Christianity. He regarded the doctrine as a great philosophical myth, embraced by Pythagoras and Plato, and, as a myth, best suited to reveal to the masses the workings of eternal justice. Schopenhauer further stressed, more in accordance with Buddhist than Brahmanic teaching, that the most accurate term for the doctrine was not "metempsychosis," which implied that a soul survived in its individuality, but rather "palingenesis," the survival of the will, as Schopenhauer would have it, or of the karmic tendencies underlying all individual lives, as Buddhist orthodoxy would have it. What perished at death, according to Schopenhauer, was the invidious illusion of the independent self, which he termed the *principium individuationis*.

Schopenhauer suggested that "we might say to the dying individual: 'You are ceasing to be something which you would have done better never to become.'" Bleak as this advice might seem, Schopenhauer was extraordinarily optimistic as to the awakening from the errors of individual, will-driven existence, which the process of death would provide as a matter of course. Quite contrary to Buddhism, he felt this would occur without regard to the karma of the life just lived:

Death is a refutation of this error and abolishes it. I believe that, at the moment of dying, we become aware that a mere illusion has limited our existence to our person. Even empirical traces of this may be seen in many states or conditions akin to death through abolition of the concentration of consciousness in the brain, and of these states magnetic sleep is the most conspicuous. When this sleep reaches the higher degrees, our existence shows itself in it through various symptoms, beyond our persons and in other beings, most strikingly by direct participation in the thoughts of another individual, and ultimately even by the ability to know the absent, the distant, and also the future, that is, by a kind of omnipresence.

By "magnetic sleep," Schopenhauer meant what we would term hypnosis. Although his arguments are highly speculative, it bears noting that his comparisons between the sleep and death states are found in Tibetan Buddhist thought, in which the practice of lucid control during the *bardo* state of dream enables the meditator to prepare for lucid passage through the *bardo* state of death. They also were mirrored, to a surprising degree, in a recent dialogue between the Fourteenth Dalai Lama and Western scientists and philosophers, the results of which were published in a volume titled *Sleeping, Dreaming, and Dying* (1997). Credit goes to Schopenhauer for first posing a Western framework for comparisons between the two fields that continues to be of interest in our own time.

Schopenhauer championed a second Eastern doctrine that, like metempsychosis or reincarnation, has since become a prominent, if not dominant, belief in the West. That doctrine might be described as support for animal rights, although in Schopenhauer's version, it more closely resembles the twentieth-century Gaia theory of the interconnectedness of all life-forms on earth. Schopenhauer wrote, in his essay "The Christian System," that the Eastern religions,

> true to the facts, recognize in a positive way that man is related generally to the whole of nature, and specially and principally to animal nature; and in their systems man is always represented by the theory of metempsychosis and otherwise, as closely connected with the animal world. The important part played by animals all through Buddhism and Brahmanism, compared with the total disregard of them in Judaism and Christianity, puts an end to any question as to which system is nearer perfection, however much we in Europe may have become accustomed to the absurdity of the claim.

In 1856, four years before his death, Schopenhauer acquired, by way of a Prussian diplomat who purchased it for him in Paris, a bronze statue of the Buddha crafted in Tibet. Schopenhauer had the black lacquer coating removed from the statue and replaced with gold plating — thus paralleling his adoring transformations of Brahmanic and Buddhistic philosophical thought. The figure delighted him, and he joked in letters to friends about how he engaged in "domestic worship" of it and had even made a "pilgrimage" to a British visitor to Germany who possessed a similar Buddha figure made in China: "Both have that famous, ortho- dox sweetness in the smile on their lips, exactly the same! The postures, the clothing, the hair, the lotus: just the same. Look here, Professor Kalb! Om, Mani, Padme, Hum!" Professor Kalb was a Sachsenhausen pastor who had bewailed the fact "that these days even Buddhism is be- ing brought onto Christian soil." Schopenhauer, in pointed contrast, looked to the day when the Indian traditions would topple the domi- nance of Christianity in Europe. He mocked the missionary efforts of the British in India, who

> send to the Brahmins English clergymen and evangelical linen-weavers, in order out of sympathy to put them right, and to point out to them that they are created out of nothing, and that they ought to be grateful and pleased about it. But it is just the same as if we fired a bullet at a cliff. In India our religions will never at any time take root; the ancient wis- dom of the human race will not be supplanted by the events at Galilee. On the contrary, Indian wisdom flows back to Europe, and will produce a fundamental change in our knowledge and thought.

Schopenhauer was clearly wrong about Christianity never taking root in India, although its influence there has never been a dominant one. But he was clearly right about the impact that Indian teachings, includ- ing Buddhism, would exercise upon the West. Despite his seemingly di- chotomous view of Indian and Christian thought, Schopenhauer took special delight in hinting that the latter was to some degree an unac- knowledged offshoot of the former — thus explaining the gulf between the Christian triune God and the strict monotheism of Judaism and Is- lam: "Because of the doctrine of the Trinity even Christians are re- proached by Mohammedans and Jews with not being pure theists. For whatever anyone may say Christianity has Indian blood in its veins, and thus has a constant tendency to be rid of Judaism."

That Schopenhauer used a racial metaphor — "Indian blood" — to express cultural and spiritual influence is not a mere literary device, but rather was intended to emphasize the link between the Aryan race of Germany and its Indian forebears. Schopenhauer was not a proto-Nazi, but he did regard Jewish monotheism — which falsely, in his view, praised a just God for the creation of a just world — with dismay and expressed that dismay, as was the intellectual fashion of his times, in racial terms, as for example in his organic metaphor of "the Christian faith, sprung from the wisdom of India, [which] overspreads the old trunk of rude Judaism, a tree of alien growth."

Other European thinkers of that era, notably the French historian and diplomat Count Joseph Arthur de Gobineau (1816–1882), laced their speculations on the common Aryan invaders of India and Germany with vicious anti-Semitism and racial theories that reduced all non-Aryan races to secondary human status. In his *Essay on the Inequality of the Human Races* (1853), Gobineau portrayed Buddhism in its Indian origins as a revolt of the pre-Aryan dark races of India against the Aryan white race, which had established Brahmanism and its strict caste system to protect its own priestly caste from racial dilution. The assault of Buddhism included the flooding of the Indian religious consciousness "with all the Buddhas, with all the bodhisattvas, and other inventions of an imagination that was all the more fecund because of its plunge into the black classes." Brahmanism ultimately prevailed in India due to the "excellence of Aryan blood," while Buddhism succeeded for as long as it did "by recruiting all the lost souls." The large numbers of living Asian Buddhists were deemed by Gobineau as belonging to "the vilest of the classes of China and its neighboring states." With Judaism as a poisonous alien growth and Buddhism as the fantasy refuge of the inferior races, the way was clear to recognize Aryan blood as the essential standard of human attainment. Gobineau went on to become one of the favorite theorists of Hitler's Third Reich.

❖

Some German disciples of Schopenhauer developed the master's insights into a movement known as "Ideological Pessimism." Its chief proponent, Eduard von Hartmann (1842–1906), posited in his *Philosophy of the Unconscious* (1869) that the "stagnated" religions of India would, paradoxically, be well suited to serve as a necessary stimulus to European Christianity, a more historically evolved creed that still needed the primal wisdom of the East: "The development of religion in the West will automatically approach that of the Indian religions as well; it will become capable of directing this ancient Aryan intellectual current into its own stream of development — something the Christian missionary activity has proven itself to be incapable of over an adequately long period of trial." Hartmann made a key point that would be increasingly echoed in the works of secular Western thinkers — that a true dialogue with Buddhism would take place in the West, rather than the East, with its overweening Christian missionary presence.

The dangers of such a dialogue, when hampered by inadequate knowledge and psychological imbalance, were illustrated by Philipp Mainländer (1841–1876), the pen name of Philipp Batz, a young German thinker who wrote *The Philosophy of Salvation* (1876) and killed himself the day after it was published. In his book, Mainländer drew upon Schopenhauer to argue that human history was a "movement from life into absolute death." Escape through nirvana could be attained by means of recognizing the primeval "will to death," which masqueraded as a "will to life" but most deeply fulfilled itself through a lifelong virginity or the taking of one's own life. The book was, in essence, a meticulously argued suicide note. Mainländer thus became a literal martyr to the cause of Buddhist "annihilation" propounded by so many Orientalists of the era.

One telling example of this lingering linkage between Schopenhauer, Buddhism, and spiritual malaise occurs in the work of Sigmund Freud (1856–1939). In his *Beyond the Pleasure Principle* (1920), Freud borrowed the term "Nirvana principle" (coined by Barbara Low, a psychoanalytic disciple of Freud) to describe an aspect of what he termed, more broadly, the "death instinct." The "Nirvana principle" sought "to reduce, to keep constant or to remove internal tension due to stimuli" by means of self-extinction. Freud had studied and admired the works of Schopenhauer and conceded that his conception of the "death instinct" had its precursive form in Schopenhauer's work: "We have unwittingly steered our course into the harbor of Schopenhauer's philosophy. For him death is the 'true result and to that extent the purpose of life,' while the sexual instinct is the embodiment of the will to live." The "Nirvana principle" thus stands as the formal incorporation, within Freudian psychoanalytic theory, of a view of Buddhist nirvana as a kind of psychic death by means of systematic elimination of the world and its stimuli.

❖

Carl Gustav Jung (1875–1961), a onetime disciple of Freud and a fellow admirer of Schopenhauer, held a far different view as to the influence of what might be called "Schopenhauerian Buddhism" within Western thought. According to Jung, its effect was to liberate the West from its long-standing Christian conviction that human effort unaided by God would always be unavailing. Schopenhauer, Jung believed, had affirmed that "ego consciousness" in and of itself could lead to liberation from the thrall of the primordial will:

> This ego consciousness is to Schopenhauer the turning point of the whole history or development of the world; if that did not exist, the world could never be redeemed. So Schopenhauer introduced an important change in the conception of the world. And it is interesting that he is really a Buddhist missionary, the first influence from the East, which is changing our conceptions in a most extraordinary way. [. . .] The whole metaphysical importance has now shifted onto man, but one could say it was really the Buddhistic influence upon the West; by that subtle and secret infection the idea is brought in that man is capable of doing something for himself.

We shall later discuss the issue of Jung's highly complex attitudes toward Buddhist thought. For now, we may observe that the phrase "subtle and secret infection" conveys some sense of the ambiguities Jung felt as to Buddhist transformations of the Western Christian psyche. It is striking that Jung regarded even the scant amount of Buddhism that Schopenhauer had gleaned through limited translations as having been sufficient to revolutionize the self-understanding of the Western psyche. Further, it was Jung, and not the Buddhist enthusiast Schopenhauer, who insisted on the absolute "metaphysical" distinction between East and West. Schopenhauer, by contrast, drew numerous parallels between Buddhism and Christianity as religions that both rejected the snares of the world. The strategy of regarding Buddhism as an "other" outside the sphere of the Western psyche, so as to delimit its accessibility — and even its advisability — for the Western psyche, would form a prominent part of twentieth-century Western responses to Buddhism, with Jung as its champion.

❖

Jung speculated that Friedrich Nietzsche (1844–1900) had drawn from Schopenhauer the central inspiration for his *Thus Spake Zarathustra* — the *Übermensch,*

> who is able to hold a mirror up to the blind will, so that the blind primordial will that has created the world may be able to see its own face in the mirror of the intellect. This is very much like the Indian idea really, like the psychological education Buddha tried to give to his time, the idea of looking into the mirror of knowledge or understanding in order to destroy the error and illusion of the world. [. . .] That is the very essence of Buddhism, and that became the integrating constituent of Schopenhauer's philosophy, where Nietzsche found it.

Whether Nietzsche's *Übermensch,* or superior man, owes anything to Buddhism or seeks rather to overcome the world-weariness that Nietzsche saw in Buddhism is a matter of debate. Nietzsche was indebted, for his knowledge of Buddhism, not only to the philosophy of Schopenhauer but also to his friendship with the German composer Richard Wagner, who for a time regarded Buddhism as superior to Christianity in grandeur. In a letter to Franz Liszt, Wagner exclaimed: "How sublime, how satisfying is this doctrine compared with Judaeo-Christian doctrine." Wagner began work on an opera, *The Victor,* based on the life of the Buddha, but never completed it. Some of its score was incorporated into *Tristan* and *Parsifal,* two overtly Christian operas. The British critic Michael Edwardes argued that the influence of Indian thought, including Buddhism, upon Wagner was such that he created "perhaps the only real synthesis of India and Europe" by a Western artist. Although this overstates the case, it does remedy the more prevalent tendency to dismiss Wagner's fascination with Buddhism as a mere phase of exoticism. On the contrary, not only was Buddhism a genuine inspiration for his music, but it also served — due to his view of Buddhism as a pure Aryan creed without Mediterranean taint — as a string to the bow of his passionate lifelong anti-Semitism, which was one of the grounds for Nietzsche's breaking off his friendship with Wagner.

Nietzsche was by no means consistent in his views on Buddhism. He borrowed from Schopenhauer's insistence on Buddhist pessimism, but he also broke more original ground in using Buddhism — as radically recast by Nietzsche — as a weapon in his ongoing attack on Christianity. In *The Anti-Christ* (1895), Nietzsche contrasted Buddhism, which he invested with a stolid heroism akin to Western Stoicism, with the weakness and evasions he saw in Christianity. The two creeds

> belong together as nihilistic religions — they are decadence religions — but they are distinguished from one another in the most remarkable way. The critic of Christianity is profoundly grateful to Indian scholars that one is now able to *compare* these two religions. — Buddhism is a hundred times more realistic than Christianity — it has the heritage of a cool and objective posing of problems in its composition, it arrives *after* a philosophical movement [Brahmanism] lasting hundreds of years; the concept "God" is already abolished by the time it arrives.

The "Indian scholars" thanked by Nietzsche were the European Orientalists whose studies of Theravada Buddhism he had consulted to a limited degree and with limited comprehension. Nietzsche declared that in Buddhism, not only God was abolished but also good and evil. While Christianity wrung its hands over sin and morality, Buddhism focused on suffering as a fact of life and set about intelligently to evade it. This view ignores the strong presence in Theravada (and all forms of Buddhism) of strictly prescribed codes of conduct for monks and laypeople that distinguish sharply between good and evil in human affairs, with karmic retribution for evil deeds.

For Nietzsche, Buddhist discipline amounted simply to avoiding the unpleasant, while nirvana was a relaxation technique so basic that it was all but inevitably achieved, given the proper climate and the proper class of human beings:

> The precondition for Buddhism is a very mild climate, very gentle and liberal customs, *no* militarism; and that it is the higher and even learned classes in which the movement has its home. The supreme goal is cheerfulness,

stillness, absence of desire, and this goal is *achieved*. Buddhism is not a religion in which one merely aspires after perfection: perfection is the normal case.

Nietzsche termed Buddha "that profound physiologist" and his religion "a kind of *hygiene*" that overcomes the baleful physical effects of the grinding emotional "*ressentiment*" that pervades human life. Paraphrasing from Friedrich Max Müller's translation of the *Dhammapada*, Nietzsche offered this concise summary of Buddhist doctrine: " 'Not by enmity is enmity ended; by friendliness enmity is ended'; these words stand at the beginning of the doctrine of the Buddha. It is *not* morality that speaks thus; thus speaks physiology." By contrast, for Nietzsche, Christianity drew "the lowest classes" and held forth spiritual ideals that "are considered unachievable, gifts, 'grace.'" Without accepting the entirety of Nietzsche's argument, it must be allowed that in the present day, the physiological effects of Buddhist practice are of great and persistent interest to Western physicians and psychotherapists.

Nietzsche was clearly mistaken both as to the ease of Buddhist attainment and the difficulties of obtaining Christian ritual grace. Although he extolled Buddhism to a degree, it held no personal appeal for him. In an ironic reversal of the "opium" metaphor used contemptuously by Diderot against Indian religion, Nietzsche was sufficiently impressed to observe that "Buddhism was making silent progress throughout Europe" and might perhaps supplant an "opiatic" Christianity. Nietzsche went further, opining that "a European Buddhism may prove indispensable" and that he himself "could be the Buddha of Europe: though admittedly an antipode to the Indian Buddha." As antipode, Nietzsche would heroically embrace what the Buddha had sought to evade through nirvana — the eternal recurrence of life and its sufferings. To embrace — to take joy in — the pains of existence would be the great affirmation of the Western *Übermensch,* after a transitional phase of "European Buddhism," during which the false hopes of Christian morality and salvation would be overcome by facing life squarely. For Nietzsche, Buddhism was the ideal means of dampening Western illusions, leaving the way free thereafter for Europe "to transvalue the values and to deify and approve the realm of becoming, the apparent world alone."

The Nietzschean vision of Buddhism — as a reasoned and passive evasion of suffering — found its way into one of the most influential works of cultural interpretation of the early twentieth century, *The Decline of the West* (1926), by the German historian Oswald Spengler. For Spengler, Buddhism was not a religion at all, but rather was of a type with Roman Stoicism and European socialism, as all three placed duty before happiness and were, at root, materialistic insofar as life on earth was their sole concern. Buddhism, Spengler believed, was the outcome of an early and steady decline in the energies of Indian civilization, "a final and purely practical world-sentiment of tired megalopolitans who had a closed-off Culture behind them and no future before them." There is an evident parallel here to the Nietzschean view of Buddhist physiological escapism.

But Nietzsche's view also encountered an eminent opponent. In *A History of Western Philosophy* (1945), Bertrand Russell set forth an imagined debate — in heaven, before a God of no designated denomination — between Nietzsche and the Buddha, in which the latter, as the representative of a human ethic based on sympathy, is given the victory. Nietzsche makes the accusation that Buddhism, like Christianity, is based on a mere negative aspiration — deliverance from suffering. By contrast, Nietzsche extols great men such as Napoleon who, through the exercise of noble will, justify through their achievements the pervasive suffering of the masses of humanity. The Buddha's response, as crafted by Russell, represents a triumph not only over Nietzsche but also over the charges of nihilism that beset Buddhism in the Europe of Nietzsche's era:

"You are mistaken, Professor Nietzsche, in thinking my ideal a purely negative one. [. . .] I, too, have my heroes: my successor Jesus, because he told men to love his enemies; the men who discovered how to master the forces of nature and secure food with less labour; the medical men who have shown how to diminish disease; the poets and artists and musicians who have caught glimpses of the Divine beatitude. Love and knowledge and delight in beauty are not negations; they are enough to fill the lives of the greatest men that have ever lived."

Russell erred in placing the Christian phrase "Divine beatitude" in the Buddha's mouth. Plainly, his language constructions were colored by his Western upbringing. But Russell was persistent in his admiration of

Buddhism. In his essay "Why I Am Not a Christian," Russell paralleled the earlier attacks of Schopenhauer on the Western consensus, in place since the time of Clement of Alexandria, as to the innate superiority of Jesus Christ to all Eastern sages:

> I must say that I think all this doctrine, that hell-fire is a punishment for sin, is a doctrine of cruelty. It is a doctrine that put cruelty into the world and gave the world generations of cruel torture; and the Christ of the Gospels, if you could take Him as His chroniclers represent Him, would certainly have to be considered partly responsible for that. [. . .] I cannot myself feel that either in the matter of wisdom or in the manner of virtue Christ stands as high as some other people known to history. I think I should put Buddha and Socrates above Him in those respects.

❖

Max Weber (1864–1920), one of the founders of modern sociology, explored both Buddhism and Hinduism with respect to their impact on Indian economic and political life. His posthumously published *The Religion of India* (1921) may be seen as a complementary study to his most famous work, *The Protestant Ethic and the Spirit of Capitalism* (1904). In the latter book, Weber examined the role of Protestant theology in creating the necessary conditions in which capitalism could be created and flourish. In doing so, Weber was not attempting to eulogize capitalism. Rather, he was examining it as a social and historical force that was reshaping the world and therefore required some degree of understanding, which meant — here was Weber's distinctive contribution — understanding the religious atmosphere in which it seemed best to function. Weber's approach to the interface of economics and religion was functional in the extreme. In 1920, he wrote tersely: "Interests (material and ideal), not ideas, directly determine man's action. But the world views, which were created by ideas, have very often acted as the switches that channeled the dynamics of the interests."

Weber argued that, in the West, rational planning and a free rein to scientific experiment had both been encouraged by the Protestant outlook. By contrast, in his analyses of Buddhism and Hinduism, Weber's foremost concern was to ask how those religions had inhibited the development of capitalism. He brought along his own cultural arrogances and relied on highly inadequate European researches, leaving his text riddled with misconceptions as to Buddhist thought. In his account of Buddhism, Weber showed himself in thrall to Schopenhauer: "All men's toil and trouble, whatever illusory cover they may use to clothe themselves before themselves and others, has, in the end, this last single meaning: the will to live. This will in its metaphysical meaninglessness is what ultimately holds life together. It is this which produces *karma*. The task is to destroy the will if one wishes to escape *karma*." Weber's sociological conclusions as to the sluggishness of Buddhist values were in neat agreement with the views long put forward by Protestant missionaries, who insisted that moribund Buddhist populations required the injection of Christian faith.

Nonetheless, Weber's emphasis on the social and economic impacts of Buddhism continues to inspire sociologists, economists, and anthropologists both in India and in the West. For Weber raised issues that have since been taken up — in a radically different manner, as we shall later examine — by the current-day Engaged Buddhism movement. One of the elements of the Eightfold Noble Path is Right Livelihood, which may be interpreted simply as earning an honest living or more broadly as participation in or resistance to prevailing economic systems. Although Weber's broad acceptance of capitalism is not always shared by Engaged Buddhists, there is a shared vision of the relevance of Buddhism to macroeconomic societal issues. That is a relatively new emphasis in Buddhist thought, Western or Eastern, and although Weber was not in the least bit personally inspired by Buddhism, he did lay the groundwork for that outlook.

❖

Martin Heidegger (1889–1976), the only Nazi to have retained his status as a great philosopher in the Western academic canon, was keenly aware of the dilemma of globalization. Heidegger referred to the "complete Europeanization of the earth and of mankind." He viewed the triumph of "Europeanization" — which he regarded with mixed feelings — as a logical outcome of the Western philosophic tradition, which had, from the time of the Greeks, emphasized objectification of, manipulation of, and dominion over the material world, with a consequent loss of awareness as to matters of inner consciousness and experience. Heidegger called this loss a "forgetfulness of being."

Such was, for Heidegger, the inescapable East-West duality. As he wrote,

> To say that philosophy is in essence Greek is the same as to say that the Occident and Europe, and they alone, are in their inmost historical course originally philosophical. This is proved by the rise and domination of the sciences. Because they originate from the inmost Occidental-European course of history, namely the philosophical, therefore they are today in a position to give their specific stamp upon the history of man on the whole earth.

At the same time, Heidegger acknowledged the onset of "the inescapable dialogue with the East Asian World." The challenge inherent in the dialogue fascinated him. For Heidegger, the quest to reach "beyond Occident and Orient" was both essential and problematic. The course he recommended, as explained by the German scholar Wilhelm Halbfass, was " '*Gelassenheit*,' a serene willingness to wait, and *not* to plan for the future."

The methodical and conclusive research of the German philosopher and scholar Reinhard May has established that the debt owed by Heidegger to his readings of Daoist and Zen Buddhist texts was far greater than Heidegger ever acknowledged in his lifetime. Indeed, "debt" is too faint a term for what became, at times, outright plagiarism. May summarized his findings, first published in 1989, in the manner of a legal brief:

> The investigation concludes that Heidegger's work was significantly influenced by East Asian sources. It can be shown, moreover, that in particular instances Heidegger even appropriated wholesale and almost verbatim major ideas from the German translations of Daoist and Zen Buddhist classics. This clandestine textual appropriation of non-Western spirituality, the extent of which has gone undiscovered for so long, seems quite unparalleled, with far-reaching implications for our future interpretation of Heidegger's work.

Graham Parkes, a senior fellow at Harvard University's Center for the Study of World Religions, served as May's English translator. Parkes adjudged that "the evidence from Reinhard May's textual comparisons suggests overwhelmingly that a major impetus for Heidegger's 'new beginning' (as he himself calls it) — for the trajectory of a path of thinking that is to lead beyond (or around or beneath) Western metaphysics — came from non-Western sources about which he maintained an all but complete silence."

The key borrowings identified by May derive principally from Daoist sources, including German translations by Martin Buber and Richard Wilhelm of the *Zhuangzi* (more familiar to Western readers, perhaps, as the works of Chuang Tzu). Heidegger also drew from an anthology of Zen Buddhist texts — the first to be translated into German — titled *Zen — Living Buddhism in Japan* (1925). The translator, the Japanese Zen Buddhist layman Ohasama Shuei, discussed therein the paradoxical nature of nirvana as a nothingness that is also the ultimate plenitude of being. Heidegger met personally over the decades with a number of Japanese and Chinese philosophers, including D. T. Suzuki. In 1946, with Paul Shih-yi Hsiao as collaborator, Heidegger commenced and abandoned a German translation of passages from the *Laozi*.

The overriding aim of Heidegger's work was to cut through the thickets of formulaic conceptions with which, he believed, philosophy had, since the time of the earliest Greek thinkers, fashioned intricate shackles for Western consciousness. There were, of course, conceptions that became central to Heidegger's own metaphysics — notably "Being" and "Nothing." May's summation of the extent of Heidegger's unacknowledged Eastern borrowings leaves no doubt that they went to the heart of his lifelong philosophical efforts:

In so far as Heidegger's work has been influenced by East Asian sources, it is not simply a matter of peripheral topics that are thought about merely incidentally. In the case of the *topos* "Nothing" it is a matter — bearing in mind the locution "Nothing and Being the Same" — of *the* major idea, the "only one" the thinker needs; a matter, then, of an idea that is new to Western thinking, and which Heidegger owes to insight into the teachings of *dao* in the *Laozi* and *Zhuangzi*. [. . .] Corresponding

Daoist– and Zen Buddhist–tinged paraphrases are to be found, in more or less encoded form, throughout the work that has been published so far.

The potential for linkage between the Zen Buddhist outlook and militarism was also a subject of fascination for Heidegger. As Parkes observed, Heidegger would likely have known of the Zen-inspired Bushido outlook through a work by Okakura Kakuzō, *The Ideals of the East with Special Reference to the Art of Japan* (1903), which was widely read in Europe and America in the first decades of the twentieth century. Okakura was an inspirational teacher to Kuki Shūzō, one of the Japanese philosophers who met frequently with Heidegger in 1920s Germany. Parkes noted the similarity between Bushido and

the existential conception of death in *Being and Time*. This characterization of the idea of "running forward" to engage one's death, in particular, reads like a passage from a Zen swordsmanship manual: "When *Dasein* by running forward to its death lets death assume power over it, it understands itself, free for death, in the superior power of its own finite freedom in order to . . . become clear-sighted for whatever might befall in the situation thus revealed. . . . Only a being that is essentially *futural* in its being, such that, free for its death and shattering itself [*zerschellend*] against it, it can let itself be thrown back on to its actual situation . . . can be *momentary* [*augenblicklich*] for 'its time.'"

It is fair to say that Western scholarship is still digesting the implications of having one of its signal thinkers indebted deeply to the East. The point was stressed by both May and Parkes that Heidegger's borrowings should not cost him his status as a great philosopher. Parkes noted rather that "the question is whether the provenance of that philosophy is as exclusively Graeco-Teutonic as its author would have us believe." May, with a clipped, subtle irony, pointed beyond provenance to the future of Heidegger studies and, by implication, the future of the study of what has been called "Western Philosophy": "In order to gain a new perspective from this 'Heidegger case,' we in the West will have to devote ourselves to *non-Western* thinking as thoroughly as to that of our own tradition, not least since Heidegger has, in his own special way, demonstrated the necessity of *transcultural* thinking."

This conclusion might be paraphrased as saying that, after the genus-and-species examinations of Hegel, after the expansive appreciations of Schopenhauer and the bristling assessments of Nietzsche, it was Heidegger who, with his thefts, brought about a deep and irrevocable enmeshment of Western thought with Eastern. It was as if Heidegger lit a fuse timed to explode sometime after his death — for surely he could not have believed that the adoration of his work would not ultimately lead to the most scrupulous researches as to its sources.

Thus far, the scholars who have probed at the borrowings have refrained from theorizing as to why Heidegger behaved as he did. There are no clear facts on which to base an answer. But in the context of this discussion of Buddhism and the West, it seems necessary to ask a few further questions, if not to answer them.

Heidegger has been the subject of furious academic debate, given the ongoing influence of his writings and the fact of his having been a public advocate of the Nazi regime of Adolf Hitler. Thus far, this debate has not addressed the possibility that Heidegger's Nazi allegiance — and the racist suppositions that underlay such allegiance — might have influenced his decision to steal from non-Aryan sources.

Heidegger was willing, very rarely, to confirm his fascination with the East. The American scholar William Barrett reported in the 1950s that "a German friend of Heidegger told me that one day when he visited Heidegger he found him reading one of Suzuki's books. 'If I understand this man correctly,' Heidegger remarked, 'this is what I have been trying to say in all my writings.'" That Heidegger owned and read the first volume of D. T. Suzuki's *Essays in Zen Buddhism* was established by the testimony of Nishitani Keiji, a Japanese philosopher who, while studying in Germany, met with Heidegger in 1938. Barrett's anecdote, admittedly secondhand, has often been regarded as implausible. But there is further testimony, from a German philosophical colleague of Heidegger, who reported that in conversation with a Buddhist monk from Thailand in 1964, Heidegger listened as the monk explained that "nothingness is not 'nothing,' but rather the completely other: fullness. No one can name it. But it — nothing and everything — is fulfillment." Heidegger's response: "That is what I have been saying, my whole life long."

It is impossible not to see the current Western reputations of Heidegger and Suzuki (who is discussed in greater detail in chapter 8) as strangely, very strangely, intertwined. Heidegger and Suzuki both supported the fascist imperialist ambitions of their respective nations. Neither of them saw in Buddhism a contradiction to their politics. Heidegger remains a controversial but firmly established member of the Western philosophical canon. Suzuki is currently rebuked for having put forth in his writings a militaristic and racialist conception of Japanese Zen Buddhism. In their works, as Heidegger himself is said to have allowed, there is an essential unity of vision.

❖

Heidegger was not the only German thinker with a Nazi affiliation to have been drawn to the teachings of Buddhism. Heinrich Harrer, the author of *Seven Years in Tibet* (1953), is the most famous — and acknowledged — example. Eugen Herrigel (1884–1955), who taught philosophy at the University of Tokyo for a time, published late in his life one of the most popular books on Zen ever written by a Westerner, *Zen in the Art of Archery* (1953), with a glowing introduction by Suzuki. Neither Suzuki in his introduction nor the author biographies in subsequent American editions of the work make mention of Herrigel's Nazi involvement. It is worth noting, in connection with the current ubiquity of the term "Zen" in Western culture, that perhaps no other book title has been imitated quite so often as Herrigel's, with the permutations ranging from "Motorcycle Maintenance" to "Dating" to "Dying."

6

THE RISE OF THEOSOPHY
AND THE "GREAT GAME"

❖

The considerable impact of the Theosophical Society on the spread of Buddhism in the West is a matter of general agreement. But disagreements continue as to just why its impact was so great and whether it ought to have had any influence at all, given the enigmatic nature and disrespectable methods of the society's founder, Helena Petrovna Blavatsky (1831–1891).

In 1899, very near the end of his life, Friedrich Max Müller, the preeminent British Orientalist of his era, who had witnessed firsthand the charismatic successes enjoyed by Blavatsky in London, offered this final exasperated assessment:

> I have often been blamed for the hard judgments which I have pronounced against Madame Blavatsky and her friends. I have been told that she and her friends have done good by rousing a new interest in their ancient philosophy among the people of India, and by attracting the attention of European thinkers towards it. If that is so, let it be to their credit; but I feel convinced that no good has ever come out of anything that is not perfectly honest and straightforward; and what a lurid light has been thrown upon the Theosophist Society at Adyar!

It is the central paradox of the Theosophical Society that its writings on Buddhism, by Blavatsky and others, were sometimes blatantly inaccurate as to matters of fact and even of basic doctrine — and yet there were many, in Europe, America, and even Asia, who were spurred by those writings to pursue a deeper understanding of Buddhist practice. The flamboyant style of Blavatsky and her followers succeeded in presenting to the West, for the first time, a Buddhism that was neither the crude pagan faith portrayed by the Christian missionaries nor the abstruse creed of nothingness detailed by Müller and his fellow Orientalists, but rather a living spiritual path that could serve the needs of Western aspirants. The flamboyance was essential to this success, for the lure of an exotic and hitherto unrevealed Dharma was just the bait needed to instill not merely interest but passion in scores of disaffected Western seekers.

❖

Blavatsky was born in the Ukraine region; her father was a military man and her mother a novelist. She married at age eighteen, but the union ended when Blavatsky left her husband to pursue travels that extended for some two decades and included considerable time in Egypt, the Caucasus, and Mediterranean Europe. According to Blavatsky, this period of roughly 1850 to 1870 also included years of occult study in Shigatse in Tibet, where resided two Mahatmas (or "Great Souls") of Indian birth, Koot Hoomi and Morya.

Whether Blavatsky ever reached Tibet cannot be confirmed, but thanks largely to the researches of the American scholar K. Paul Johnson, it is clear that she did make contact with a number of spiritual teachers during these decades, including Paulos Metamon, a Coptic magus; the Jewish Egyptian Sufi, Freemason, and playwright James Sanua; Sanua's teacher, the Sufi Jamal ad-Din al-Afghani; and the French spiritualist and occultist Victor Michal. But there are no known contacts with Buddhists prior to her founding, with Henry Steel Olcott, of the Theosophical Society in 1875 and the publication of her first major work, *Isis Unveiled* (1877). In a November 1877 letter, Blavatsky took great care to distance herself from the term "Spiritualism" that she had so recently extolled:

> Let us settle, once and for all if you please, as to the word "Spiritualist."
> I am not one — not at least in the modern and American sense of the
> word. I am a Svabhavika, a Buddhist pantheist, if anything at all. I do not

believe in a *personal* God, in a direct Creator, or a "Supreme"; neither do I confess to a *First* cause, which implies the possibility of a *Last* one — and if so, then what comes next? I believe in but one eternal, indestructible substance, the Svabhavat, or invisible, all pervading matter, whether you call it God, or many Gods in partnership.

In 1878, Blavatsky and Olcott voyaged to India, where they promptly founded a journal, the *Theosophist*. After a year of extensive travel in both India and Sri Lanka, during which time Theosophical Society membership swelled in those lands, Blavatsky and Olcott underwent, on May 25, 1880, a *pansil* ceremony in which they swore — the first known Caucasians ever to do so — to follow the Five Vows of Buddhism. Presiding was H. Sumangala Unnanse, chief monk of the Theravada temple at Adam's Peak in Sri Lanka. Olcott later explained the spirit in which he and Blavatsky had taken their vows: "If Buddhism contained a single dogma that we were compelled to accept, we would not have taken the pansil nor remained Buddhists ten minutes. Our Buddhism was that of the Master-Adept Gautama Buddha, which was identically the Wisdom Religion of the Aryan Upanishads, and the soul of all the ancient world-faiths." It was, both Blavatsky and Olcott believed, the role of the Theosophical Society to discern and foster this essential truth in Buddhism, and to ignore or rebuke as "debased" those Buddhist practices that seemed insufficiently universalist.

In the decade that followed, the influence of the Theravadan Unnanse would fade for Blavatsky. She soon claimed to be receiving teachings from two great Mahatmas — Koot Hoomi and Morya — who lived in the fastnesses of Buddhist Tibet, where, as Blavatsky told it, "initiated Arhats retired after the Master's [Buddha's] death" to preserve the esoteric heart of Buddhist wisdom and to "teach all that is now called Theosophical doctrines, because they form part of the knowledge of the initiates." Blavatsky regarded "Northern" Buddhism as far superior to the Theravada school, in which "the truth has been sacrificed to the dead-letter by the too-zealous orthodoxy of Southern Buddhism." The procedure for receiving what became known as the "Mahatma Letters" — written missives from Koot Hoomi and Morya — involved a long-standing practice of Western magic: the peering by an initiate into a mirror or crystal, within which may be perceived a spirit writing, which may then — through "precipitation," as Theosophical practice termed it — be transcribed.

A. P. Sinnett, the president of the London Lodge of the Theosophical Society, published *Esoteric Buddhism* (1883) to convey to the world at large the inner truths of Buddhism as taught by the Mahatmas. For Sinnett, Buddhism was not a distinct historical religion, but rather "the doctrine of the Buddhas, the Wise, i.e. the Wisdom Religion." True Buddhism was the eternal esoteric core of all religions, now revealed anew by the Theosophical Society. The purest of Buddhist teachings had, until the time of Sinnett's writing, "been jealously guarded as a precious heritage belonging to regularly initiated members of mysteriously organized associations" — to Buddhists, one might say. As for the sources of his own knowledge, Sinnett offered an English gentleman's references: "All my inquiries into the subject have convinced me that the Tibetan Brotherhood is incomparably the highest of such associations, and regarded as such by all other associations — worthy of being looked upon themselves as really 'enlightened' in the occult sense of the term." And as for the state of nirvana, Sinnett could assure Western readers leery of encountering nothingness that nirvana was deliciously the opposite — "a sublime state of conscious rest in omniscience." But if Sinnett had hoped to please Blavatsky with his book, he failed. It was her private opinion that Sinnett had revealed overly much of the teachings.

The Society for Psychical Research, based in London, resolved to investigate the grand claims to wisdom of Theosophy by sending Dr. Richard Hodgson to Adyar. His report, published in 1886, declared that Blavatsky had written the "Mahatma Letters" in her own disguised hand, that the delivery of the letters was accomplished not through occult phenomena but by fraud, and that the alleged Mahatmas did not in fact exist. The glamour cast by that mythic fabrication underlay the broad appeal of Theosophy in India, Europe, and North America. In the immediate months and years after Hodgson's report, the society suffered a massive loss of membership.

❖

One organization that drew disaffected Theosophical Society members was the Hermetic Brotherhood of Luxor, an occult order that emphasized the integral role of sexuality in physical and spiritual well-being and circulated the writings of Paschal Beverly Randolph (1825–1875) so as to instruct its members on specific techniques of esoteric sexual practice. This emphasis was in sharp contrast to the Victorian prudishness of the Theosophical Society. Randolph, a nineteenth-century African American born in the slums of New York City, first rose to prominence as a master of mediumistic trance who performed before European royalty. He was also a novelist, an educator who worked with black freedmen during the Civil War, and a prominent Rosicrucian, who claimed to be restoring the true wisdom of that venerable order, which, in Randolph's view, had included Hermes Trismegistus, Thoth, and the Buddha, among many others.

In the course of his travels in Europe, Egypt, and the Ottoman Empire, Randolph became personally acquainted with a wide range of spiritual teachers, including, in the late 1850s, the British writer Hargrave Jennings, an audodidact whose bizarre conception of Buddhism influenced not only Randolph but a host of other American and European occultists of the late nineteenth century. In *The Indian Religions; or, Results of the Mysterious Buddhism* (1858), Jennings drew a parallel between Buddhism and spiritual phallic worship, thus following in the footsteps of the Irish scholar Henry O'Brien, discussed in chapter 4. But Jennings won a far greater readership due to his penchant for murkily hinting at the grandest of mysteries:

> The old Buddhists — as equally as the ancient believers in the doctrine of the Universal Spiritual Fire — held that Spirit Light was the floor or basis of all created things. The material side or complement of this Spiritual Light being Fire, into which element all things could be rendered; and which (or Heat) was the motive of all things that are. They taught that matter or mind — as the superflux — as the sum of sensations, or as natural and unreal shows of their various kinds — were piled, as layer on layer or tissue on tissue, on this immutable and immortal floor or groundwork of Divine Flame, the Soul of the World.

Randolph also made personal contact with Buddhist practitioners. In his *After Death* (1868), he claimed to have joined an unnamed Buddhist group "of the better land" (perhaps a Chinese Pure Land *sangha* in America) for an unspecified time, only to break from them at last because of their refusal to believe in the immortality of souls:

> Once, when *en rapport* with a vast brotherhood of learned Buddhists, of the better land, they taught, and I believed, that there would come a period when man would be so pure and perfect as to lose his identity, and be swallowed up in God — be absorbed into the Great Brahm, a component of whom he would then become. Somewhere, in one of the many books I have written, that idea has its place.[. . .] I now believe in our continued existence as humans, — in ascending orders and hierarchies.

❖

Despite the loss of prestige and membership suffered by the Theosophical Society, Blavatsky was, by her own account, somewhat relieved by the public disclosures brought forth by the Society for Psychical Research. In an 1886 letter to Sinnett, Blavatsky emphasized that the latter society's investigator, Hodgson, had failed to identify the actual living sources behind the letters, and hence had left undisturbed the living sources of the wisdom to which she had devoted her life: "What saved the situation in the *Report* is that the Masters *are absolutely denied.*"

In spite of the fraudulent methods employed in the creation of the "Mahatma Letters," there were living personages from whom, in the 1880s, Blavatsky received Buddhist teachings. Although the identities of those who contributed to the content of the "Mahatma Letters" cannot be established, K. Paul Johnson speculated cogently that the two key figures involved — the "real" Morya and Koot Hoomi — were, respectively, Ranbir Singh and Thakar Singh. Ranbir was a Hindu maharaja of Kashmir who promoted religious tolerance among his populace of Hindu, Muslim, Buddhist, Sikh, and Christian believers. He may have facilitated contact between Blavatsky and Tibetan Buddhist teachers and texts. Thakar was a Punjabi reformer who promoted Sikh education and cultural awareness. He was also an opponent of Christian missionary efforts and of the Raj. Neither Ranbir nor Thakar wrote the "Mahatma Letters," but both served as inspirations to Blavatsky, who in all likelihood was their principal author.

The choice of Tibet as Blavatsky's sources' alleged place of residence was based in part on convenience — Shigatse was not within reach of any but the most curious visitors. There was an emotional link as well, for Blavatsky, as a child, had been taken by her grandfather, a Russian imperial administrator, to visit lands near Astrakhan settled by the Kalmucks, a tribe that practiced Tibetan Buddhism. Blavatsky met Prince Tumen, the Kalmuck leader, and a Tibetan lama in attendance on the prince. They left an impression on her.

But there was a third, more pertinent basis for the choice of Shigatse. Leaving aside her own unproven assertion of years spent studying in Tibet, there remains clear evidence that two men with whom Blavatsky was well acquainted, Sarat Chandra Das and Ugyen Gyatso, had made contact with Tibetan Buddhists in Shigatse. Das, a Hindu Indian educator and author who published an account of his travels to Lhasa and central Tibet, was the most masterful of the *pundits,* or British-trained Indian spies, who, while posing as seekers of Buddhist wisdom, gathered information for the Raj. Gyatso, a lama of Tibetan ancestry, found work in the Bengal Education Department, where Das also was employed. Thereafter, the Raj made them an espionage team. Their first journey to Tibet was in 1879, and their chief destination was Shigatse, to which they returned in 1881. Gyatso made a further solo foray into Tibet in 1883, returning with a detailed guide to Tibetan geography.

While fulfilling their missions, Das and Gyatso also pursued their genuine shared interest in mastering the Tibetan language and studying Tibetan Buddhism. In 1892, more than a decade after returning to India, Das founded the influential Buddhist Text Society. He also compiled, with the help of Gyatso, a Tibetan-English dictionary. Das ultimately received the Companion of the Order of the Indian Empire, ostensibly for his cultural achievements. But his true fame rests in Rudyard Kipling's use of him as the model for the fictional Indian master spy Hurree Chunder Mookerjee in the novel *Kim* (1901).

In that novel, Kipling also created the first fully drawn Buddhist character in English literature, a Tibetan lama — he is never given a name — with whom the young orphan Kim journeys through India. Kim imbibes the depths of Buddhist wisdom from the lama, whose *chela,* or devoted student, Kim becomes. The characterization is not free of unintended caricature. The most prominent example of this is the Tibetan lama's bizarre espousal, early in the narrative, of the standard deprecatory view of "Northern" Buddhism held by British Orientalists. In Tibet, the lama laments, "the Old Law was not well followed; being overlaid, as thou knowest, with devildom, charms, and idolatry." Nonetheless, Kipling, a Freemason whose views on religious tolerance were in advance of most of his contemporaries', fashioned, in the narrative of *Kim,* a portrayal of Buddhism that exceeds in sympathy even Edwin Arnold's *Light of Asia.* For Kim, a boy of Anglo-Irish heritage, becomes — in essence, though not as a matter of formal ritual — a convert to Tibetan Buddhism, or at least the Tibetan Buddhism of Kipling's imagination.

The chief — and unwitting — assistance to the espionage efforts of Das and Gyatso in and around Shigatse came from Sengchen Tulku, an esteemed lama and minister to the Panchen Lama. Sengchen took the travelers at their word that they were interested students of Buddhism. As Sengchen administered the extensive Tashilhunpo monastic library, Das was able to obtain numerous Sanskrit Mahayana texts with Tibetan annotations — a trove largely unknown to the West. It was by means of Das and his scholarly labors that Blavatsky was able to obtain Tibetan Buddhist teachings of genuine value.

If this seems an overstatement, consider the fate of her book *The Voice of the Silence* (1889), which consisted, according to Blavatsky, of excerpted translations from *The Book of the Golden Precepts,* which she described as "one of the works put into the hands of mystic students in the East." (The original text of this putative work has never come to light.) The style of these "translations" strongly resembles that of Blavatsky's original works — an impassioned and insistent teaching voice, as in this passage on Buddhist realization:

> Believe thou not that sitting in dark forests, in proud seclusion and apart from men; believe thou not that life on roots and plants, that thirst assuaged with snow from the great Range — believe thou not, O devotee, that this will lead thee to the goal of final liberation. [. . .] The blessed ones have scorned to do so. The Lion of the Law, the Lord of Mercy [the Buddha], perceiving the true cause of human woe, immediately forsook the sweet but selfish rest of quiet wilds. [. . .] Sow kindly acts and thou shalt reap their fruit. Inaction in a deed of mercy becomes an action in a deadly sin.

Regardless of its actual origins, an impressive array of Asian Buddhist experts, including D. T. Suzuki, testified that *The Voice of the Silence* was a worthy presentation of Mahayana teachings. A 1927 edition of the book was published by the Chinese Buddhist Research Society in Beijing at the urging of the Ninth Panchen Lama (who included a prefatory verse of his own urging "all beings to enter the path"). In 1989, a centenary edition of the book was published with a foreword by the Fourteenth Dalai Lama, who wrote of having first met with Theosophists in the 1950s and having since "had the pleasure of sharing my thoughts with Theosophists from various parts of the world on many occasions. I have much admiration for their spiritual pursuits. [. . .] I believe that this book has strongly influenced many sincere seekers and aspirants to the wisdom and compassion of the Bodhisattva Path." To place this praise in fair context, it must be remembered that the Dalai Lama was not here endorsing all that Blavatsky had written on Tibet. He considered the Frenchwoman Alexandra David-Neel, a onetime Theosophist and a famous twentieth-century traveler to Tibet, to be "the first to introduce the real Tibet to the West."

During the late 1800s, Britain, Russia, and China were engaged in a competition, called the "Great Game" by Kipling and others, to gain the upper hand in central Asia, particularly Tibet, which was seen as strategically vital for control over southern and eastern Asia. For its part, Tibet was exceedingly anxious to evade British or any other foreign domination. Just how anxious is conveyed by the fate meted out — by order of the Thirteenth Dalai Lama — to Sengchen Tulku once his unwitting service to Das and Gyatso was discovered. The British historian Peter Hopkirk wrote:

He was arrested, imprisoned, flogged, then flung — still living and with his hands tied behind his back — into the Tsangpo [River]. The hands and feet of his servants had been cut off, their eyes gouged out, and they were left to die in agony. Furthermore the official himself [Sengchen], a high-ranking lama at the head of a monastery, was condemned posthumously to eternal damnation — a punishment more to be dreaded than death by a devout Tibetan Buddhist. When, soon after his execution, his reincarnation appeared in a small boy, the child was callously abandoned.

Frontier officials who had let the intruder [Das] past the check-point were also severely punished, and nineteen years later two other men who had been implicated were still in chains in a Lhasa dungeon.

Such was the cost of the transmission of Tibetan Buddhist teachings to Blavatsky and the Theosophical Society.

❖

It was not Blavatsky and her followers, however, but the renowned Christian apologist G. K. Chesterton (1874–1936) who exemplified the mainstream Edwardian response to Buddhism. As Chesterton emphasized, Christendom — led by the British Empire — believed in the dual enlivening possibilities of societal progress and of heavenly redemption. By contrast, the Buddhist aspiration to rid oneself of earthly desires, without hope — as Chesterton viewed it — of a better hereafter, was tantamount to a despairing hatred of existence. Chesterton was at pains to controvert those Western thinkers who had begun to posit that Christianity and Buddhism were, at root, one in their spiritual outlook. It had been argued, Chesterton recounted with satiric glee,

> that both Christ and Buddha were called by the divine voice coming out of the sky, as if you would expect the divine voice to come out of the coal-cellar. Or, again, it was gravely urged that these two Eastern teachers, by a singular coincidence, both had to do with the washing of feet. You might as well say that it was a remarkable coincidence that they both had feet to wash. [. . .] That Buddhism approves of mercy or of self-restraint is not to say that it is specially like Christianity; it is only to say that it is not utterly unlike human existence. [. . .] All humanity does agree that we are in a net of sin. Most of humanity agrees that there is some way out. But as to what is the way out, I do not think that there are two institutions in the universe which contradict each other so flatly as Buddhism and Christianity.

For Chesterton, and for the dominant majority of like-minded Western religionists, Buddhism represented nothing so much as a failure of nerve — an ignoble flight from reality.

Blavatsky always retained a flagrant arrogance toward Christian apologists and Orientalist scholars alike, whose knowledge of Buddhism could not compare — she was certain — to her own. To be sure, the limitations of that knowledge made Blavatsky, at times, as misleading and biased an interpreter of Buddhism as any Orientalist. Her insistence on the superiority of "Northern" Buddhism was coupled with an ignorance of the range of Buddhist practice in China and Japan. Hence Blavatsky could assert that the Sukhavati, or Western Paradise, of Pure Land Buddhism was believed only by "the uneducated rabble."

But Blavatsky did find, and transmit in her own style, Tibetan Buddhist teachings hitherto unknown to her readers. The war in the West between the esoteric and academic approaches to Buddhism had been declared. The academicians would do their part by continuing — to the present day, with rare exceptions — to treat Theosophy and Blavatsky as unworthy of address.

❖

Colonel Henry Steel Olcott (1832–1907) became what seems a startling anomaly to current sensibilities — an American Theosophist and convert to Theravada Buddhism, whose work on behalf of the Sinhalese Buddhist Revival in British Ceylon, including the design for what is now the Sri Lankan flag, is still commemorated in Sri Lanka each February 17 by way of prayers in Theravada temples. In Sri Lankan schoolrooms, students are not only familiar with Olcott's photograph but also receive religious training from his *Buddhist Catechism* and respectfully refer to him as the "White Buddhist." In India, where Olcott also worked for religious reform and revival of both Buddhism and Hinduism, his birthday continues to be celebrated in Adyar, the suburb of Madras in which the headquarters of the Theosophical Society was established by Olcott and Blavatsky.

Yet Olcott is scarcely remembered in his native land. His résumé might have attracted greater interest from historians had it not included fascinations with spiritualism, Theosophy, and Buddhism — all three viewed as disreputable by the prevailing American culture during Olcott's lifetime and, indeed, to this day. But if his name remains obscure in the West, his impact has not, for Olcott was the first Western Buddhist to take a leadership role in the Asian Buddhist community and to claim sufficient commitment to the Dharma to teach it to Asians and

Westerners alike. This latter claim has since raised hackles among many Asian and Western Buddhists, not only because of the hubris involved — and hubris it can fairly be seen to be — but also because of the perceived transformation of Buddhist teaching in the hands of Olcott, an American Protestant born and bred. Both Olcott and his ally (for a time), the Sri Lankan lay Buddhist leader Anagarika Dharmapala, have been accused of promulgating a "Protestant Buddhism" — one that stresses and celebrates economic and political endeavor as opposed to the reclusive monastic practices of the Theravada tradition. It has been frequently noted that this "Protestant Buddhism" was an influential forebear of the Engaged Buddhism of today — although the former embraced capitalism without critical complaint, while the latter is decidedly critical of the capitalistic world economy.

Olcott was born into a New Jersey Presbyterian family but held heterodox religious views and yearnings from his early teens. During the Civil War, he served in the Union army as a signals officer. After the war, he launched successful careers in New York as both a reformist attorney and a journalist. In the latter role, he reported the spiritualist claims of contact with the dead which were then so prominent a topic of discussion and wonder. In his writing, Olcott took the stance of an occult believer distressed by the shams of fraudulent mediums. The shared dream of reforming spiritualism led to his friendship with Blavatsky.

The two first met in New York in 1873. Plainly, Blavatsky and Olcott were kindred spirits in terms of their devotion to esoteric wisdom. Whether they had an affair is not known, but the presence of at least a tacit erotic current between them seems clear from the fact that, for the remainder of the decade, their marriages fell into disarray while they remained devoted to each other — often sharing living quarters in New York and other global venues — and to the cause of the Theosophical Society, which they founded in 1875. Blavatsky was the expansive thinker and public speaker, while Olcott served as the canny backstage strategist. Under their guidance, the Theosophical Society achieved a rapid international success that remained the envy of subsequent Western occult sodalities.

Olcott began corresponding with Asian spiritual leaders in 1877. When he and Blavatsky landed in Bombay in February 1879, Olcott's first action, as he later wrote, "was to stoop down and kiss the granite step; my instinctive act of pooja! For here we were at last on sacred soil." The Raj was at first suspicious of Olcott and the Theosophists, going so far as to order surveillance of them. But in the summer of 1879, Olcott met with Sir Richard Temple, the British governor of Bengal, to assure him that the activities of the Theosophists would in no manner conflict with British rule. The surveillance ceased, and Olcott was as good as his word — his mission was religious, not political, reform, and he remained blithely confident that he could keep such matters separate in a colonial and missionized southern Asia.

Olcott was a formidable advocate on behalf of Asian spiritual wisdom. In an early issue of the *Theosophist* — a monthly journal widely read by English-speaking Indians and featuring determinedly eclectic writings by Hindu, Zoroastrian, Muslim, and Buddhist authors — Olcott set forth a defiant challenge to Christianity: "There is no adequate proof to my mind either that Jesus was the Son of God, that he said or did the things ascribed to him, that either one of the four gospels is anything better than a literary fabrication, or that Jesus ever lived. . . . [Christianity] is a bad religion and fosters every sin and vice against which its ethical code inveighs." In his later years, Olcott repented his anti-Christian polemics and urged Buddhist leaders such as Dharmapala to refrain from indulging in the same tactics. Dharmapala refused to do so, but then he was embedded in a cultural struggle to which Olcott, for all his sympathy, remained an outsider.

According to an 1815 treaty, the British terms of rule of Ceylon included an express promise that the Buddhist religion "is declared inviolable, and its rites, Ministers and Places of Worship are to be maintained and protected." But by the 1830s, the view of Anglican and other Christian missionaries that India and Ceylon could be more securely ruled were they Christianized had begun to prevail in practice. Hence, by the time Olcott and Blavatsky visited Ceylon in 1880, Christian control of the schools, as well as of civil service functions such as registry of births and marriages, had created a crisis for Buddhist clergy and lay believers. The Sinhalese Buddhist revival had already begun in the years prior to their visit, but there is no question that Olcott stirred it to greater successes by his public lectures and his help in founding independent Buddhist schools.

Olcott's newfound commitment to Ceylon aroused the opposition of

Blavatsky, who claimed that the needs of the Theosophical Society — as declared by the Mahatmas themselves — mandated Olcott's return to the West. Olcott broke with Blavatsky on this matter, embarked on another Ceylon-wide lecture tour, and pursued the approval of Sinhalese Theravada Buddhist teachers for his newly composed *Buddhist Catechism*.

Olcott was, in his Asian efforts, an organizer on a grand scale, although he could never repeat the success that he and Blavatsky had achieved with the Theosophical Society. In Ceylon, he sought to unify the three most prominent Theravada schools into the Buddhist Ecclesiastical Council, which he hoped could contend with the organized efforts of the Christian missionaries in shaping the island's educational policies. In addition, in an attempt to merge the energies of the Theosophical Society with the realities of Sinhalese culture, Olcott founded Buddhist Theosophical Societies for laypeople. In the final decade of his life, he launched the pan-Asian International Buddhist League and proposed a society called the United Buddhist World to stimulate dialogue between Eastern and Western Buddhist practitioners. Olcott even conceived of a Universal Brotherhood of Humanity, which came to naught when its founders quarreled among themselves. He sought to level differences in the pursuit of certain uniting principles — clarity, passion, activism. To these ends, Olcott was prepared to combat Asian divisions in Buddhist practice, as well as the incursions of the Christian West.

In 1890, Olcott reached his apogee as a proponent of Buddhist ecumenism. At a conference held in Adyar, Buddhists from Ceylon, Bangladesh, Burma, and Japan — including representatives of both the Theravada and Mahayana schools — voted to accept the fourteen-point "Buddhist Platform" drafted by Olcott, which he believed contained the essence of the Dharma. This victory confirmed Olcott's hopes for the conference — the creation of "a religious pact of the Buddhist nations, and the unification of the two schools of Buddhistic Philosophy." His biographer Stephen Prothero argued that Olcott's platform

> encompassed an intriguing concatenation of traditional Buddhist and modern western values. In addition to a restatement of the Four Noble Truths and the Five Precepts for lay Buddhists, the fourteen propositions included: an affirmation of religious tolerance and of the evolution of

the universe, a rejection of supernaturalism, heaven and hell, and super-stition, and an emphasis on education and the use of reason.

But it would be only fair to add that these latter values had long been held by many Theravada and Mahayana Buddhists and were hardly im-ported wholesale from the West. Rather, Olcott's achievement was to fashion grounds for abstract doctrinal consensus in which his Western reformist agenda could be merged with the Dharma. For a brief time, as long as the abstractions were not put to the test of real-life application, the consensus held.

Eventually, however, Olcott came to be seen as culturally intrusive by Asian Buddhist leaders, many of whom had early on welcomed his ef-forts. Dharmapala was the most dramatic example. Once mentored by Olcott, he later viewed the older man as bound up in Western concep-tions of religious universalism — and therefore rooted insufficiently in Asian Buddhism and too prone to compromise with Western Christians.

❖

Anagarika Dharmapala (1864–1933) — whose full Buddhist name means "wandering protector of the Dharma" — met Olcott and Blavatsky when he was only nineteen, during their 1880 visit to Ceylon. Born David Hewavitarne, to a pious Sri Lankan Buddhist family, Dharmapala had received and then rejected the training of the Christian missionary schools. Theosophy seemed to him the best path to a living source of Buddhist wisdom. For her part, Blavatsky was so convinced of the potential of the boy that she planned to accept him as her personal *chela* — despite the disapproval of the boy's father. Blavatsky even told the father that his son would die if he did not accompany her back to Adyar. She then changed her course, advising instead that Dharmapala remain in Ceylon, study the Theravada texts of his native land, and de-vote himself to the betterment of the world.

One of the causes that Dharmapala took up, inspired by the writings of Sir Edwin Arnold, was the restoration of the Bodh Gaya shrine and sacred grounds to Buddhist hands. To that end, he founded, in Colombo in 1891, the Bodh Gaya Maha Bodhi Society, with the Theravada monk Unnanse (who had administered the *pansil* vows to Blavatsky and Olcott) as its president and Olcott as its director. The far younger Dharmapala served as its secretary and organized an international Buddhist conference at Bodh Gaya, attended by Buddhist delegates from China, Chittagong, Japan, and Ceylon. Little headway was made with the Raj, which was far more interested in pleasing native Hindus than in placating foreign Buddhists. But the Bodh Gaya cause won the support of the Thirteenth Dalai Lama and other eminent Buddhists, thus serving, despite its ongoing political failure, as an ecumenical force among long-separated Asian Buddhists.

Dharmapala attended, as a representative of Sinhalese Theravada Buddhism, the World Parliament of Religions in Chicago in 1893. This event is often regarded as a turning point in Western public awareness of Buddhism, after which fascination with this strange new Asian religion intensified dramatically. That is an overstatement, as it ignores the prior successes of Blavatsky. But it is certainly true that Buddhism won great attention at the World Parliament. Buddhist leaders were in ample attendance, including not only Dharmapala but also representatives of five Japanese sects — Jodo Shinshu, Nichiren, Shingon, Tendai, and Zen. The alliance between Buddhism and the Theosophical Society was still firm, as evidenced by a ceremony sponsored by the society just days after the World Parliament, in which Dharmapala received the vows of Charles T. Strauss, from a New York City Jewish family, as the first American to convert, in America, to Buddhism.

By 1896, Dharmapala had broken with Olcott and the Theosophical Society to pursue a broad revivalist approach to Buddhism that would later be termed, both with deprecation and admiration, "Protestant Buddhism." Dharmapala conducted three successful lecture tours in America, during the last of which, from 1902 to 1904, he received an extraordinary tribute from Harvard professor William James, a founding figure in modern philosophy and psychology. Dharmapala attended one of James's classes, upon which James declared, "Take my chair. You are better equipped to lecture on psychology than I." After Dharmapala gave a talk on Buddhism, James said, "This is the psychology everybody will be studying twenty-five years from now." Had James extended his time estimate to a century later — the present day — he would have been largely correct, given the current prominence of Buddhist teachings in Western psychotherapy.

Dharmapala was acclaimed in his time in the West, but his most significant legacy lies in his decades of political activism in his native land. A lay Buddhist (until ordination as a monk just prior to his death in 1933), Dharmapala sought to reconcile traditional codes of Buddhist conduct with the realities of a newly emerged capitalist colonial economy. At the same time, he emphasized the proud Buddhist history of Sri Lanka, meaning, for Dharmapala, the proud history of the Sinhalese people. As the Harvard anthropologist Stanley Jeyaraja Tambiah noted, for Dharmapala "nationalism, Buddhism, Sinhala language, and Sinhala race had been fused into a single indivisible reified entity." Tolerance for other races and religions was lacking, in part in response, as Tambiah noted, to widespread "Christian missionary denunciation of 'heathen' beliefs and practices."

In *Sinhala Bauddhaya,* a journal controlled by Dharmapala, sentiments such as this, from a 1912 piece, flourished: "From the day the foreign white man stepped in this country, the industries, habits, and customs of the Sinhalese began to disappear and now the Sinhalese are obliged to fall at the feet of the Coast Moors and Tamils." The journal was banned by the British for its role in inflaming sentiments that led to extensive rioting in Ceylon in 1915. In a subsequent letter to the colonial secretary of state, Dharmapala cast blame for the riots on the Muslim populace, of whom he wrote:

The Muhammadans, an alien people who in the early part of the nineteenth century were common traders, by Shylockian methods became prosperous like the Jews. The Sinhalese, sons of the soil, whose ancestors for 2,358 years had shed rivers of blood to keep the country from alien invaders, . . . today . . . are in the eyes of the British only vagabonds. . . . The alien South Indian Muhammadan comes to Ceylon, sees the neglected, illiterate villagers, without any experience in trade, without any knowledge of any kind of technical industry, and isolated from the whole of Asia on account of his language, religion, and race, and the result is that the Muhammadan thrives and the sons of the soil go to the wall.

Dharmapala had taken in — and then expertly spat back — every hate-filled stereotype of the British colonials and the Christian teachers.

At his death, forty-two years after the founding of the Maha Bodhi Society, Dharmapala vowed to reincarnate as a Brahman so as better to continue the fight within India for the Buddhist liberation of Bodh Gaya. That fight ended before a reincarnated Dharmapala would have had time to reach maturity.

One of the more interesting responses by a non-Buddhist Indian to the issue of Bodh Gaya had been offered in 1923 by Mohandas K. Gandhi, then practicing law in South Africa. There was "no doubt that the possession of the Temple should vest in the Buddhists," Gandhi wrote, with the practical caveat that nothing could be done until "India comes into her own." Gandhi would, in the decades to come, prove to be the leader to bring India into her own. The year after he was assassinated, in 1949, the Indian government tendered Bodh Gaya to Buddhist control.

Sinhalese Buddhist nationalism has continued in force to the present day, and tensions — sometimes escalating into violence — between the Sinhalese and Tamil populations have proven a major obstacle to economic and cultural development in Sri Lanka. This is not to place blame exclusively on Sinhalese Buddhists, but rather to observe that Buddhism, like all religions, can serve as a medium in which nationalism and racism thrive — a fact sometimes forgotten by those in the West who see in Buddhism an ahistorical purity that it does not, and could not, possess.

❖

The political realities of the British Raj, with its control of India and Ceylon and its ambitions toward Tibet, decisively influenced the development of Theosophy. Blavatsky employed the *pundits* of the Raj to gain knowledge of Tibetan Buddhism, as Olcott at once mollified and challenged the British rulers of Ceylon while promoting his reformed version of Buddhism.

Quite beyond the confines of Theosophy, however, Tibet emerged, in the late nineteenth century, to become a central preoccupation for the West in two distinct yet interrelated senses. The Western imperial powers grew to covet Tibet as a holding, and the Western public — spurred on by accounts of Forbidden Lhasa and a mysterious, seldom-photographed Dalai Lama — grew to see it as the locus of the hidden arcane wisdom of the ages. It is to these developments — a kind of parallel history to the myth-laden rise of Theosophy — that we now turn.

❖

Through most of the nineteenth century, the chief concern of the Raj regarding Tibet was to ensure its neutral stability as a buffer state to the north. The Chinese had been recognized by the British as suzerains of Tibet, but that was a nominal concession, for the British conducted their relations with Tibet without regard to Chinese permission or opinion, in accordance with standard British treatment of the Manchu rulers on all matters affecting British political and economic interests. For its part, China sought to maintain its influence in Tibet by informing the Dalai Lama that the Christian governments and missionaries of Britain and the other Western nations sought the demise of Tibetan Buddhism, a claim as to which there was some truth.

Tibet had adopted an isolationist course toward the West since 1792, when Tibet was overrun by Nepalese Gurkha forces and called upon China for military assistance, which was rendered successfully — but at the cost of an ongoing Chinese *Amban* (minister) being stationed in Lhasa. The Chinese insisted that the British had instigated the Nepalese attack and thus the Tibetans remained in need of Chinese protection.

Even in these straitened political circumstances, one young British traveler managed an early journey to Lhasa. Thomas Manning, a Cambridge University dropout who worked for the East India Company in London, dreamed of journeying to China and Tibet. His friend, the English essayist Charles Lamb, sought to dissuade him from seeking the wonders of the Orient, as they were "all poet's invention. Pray try to cure yourself. Take hellebore. Pray to avoid the fiend. Read no more books of voyages, they are nothing but lies." Lamb's judgment here rather strangely resembles the verdict of certain current Western scholars who find pervasive exoticism and distortion in the Orientalist writings of the period. But Manning would not be dissuaded. He got himself assigned to the Chinese branch of the East India Company in 1808, spent three years acquiring a knowledge of Chinese customs and language, and then requested official British sponsorship for his plan to reach Lhasa in the disguise of a Chinese physician. Angered by the prompt refusal, Manning set out on his own from Bhutan — and succeeded.

The city of Lhasa itself he found unprepossessing: "Dirt, dirt, grease, smoke. Misery, but good mutton." Manning revealed his British status in order to obtain interviews with the five-year-old Ninth Dalai Lama, Lungtok Gyatso (1806–1815), and it was in these interviews that Manning found his reward. Of their first meeting, Manning wrote:

> Beautiful youth. Face poetically affecting; could have wept. Very happy to have seen him and his blessed smile. [. . .] He enquired whether I had not met with molestations and difficulties on the road, to which I promptly returned the proper answer. I said that I had had troubles, but now that I had the happiness of being in his presence they were amply compensated, I thought no more of them. I could see that this answer pleased both the Lama and his household peoples.

Manning was interested in pursuing the study of Tibetan Buddhist texts with the assistance of a lama, but the Dalai Lama seems, by Manning's own account, not quite to have trusted this request from an undocumented British envoy: "No doubt my grim beard and spectacles somewhat excited his risibility." The Chinese were entirely unconvinced of Manning's motives, and after some months in Lhasa, he was arrested and deported. Roughly a century later, Sir Charles Bell, the British political representative in Tibet, adjudged, perhaps harshly, that "Manning, the eccentric Englishman who visited Lhasa in 1811, cannot be said to have strengthened the connexion" between Britain and Tibet, which was indeed the achievement of Bell in the first decades of the twentieth century. But Manning, with his ardor, endures — if not as a diplomatic success, then as a prototype of the spiritual seeker for whom the Himalayas were a lure, not an impasse.

Nonetheless, the Tibetan policy through the close of the century remained one of strict isolation from the West. Even trade contacts were viewed as potential threats to the Tibetan Buddhist culture. Ironically, nothing could have been so well calculated to spur interest in Tibet than to make it inaccessible after nearly two centuries — from the time of the first Jesuits to the late eighteenth century — of paying hospitable welcome to those Western visitors who had managed to come so far. The fantasy of an isolated and spiritually mysterious Tibet — which became a spiritually *advanced* Tibet by the early twentieth century, as the fantasy turned inward — led dozens of disguised Western travelers (whose subsequent books were read avidly) to seek out Lhasa.

The political focus of the Great Game was brought to bear on Tibet in 1899, when British intelligence became aware of repeated trips between Lhasa and St. Petersburg by Agvan Dorzhiev (1854–1938), a Buriat Mongol raised within the Russian empire as a Buddhist. At age nineteen, Dorzhiev journeyed to Lhasa and established himself as a monastic student despite stringent prohibitions against foreign residents. His success in blending into Tibetan culture may be measured by his ascension into the inner court of the Thirteenth Dalai Lama, Thubten Gyatso (1876–1933), whose chief political adviser Dorzhiev became in 1895. Dorzhiev saw himself as a sincere advocate of both the Tibetan and the Russian causes, as he believed that the "White Tsar" of Russia — whom Dorzhiev also termed the "Bodhisattva-tsar," thus tacitly placing him alongside the Dalai Lama as an incarnation of the Buddha of compassion — could defend Tibet, as China no longer could, against the encroachments of the British, while also offering benign autonomous shelter to Tibetan Buddhism. Dorzhiev was disappointed in his diplomatic efforts: Russia and Tibet would form no alliance. But Dorzhiev plays a role in our narrative other than as a masterful emissary/spy; he also became the principal teacher, or root guru, of Geshe Wangyal, a Tibetan teacher of great renown. Geshe Wangyal later fled from Chinese-occupied Tibet and founded, in Freehold Acres, New Jersey, in 1955, the first Tibetan Buddhist monastery in the United States. As for Dorzhiev, he died in 1938 in Joseph Stalin's Gulag.

The official Russian stance as to Dorzhiev's visits was that they were purely religious in character — a means by which Nicholas II could stay abreast of the needs of the Buriat Buddhists of Siberia. Britain, now guided in the region by Lord Curzon, the new viceroy of India, took the view that these visits were intended to further Russian aspirations in Tibet, which would, if successful, threaten India itself. But there were further causes for Curzon's displeasure with Tibet. Twice the missives he had sent to the Dalai Lama proposing trade relations had been returned to him unopened. In early 1903, a British trade mission with a small military escort set forth under the command of Colonel Francis Younghusband.

It proceeded as far as Khamba Dzong, just within Tibet's border. The Tibetans refused to negotiate, and after some months the mission returned to India, handing Curzon yet another humiliation, which he refused to bear.

In December 1903, Younghusband again crossed into Tibetan territory, this time with an escort of one thousand Gurkha and Sikh troops under the command of Brigadier General James Macdonald. Slaughters ensued at Guru, the Red Idol Gorge, Karo Pass (at 16,000 feet, the highest site of a major battle in history), and Gyantse. In each case, Tibetan troops armed with matchlock rifles were mowed down by British machine guns. Total casualties suffered by the Tibetans: some 1,600 dead and wounded. Total casualties for the British troops: 9 dead and 43 wounded. The economic superiority of the British also exacted its toll. As Tsepon W. D. Shakabpa noted,

> The morale of the Tibetan army began to suffer for various reasons. It soon became well-known in U-Tsang that the British provided medical aid to the Tibetan wounded, who were later given cash and presents and then set free. Younghusband was known to be sympathetic with the Tibetan soldiers. Moreover, the fact that the British paid well for firewood, grain, and fodder impressed the local inhabitants.

On August 3, 1904, Younghusband fulfilled his long-held personal ambition of entering Lhasa, the Forbidden City no longer. The Dalai Lama had been forced to interrupt an intended three-year meditation to escape the city, thus making it impossible for Younghusband to find anyone with whom to negotiate the trade and access concessions that he had been ordered to obtain. The Chinese now stepped forward to appoint an elderly regent who would act in the stead of the Dalai Lama, whose flight, the Chinese held, constituted a de facto abandonment of his leadership post. A contrary Tibetan version of these events has the Dalai Lama himself appointing the regent prior to leaving Lhasa for Mongolia to the north. Sir Charles Bell, who served in Tibet in the years following the Younghusband expedition and befriended the Thirteenth Dalai Lama, offered this account: "The Chinese government took the opportunity of issuing a proclamation deposing the Dalai Lama. This the Tibetans entirely declined to recognize. They bespattered the proclamation with dirt and, throughout the long exile of His Holiness, continued to refer to him all important questions affecting the welfare of the country."

The newly appointed regent came to serve both British and Chinese interests, as the Chinese wanted British troops to depart from Tibet, treaty in hand, as soon as possible — which they did, a mere seven weeks after their arrival. But many of the treaty points obtained by Younghusband were, within a year, unilaterally watered down by Britain itself, which no longer viewed Russia, now defeated in the Russo-Japanese War, as its principal rival in Asia. Germany was the dreaded new foe, and Russia could be placated in Tibet. There was, after all, a reason why central Asian politics were called the Great Game by the participants themselves. By the end of the decade, the European powers had found issues closer to home over which to quarrel — issues that would escalate into the First World War. As for Tibet, due to the weakness of the tottering Manchu dynasty, it was able to expel, in 1913, Chinese troops that had invaded three years earlier. In 1950, however, China would again invade Tibet and remain, continuing to control the country to this day.

The story of Colonel Younghusband, and the lasting impact of Lhasa on him, strays outside the political maneuvering that led to his military incursion of Tibet. As Younghusband later wrote, he had, on his final day in Tibet, received an image of the Buddha from the Tibetan regent:

> He was full of kindliness, and at that moment more nearly approached Kipling's Lama in "Kim" than any other Tibetan I met. We were given to understand that the presentation by so high a Lama to those who were not Buddhists of an image of Buddha himself was no ordinary compliment. And as the reverend old Regent rose from his seat and put the present into my hand, he said with real impressiveness that he had none of the riches of this world and could only offer me this simple image. Whenever he looked upon an image of Buddha he thought only of peace, and he hoped that whenever I looked on it I would think kindly of Tibet.

Later that day, alone on horseback in the Himalayan outskirts of the city, Younghusband the conqueror was transformed in his view of the conquered:

As I now looked towards that mysterious purply haze in which the sacred city was once more wrapped, I no longer had cause to dread the hatred it might hide. From it came only the echoes of the Lama's words of peace. And with all the warmth still on me of that impressive farewell message, and bathed in the insinuating influences of that dreamy autumn evening, I was insensibly suffused with an almost intoxicating sense of elation and good-will. This exhilaration of the moment grew and grew till it thrilled through me with overpowering intensity. Never again could I think evil, or ever again be at enmity with any man. All nature and all humanity were bathed in a rosy glowing radiancy; and life for the future seemed nought but buoyancy and light. [. . .] And that single hour on leaving Lhasa was worth all the rest of a lifetime.

But Younghusband did not regret the British incursion, which he felt justified by the aim of uniting humankind: "Independence, indeed, we may respect, but surely not isolation. To individuality we may allow the fullest play, but hardly to unsociality."

Younghusband was later knighted for his service in India. He resigned from the military in his late forties to pursue the goal of religious harmony, founding, to this end, the World Congress of Faiths. Younghusband died in 1942. The statue of the Buddha that the Tibetan regent had given him remained his most prized possession, and his daughter placed it on his coffin. Upon his tombstone was a carved relief of the Lhasa he had unveiled to the West in 1904, and below it this text: "Blessed are the pure in heart, for they shall see God."

Yet it was not Younghusband who would have the greatest impact on his contemporaries in their understanding of Tibetan Buddhism. Instead, it was the chief medical officer on Younghusband's expedition. Laurence Austine Waddell, of Scottish Presbyterian background, who emerged as the leading savant in the field with the publication of *The Buddhism of Tibet, or Lamaism* (1895). While stationed in Darjeeling in the 1880s, Waddell took a pronounced — perhaps even an obsessive — interest in the history and doctrines of Lamaism, while at the same time maintaining a hearty distaste for what he viewed as a priest-driven degenerative form of Buddhism that indulged in devil worship. He also made much of the supposed parallels between Lamaism and Catholicism, terming the Dalai Lama the "Lamaist Pope."

Waddell undertook tremendous labors over many years to research his book, which on numerous particulars can still be informative. In his preface, he spoke of his labors just briefly, but with a kind of rapture:

> One of the few Europeans who have entered the territory of the Grand Lama, I have spent several years in studying the actualities of Lamaism as explained by its priests, at points much nearer Lhasa than any utilized for such a purpose, and where I could feel the pulse of the sacred city itself beating in the large communities of its natives, many of whom had left Lhasa only ten or twelve days previously.

Waddell went so far as to procure surreptitiously his own personal Buddhist temple in Tibet, complete with living Buddhist clergy. As he explained,

> Realizing the rigid secrecy maintained by the Lamas in regard to their seemingly chaotic rites and symbolism, I felt compelled to purchase a Lamaist temple with its fittings; and prevailed on the officiating priests to explain to me in full detail the symbolism and the rites as they proceeded. Perceiving how much I was interested, the Lamas were so obliging as to interpret in my favour a prophetic account which exists in their scriptures regarding a Buddhist incarnation in the West. They convinced themselves that I was a reflex of the Western Buddha, Amitabha, and thus they overcame their conscientious scruples, and imparted information freely.

Whether the lamas had "convinced themselves" or were moved by his having financed a place of Buddhist worship, Waddell did acquire an access that exceeded what Blavatsky had attained through her *pundits.* Yet Waddell's understanding of Tibetan Buddhism remained pervasively flawed. For example, he viewed the wrathful deities of Tantrism as literal punitive demons requiring incessant appeasement. The meditational aspects of Tibetan Buddhism, in which wrathful demons serve to channel the negative emotional energies of the aspirant to higher ends, are all but absent from his book. Its abrupt conclusion, after nearly six hundred pages documenting his dedication as a field-worker and translator from the Tibetan, is mystifying in that it leaves one wondering what drove him all those years:

Still, with all their strivings and the costly services of their priests, the Tibetans never attain peace of mind. They have fallen under the double ban of menacing demons and despotic priests. So it will be a happy day, indeed, for Tibet when its sturdy overcredulous people are freed from the intolerable tyranny of Lamas, and delivered from the devils whose ferocity and exacting worship weigh like a nightmare upon all.

The triumph of the Younghusband mission seemed, to Waddell, to bode well for the future of Tibet. In his *Lhasa and Its Mysteries* (1905), published after Waddell's return to London, he provided one of the most detailed British accounts of the expedition. On the demise of Forbidden Lhasa, Waddell waxed poetic: "Her closed doors are broken down, her dark veil of mystery is lifted up, and the long-sealed shrine, with its grotesque cults and its idolised Grand Lama, shorn of his sham nimbus, have yielded up their secrets, and lie disenchanted before our Western eyes. Thus, alas! inevitably, do our cherished romances of the old pagan world crumble at the touch of our modern hands!" Waddell was, however, favorably impressed by the same regent who so affected Younghusband, and he conceded that "in the University, which must ere long be established under British direction in Lhasa, a chief place will surely be assigned to studies of the origin of the religion of the country." In this hope of extending northward the Indian colonial model, Waddell was betrayed by the lessening of British interest in Tibet.

❖

The Great Game only seemed to abate, for in truth it continued on for two more decades in the altered form of archaeological plunder. Turkestan, a key center of the early Mahayana Buddhist migration north of India, stood at the center of a range of newly discovered — from the Western perspective — central Asian sites containing artistic and manuscript treasures.

The two most famous of the many participants — including American, French, German, and Japanese representatives — in this scientifically sanctioned course of ransacking were Sir Aurel Stein — Hungarian born, British naturalized — and the Swedish explorer Sven Hedin. As Peter Hopkirk observed,

The men who carried off all these treasures had few qualms about the rightness of what they were doing. Nor, it should be said, did the governments or institutions (including the British Museum) which sent them. At the time they were lionized and honoured for their remarkable discoveries and unquestionable contributions to the scholarship of Central Asia and China. Stein and Hedin, neither of whom was British born, even received knighthoods.

Plunder has been, historically, how great collections of art have been built worldwide, with particular recent success in the West. The immorality of the Western seizures is as fixed a cultural view in China and elsewhere in Asia as is the evil of slavery in the Western world — which is to say, it is not considered a matter for debate. Without seeking to defend the plunderers, it is worthy of mention that there were others, over the centuries, who carried off or destroyed central Asian Buddhist relics, notably the Muslim invaders, and further that the indigenous Turkestan populations were themselves known to take what building materials they needed from the falling and abandoned Buddhist temples of the region, as well as objects of precious metal that could be sold or resmelted. Earthquakes had taken their toll at certain sites as well. The Manchu dynasty, in the early twentieth century, exercised desultory control over its far western provinces and showed little early interest in deterring the Western plunderers. And the more often they came — until countermeasures were at last enacted in the mid-1920s — the more vigorous grew the Chinese black market in which relics were sold to Western buyers.

A substantial collection of Chinese wall paintings and manuscripts brought to Germany in the early twentieth century by Albert von Le Coq were housed in an ethnographic museum — precisely the environment to preserve such treasures, the Western argument went. The museum was destroyed by Allied bombing during World War II. A somewhat similar fate befell the Buddhist art collection brought back to Japan, in the same era, by Count Kozui Otani, a leader of the Japanese Jodo Shinshu sect. Portions of that collection have been lost for decades, with theories of their potential whereabouts abounding. The most recent notable chapter in the story of the prized and besieged Buddhist shrines of central Asia took place in the Bamian Valley of Afghanistan in March 2001, when two large (174-foot and 125-foot) Buddha statues carved into a cliff face were dynamited by the Taliban regime. The subsequent shift in leadership brought about by the coalition forces led by the U.S. military in 2002 has encouraged a team of scientists from the Swiss Federal Institute of Technology to propose a plan for rebuilding the statues with concrete and plaster. Exact standards can allegedly be assured through the combined use of old photographs and specialized software. The estimated cost is $30 million per statue. At this point, the cycles of plundering turn back upon themselves, raising the question of what restoration can truly mean after so many uprootings.

The Taklamakan Desert — in which had once prospered the oasis cities of the southern Silk Road — drew the greatest interest from Western archaeological expeditions. Located in what is now the far western region of China, the desert borders Tibet and India to the south, Afghanistan and Pakistan to the west, and Kazakhstan, Kirghizia, Mongolia, and Tajikistan to the north. From this region, the Mahayana teachings were spread to the above-mentioned lands, although the subsequent expansion of Islam largely drove Buddhism from all but Mongolia, China, and Tibet. The German archaeologist Christoph Baumer, a recent explorer of the region, described the climatic transformations that led to the preservation of a lode of archaeological riches:

> Oases that were flourishing barely two thousand years ago, wealthy cities and blue lakes are nowadays ruins that are covered by sand, and riverbeds have long since dried out in the midst of the quiet solitude of the desert. [. . .] Even at the time when Marco Polo travelled east along the Southern Silk Road to the court of Kublai Khan, important oases such as Naya, Karadong and Loulan had already been deserted for almost a thousand years.

All told, the Taklamakan sites unearthed by Hedin, Stein, and others contained a vast and unparalleled gallery and library of central Asian and Chinese Buddhism over the course of a millennium. The difficulties of digs in the Taklamakan Desert were immense, but then again, the desert sands made possible the discovery of relics made of wood, clay, cloth, and paper that would have been impossible in temperate climates.

Kumran Banyas, a Uighur Muslim born in 1886, had as a young man been employed in expeditions of both Hedin (1900–1901) and Stein (1914) to the Taklamakan Desert. He was 108 years old when he was interviewed by Christoph Baumer. When Stein's name was mentioned, Kumran asked if Baumer meant the "robber of the Miran paintings." Baumer further reported:

> With an agitated voice he [Kumran] compares the two explorers: "Etzin [Hedin] most of all was interested in land survey, in mapping and photographing, while Stein endeavoured to take away as many objects as possible. He promised a reward to every excavation labourer if he could find something. He also removed the paintings from the Miran temple ruins. Together with other workers, as for instance Tokta Akhun, I have helped for days to carefully wrap statues, coins, writings and paintings in cotton wool and to pack them in large crates that were then transported to Kashgar." Kumran's words clearly show that he was not sympathetic to Stein.

In fairness, Hedin did his share of taking away "as many objects as possible," although he also conducted exploratory expeditions of a kind that did not interest Stein, for whom archaeological finds were the unquestioned aim. There were obvious similarities between the two men: both were short and slight; both were lifelong bachelors and prolific chroniclers of their own expeditions; both were foreigners knighted by the British throne; both lived into their eighties to see their fame in eclipse. Both also had Jewish ancestry and confronted, in divergent ways, the European anti-Semitism of their times — Stein through assimilation, Hedin by a staunch pro-German stance during both the First and Second World Wars. In both cases, Hedin earned the hatred of a considerable number of his Swedish countrymen.

As it was Stein whose hauls of Buddhist art, manuscripts, and relics were most extraordinary, we shall focus on him here as the exemplar of the era. He was born Marc Aurel Stein in Budapest in 1862 to a Jewish family that had the baby baptized as a Christian for the sake of opening the European world to their son. Stein remained a Christian all his life, later becoming an Anglican. As a boy, he was enchanted by tales of the conquests of Alexander the Great. As a young Hungarian student, he was impressed by the writings of his countryman Alexander Csoma de Körös, in particular his unyielding fortitude in traveling by foot to Tibet.

Stein emigrated from Hungary to India in 1888 and joined the Raj education service in Lahore, where he befriended John Lockwood Kipling, the father of Rudyard and the curator of a museum of Gandharan and other Buddhist antiquities — a museum portrayed as the "wonder house" in *Kim,* in which a curator based on Kipling shows the visiting Tibetan lama the British collection of Buddhist art and relics. Kipling served the same role with Stein, thereby opening to him the archaeological possibilities of the region. Stein's taking of British citizenship was a natural outcome of his employment by various Raj universities, under whose auspices he was able to satisfy the Chinese authorities as to the respectably scholarly goals of his expeditions of 1900, 1906, and 1914. The bulk of Stein's finds were delivered to the British Museum in London.

The strategies of Stein and his contemporary Hedin differed markedly when it came to cooperation with the Chinese, a matter in which Stein was a determined hard-liner. This showed itself most strongly when Stein attempted his fourth and final expedition, an abortive one, to central Asia in 1931. Baumer wrote:

> Chinese university circles of that time were angry with Stein's earlier "looting" of Dunhuang because he had bought tons of ancient documents at a ridiculous price from the unsuspecting guard of the cave temples in 1907 and 1915. In this difficult situation, Stein lacked the diplomacy and also the willingness to compromise. Quite unlike Sven Hedin, who under most difficult conditions between 1926 and 1935 had successfully headed the great Sino-Swedish "field university" by integrating Chinese scientists in his expedition, Stein insisted in travelling only in the company of local Uighurs.

Stein was this time refused access, the first and only failure of his career.

The designation of "tons" of documents acquired on his prior trips is no exaggeration. Stein later wrote of his Dunhuang expedition that one of his tactics to win the confidence of the Daoist priest in charge of the cave manuscripts was to stress his own "devotion, genuine enough, to Buddhist lore and Hsuan-tsang's [Xuanzang, a revered Chinese Buddhist pilgrim] blessed memory." The qualification "genuine enough" leaves one to assume that Stein was playing with language, for his devotion to Buddhism consisted solely in the acquisition and display of its artifacts. As Stein recounted, "My time for true relief came when, some sixteen months later, all the twenty-four cases, heavy with manuscripts, and five more filled with carefully packed paintings, embroideries and similar art relics, had safely been deposited in the British Museum in London." The cost of the acquisition to the British public was £130, which included, among a literal embarrassment of riches, a woodblock copy of the *Diamond Sutra* published in 868, making it the earliest printed book in existence, antedating the Gutenberg Bible by some six centuries.

Such were the final spoils of the Great Game.

7

TRANSCENDENTALISTS, CHRISTIAN MISSIONARIES, AND ASIAN BUDDHIST IMMIGRANTS TO AMERICA

❖

Two events of little note but rippling effect occurred in 1844. One of these was a lecture, titled "Memoir on the History of Buddhism," to the American Oriental Society in May 1844 by Edward Elbridge Salisbury, a Yale professor of Arabic and Sanskrit and a former student of Eugène Burnouf in Paris. This was the inauguration of official academic interest in Buddhism in America.

Perhaps of greater importance was the publication, that same year, in the *Dial* — the foremost journal of the transcendentalist movement — of excerpted translations from Burnouf's French version of the *Lotus Sutra*. The unidentified translator was the editor of the *Dial,* Elizabeth Palmer Peabody, and her excerpts made Buddhism known to her fellow transcendentalists in a more direct manner than ever before.

Among the readers of the *Dial* was Henry David Thoreau, who for a considerable time after his death was mistakenly believed to have been the translator of the Burnouf excerpts. The basis for this stemmed in part from Thoreau's brief musings on Buddhism in *A Week on the Concord and Merrimack Rivers* (1849) and *Walden* (1854). His most telling observation came in the former, when Thoreau underscored his rejection of Christian dogma while confessing a fondness for the outlook of the Buddha:

I trust that some may be as near and dear to Buddha, or Christ, or Swedenborg, who are without the pale of their churches. It is not necessary to be Christian to appreciate the beauty and significance of the life of Christ. I know that some will have hard thoughts of me when they hear their Christ named beside my Buddha, yet I am sure that I am willing they should love their Christ more than my Buddha, for the love is the main thing, and I like him too. "God is the letter Ku, as well as Khu." Why need Christians be still intolerant and superstitious?

But Thoreau knew far more about Hinduism than Buddhism, having read Charles Wilkins's translation of the Bhagavad Gita, as well as excerpts from the Vedas. All spiritual teachings were of interest to Thoreau, including those of the Neoplatonics and the Sufis. Thoreau the keen-eyed contemplative has since become a source of inspiration for many American Buddhists. But Thoreau did not view himself as a Buddhist. An 1850 entry in his *Journal* put the matter plainly:

> I do not prefer one religion or philosophy to another. I have no sympathy with the bigotry and ignorance which make transient and partial and puerile distinctions between one man's faith or form of faith and another's — as Christian and heathen. I pray to be delivered from narrowness, partiality, exaggeration, bigotry. To the philosopher all sects, all nations, are alike. I like Brahma, Hari, Buddha, the Great Spirit, as well as God.

Ralph Waldo Emerson was aware of Buddhism, but it did not stir him as had his reading of the Bhagavad Gita. That sacred text served as the inspiration for one of Emerson's finest poems, "Brahma," in which, as in this stanza, the immanence of deity in all things is rendered with a joyous dancelike rhythm:

> *They reckon ill who leave me out;*
> *When me they fly, I am the wings;*
> *I am the doubter and the doubt,*
> *And I the hymn the Brahmin sings.*

For Emerson, the Vedanta meshed smoothly with his own transcendentalist outlook, which beheld the workings of God in the workings of nature and stressed the role of spiritual intuition alongside that of intellect. Emerson held that intuition, as well as science, could discern laws in nature. In his controversial 1838 address to the graduating class of Harvard Divinity School (it was thirty years before Harvard asked him back), Emerson argued for the benign or shocking — depending on one's views on revealed religion — equivalence of God and the laws of nature. His account of one of these laws closely resembles the law of karma broadly shared by Hindus and Buddhists, although Emerson was likely not yet aware of the parallel:

> The intuition of the moral sentiment is an insight of the perfection of the laws of the soul. These laws execute themselves. They are out of time, out of space, and not subject to circumstance. Thus in the soul of man there is a justice whose retributions are instant and entire. He who does a good deed is instantly ennobled. He who does a mean deed is by the action itself contracted. [. . .] A man in the view of absolute goodness, adores, with total humility. Every step so downward, is a step upward. The man who renounces himself, comes to himself.

Emerson regarded Buddhism — as he came to understand it through the writings of the Orientalists — with a degree of repugnance, as a kind of rooted life pessimism. He did recognize that there was common moral ground — based on common causal or karmic suppositions — between Buddhism and transcendentalism: "The Buddhist who thanks no man, who says, 'Do not flatter your benefactors,' but who, in his conviction that every good deed can by no possibility escape its reward, will not deceive the benefactor by pretending that he has done more than he should, is a Transcendentalist." But Emerson would not concede that the Buddhist outlook, which he viewed as excessively systematized, was capable of properly comprehending, as could transcendentalism, the breadth and depth of divine reality: "Nature will not be Buddhist: she resists generalizing, and insults the philosopher in every moment with a million of fresh particulars."

Within the transcendentalist movement, there was only one figure who engaged deeply with Buddhism — James Freeman Clarke (1810–1888), friend of Theodore Parker, Margaret Fuller, and William Henry Channing. Clarke was a Unitarian minister, antislavery activist, and university lecturer on the history of religions, and he wrote the most widely accepted American version of Buddhist thought of the late nineteenth century. In his two-volume magnum opus *Ten Great Religions* (1871, 1883), Clarke sought to summarize and compare the religions of the world. Protestant Christianity was his unsurprising choice as the highest development of religion, but he also praised Buddhism as "the Protestantism of the East." This flew in the face of the standard Western emphasis on Catholic sacerdotal parallels. But Clarke argued that

> deeper and more essential relations connect Brahmanism with the Romish Church, and the Buddhist system with Protestantism. The human mind in Asia went through the same course of experience, afterward repeated in Europe. It protested, in the interest of humanity, against the oppression of a priestly caste. Brahmanism, like the Church of Rome, established a system of sacramental salvation based on personal character. Brahmanism, like the Church of Rome, teaches an exclusive spiritualism, glorifying penances and martyrdom, and considers the body the enemy of the soul. But Buddhism and Protestantism accept nature and its laws, and make a religion of humanity as well as of devotion.

One could hardly make a better case to Protestant America on Buddhism's behalf. But Clarke was also careful to cite fundamental flaws. He found no Buddhist moral vision comparable to that of the Christian teachings, and worse still, he found no hope of salvation: "The superiority of Christianity is to be found in its quantity, in its fulness of life. [. . .] It fills up the dreary void of Buddhism with a living God; with a life of God in man's soul, a heaven here as well as hereafter." Nonetheless, Clarke's bold linkage of the Protestant outlook with Buddhism helped to create an accepting attitude toward Buddhist teachings among the educated readers who were his audience.

❖

A still more heterodox Western assessment of Buddhism was offered by Richard Maurice Bucke, a Canadian psychiatrist. In his *Cosmic Consciousness: A Study in the Evolution of the Human Mind* (1900), Bucke sought to demonstrate that there existed a common core of experience behind all cultural forms of mysticism. One of his case studies was the Buddha, whose nirvana was, for Bucke, merely another term for "Cosmic

Consciousness." Like Clarke, Bucke felt able to encapsulate Buddhism with ease, but unlike Clarke, he found hope aplenty in the Buddhist vision:

> The whole of Buddhism is simply this: There is a mental state so happy, so glorious, that all the rest of life is worthless compared to it, a pearl of great price to buy which a wise man willingly sells all that he has; this state can be achieved. The object of all Buddhist literature is to convey some idea of this state and to guide aspirants into this glorious country, which is literally the Kingdom of God.

His years of friendship with Walt Whitman — the focus of the longest case study in the book — convinced Bucke (one of Whitman's literary executors) that Whitman — not the Buddha, Moses, Jesus, or Mohammed — was the greatest example of Cosmic Consciousness in recorded human history. I wish to be clear that although I do not concur with Bucke's view, neither do I scorn it; there are many who have found in Whitman's life and writings a wellspring that is unique. It was on behalf of this uniqueness that Bucke argued.

The Buddha, according to Bucke, had not learned to fully control Cosmic Consciousness, but rather had been partially defeated by it, as evidenced by his negative view of humankind in its unenlightened state. By contrast, according to Bucke, "it may be that Walt Whitman is the first man who, having Cosmic Consciousness very fully developed, has deliberately set himself against being thus mastered by it — determining, on the contrary, to subdue it and make it the servant along with simple consciousness, self consciousness and the rest of the united, individual SELF."

These comparisons by Bucke were offered in a book published after the poet's death. As for Whitman himself, Buddhism was of little interest, if we may judge by the paucity of his writings and remarks upon it. But he was not indifferent to the economic and cultural plight of the Chinese Buddhist railroad laborers brought to America and strongly opposed the exclusionary laws passed against them. Like Emerson, Whitman was more familiar with Hindu than with Buddhist teachings. And like Thoreau, Whitman would favor no creed over another. He once recounted that "when I was a young fellow up on the Long Island shore I seriously debated whether I was not by spiritual bent a Quaker? — whether if not one I should become one? But the question went its way again: I put it aside as impossible: I was never made to live inside a fence."

Whitman insisted on his own broad religiosity that took in all world spiritual paths. In "Song of Myself," he portrayed himself, in the manner of a tall-tale boast, as having swallowed whole the entire parade of human-created divinities:

Magnifying and applying come I,
Outbidding at the start the old cautious hucksters.
Taking myself the exact dimensions of Jehovah,
Lithographing Kronos, Zeus his son, and Hercules his grandson,
Buying drafts of Osiris, Isis, Belus, Brahma, Buddha,
In my portfolio placing Manito loose, Allah on a leaf, the crucifix engraved,
With Odin and the hideous-faced Mexitli and every idol and image,
Taking them all for what they are worth and not a cent more,
Admitting they were alive and did the work of their days,
(They bore mites as for unfledg'd birds who have now to rise and fly and sing
for themselves,)
Accepting the rough deific sketches to fill out better in myself [. . .]

Given the all-but-total Christian dominance of the American discourse of that era, Whitman's broader sense of spiritual identity perhaps spoke more loudly to readers of his time than it does to us. Certainly, it spoke to Emerson, who, after his first reading of *Leaves of Grass* in 1855, wrote that the book was "so extraordinary for its oriental largeness of generalization, an American Buddh." But an "American Buddh" who felt free to reshape Buddhism — and all other religions — in the service of his individual vision. That is an outlook that recurs in the Western Buddhism of our own time.

❖

Emerson had insisted on his distance from Buddhism. But those who write are not always remembered as they might wish. William James, in his classic work *The Varieties of Religious Experience* (1902), declared that Emerson and the Buddhists shared the same spiritual view — that reality was guided by immutable divine laws rather than by a personal creator god. James did, in due accordance with the Orientalists, note the emotional tone difference between "Emersonian optimism" and "Buddhistic pessimism." But then, in his postscript to the book, in which he explored his own personal convictions, there came a rather remarkable confession — for it was in the style of a confession that James, a Harvard professor, admitted to preferring the doctrine of karma to the Christian framework of providence:

I am ignorant of Buddhism and speak under correction, and merely in order the better to describe my general point of view; but as I apprehend the Buddhistic doctrine of Karma, I agree in principle with that. [. . .] I state the matter thus bluntly, because the current of thought in academic circles runs against me, and I feel like a man who must set his back against an open door quickly if he does not wish to see it closed and locked. In spite of its being so shocking to the intellectual tastes, I believe that a candid consideration of piecemeal supernaturalism [James's own descriptive term for "karma"] and a complete discussion of all its metaphysical bearings will show it to be the hypothesis by which the largest number of legitimate requirements are met. That of course would be a program for other books than this.

Having said that, James never again wrote on the theme.

James was not the first among his fellow Bostonian intellectuals to manifest an interest in Buddhism, nor did his interest by any means run the deepest. Ernest Fenollosa (1853–1908) and William Sturgis Bigelow (1850–1926) were two Boston Brahmins who became Buddhist converts largely due to the aesthetic beauties, disallowed in American Protestant worship, which flourished in Japanese esoteric Buddhism.

It was Fenollosa's aim to promote "the future union" of Eastern and Western spirituality and aesthetics. He became, in his era, the preeminent Western interpreter of Japanese art to the West, both through his writings and through his years as an astutely acquisitive curator for the Department of Oriental Art of the Boston Museum of Fine Arts, for which he assembled a collection of Japanese art unrivaled in the West in its time. Fenollosa's buying tours took him to impoverished Japanese rural temples — the modernizing Meiji legislation had diminished the sources of their funding — where Buddhist paintings and sculpture often lay ignored, enveloped in dust and rodent droppings. He did attempt — once his own acquisition work was complete — to alert the Japanese government about the need to protect the artistic treasures of the nation.

Fenollosa is known to many readers through his posthumous influence on Ezra Pound, who in 1912 gained permission from Fenollosa's widow to study his unpublished papers. In 1920, Pound edited and published Fenollosa's essay *The Chinese Written Character as a Medium for Poetry,* which theorized that all Chinese characters were in essence pictograms of the object or concept they signified. Fenollosa overstated his case — only a minority of characters match up with his theory — and as a result incurred the scorn of Western scholars who reviewed the work. But as a matter of poetic theory, Fenollosa's essay was a brilliant success, having served Pound as a "found" manifesto of Imagism. The poems in Pound's *Cathay* (1915), fueled by his reading of Fenollosa, earned the dictum of T. S. Eliot that "Pound invented Chinese poetry for our time." The irony of Pound's championing of Fenollosa is that Pound found little to admire in Fenollosa's commitment to Buddhism; "damn bhuddists," Pound called them in *The Cantos,* in which Confucian thought, for which Fenollosa had a low regard, was offered as a palliative to Western chaos and decay.

Bigelow, a graduate of Harvard Medical School, soon rejected the medical career for which he was temperamentally unfit. With the wealth of his family behind him, he traveled to Paris, began collecting Japanese art there, and was so moved by it that in 1881 he traveled to Japan, where he lived for eight years. In 1885, he formally avowed, along with his friend Fenollosa, acceptance of the teachings of Tendai and Shingon Buddhism. In these teachings, Bigelow found a resemblance to Emerson, but with the remarkable addition of vivid Tantric meditational practices. He wrote, "In Tendai and Shingon they use the old forms of Northern Buddhism. Have kept the ritual very closely. Very beautiful ritual."

After his return to Boston, Bigelow maintained traditional Brahmin social relations while practicing his Tantric Buddhism in private. His friends included Henry Adams, Henry Cabot Lodge, Theodore Roosevelt, and Isabella Stewart Gardner. Bigelow lived well but seemed to enjoy himself most when outside the strict confines of Boston, at his summer home on the tiny island of Tuckernuck, just west of Nantucket. Aquatic sports, fine wine and cuisine, Japanese Buddhist art, and a recondite 3,000-volume library — all were afforded to his male-only guests, with only one requirement laid down by the host: formal dress for dinner. Bigelow had his definite wardrobe preferences, even unto death: his family was displeased at his choice of cremation in Buddhist priestly robes. Bigelow's stipulations as to the handling of the ashes were meticulous. Half would be buried in the ancestral Mount Auburn Cemetery in Cambridge. Half would be shipped to Japan, to rest alongside the grave of Fenollosa at Mi-idera, a Buddhist temple with a view of Lake Biwa.

Both Fenollosa and Bigelow developed close friendships with Okakura Kakuzō, a student of Fenollosa in the 1880s, who thereafter emerged as an influential voice in the West on behalf of Japanese aesthetics and religion. Okakura recognized that the enthusiastic purchases of Fenollosa and others represented a threat to the Japanese cultural heritage. In 1884, he successfully urged upon the Meiji government the passage of the National Treasures Law. At the same time, Okakura was quite willing to work on behalf of Western plunderers of Chinese art, which remained inadequately protected. In 1905, with the support of Bigelow, Okakura was hired by the Boston Museum of Fine Arts to serve as adviser and later curator of its Chinese and Japanese art collections until his death in 1913.

Okakura made several purchasing tours of China, which took on a sort of legendary status among Boston museum patrons. The American critic E. F. Bleiler wrote:

> His trips to China would probably make fine novels, if half the rumors that one hears about them are true. He traveled in disguise, with a false pigtail, trusting to his mastery of Chinese to carry him through the unsettled country. He managed to obtain fabulous art treasures at a time when Chinese collectors were hiding their possessions in panic to avoid confiscation. Without these trips, it is safe to say, our American collections of Chinese art would be considerably poorer.

Okakura wrote two memorable books in his adopted tongue of English — *The Ideals of the East with Special Reference to the Art of Japan* (1903) and *The Book of Tea* (1906). The latter work remains popular, with readers drawn to its brevity and cadenced exactitude in describing the aesthetics of the Japanese tea ceremony. The former was also widely circulated and gave Western readers an early perspective on the linkage between Zen Buddhism and the Bushido code of the samurai class.

Just three years after Okakura's death, in 1916, the Boston Museum of Fine Arts hired yet another savant to work with its Oriental collections. Ananda Coomaraswamy (1877–1947) remained with the museum for the remaining three decades of his life. The son of a knighted colonial Hindu and an English mother, Coomaraswamy was born in British Ceylon, studied natural sciences and geology in London, and returned to his homeland in 1902 to serve as the Director of the Mineralogical Survey. His interests thereafter shifted toward the arts, and he soon became one of the most respected art historians of his time, as well as an eminent writer on issues of comparative religion. In *Buddha and the Gospel of Buddhism* (1916), one of the most widely read accounts of its era, Coomaraswamy placed Buddhism as a mere variation on the broad scheme of Hindu thought as expressed in the Upanishads and the later Vedanta philosophy of Shankara. Despite the pointed appropriation of its title, the book does not address Christianity in any detail. Refraining from Buddhist-Christian comparisons was unusual for the time and perhaps stressed Coomaraswamy's determination that the Indian wisdom traditions of which he wrote should be viewed within their own settings.

❖

Whereas American writers such as Emerson, Thoreau, and Whitman had considered what Buddhism had to say, it was Lafcadio Hearn (1850–1904) who first brought it into American literature as an inspired imaginative vision. Hearn was born on the Ionian island of Santa Maura to an Irish surgeon major of the British army and a Greek mother renowned for her beauty. Shortly after his birth, his father was ordered to the West Indies. At age two, his mother took him to Dublin, from which, two years later, she departed forever, leaving the boy under the care of his paternal great-aunt, a strict Roman Catholic with whom he quarreled. The young man was educated in France and England and lost the sight in one eye in a playing-field mishap. The blinded eye whitened, and the surviving eye bulged from the added strain, leaving the short and slight Hearn self-aware and vulnerable.

At age eighteen, his family paid his passage to America, where he was expected to make his own way. After a year of living on the streets, he found his métier in journalism, winning success as a feature writer and columnist in Cincinnati and New Orleans. In the latter city, his interest in Buddhism emerged, as did his penchant for dovetailing Buddhism with the evolutionary philosophy of the British thinker Herbert Spencer, whom Hearn revered. So enthusiastic did Hearn become that he began to write columns devoted to Buddhist ideas in the *New Orleans Times-Democrat,* which consequently became known in the sermons of the New Orleans clergy as the "Infidel Sheet." In 1883, Hearn declared that "Buddhism in some esoteric form may prove the religion of the future. . . . I have the idea that the Right Man could now revolutionize the Occidental religious world by preaching the Oriental faith." In particular, Hearn was convinced that the mesh — as Hearn perceived it — between the Buddhist doctrine of reincarnation and the scientific doctrine of evolution could produce an upheaval in the Western spiritual outlook.

In 1890, on assignment from *Harper's Magazine,* Hearn traveled to Japan, which he soon recognized as his spiritual homeland. In an early letter from Japan, Hearn revealed the process of his initial immersion in the new culture:

> The religion seized my emotions at once, and absorbed them. I am steeped in Buddhism, a Buddhism totally unlike that of books — something infinitely tender, touching, naif, beautiful. I mingle with crowds of pilgrims to the great shrines; I ring the great bells; and burn incense-rods before the great smiling gods. My study is confined to the popular religion, so far, and its relation to popular character and art.

Hearn distinguished, in Japanese Buddhism, between the "popular religion" of the ritualistic and theistic masses and the "Higher Buddhism," with its philosophic outlook that was compatible with Spencer. But there were transformations for which even Spencer had not prepared him. In his writings, Hearn charted his own progress from Occidental to Oriental — for he claimed to be able to write with a Japanese sensibility — a progress that included a deepened familiarity with Buddhist beliefs. In 1895, he marked the ongoing transformation:

When one has lived alone five years in a Buddhist atmosphere, one naturally becomes penetrated by the thoughts that hover in it; my whole thinking, I must acknowledge, has now been changed, in spite of my long studies of Spencer and Schopenhauer. I do not mean that I am a Buddhist, but I mean that the inherited ancestral feelings about the universe — the Occidental ideas every Englishman has — have been totally transformed. There is yet no fixity, however: the changes continue, — and I really do not know how I shall feel about the universe later on.

Hearn married a Japanese woman of a samurai family, Setsuko Koizumi, and became a Japanese citizen in 1896, taking the name Koizumi Yakumo by which he became known to Japanese readers when his works were at last translated into Japanese in the 1930s. In 1897, he was appointed professor of English literature at the Tokyo Imperial University, all the while continuing to produce essays on Japanese culture that appeared in Western venues such as the *Atlantic Monthly*. Hearn remained in Japan until his death, writing prolifically of all aspects of his new land. Given his own early history of poverty and grimy crime reportage in the United States, it is of interest that Hearn believed the Japanese slums far less horrific than those of the West — in sharp contrast to the usual view of Oriental squalor offered by Christian missionaries of the time. He was given a Buddhist funeral, a pervasive practice in Japanese society at the time.

Hearn's works remain revered in Japan, where he is regarded not only as a preeminent Western interpreter of that country but also as a master stylist and storyteller. His posthumous reputation in the West is largely that of a belle-lettristic exoticist. In recent decades, the problem has been compounded by suspicions that Western writers cannot penetrate the realities of Eastern peoples. But Hearn is deeply respected by the Japanese themselves, in part, as the historian Yuzo Ota discerned, due to aspects of Hearn's vision that seduced Japanese and Westerners alike:

Paradoxical as it may seem, is it not his [Hearn's] emphasis on the virtual impossibility of understanding the Japanese which is one of the important factors that explains Hearn's continued popularity as a Japan interpreter both inside and outside Japan? Hearn's interpretations fit into preconceived ideas on the part of many of the Western readers as reflected in phrases, such as "inscrutable Orientals" and "the mysterious East" and thus was and is easily digestible. It also fits into the deep-rooted assumption on the part of many of the Japanese readers that Japanese culture is so unique that only the Japanese can understand it properly. His writings flatter their desire to be thought to be unique and different from the world.

Hearn admired and even romanticized Buddhism, but he never felt himself to be a Buddhist, although he did write, during his years in Japan, that "if it were possible for me to adopt a faith, I should adopt it." What drew Hearn most powerfully to Buddhism was its evolutionary role in the growth of a nonsectarian world religion embracing scientific reason and spiritual tolerance. Hearn felt that Christian missionaries falsely put forth their religion as providing the greatest solace for those afflicted by life's sufferings, by means of the Christian assurance of an eternal soul. He wrote in rebuttal:

The doctrine of the impermanency of the conscious Ego is not only the most remarkable in Buddhist philosophy: it is also, morally, one of the most important. Perhaps the ethical value of this teaching has never yet been fairly estimated by any Western thinker. How much of human un-happiness has been caused, directly and indirectly, by opposite beliefs — by the delusion of stability, — by the delusion that distinctions of char-acter, condition, class, creed, are settled by immutable law, — and the delusion of a changeless, immortal, sentient soul, destined, by divine caprice, to eternities of bliss or eternities of fire.

Hearn's writings left their mark on Western readers seeking to pene-trate the mysteries of Japanese Buddhist practice. One such reader, the American poet Kenneth Rexroth, offered this homage: "It would be up to more scholarly and less imaginative writers to begin to translate and preach specific Buddhist doctrines, but Hearn has done much to translate the spirit of Japanese Buddhism and to prepare Western society for it."

❖

Hearn's appreciation, as a Westerner, of traditional Japan found its mirror opposite in the hostility to Westernization that dominated the Japanese Meiji era. A major wave of Christian conversions had taken place subsequent to the reopening of Japan to the West in 1858, but a backlash of substantial vehemence arose in the 1880s. As the Japanese historian Masaharu Anesaki explained,

"Down with frivolous Europeanization!" "Keep to our national heritage!" "Japan for the Japanese!" became the watchwords of the time. The pioneer in this movement was a group of young Buddhists and others who had been educated in the anti-Christian University of Tokyo, and their journal *Nippon-jin* ("The Japanese") became a beacon light of the nationalistic movement. [. . .] To these banners flocked not only Buddhists and Shintoists, but also Confucianists and agnostics, priests and lawyers, professors and students, making common cause against Europeanization and Christianity.

The renewed conviction that Buddhism was central to the future of Japan overcame the long-standing disdain with which Japanese intellectuals had treated its teachings — and the perceived degeneracy of its clergy — since the late eighteenth century. A maxim of Honda Toshiaki (1744–1821), who judged religions on their use to society, suffices to give the feeling of the Japanese literati of the prior era: "Buddhism usually has the effect of causing people to waste their time in utter ignorance." By contrast, Inoue Enryo (1858–1919), the most influential writer of the Japanism movement, argued that Buddhism was to be culturally revered because it was "chief among the important factors that make Japan Japan; maintaining and propagating Buddhism is the best way that the Japanese can be made Japanese and that the Japanese can be made independent." Inoue held to his stance in the face of objections that Buddhism, with its foreign origins, could scarcely constitute the essence of Japan. In this respect, the Christian missionizing effort in Japan can be seen as having encouraged an impassioned Buddhist revival. James B. Pratt, an American Protestant scholar who in the 1920s journeyed to Asia to study Buddhism firsthand, observed that Christianity "has been a stimulant to Buddhism, rousing it to renewed life and effort by the very fact of its rivalry. Two earnest Japanese Buddhists of my acquaintance, both of them professors in Buddhist seminaries, assured me — and each quite spontaneously — that Japanese Buddhism owed a large debt of gratitude to the Christian missionaries."

As for Inoue, he went on to found a college for the training of Japanese Buddhists in Western philosophy, so as to prepare them to counter the arguments of Western missionaries. But there were times when affinities on philosophical issues could create a bridge between Buddhists and Christians. In 1896, in common cause against agnosticism and atheism, representatives of the two religions, joined by Shintoists, formed the Teiyu Ethical Society, which sought to rejuvenate all Japanese religious practices — practices that, the society argued, had become tainted by sectarian and nationalistic concerns. Out of this common cause there arose, among some Japanese Christians, the aim, described by Anesaki, of "'restoration of Christianity to the Oriental consciousness,' on the ground that Christ himself was an Oriental and the Occidental civilization is not entirely Christian." The looking inward to a traditional Japan could thus lead — contrary, perhaps, to the expectations of the Japanism theorists — to the embrace of Christian as well as Buddhist and Shinto practice.

❖

Paul Carus (1852–1919) was the most prominent American spokesman on behalf of Buddhism at the turn of the century. Henry Steel Olcott had drawn those with a penchant for esoteric wisdom to his blending of Theosophy and Buddhism. But Carus served as the advocate for Buddhism as it entered the court of American public opinion as manifested in the journals and lecture halls of the day. Carus was careful never to declare himself as a Buddhist or a religionist of any type. Rather, he defended Buddhism on rationalist grounds as offering insights of interest to freethinking readers. Carus was esteemed by Asian Buddhists of the period, including D. T. Suzuki, who were eager to bring their teachings to America. But then Carus was himself an immigrant, having been born into a pious Protestant German family whose beliefs he came to reject, thereby costing him both the regard of his father and his teaching position in Germany. After earning a degree at the University of Tübingen, Carus came to America in 1884 for the purpose of promoting, in what he felt was a more receptive land, his doctrine of reasoned religious liberalism.

In 1887, he became the editor of the *Open Court,* a prominent journal of its day, as well as the managing editor of the Open Court Press (still in existence), which specialized in the publication of philosophical and scholarly texts. This was the ideal platform from which Carus could conduct his ongoing critique of Western religious suppositions. For him, Buddhism served as an ideal means to that end, as its philosophies undermined the greatest of all Western suppositions — the alleged supremacy of its divinely received religions. Carus argued not for the supremacy of Buddhism, but rather for an open competition between Christians and Buddhists for Western adherents, a competition that could, Carus believed, provoke the evolution of a new religion based on reason and greater than either of its precursors.

The Gospel of Buddha, compiled by Carus largely from the Pali Canon, went through thirteen printings by 1915, was used in Buddhist schools and temples in both Japan and Sri Lanka, and won the praise of Shaku Sōen, the Zen abbot of the Engakuji monastery in Kamakura, who had his disciple D. T. Suzuki translate it into Japanese. Carus's *Gospel* was a honed philosophic version of Buddhism from which ritual and supernatural beliefs, such as one might find among living Asian Buddhists, had been carved away, leaving only a platform of compassion worthy to set beside the Christian Gospel. Although Carus's support of the Dharma won the admiration of Asian Buddhists, his refusal to declare himself a Buddhist was a source of frustration to them. In an 1896 letter, Carus explained his stance to Anagarika Dharmapala by drawing on the example of the recent World Parliament of Religions: "I am, as it were, a religious parliament incarnate. To say that I am a Buddhist and nothing else would be a misstatement, and, indeed, it would be un-Buddhistic, it would be against the teachings of the Buddha himself. In this sense we read in Ashoka's twelfth edict: 'The beloved of the gods honors all forms of religious faith.'"

Carus was not averse to lecturing American and Asian Buddhists alike on the truths of the pure Pali doctrine. On one occasion, he chastised Dharmapala for the vehemence of his attacks on Christian missions: "The charges which are made in these remarks against Christianity are not true, and even if they were true they ought to be expressed in a different way. Buddha certainly would not have used this language."

Without wishing to justify the intolerance of Dharmapala's attacks, nor to deny the wisdom in Carus's response, we shall now turn to the Protestant missionaries and their views on Buddhism, to show that there were unfortunate conceptions on both sides.

◈

The onset of large-scale Protestant missionary efforts in nineteenth-century Asia differed markedly, in political context, from the Catholic beginnings some four centuries earlier. Europe had established itself as sovereign ruler across nearly all of southern Asia. China was a crumbling empire made subject to repeated European military encroachments and the forcible imposition of a poisonous opium trade that enriched the coffers of the British Empire. Protestants who had been blocked from China by imperial edict were now expressly invited — pursuant to the 1858 Sino-British treaty imposed on China after its defeat in the Second Opium War. Equivalent provisions appeared in treaties between China and three other Western nations — Russia, France, and the United States — that same year. At once, the doors had swung open to missionary efforts, protected by Western superiority in arms.

A similar fate was endured by Japan, which had maintained more than two centuries of isolation from the West. Preston A. Laury, in *A History of Lutheran Missions* (1899), described with relish the 1857 naval mission that broke the Japanese resolve. Commodore Perry, Laury wrote, "arrived in Yeddo Bay with the American colors flying, the open Bible on the capstan and singing the one hundreth [sic] Psalm. This circumstance was an indication of the future triumph." By the treaty imposed in 1858, Japan opened a select few of its seaports to residence by foreigners. Within a decade, eight Protestant missionary societies were functioning in Japan, most of them established by Americans.

◈

There were Chinese Catholics who had, since the debacle of the Jesuit Rites Controversy (see chapter 3), weathered the isolation from the West and kept true to their faith. Indeed, some 150,000 Chinese Catholics continued privately to practice their faith into the nineteenth century. This remnant aside, Protestants and Catholics now competed on terms of relative equality in China for the first time. The onset of Protestant missionary efforts produced an estimated 37,000 converts by 1889, an estimate that grew to 178,000 by 1905 — an impressive rate of progress if one leaves aside the size of the total Chinese population. But anti-Christian feeling in China grew rather than lessened. More than 200 anti-Christian riots were recorded in the late 1800s, culminating in 1900 with the Boxer Rebellion, in which some 200 Western missionaries and 30,000 Chinese Christians were killed.

The Protestant missionaries endured and, in the early twentieth century, somewhat flourished. The number of Western Protestant missionaries grew to 5,000 by 1925, while the tally of Chinese converts climbed to 536,000 by 1936. The Protestants borrowed the Jesuit strategy of converting those in power: both Sun Yat-sen and Chiang Kai-shek, the founding leaders of the Chinese republic, became Christians. The American writer Pearl S. Buck, winner of the Nobel Prize for Literature in 1938 and midcentury shaper of American conceptions of China, was both the daughter and the wife of missionaries to that nation.

The attitudes of the Protestant missionaries reflected the arrogance of the Western colonial empires. The Jesuits had not lacked for assurance as to the absolute truth of their religion and the superiority of European culture, but they had approached Japan and China as venerable cultures worthy of respect and even accommodation. The Protestant viewpoint was that the cultures of Asia were stagnant and as greatly in need of a thorough reformation as Europe had been in the time of Martin Luther. The Jesuits had studied Asian religions with an aim of undermining and overthrowing its arguments. The Protestants took little interest in the intricacies of the pagan creeds that were to be superseded.

The most influential of the nineteenth-century Protestant missionary-authors on Buddhism was the Reverend Robert Spence Hardy, a British Wesleyan who had spent two decades (1825–1845) in colonial Ceylon. Buddhism, the dominant religion of Ceylon, had been for Spence Hardy the burden to be overcome. His task was made more onerous by the divided Christian efforts on the island. Despite the exclusive support of the British government for Protestant missions, the prior work of the Jesuits under the Portuguese empire had left Catholicism as the strongest European faith in Ceylon, with roughly 150,000 converts in 1850. By contrast, Wesleyan conversions numbered less than 5,000 during Spence Hardy's era, while Anglican efforts lagged farther behind.

Still more dire, the prior tolerance of the Sinhalese Buddhist priests toward Christian missionaries was eroding. As Spence Hardy, after his return to England wrote in 1866, the Buddhist clergy

> have purchased presses and type, and possess printing establishments of their own. They now refuse to render any assistance to the missionaries, as before, in explaining the native books, or lending those that are in their libraries for transcription. [. . .] Tracts, pamphlets, and serials issue in large numbers from the Buddhist presses. The king of Siam, and one of the native chiefs in Kandy, have contributed largely toward their publication. They present some arguments which are new and ingenious; but the defiant and blasphemous expressions they contain, against the sacred name of "Jehovah," are probably the most awful ever framed in human language.

But Spence Hardy was nothing if not "defiant and blasphemous" to Buddhism in turn. He conducted extensive researches on the early Sanskrit and Pali texts so as to ease the task of future Christian missionaries by instructing them on the tenets — and errors — of Buddhism. There were times when the weariness of explicating Buddhist absurdities showed itself in the style of presentation:

> These are the characteristics of nirwana [sic]. That which is void, that has no existence, no continuance, neither birth nor death, that is subject to neither cause nor effect, and that possesses none of the essentialities of being, must be the cessation of existence, nihilism, or non–entity. Thus dark is the ignorant pall thrown by ignorant man over his own destiny; but the thought is too sad to be dwelt on, and we turn away from its painful associations, that we may listen to the voice of one who had seen in reality visions that were only feigned to have been seen by Buddha: "Behold, I shew you a mystery." But thanks be to God, which giveth us the victory, through our Lord Jesus Christ.

The charge that the Buddha had "feigned" his enlightenment was supported, Spence Hardy believed, by the manifest absurdity of Buddhist texts and teachings. That he could have gone to such lengths to chronicle those absurdities, however inadequately, was at least a tacit tribute to the strength of the Buddhist adversary faced by Christendom in Asia, though Spence Hardy was convinced that the time would come when "the now myriad-worshipped Buddha will not have a single votary."

The rhetoric of certainty pervaded the writings of the Protestant missionaries, who must have been daunted by the sheer number of souls needing saving in Asia but would confess to no despair. Thus the American missionary J. M. Thoburn made, in 1895, predictions in the manner of a confident industrialist: "The time is very near when converts will be added in India at the rate of one hundred thousand a year, and twenty-five thousand a year in China." Edward Thomson, a bishop of the Methodist Episcopal Church, echoed the former enthusiasm of Francis Xavier and Matteo Ricci for the particular racial fitness of eastern Asian peoples to receive the Gospel: "Next to the Caucasian, the Mongolian is, both intellectually and physically, the best variety of the human race, and the Chinese are the best part of the Mongolian family." Thomson believed that he was witnessing, in his own time, the last stand of Buddhism in the East, due largely to its unsound strategy of permitting Christian missionaries such as himself to operate freely:

> Buddhism prevails in Ceylon, Farther India, Thibet, China, Japan. That it is declining is pretty evident. Once it was exceedingly active and diffusive, having not only priests, but kings and queens engaged as propagandists. It is now stationary. Who has heard of any missionary movement of Buddhism within the last century? One of its leading principles is the toleration of other religions. It even teaches respect and reverence for other forms of faith. Its whole flank is therefore exposed.

The sense of the Protestant missionaries was that they were liberating those who had for millennia been oppressed by Buddhist nihilism and degeneracy. Arthur H. Smith, an American Protestant missionary to China in the early twentieth century, held that Buddhist monks had systematically exploited the Chinese population by obtaining, under pious pretense, lands that were then used "in order to support in idleness, gambling, opium-smoking, and vice social vampires who add nothing to the common weal, but suck the life-blood of China." The employment of a vampiric metaphor for Buddhist monks was not an entirely original conception, as it had previously been used in Protestant polemics against Catholicism. Smith's summation of the state of affairs in Chinese Buddhist nunneries was a trace kinder, perhaps out of chivalry. He allowed that "there may be virtuous women among them, but the shrewd adage runs: Ten Buddhist nuns, and nine are bad; The odd one left is doubtless mad."

Certain among the Protestant missionaries acknowledged the moral difficulties that arose from serving both as teachers of the Gospel and as representatives of a rapacious European colonialism, under the military protection of which their mission houses were established. The linkage was plainly problematic, for it was difficult to preach the Word if one confessed that the European civilization that had lived the longest with Christian teachings had failed to become truly civilized through them. The greatest protest from missionaries was directed at the active promotion, by Western colonizers in Asia, of widespread alcohol and opium consumption. Britain, the most egregious perpetrator, encouraged opium production in India as a means of creating revenue by which it could purchase Chinese tea and silk. Opium had been cultivated and smoked in China for several centuries, but its usage increased sharply in the late eighteenth century, due to vigorous British marketing of Indian opium, widely regarded as superior in quality. The Chinese imperial government sought to stem the tide of addiction by making both opium use and importation capital offenses. In 1839, the destruction by the Chinese of large quantities of British-owned opium held in storage in Canton led to British military retaliation. The First Anglo-Chinese War, better known as the First Opium War, ended in 1842 with the abject defeat of China and the imposition of the Treaty of Nanking, which ensured an untrammeled market for opium sales.

In 1888, at a missionary conference held in London, the British Reverend J. Hudson Taylor, founder and director of the China Inland Mission, gave a speech in which he summarized the damage: "You may go through China, and you will find thousands — I can safely say tens of thousands — of towns and villages in which there are but small traces of the Bible or of Christian influence. You will scarcely find a hamlet in which the opium-pipe does not reign." The missionary sisters Mary and Margaret W. Leitch reported to the conference that one elderly Chinese woman had declared indignantly that "we don't want your opium and we don't want your Christ." What made matters worse, as the Leitch sisters conceded, was that Hindus and Buddhists alike had forbidden, with broad effectiveness, the use of strong drink and intoxicants in India and China prior to the advent of the British Empire.

❖

As the Orientalist scholars of this period were very often Christians, their conclusions on the comparative worth of Buddhist and Christian teachings tallied nicely with those of the Protestant missionaries. Sir Monier Monier-Williams, in his Duff Lectures delivered in Edinburgh in 1888, reassured his audiences that nothing in his lengthy analyses of Buddhist lore could be viewed as a threat to the ultimate triumph of Christendom:

> Here, then, is the first great contrast. When the Buddha said to his converts, "Come (ehi), be my disciples," he bade them expect to get rid of suffering, he told them to stamp out suffering by stamping out desires. When the Christ said to His disciples, "Come, follow Me," He bade them expect suffering. He told them to glory in their sufferings — nay, to expect the perfection of their characters through suffering. [. . .] What shall I do to inherit eternal life? — says the Christian. What shall I do to inherit eternal extinction of life? — says the Buddhist.

Edward Caird, master of Balliol College, Oxford, in presenting his Gifford Lectures to the University of St. Andrews from 1890 to 1892, adapted the Darwinian paradigm to create what he believed to be a scientific approach to religious history. When comparing the doctrinal developments of the world religions, one could assess their respective greatness simply by asking of each: "'How much truth has been brought to expression, and with what inadequacies and unexplained assumptions?'" Just what "truth" might be was plain to Caird, who saw all of humanity searching, under different religious guises, "for the one principle of life which masks itself in all these varied [religious] forms, and which through them all is striving towards the complete realization of itself." This one principle was God, the ultimate end of all knowledge.

Caird bestowed the highest evolutionary laurels on Christianity, as it blended objectivity (reverence for and knowledge of the world) with subjectivity (recognition of the complex depths of the human spirit) in Jesus Christ:

The infinite pitifulness of Jesus to the sorrows and evils of humanity, his absolute confidence in the possibility and even the necessity of their being remedied, and the way in which he bases his confidence on the love of God to man, and on his own unity as man with God — these, taken together, make up a faith beyond which religion cannot go, except in two ways, namely, in the way of understanding them more adequately, and of realizing them more fully.

Buddhism, in Caird's view, was rooted in the subjective aim of extinguishing self and suffering; hence "Buddhism had power only as a protest or a negative deliverance from the world, which led to no positive regeneration of it. Subjective religion is valuable mainly as a stage of transition, from a lower religion which is merely objective, to a higher religion which is both objective and subjective." Thus was Buddhism scientifically encompassed as a waypoint on the road to Christian truth.

Such evolutionary proofs did not always convince the doubters who had emerged in the West itself. With increasing knowledge of Buddhism and other non-Western religions, questions more frequently arose as to the necessity for missionary labors to Asian nations already amply equipped with spiritual creeds. The defense most frequently offered by missionaries and their lay supporters was that the spread of Christianity was necessary on moral and economic as well as religious grounds. Burton Holmes, a popular American travel writer in the 1910s, gave vent, in his portrayal of China, to the disgust that any right-minded visitor must feel in viewing the practice of Chinese religion with its Tibetan influences:

As for Buddhism, in the abstract it is beautiful — but to what depths of degradation is it not sunk in the Celestial Empire? There it is represented by a horde of ignorant, filthy priests, droning in the dilapidated temples, looking with hungry eyes at the inquisitive foreigners whom they pursue with savagely insistent demands for offerings of money. Playing upon the abject superstition of a populace more ignorant than themselves, these shaven-pated Lamas are among the curses of the land. If one would be convinced of the utter demoralization of the priesthood of Gautama's faith, let him visit, as we did, the great Lama Temple in the far northeastern corner of the Tatar City, and study there the inane, vicious visages of the "holy men." It is like entering the haunt of birds of prey — now frightened into harmlessness, but retaining all the instincts of the vulture and the buzzard. [. . .] Even the irreligious must admit that China needs a new religion if only as *a means of escape* from the thralldom of tradition.

Escape from such thralldom, as the West viewed it, was extraordinarily difficult for those Chinese persons still bonded to a traditional Buddhist family. The Reverend Andrew Gih, a Chinese evangelist of the 1920s, recounted the testimony of one young man, John Shih, who had been beaten repeatedly by his Buddhist father and had his Bible ripped from his hands and torn to shreds by his Buddhist wife. What finally spurred the young man's departure from home was this tragic and transcendent scene:

One day after dinner I was seated in my room when my father came in and struck me over the head until the blood poured from my nose. He kicked and pummelled me until at last the family came and pulled him off. Hitherto I had been unwilling to leave home because I felt I had not yet "resisted unto blood." But now I was content to go, although of course the little blood I shed was of no moment. How infinitely precious is the blood of the Lord Jesus which can cover the whole earth and save every living soul!

❖

At the turn of the twentieth century, standard Western estimates placed some 500 million people — roughly 40 percent of the world's population — as Buddhists. This was inflated, as it included the entire population of China and hence ignored the pervasive Chinese amalgam of Confucianism, Daoism, and Buddhism, which did not always include a pronounced allegiance to the latter. The Shinto population of Japan was blended into the Buddhist head count as well. But such fine points were hardly the concern of Christian missionaries, who highlighted instead that the world's Christian population, even including the Greek Orthodox Church, was a mere 26 percent. "Mohammedans," at roughly 13 percent, were a particularly difficult field for missionary endeavor and seemed likely to remain so.

The conviction began to dawn on many in Christendom that their primary rival for the religious sustenance of humankind was Buddhism, the selfsame obscure religion that the scholars of Europe had been painstakingly mapping out for nearly a century. Moreover, there was mounting concern that the popularity of Edwin Arnold's *Light of Asia* and other sympathetic literary works, the laudatory accounts of Buddhism by the Theosophists, and the publicity splash made by Buddhist leaders at the World Parliament of Religions in Chicago had combined to bring about a challenge to Christendom on its own soil and directed at white Americans.

There was, within that populace, a reasonably broad reading public that was taking in, to some degree, what Buddhism had to say. As the American historian Thomas Tweed observed,

> If we considered only the popularity of three books we might have to conclude that a significant number of Americans had some personal interest — Arnold's *The Light of Asia* (1879), Olcott's *Buddhist Catechism* (1881), and Carus's *The Gospel of Buddha* (1894). All three had sizable circulations and were cited frequently. Carus's *Gospel of Buddha* went through thirteen editions by 1910, and Olcott's *Buddhist Catechism* went through more than forty editions before the author died in 1907. [. . .] Arnold's poetic life of the Buddha sold between five hundred thousand and one million copies.

Tweed estimated that there were, in the years 1893 to 1907, two thousand to three thousand Euro-Americans who regarded themselves as Buddhists to a degree, while tens of thousands more were sympathetic. That sympathy seldom extended to the hundreds of thousands of Asian Buddhists actually living in America.

❖

The great wave of Chinese immigration to the United States, spurred by the desire for cheap imported labor for railroad construction, began in the 1850s and officially terminated with the passage of the bluntly titled Chinese Exclusion Act of 1882. At its peak, the Chinese labor force in America numbered some 200,000, largely based on the West Coast. Presumably, a good many considered themselves Buddhists of either the Ching-t'u (Pure Land) or Chan (Zen) sect. But statistics were not kept as to Buddhist affiliations or places of worship of the immigrant Chinese community. Their geographical isolation in America and the failure of Chinese Buddhists to concern themselves with their emigrant members led to a substantial degree of Christian assimilation among second- and third-generation Chinese American families.

The Chinese Exclusion Act, a panicked racist response by Euro-Americans who feared that Chinese workers would come to dominate the labor market in the West, suspended formal immigration options. Ten years later, in 1892, the Geary Act raised further legal thickets. The combined effect of the federal legislation was to suspend all further Chinese immigration, to preclude any Chinese laborers already on American soil from obtaining U.S. citizenship, and to mandate that all such laborers register themselves and carry photographic identification at all times. No other resident population in America was subjected to such requirements. The lack of citizenship effectively eliminated any voice in the American political process. The Chinese working population was very predominantly male but was precluded by anti-miscegenation laws from marrying non-Chinese women. Lynchings and other attacks on Chinese were commonplace in the western United States, reaching a peak in 1885 in Rock Springs, Wyoming, where twenty-eight Chinese were killed and some three hundred more driven from town. The railroad, mining, and factory jobs held by Chinese workers — at dreadful wages — were not generally of interest to the American workforce. But the insistence on a "Yellow Peril" that would strip America of its jobs and wealth took its toll.

According to the 1890 U.S. census, roughly 107,000 Chinese were living in America; some three-quarters of them resided in California, where 178 religious shrines, reflecting Buddhism in varying syncretistic degrees, had been established. But as that decade proceeded, the federal legislation accomplished its purpose: the number of Chinese workers declined by about 15 percent, and fears subsided. An improved public feeling toward the Chinese was further encouraged by a shift in American foreign policy, initiated by Theodore Roosevelt, that favored Chinese interests over those of an expansionist Japan, which was seen as threatening recently acquired American territories in the Philippines and Hawaii. Five decades later, however, fear of a Chinese "Yellow Peril" would return to American life with the rise of Mao Zedong.

❖

Japanese immigration to America commenced in strength in the 1890s, with some twenty thousand responding to the ongoing call for railroad workers. As in the case of Chinese immigrant labor, reliable statistics are lacking, but certainly a large number of the newly arrived Japanese workers were affiliated with Jodo Shinshu (True Sect of the Pure Land) or other Pure Land Buddhist sects. In contrast to the Chinese immigrants, ties remained strong between Japanese American Pure Land Buddhists and their homeland, due to ongoing Japanese missionary efforts in the United States. In keeping with the example of the Christian missionaries in both Japan and the American West, Japanese Pure Land missionaries adapted American Protestant customs to their own benefit — hence the creation of the Young Men's Buddhist Association (YMBA) in San Francisco in 1898. The YMBA founded branches in Japan and China during the same period and for the same reason — to counter successful Christian conversion efforts among the young. Also in 1898, and again in San Francisco, the first legally created Buddhist temple in the United States was opened to the public — a public that included, in this and subsequent temples in the city, interested Euro-Americans. To appeal to this group, Japanese Pure Land missionaries created the Dharma Sangha of Buddha organization and an English-language magazine, the *Light of Dharma*.

In 1899, Japanese Jodo Shinshu missionaries established the North American Buddhist Mission — later renamed the Buddhist Churches of America — which still exists today. In California and elsewhere, however, political controversy arose from the fact that Shintoism, with its worship of the perfected mikado, or emperor, was seen as having blended with Jodo Shinshu worship, thus fostering alien allegiances on U.S. soil. As the Protestant historian Martin E. Marty described the mood of the time, "California Senator James D. Phelan in 1920 told the House Committee on Immigration that the seventy-six Buddhist temples in California were 'regularly attended by "Emperor-worshippers" who believe that their Emperor is the over-lord of all.' "

The political and social pressures to abjure public Shinto and Buddhist worship were intense. But Buddhist communities were created and sustained by what came to be generations of Asian Americans. In 1992,

Ryo Imamura, a Jodo Shinshu priest whose father, Enryo Imamura, served as spiritual head of the Buddhist Berkeley Church, wrote on behalf of the early Buddhist immigrants to America:

> I would like to point out that it was my grandparents and other immigrants from Asia who brought and implanted Buddhism in American soil over 100 years ago despite white intolerance and bigotry. It was my American-born parents and their generation who courageously and diligently fostered the growth of American Buddhism despite having to practice discreetly in hidden ethnic temples and in concentration camps because of the same white intolerance and bigotry. It was us Asian Buddhists who welcomed countless white Americans into our temples, introduced them to the Dharma, and then often assisted them to initiate their own Sanghas, when they felt uncomfortable practicing with us. . . . We Asian Buddhists have hundreds of temples in the United States with active practitioners of all ages, ongoing educational programs that are both Buddhist and interfaith in nature, social welfare projects . . . everything that white Buddhist centers have and perhaps more.

❖

According to the 1920 U.S. census, there were some 110,000 Japanese in America, a number that came to be perceived as dangerously high. Despite testimony from Jodo Shinshu clergy such as Bishop Koyu Uchida, who stressed to the House Committee on Immigration that the Buddhist Mission was not only independent from Shintoism and the emperor but also recognized "the necessity of the Americanization of our people," Congress enacted exclusionary legislation against further Japanese immigration in 1924.

It was in this political climate that the introduction of Japanese Zen Buddhism into the United States — and from there to the rest of the West — took place.

8

JAPANESE ZEN MISSIONS
TO THE WEST

❖

The first Japanese Zen master to have an impact on the American public was Shaku Sōen (1859–1919), a Rinzai Zen priest. Sōen composed a very brief autobiography, which tells in the third person of his early Zen training:

> This fellow was a son of Nobusuke Goemon of Takahama, the province of Wasaka. His nature was stupid and tough. When he was young, none of his relatives liked him. When he was twelve years old, he was ordained as a monk by Ekkei, Abbot of Myoshin Monastery. Afterwards, he studied literature under Shungai of Kennin Monastery for three years and gained nothing. Then he went to Mii-dera and studied Tendai philosophy under Taiho for a summer, and gained nothing. After this, he went to Bizen and studied Zen under the old teacher Gisan for one year, and attained nothing. He then went east, to Kamakura, and studied under the Zen master Kosen in the Engaku Monastery for six years, and added nothing to the aforesaid nothingness. [. . .] Such a wandering mendicant! He ought to repay the twenty years of debts to those who fed him in the name of Buddhism.

Which indeed Sōen sought to do.

Imakita Kōsen (1816–1892), Sōen's teacher, had emerged as a leading Rinzai Zen master in Meiji Japan. During the late nineteenth century, the status of Buddhism in Japan had markedly declined. There was government hostility toward a Buddhist creed now attacked as a decadent "foreign" element hindering the push within Japan toward greater urbanization and industrialization — a push that disrupted the agrarian classes on which Buddhist monasteries depended for their support. Kōsen was among those who argued that the fault lay not with Buddhist teachings, but with a corrupted clergical hierarchy. The answer was to reinvigorate Buddhism, which meant not only reforming the monasteries but also reaching outside the monastic system to impart Buddhist teachings to long-neglected Japanese laypeople — that is, the very population so ardently courted by Christian missionaries during the same era. To these ends, Kōsen served, during the 1870s, as a high-ranking member of the Ministry of Doctrine, while still presiding as chief abbot at the Engakuji Rinzai monastery. His Buddhist reform movement aimed at competing more effectively with Christianity not only in Japan but in the West as well.

When Kōsen died in 1892, Sōen, age thirty-three, succeeded him as the abbot of Engakuji. Sōen had already revealed an unusual range of intellectual interests for a Zen monk by obtaining a degree from Keio University in Tokyo, where Western studies were emphasized, and thereafter spending two years in Sri Lanka studying Pali — proof of a reformist outlook committed to reexamining the oldest Buddhist texts. The following year, Sōen attended the World Parliament of Religions in Chicago, where he and his fellow Japanese Buddhist delegates won the respectful interest of journalists and the American public. They returned to Japan to public acclaim. As Ohara Kakichi, a Japanese writer of the time, exulted, the doors had been opened for "Buddhism in Japan in the Far East to turn the wheel of the Dharma in America in the Far West."

Sōen was not averse to speaking his mind to his American audiences. In 1896, he wrote a letter of protest — published in Paul Carus's journal, *Open Court* — against the characterization (by John H. Barrows, the Protestant theologian and chief organizer of the World Parliament of Religions) of Buddhism as a nihilist creed. As for Barrows's attribution of "supernatural" powers to Christ, as opposed to mere "natural" powers to Buddha, Sōen's response was not conciliatory:

We may grant that Jesus Christ is the greatest master and teacher that appeared in the West after Buddha, but the picture of Jesus Christ as we find it in the Gospel is marred by the accounts of such miracles as the great draft of fishes, which involves a great and useless destruction of life (for we read that the fishermen followed Jesus, leaving the fish behind), and by the transformation of water into wine at the marriage-feast at Cana. Nor has Jesus Christ attained to the calmness and dignity of Buddha, for the passion of anger overtook him in the temple, when he drove out with rope in hand those that bargained in the holy place. How different would Buddha have behaved under similar conditions in the same place! Instead of whipping the evil-doers he would have converted them, for kind words strike deeper than the whip.

In 1904, during the Russo-Japanese War, Sōen, like many of his fellow Buddhist clergy, served as a Buddhist chaplain for Japanese troops. That December, in *Open Court,* Sōen published an essay (translated into English by D. T. Suzuki) titled "At the Battle of Nan-Shan Hill." In this essay, he portrayed Japanese involvement in the war as both politically necessary and manifestly just: "War is an evil and a great one, indeed. But war against evils must be unflinchingly prosecuted till we attain the final aim. In the present hostilities, into which Japan has entered with great reluctance, she pursues no egotistic purpose, but seeks the subjugation of evils hostile to civilization, peace, and enlightenment." Sōen went on to examine the Buddha-nature of battlefield death:

> Were it not for the belief that the bloom of truly spiritual light will, out of these mutilated, disfigured, and decomposing corpses, return with renewed splendor, we would not be able to stand these heart-breaking tribulations even for a moment. Were it not for the consolation that these sacrifices are not brought for an egotistic purpose, but are an inevitable step toward the final realization of enlightenment, how could I, poor mortal, bear these experiences of a hell let loose on earth?

Militarism viewed as a path to enlightenment is a troubling perspective for many present-day Western and Eastern Buddhists, for the reason that it is a desecration of the nonviolent Dharma taught by the Buddha. I shall explore this issue in greater depth shortly, when discussing D. T. Suzuki. For now, note that such views on war as Suzuki later expressed were held in common with his master, Sōen, among others. Yasutani

Haku'un Roshi, the Japanese Zen master whose students included three eminent modern-day American Zen teachers — Robert Aitken (b. 1917), Philip Kapleau (1912–2004), and Bernard Glassman (b. 1939), the latter two of Jewish ancestry — was not only a militarist but also a fervid anti-Semite. This is not in the least to impute his value to those three men, but rather to note that the importation of Japanese Zen into America was laden with background politics that seems — by the testimony of numerous living students, including Aitken and Glassman — not to have been reflected in the Yasutani Roshi they encountered as an efficacious teacher of the Dharma.

There was only one prominent contemporary Western response to Sōen's views on war that dared to contest his status as a true representative of the Buddha's teaching. Leo Tolstoy, in his essay "Bethink Yourselves!" written during the Russo-Japanese War, portrayed that war as "the perversion of both the Christian and the Buddhist teaching" and identified Sōen, in particular, as an example of a Buddhist who had betrayed the Dharma:

> Nor do the Japanese theologians and religious teachers lag behind our European ones. As their military men are up to date in the technique of armaments, so are their theologians up to date in the technique of deception and hypocrisy — not merely tolerating but justifying murder, which Buddha forbade. The learned Buddhist Soyen-Shaku [. . .] explains that though Buddha forbade manslaughter, he also said [. . .] that to bring the discordant into harmony it is necessary to fight and kill people.

But Tolstoy's views on the war and Buddhism were both ignored at the time.

Sōen traveled to America in 1905–1906 to present a series of talks that were published as *Sermons of a Buddhist Abbot.* D. T. Suzuki accompanied him as translator. Sōen's viewpoints, as quoted above, aroused no controversy during his tour. One possible reason for this is that Sōen's rhetoric on war so resembled that of the Christian and Jewish clergy of America during times of national conflict that it passed as standard fare. Also, few Westerners possessed sufficient knowledge to examine Sōen's teachings within the broader context of historical Buddhist practice. Sōen would have thought little of such a comparative approach; as he stated in one lecture, "What I firmly believe is that in the Buddhism of Japan today are epitomized all the essential results reached through the unfolding of the religious consciousness during the past twenty or thirty centuries of Oriental culture." To Japan thus went the honor of preserving — and now bestowing — the quintessence of Buddhism.

❖

Sōen did not return to America after his 1905–1906 tour. He died at age sixty in Kamakura. But he had taken care to create a lineage of students to continue the work of Zen teaching in the United States. Of these students, Nyogen Senzaki (1876–1958) was the most enigmatic, with a life filled with shifts and sorrows through which he maintained a dedication to Zen and to his teacher, Sōen, that was remarkable, given his utter isolation in the New World.

Senzaki was born in northeastern Siberia. The identity of his father remains unclear; he is variously described as Russian or Chinese. His mother was Japanese. As a baby, he was found lying beside the frozen body of his mother by a Japanese Buddhist monk traveling in Siberia. The monk brought the baby back to Japan, where he was adopted by a ship carpenter named Senzaki. The boy was drawn to Buddhist teachings, and at age twenty he resolved to find a suitable teacher of the Dharma. That teacher was Sōen, who was also teaching D. T. Suzuki during the same period (mid-1890s). The two young men came to know each other when they practiced *zazen* (Zen meditation) together. In 1897, Suzuki departed for America, where he would reside for eleven years, working closely with Paul Carus and his Open Court Press. Senzaki studied under Sōen for five years, then left the monastic life to found a kindergarten in a Buddhist temple in Hirosaki. He called his little school a "Mentorgarten," a name he would later apply to his Los Angeles *zendo* (meditation hall).

Senzaki and Suzuki traveled with Sōen during his lecture tour of the United States, but with a great difference in their status and duties. Suzuki was Sōen's translator and social liaison; Senzaki did maintenance chores in a stylish coastal house just outside San Francisco in which the Sōen contingent was lodged. The Japanese Rinzai master Eido Shimano Roshi, who served as a posthumous editor of Senzaki's manuscripts, wrote that some mystery surrounds the extent of the teacher-student relationship between Soyen [Sōen] Shaku and Nyogen Senzaki. [...] He [Senzaki] was extremely devoted to his [Sōen's] memory, and had nothing but praise and gratitude for this great Zen master. But what of Soyen Shaku's opinion of Nyogen Senzaki in America? I have searched through Soyen Shaku's diary of this time and have found very little mention of Nyogen Senzaki. Dr. Suzuki, in contrast, is mentioned on almost every page with much praise and admiration for his work in America. [...] Soyen Shaku's last entry concerning Nyogen Senzaki is dated August 3, 1905, and rather unconcernedly states, "Mr. Nyogen Senzaki left [...] [the coastal] home because the work was too hard for him."

But Senzaki left his own written record of that day. Nearly fifty years later, in a 1954 commemoration of his teacher, Senzaki recalled that after he was dismissed from the house, Sōen accompanied him into San Francisco, where Senzaki, with his severance pay, was to find a hotel in which to live. According to Senzaki, as the two men walked through Golden Gate Park, Sōen told his student, "This may be better for you instead of being hampered as my attendant monk. Just face the great city and see whether it conquers you or you conquer it." Sōen then walked away, and Senzaki was alone.

Senzaki never forgot his teacher or the task with which he had been entrusted, which was to teach Zen to Americans. There was, however, one proviso: Senzaki was forbidden from so much as speaking the word "Buddhism" aloud for seventeen years. The reason for this was revealed in a 1901 assessment of Senzaki by Sōen: "He has to walk a long way to become a Jofukyo [a monk praised in the *Lotus Sutra*] but, at least, I consider him as trailing along. [...] Nyogen will not live each day in vain so long as he keeps the Four Vows with him."

Senzaki obeyed his teacher's proviso, earning his living all the while through a series of menial jobs. As he later wrote,

For seventeen years, I have simply walked through many areas of American life, making myself a grass of the field, doing Zazen alone in Golden Gate Park, or studying hard in the public library of San Francisco. Whenever I could save money, I would hire a hall and give a talk on Buddhism. In 1922, I named our meeting place "the floating Zendo." At last, I established a Zendo in 1928 which I have carried around with me like a silkworm in a cocoon. Then I came to Los Angeles in 1931. The silk thread is surrounding me, still unbroken.

In Los Angeles, Senzaki established a *zendo* at 441 Turner Street. His assessment of his accomplishments was as dour and detached in tone as that of his teacher, Sōen, in his own autobiography. Senzaki wrote: "I was left in America to do something for Buddhism, but as you all know, my work is very slow and I have neither an aggressive spirit nor an attractive personality to draw crowds. [. . .] America had to pick up this monk — a poor potato. I am very sorry about it."

During World War II, Senzaki, as a Japanese American, was interned in a camp in Heart Mountain, Wyoming. The racist internment policies enforced against Japanese Americans in this era produced grievous harms — economic, psychological, and political — that have endured to this day. The elderly Senzaki, a poet who wrote in Chinese, Japanese, and English, took a stance that considered only the fate of the Dharma in America:

> All Japanese faces will leave California to
> support their government
> This morning the winding train, like a big
> black snake,
> Takes us away as far as Wyoming.
> The current of Buddhist thought always runs
> eastward.
> This policy may support the tendency of the
> teaching.
> Who knows?

The answer would seem to be, in cautious but comfortable hindsight, that the policy did nothing to support the teaching. After the war, Senzaki returned to Los Angeles, where he continued his work until his death in 1958. He returned to Japan only once, in 1956, fifty years after parting company with Sōen in Golden Gate Park.

Senzaki left relatively little by way of a written legacy. *Zen Flesh, Zen Bones: A Collection of Zen and Pre-Zen Writings* — which consisted almost wholly of collaborative translations, in poetry and prose, by Senzaki and one of his Western students, the American poet Paul Reps — was first published in the 1930s and became a widely read and beloved introduction to Zen in the West. Indeed, it remains briskly in print today. Reps, in his foreword, expressed his gratitude "to Nyogen Senzaki, 'homeless monk,' exemplar-friend-collaborator, who so delighted with me" in the work of translation. Even so, for decades its title page featured "Compiled by Paul Reps" as the sole authorial listing, for reasons that are still unclear. Current editions of the book credit both men as compilers. During his lifetime, however, the "homeless monk" enjoyed a largely anonymous publishing success, which may well have suited him just fine.

❖

If Senzaki was an exemplar of the slow blossoming of Zen training, his younger contemporary Sokei-an Sasaki (1882–1945) was the archetype of the imaginative artist and thinker who submits after struggle to the discipline of Zen. He was born into a well-to-do Japanese family. His father, who died when Sokei-an was fifteen, was a Shinto priest. In his late teens, Sokei-an trained both in sculpture and the performing arts. Then, at nineteen, he commenced Zen lay training with Ryomokyo-kai, a group founded by the Rinzai master Kōsen, the teacher of Sōen, from whom Suzuki and Senzaki had received their training. Sōen's successor, Sokatsu Shaku (1870–1954), became Sokei-an's first Rinzai teacher in 1901. Five years later, Sokatsu invited fourteen young men and women, including Sokei-an, to join him in bringing Zen to America.

The timing of their arrival in San Francisco was inauspicious, coming just after the earthquake of 1906. The shattered city had no jobs to offer to the newly arrived contingent from Japan. Sokatsu believed that he had solved the problem when he procured a small farm in nearby Hayward and established what can be viewed in retrospect as the first Zen commune in the West, with all the members working at growing strawberries and other cash crops in soil that had been left badly depleted by the previous owner. It did not help matters that neither Sokatsu nor his lay students knew anything about farming. As the disaster progressed, Sokei-an left the group and went off to study painting in San Francisco. During this period, he met Senzaki. The two became lifelong friends and, now and then, in a playful spirit, friendly rivals.

When Sokatsu abandoned the farm and established a *zendo* on Sutter Street in San Francisco, Sokei-an returned, apologized to his teacher, and resumed training. With the approval of Sokatsu, Sokei-an married Tome, a fellow group member. In 1908, Sokatsu returned to Japan. Within two years, the remainder of the group followed, with the exception of Sokei-an and Tome, who thereafter had two children. Tome cared little for America and did not want their second child to be born there, leading her to return abruptly to Japan. This trip was facilitated by Sokei-an's aging stepmother, who supported Tome and the children; in return, Tome cared for the older woman. The separation from the children wrenched Sokei-an, but a sense of mission had been established by his teacher. As Sokei-an later explained,

He [Sokatsu] told me: "North America is the place where Buddhism will be spread in the future. You should stay here and familiarize yourself with the attitudes and culture of this land. Be diligent! If in the future no one else appears, the responsibility will be yours!" Following my teacher's instruction, I wandered all over the United States for more than ten years and finally understood the ways of this country.

Sokei-an moved to New York in 1916 and became a Greenwich Village poet, supporting himself by writing stylishly satirical pieces for the Japanese newspaper *Chuokoron*. Among the Western bohemians he chronicled during this period were Maxwell Bodenheim and Aleister Crowley. As he took in an appreciation of American ways, Sokei-an also came to a heightened sense of the value of traditional Rinzai Zen training. Later he would write of a moment of epiphany while walking in New York in 1920: "I saw a dead horse in Sixth Avenue. I went by and saw the physical details — a dead horse lying on the pavement. Something happened. In that moment, nothing was left in my mind. In August 1920, I sailed for Japan. Sokatsu agreed with the validity of my experience and gave me the seal [upon the *inka,* or diploma of attainment]."

In 1922, Sokei-an returned to New York. Gradually, he attracted a small group of students by giving lectures at the Orientalia Bookstore on East Fifty-eighth Street, across from the Plaza Hotel. He returned to Japan in 1928 to receive ordination as a Zen master, then resumed his work in New York, establishing a *zendo* on West Seventieth Street — a one-room walk-up apartment with a tiny kitchen in which Sokei-an both lived and taught.

Through his writings and lectures, Sokei-an left a terse but vivid portrait of the life of a Zen Buddhist missionary living in cultural isolation in Depression-era New York. After a visit from his friend D. T. Suzuki, by then a successful author and lecturer, Sokei-an compared the public roles of Suzuki and himself: "On February 22, 1936, I gave a lecture before the Japan Society of Boston. It seemed to me that they did not understand my address: they could not understand which was the tail, which was the head. [. . .] The tea ceremony is what Americans think Japan is, and when Dr. Suzuki takes seventy-five dollars for a lecture, he must give them that and not Zen." Sokei-an was determined to teach Zen to Americans in a manner as closely akin as possible to traditional Rinzai methods:

> I am often asked by American people, "I have heard that you have organized a religious center." "Yes." "What are your activities?" "What do you mean?" "Well, any social work?" "No, I am not doing anything." "Then how can you call it religion?" To popularize Buddhism is very dangerous. If I popularize my Buddhism here and give dinners and dancing, perhaps I can move into 42nd Street, but Buddhism will be annihilated.

Critics of Sokei-an's teaching method included a prominent Western Buddhist of the era, Dwight Goddard, a onetime Protestant missionary in southern China who ultimately converted to Buddhism. In 1928, Goddard spent several months at the Zen monastery of Shokoku-ji in Kyoto, where he was accorded the title "monk-novice." After his return to America, he worked as a Western missionary on behalf of Buddhism. His *Buddhist Bible* (1932), compiled from various published translations and later expanded to include new Mahayana translations by Goddard in collaboration with the Chinese Bhikshu Wai-tao, served for four decades as perhaps the most widely read Western anthology of Buddhist texts. Jack Kerouac, for example, studied it intently.

In 1934, Goddard created the Followers of the Buddha, an organization devoted to the establishment of two Zen Buddhist monasteries — one at Goddard's farm in Thetford, Vermont, and the other at a donated retreat near Santa Barbara, California. The plans fell through, but Goddard was motivated in his efforts by his conviction that there was a weakness in the Zen teaching styles of Senzaki and Sokei-an for American students: "Coming under the influence of Buddhism for only two or three hours a week and then returning to the cares and distractions of the worldly life, they fall back into the conventional life of the world." This debate continues in the West today, and Zen (and other Buddhist) monastic candidates from the West remain relatively few. The Zen training approach of Sokei-an, which accommodated lay practice, has prevailed.

Sokei-an proved adept at blending traditional rigor with flexibility. He produced translations for his American students of classic texts such as *The Platform Sutra of the Sixth Patriarch* and *The Record of Rinzai*. But early on, he concluded that the Americans could not withstand the rigors of Japanese *zazen* postures and conducted seated meditation sessions instead. Sokei-an was clearly willing to address the specific needs and limitations of Western students. Indeed, it was in answer to those needs, as he perceived them, that Sokei-an, against the wishes of his teacher, Sokatsu, gave up his lay status and became an ordained Zen Buddhist priest in 1933. Deeply angered, Sokatsu disowned his disciple for a time.

Sokei-an confessed his personal sorrow over his failure to have trained a Dharma heir of his own. Yet the onetime poet and essayist disdained to publish books on Buddhism, and his lectures to his students were collected only years after his death. In one of them, he declared:

> At this time, I cannot take the Oriental attitude toward my disciples in this country because this is just the dawn before true discipline begins. When I come to this country again in the next incarnation, it will be different! [. . .] Today a student may come to the temple to meet a Zen master. He may spend a year or two without passing a koan, and then he will go home and read some books — perhaps write a book himself — and become a famous scholar! Another will meditate in a corner and think, "Oh, I am in touch with the White Brotherhood in Tibet — wonderful!" And he will spring from his seat and write a book, claiming to be a great master.

The jibe at the Theosophist type of Esoteric Buddhist is clear. The reference to the student-become-scholar was likely a veiled criticism of Alan Watts, whom Sokei-an came to know well in the late 1930s. Watts had published *The Spirit of Zen*, an evocative and intelligent portrayal of

Zen practice, while still a young man in London. When he moved to New York, he attended the First Zen Institute — as Sokei-an's *zendo* came to be designated — for a few weeks, engaging in regular *sanzen* (private interviews between master and disciple) with Sokei-an. Things did not go well. Watts, who could not solve a single koan, felt himself under intolerable pressure from Sokei-an, and their final *sanzen* ended in a shouting match.

The version of these events offered by Watts in his autobiography, *In My Own Way* (1972), is valuable for its perspective on Sokei-an. It is also markedly uncomfortable in tone. Watts insisted that he had asked Sokei-an to be his Zen teacher because he was the only such teacher available, "although in Asia it is often the custom to shop around for a teacher with whom one feels a special rapport." Sokei-an taught students according to the Rinzai method, first perfected by the Japanese Zen master Hakuin, which stressed the solution of koans. Watts preferred the less structured approaches of other Japanese masters, such as Bankei. Nonetheless, Watts kept up the koan studies for some weeks "contrary to my lone wolf inclination to find my own way." At last, he resolved to employ his own methods: "I decided, therefore, to change my approach and study with Sokei-an without his knowing it. I wanted to observe a Zen master in his personal everyday life, and for this I had ample opportunity, since he visited us often at the hotel, and accompanied us to restaurants and for drives about the countryside."

The ample opportunities stemmed from the fact that Watts's wife Eleanor was the daughter of Ruth Fuller Everett, who became Sokei-an's lover and ultimately married him just before his death in 1945. As Ruth Fuller Sasaki, she was active for two decades more as a writer and teacher on Zen. Whether Sokei-an was unaware of being observed by Watts is open to doubt. The portrayal Watts went on to provide was of a vivid and robust Zen master at home with himself and the world, happy to have fallen in love, and now and then fond of shocking Western sensibilities by using a fart joke to illustrate a point of the Dharma. Watts concluded: "If I have stressed the wayward elements of Sokei-an's personality, it is only because I felt that he was basically on the same team as I; that he bridged the spiritual and the earthy, and that he was as humorously earthy as he was spiritually awakened." The sense of awkwardness, of ruffled sensibility and pride, persists in this explanation.

Sokei-an, like Senzaki, was interned during the war. He was sent first to Ellis Island, in June 1942. The exposed climate was not good for a man in his sixties with a weakening heart and high blood pressure. As his health declined, his New York students and supporters pressed his case with the U.S. government, securing a release in 1943. But Sokei-an continued to decline, and he died in May 1945, just after giving an evening lecture.

❖

Whereas Senzaki and Sokei-an labored with the practical difficulties of training Americans in Zen, D. T. Suzuki (1870–1966) succeeded in reaching a broad public in Europe and America. There is no dispute that the writings and lectures of Suzuki were the foremost factor in the increase of interest in and sympathy toward Zen in the West in the first half of the twentieth century.

Suzuki was born into a family with strong traditional ties to the medical profession. His father, a doctor, died when Suzuki was six, leaving his family in poverty. In his teens, Suzuki had contact with Greek Orthodox missionaries, who urged on him a copy of a Japanese translation of Genesis. He later wrote:

> I read it, but it seemed to make no sense at all. In the beginning there was God — but why should God create the world? That puzzled me very much. [. . .] I went to another missionary, a Protestant this time, and asked him this same question. He told me that everything must have a creator in order to come into existence, and hence the world must have a creator, too. Then who created God, I asked. God created himself, he replied. He is not a creature. This was not at all a satisfactory answer to me, and always this same question has remained a stumbling block to my becoming a Christian.

Suzuki studied Zen at Engakuji first under Kōsen and then, after 1892, under Sōen. Pursuant to the lay outlook of his teachers, Suzuki also attended Tokyo Imperial University, although he did not complete his degree. At this time, Suzuki entered into an admiring correspondence with Paul Carus, whose philosophical portrayal of Buddhism seemed to Suzuki an ideal portal for the importation of Zen to the West. In 1896, Suzuki was enabled, through Sōen's influence, to travel to the United States to study under Carus and to assist editorially with the Open Court Press.

In the weeks before leaving Japan and his teacher, Suzuki felt a heightened resolve to press on with his koan meditation. His specific koan was *Mu*. That koan, created by the Chinese T'ang dynasty Zen master Joshu (778–897), was later described by Suzuki in a scholarly lecture:

> [Joshu] was once asked by a monk, "Has a dog the Buddha-nature?" Answered the master, *"Mu!" "Mu!"* (*wu*) literally means "no." But when it is used as a koan the meaning does not matter, it is simply *"Mu!"* The disciple is told to concentrate his mind on the meaningless sound *"Mu!"* regardless of whether it means "yes" or "no" or, in fact, anything else. Just *"Mu!" "Mu!" "Mu!"*

The design of the koan exercise was to frustrate any attempt at an answer relying on philosophical analysis with its dualist categories. In an autobiographical essay, Suzuki described his own struggles with the koan and the experiential manner in which they were resolved.

> Up until then I had always been conscious that *Mu* was in my mind. [. . .] But towards the end of that *sesshin,* about the fifth day, I ceased to be conscious of *Mu*. [. . .] That is the real state of samadhi. But this samadhi alone is not enough. You must come out of that state, be awakened from it, and that awakening is *Prajna*. That moment of coming out of the samadhi and seeing it for what it is — that is satori. When I came out of that state of samadhi during that *sesshin* I said, "I see. This is it."

His realization was thereafter confirmed by Sōen.

Suzuki's account exemplifies an outlook that exasperated numerous critics both during and after his lifetime — that is, his insistence that Zen enlightenment falls outside all historical and linguistic criteria as an ultimate state of consciousness understood only by those who have experienced it. As the French scholar Bernard Faure argued,

> The assumption that there is an "essence" of Buddhism, a kind of perennial Dharma to which only "authentic" masters would have access, is to be rejected as ideologically suspect. It is interesting to note that, despite

its supposedly unconditioned character, the "pure experience" of awakening is said [by Suzuki] to be inaccessible to the isolated practitioner and can only be triggered with the guidance of a master affiliated to the orthodox tradition.

This argument has its merit, as it challenges the validity of grandiose spiritual claims, Buddhist or otherwise. But ideological suspicions alone cannot dismiss the substantial historical evidence that orthodox "conditioned" means of training — what other means but "conditioned" ones are available to humankind? — can now and then lead to "unconditioned," "enlightened," or "mystical" states readily recognizable across cultures. There is perhaps a further issue at work here, and that is the nature and quality of the knowledge of the Dharma that may be claimed by present-day Buddhologists, Western and Eastern alike. If Suzuki is correct, mere scholarly analysis is inherently marginalized, while the utterances of those who have attained enlightenment are forever privileged — beyond the critique of even the most brilliant academician who has not the requisite experience. Buddhologists have at times responded fiercely to this claim of inaccessibility.

❖

During his early twelve-year stay in America, Suzuki wrote his first major work, *Outlines of Mahayana Buddhism* (1907), in which he sought to place the experience of satori within the pancultural theory of mysticism proposed by William James in his *Varieties of Religious Experience*. Suzuki remained an extraordinarily prolific writer for fifty years thereafter. In 1911, he married Beatrice Erskine Lane (1878–1938), an American who was a member of the Theosophical Society and ultimately wrote respected works on Zen and Shingon Buddhism. Husband and wife influenced each other's interests, for Suzuki became a member of the Order of the Eastern Star, an offshoot of the Theosophical movement led by Annie Besant, which proclaimed Jiddu Krishnamurti to be the new World Teacher (until 1929, that is, when Krishnamurti resigned the post and the order, then went on to a distinguished career as an unaffiliated spiritual teacher). Even after Krishnamurti's resignation, Suzuki remained involved with the Theosophically inspired Mahayana Lodge in Osaka. During this period, Suzuki was sufficiently fascinated by the writings of Emanuel Swedenborg to translate several of his works into Japanese and to assist in founding the Japanese Swedenborg Society in 1914. His admiration for Helena Blavatsky and her book *The Voice of the Silence* has already been discussed in chapter 6. But Suzuki's interest in heterodox Western spiritual thought dwindled to nothing in the latter decades of his life, as his identification of Zen with Japanese culture and imperialism intensified.

By the 1930s, Imperial-Way Buddhism had emerged as a powerful cultural force in Japan. According to the Australian Soto Zen priest Brian Victoria, this form of Buddhism "represented the total and unequivocal subjugation of the Law of the Buddha to the Law of the Sovereign. In political terms, it meant subjugation of institutional Buddhism to the state and its policies." In practice, of course, this included the militaristic policies that fostered the Japanese alliance with Nazi Germany. Suzuki was an active proponent of Imperial-Way Buddhism for more than a decade, as he acknowledged in a 1946 postwar lecture delivered in Japan:

> Both before and after the Manchurian Incident [of 1931] all of us [Japanese Buddhists] applauded what had transpired as representing the growth of the empire. [. . .] At that time everyone was saying we had to be aggressively imperialistic. They said Japan had to go out into the world both industrially and economically because the country was too small to provide a living for its people. There simply wasn't enough food; people would starve.

But Suzuki did not limit the political confines of Zen practice to service of the Japanese empire. On the contrary, he believed that Zen could meld successfully with any political ideology:

> Zen has no special doctrine [. . .] except that it tries to release one from the bondage of birth and death, by means of certain intuitive modes of understanding peculiar to itself. It is, therefore, extremely flexible in adapting itself to almost any philosophy and moral doctrine as long as its intuitive teaching is not interfered with. It may be found wedded to anarchism or fascism, communism or democracy, atheism or idealism, or any political or economic dogmatism.

This quotation, which many present-day Western Buddhists and Bud-dhologists find reprehensible, is nonetheless a true summary of the history of Zen Buddhism in Japan, which has included rapt alliances with the shogunate, the emperors, and even — in the first decade of the twenti-eth century, through the efforts of the Soto priest Uchiyama Gudo and other Buddhist clergy — socialism and anarchism. This latter alliance, opposed by the vast majority of Zen and other Japanese Buddhist clergy, ended in the hanging of Gudo. Unpleasant as Suzuki's words are, they reflect an essential truth as to the metamorphoses of which Zen, when framed ahistorically and amorally as by Suzuki, is capable. As John Daido Loori, the present abbot of Zen Mountain Monastery in New York, ac-knowledged, "Buddhism is not immune to the kind of distortions that have been used throughout human history by virtually all of the world's religions to justify so-called holy wars." This raises the off-putting ques-tion of whether instances of religious support of warring governments can be accurately described as "distortions" when they have been pre-sent throughout human history. Given the history of Buddhist-inspired or Buddhist-sanctioned violence in Sri Lanka and Tibet, it is clear that Buddhists do not always equate the Dharma with pacifism. Buddhists, like Christians and other religionists, are not always in accord with the teachings of their founder, who clearly taught the need for restraint.

It is wishful thinking to accord to Suzuki and a handful of fellow Japanese writers on Zen the accomplishment of inventing an entirely novel construct that could dovetail its teachings with the extremes of militarism. As Brian Victoria stressed,

Looking at this period in isolation from its historical antecedents suggests that a phenomenon such as Zen's endorsement of Japanese militarism can be explained solely by the events of the Meiji period and thereafter. Indeed, some present-day observers have adopted this viewpoint and maintain that this phenomenon was no more than a momentary aberra-tion of modern Japanese Zen or its leaders. More informed commenta-tors such as Ichikawa Hakugen, however, make it clear that the unity of Zen and the sword has deep roots in Zen Buddhist doctrine and history.

Takuan Soho (1573–1645), for example, was a renowned Zen teacher who composed a classic manual on Zen and swordsmanship, *The Unfettered*

Mind. This is not to say, as Suzuki did, that Zen and the code of the samurai are essentially one. Zen is far too diverse in its forms and teachings to be so reduced.

❖

Suzuki's most famous works are his three-volume *Essays in Zen Buddhism* (1927, 1933, 1934), *Mysticism: Christian and Buddhist* (1957), and *Zen and Japanese Culture* (1959). He also served as editor of the English-language journal the *Eastern Buddhist,* which he founded in 1921 and guided until the outbreak of World War II. His status, in both the West and Japan, as a scholar on Zen was unsurpassed during his lifetime. The eminent British historian Arnold Toynbee opined that the Western encounter with Zen spurred by Suzuki would, in the future, be viewed as comparable in importance to the development of nuclear energy. In his home country, Suzuki received an honorary doctorate from Otani University in Kyoto and the Cultural Medal from the emperor, to whom Suzuki presented lectures on Zen in 1947. Suzuki spent extensive time in the West, including two long residencies in the United States (1897–1909 and 1949–1958). The earlier stay represented his apprenticeship, under Carus, in the art of communicating the East to the West. During the postwar 1950s, his missionary efforts flourished, and he was not only read but also revered.

Christmas Humphreys, a prominent British Buddhist, first met Suzuki when the latter addressed the World Congress of Faiths in London in 1936. Thereafter, Humphreys served as Suzuki's European literary agent. His assessment of Suzuki mirrored that of many Western Buddhist scholars and practitioners of the time:

> In fifty years in the field of Buddhism I have been privileged to meet at least five men of great spiritual and scholastic attainment, but of only one of them is it true that his master gave him, at the time of his attainment, the name Daisetz, which means "great humility." Working closely with him, listening to explanations often illustrated on the back of an envelope, one for a moment "understood."

Suzuki's writings on Zen were far and away the best then available in the West. He produced a valuable translation and commentary on the

Lankavatara Sutra and was, in his less polemical writings, astute in pointing to the continuities between Indian Mahayana texts, Chinese Chan teachings, and the approaches of Japanese Zen. Suzuki was also a gifted stylist and translator, whose best works afford pleasure as well as knowledge. His appreciations of Japanese culture are sensitive and replete with valuable detail. Without question, he favored his Rinzai school of Zen over the Soto school, which he largely ignored and otherwise deprecated. Indeed, during his public lectures in the United States in the 1960s, he insisted that the great Soto master Dogen had never achieved enlightenment and hence that his works were unworthy of serious attention, a stance with which no current Zen thinker would agree. It is worth recalling — not as a justification for Suzuki, but rather to emphasize the changing nature of historical frameworks — that Dogen (1200–1253) had largely been forgotten in his home country until his scholarly rediscovery in the 1920s. It is also worth noting the irony that Suzuki's popularization of Zen in the West spurred appreciation of Dogen's writings as well. As the German scholar Edward Conze wrote in 1968, two years after Suzuki's death, "As a direct result of Suzuki's books on Zen there is now a flourishing Zen movement all over the world, and this movement has caused an immense interest in those aspects of Zen not covered by Suzuki."

The key point here is that the Zen "movement" created so successfully by Suzuki was never under his doctrinal control. The Western fascination with Zen took on its own momentum. A remarkable episode that illustrates the nature of Suzuki's powerful but permeable influence was recounted in a 1958 letter by Jack Kerouac. In the 1950s, Kerouac was a highly serious student of Buddhism, the teachings of which permeated several of his works, most notably the novel *The Dharma Bums* (1958). In a letter to the poet Philip Whalen — who some three decades later would become an American Zen abbot — Kerouac described a visit he paid to Suzuki at his New York apartment. Suzuki had learned of Kerouac's expressed affinity for Zen and extended the invitation so as to assess for himself what the fuss over the famous Beat writer was about. Kerouac, accompanied by Allen Ginsberg and Peter Orlovsky, received green tea brewed and whisked by Suzuki. The three poets, in turn, composed spontaneous haiku for their celebrated host. As they were departing, Kerouac suddenly realized he [Suzuki] was my old fabled father from China and I said, "I would like to spend the rest of my life with you sir," and he said "Sometime." And he kept pushing us out the door, down the stairs, as tho impatient [. . .] but then when we were out on the street he kept giggling and making signs at us through the window and finally said "Don't forget the tea!" And I said "The Key?" He said "The Tea."

All this reads as suitable Beat spontaneity, but there was a bitter aftertaste, as expressed by Kerouac in a letter some three months later to the poet Gary Snyder, a serious student of Zen Buddhism. Snyder had been the model for Japhy Ryder, the backpacking open-road American Buddhist protagonist of *The Dharma Bums,* but both Snyder and Ruth Fuller Sasaki, the widow of Sokei-an, found fault with the book for the liberties it took with its depictions of Buddhist teachings. Kerouac fought back, and his counterattack included D. T. Suzuki, although Suzuki had not overtly criticized the book:

> For Mrs. Sasaki to say that "it was a good portrait of Gary but he doesn't know *anything* about Buddhism" is just so fuckin typical of what's wrong with official Buddhism and all official religions today — woe, clashings, divisions, sects, jealousies, formalities, do-goodism, actionism, no repose, no universal love-try, no abandoning of arbitrary conceptions for a moment. Even Suzuki was looking at me through slitted eyes as tho I was a monstrous impostor of some kind (at least I feel that, I dunno). Why should the Japanese make the chief claim on Buddhism when it came from an Aryan Indian, and Bodhisattva Bodhidharma came from the West?

The seemingly racist "slitted eyes" emphasis should not entirely overshadow the vital point raised here by Kerouac, who had a profound respect for the Asian Buddhist tradition. Kerouac was insisting that, historically, Buddhism has always been in a process of evolution and that the emerging nature of American Buddhism was as worthy of respect as the venerable Asian traditions. As long as Zen was studied as an exotic other, it could never take on genuine life. Kerouac's response here indirectly addresses — three decades in advance — the spate of Western scholarly criticisms that emerged in the 1990s over Suzuki's chauvinistic portrayals of Japanese Zen and its link to Japanese nationalism.

The criticisms are valid, but they overshadow the key fact that earlier Western readers of Suzuki were often able to take what they could use without accepting his dogmatic limitations. Broad cultural influences, such as the interest spurred by Suzuki's writings, are by their nature diffuse and heterodox. Suzuki's theories on Zen interested Western readers far less than his translations of the scriptures, teaching stories, and koans of the Zen tradition. Western readers would brook no obstructions to their enthusiasm, and obstructions there were, such as this statement by Suzuki — he could not have put it plainer — in his essay "An Interpretation of Zen-Experience," submitted in 1939 to an East-West philosophical conference:

> The only thing, let me repeat, we can state here about Zen is that it is an altogether unique product of the Oriental mind, refusing to be classified under any known heading, as either a philosophy, or a religion, or a form of mysticism as it is generally understood in the West. Zen must be studied and analyzed from a point of view which is still unknown among Western philosophers, and I am sure the study will give us a rich yield, not only in philosophy and the science of religion, but also in psychology and allied studies.

Thus, for the West to understand Zen, it would need, spiritually speaking, to start over.

One of the principal means by which Suzuki was able to rouse enthusiasm for Zen in the West was his embrace of a psychological approach to its teachings. Suzuki was not only an appreciative student of William James, but he was also a ready advocate of merging what he perceived to be the shared insights of Zen and the psychoanalytic theories of Freud and Jung, which stressed the debilitating and creative roles of the unconscious. As the German Jesuit scholar Heinrich Dumoulin noted,

> The reception of Zen in the West happened at a time in which Western psychology, through its new discoveries, had aroused uncommon general interest. [. . .] Many Westerners were ready to join their Eastern counterparts in a common exploration of the *terra incognita*. It was in no small measure due to modern psychology that Oriental meditation spread so

rapidly in the West. This conjunction was facilitated by D. T. Suzuki's openness to and understanding of modern psychology, which was still an avant garde movement when he first encountered it during his formative years in America.

Suzuki was willing to equate the source of Buddhist wisdom with the unmediated experience of the unconscious mind. In a 1934 essay, he stated flatly: "The sutras, especially Mahayana sutras, are direct expressions of spiritual experiences; they contain intuitions gained by digging deeply into the abyss of the Unconscious, and they make no pretension of presenting these intuitions through the mediumship of the intellect." But Suzuki was careful to distinguish between the treatment of unconscious disorders — the task of psychoanalysis — and the disciplined conquest of the unconscious that Zen enlightenment entails: "When this liberation takes place, we have the 'trained' unconscious operating in the field of consciousness. And we know what Bankei's 'Unborn' or the Chinese Zen master's 'everyday mind' is."

Suzuki's willing alliance with Western psychology was in stark contrast to his determination always to distinguish sharply between Buddhist and Christian spiritual teachings. He closely followed the views of his teacher Shaku Sōen in this regard. In *Mysticism: Christian and Buddhist,* billed on the dust jacket by its American publisher as Suzuki's affirmation "that the superficial differences between Zen, Shin [Pure Land] and Christian schools are vastly less important than the fact that all three express the same fundamental insights," Suzuki argued for the exact opposite view. While granting that the fourteenth-century German mystic Meister Eckhart had given, in his sermons, insights capable of being mistaken for Zen teachings, Suzuki made it clear that "as far as I can judge, Eckhart seems to be an extraordinary 'Christian.'" As for more orthodox Christian teachings, Suzuki ticked off their comparative shortcomings to Buddhist wisdom: "Being combative and exclusive, Christianity tends to wield an autocratic and sometimes domineering power over others, in spite of its claim to democracy and universal brotherhood. [. . .] But there is no doubt that Buddhism is a religion of peace, serenity, equanimity, and equilibrium. It refuses to be combative and exclusive."

A graphic example of Suzuki's polite but firm disrespect for the abilities of Christian thinkers to grasp Zen realities appears in a 1959 dialogue, by means of written exchanges, between Suzuki and Thomas Merton, which was published in Merton's *Zen and the Birds of Appetite* (1968). Merton was respectful in the extreme and hesitant as to the adequacy of his understanding of Zen Buddhism. Suzuki, for his part, drew yet another sharp distinction between the two religions: "There are two types of mentality which fundamentally differ one from the other: (1) affective, personal and dualistic, and (2) nonaffective, nonpersonal and nondualistic. Zen belongs to the latter and Christianity naturally to the former." Merton, in Suzuki's view, exemplified this divide by failing to comprehend the richness of Zen spiritual insight: "Father Merton's emptiness, when he uses this term, does not go far enough and deep enough, I am afraid. [. . .] Father Merton's emptiness is still on the level of God as Creator and does not go up to the Godhead [the absolute experience of reality offered by Zen]." Merton accepted the rebuke as a necessary lesson: "It is clear that the strongly personalistic tone of Christian mysticism [. . .] generally seems to prohibit a full equation with Zen experience." Merton would continue to pursue his studies of Zen and other forms of Buddhism. His later encounter with Thich Nhat Hanh, to which we will come shortly, proved a more fruitful exchange.

❖

During the 1960s, so-called Zen centers — a very few monastic, most not — were established in major cities such as New York, San Francisco, and Los Angeles. Those centers were run by transplanted Japanese Zen roshis (spiritual leaders), who struggled to overcome language and cultural barriers so as to reach Western students.

Among the postwar wave of Zen missionary teachers, the most charismatic and successful was unquestionably the Soto Zen priest Shunryu Suzuki, founder of the San Francisco Zen Center and author of *Zen Mind, Beginner's Mind* (1970), a selection from his talks to his students, which remains unsurpassed as an introduction to Zen for Western readers. Shunryu Suzuki was casual, even humorous, yet direct in tone, and he did not soft-pedal the distinctions between Buddhist practice and Western ethical conceptions that failed to take into account the fluid uses to which mental energies can be put for the sake of attainment:

Even to have a good thing in your mind is not so good. Buddha some-times said, "You should be like this. You ought not to be like that." But to have what he says in your mind is not so good. It is a kind of burden to you, and you may not actually feel so good. In fact to harbor some ill will may even be better than to have some idea in your mind of what is good or of what you ought to do. To have some mischievous idea in your mind is sometimes very agreeable. That is true. Actually, good and bad is not the point. Whether or not you make yourself peaceful is the point, and whether or not you stick to it.

Shunryu Suzuki first came to America in 1959, assigned as the new priest for Sokoji, a temple with a Japanese American congregation lo-cated at 1881 Bush Street in San Francisco. He did not arrive as a pres-tigious person; he had no great status among the Soto Zen clergy in Japan, although he had served as abbot of Rinso-in, a Soto temple in Yaizu. During World War II, his stance, as described by his biographer and American disciple David Chadwick, was that "there was little he could do. He didn't oppose the war, didn't oppose the government, didn't advocate surrender, didn't say that Japan was wrong. He didn't want Japan to lose the war, he just wanted it to be over. He was torn be-tween his belief in Buddhism and peace, and his devotion to Buddhism and country."

Shunryu Suzuki persistently expressed a desire for a position as a mis-sionary in America; he studied English for several years prior to his 1959 appointment in San Francisco. His new congregation soon grew to in-clude Zen aspirants from all parts of the Bay Area who were drawn to the new teacher. As Mel Weitsman, an American Zen abbot and former disciple of Shunryu Suzuki, observed,

During his twelve years here, his command of the language became bet-ter and better. Though he often had to grope for just the right expres-sion, he usually found it. But even when searching for the right expression he was always eloquent. In fact, someone who heard him give a talk in Japanese and a talk in English on the same day found the English talk far more innovative and compelling — perhaps even helped by the fact that English was not his native language.

The response Shunryu Suzuki struck with American students led to the founding of the San Francisco Zen Center, which in 1969 established new quarters at 300 Page Street. During this period, land for the first Zen Buddhist monastery in America — Zenshinji, the Tassajara Zen Mountain Center, in the Los Padres National Forest in central coastal California — was purchased, thanks to financial support elicited by Shunryu Suzuki's teachings. He worked on the construction of the monastic facilities, hauling large stones found locally for use as building material. As Weitsman recalled,

> His wife, Mitsu-san, came down from San Francisco in that summer of 1970 and was very worried about him. She knew he was very ill and thought he was working too hard. Sometimes when she would pass by he would pretend that he was resting and then go back to moving stones. She once chastised him, using the familiar name for an abbot: "Hojo-san! You are cutting your life short!" He replied, "If I don't cut my life short, my students will not grow."

Shunryu Suzuki died in 1971, leaving his Dharma heir, Zentatsu Richard Baker, as the new roshi of the San Francisco Zen Center and of Tassajara.

From the San Francisco Zen Center has branched strains of American Zen that show signs of endurance. When confused with D. T. Suzuki, Shunryu Suzuki would say, "No, he's the big Suzuki, I'm the little Suzuki." Both men proved to be gifted Zen missionaries — D. T. Suzuki as a disseminator of Zen thought, Shunryu Suzuki as an approachable embodiment of it. Taizan Maezumi Roshi, a Japanese Zen master who founded the Los Angeles Zen Center, offered this tribute to Shunryu Suzuki:

> There's Page Street in the city and Tassajara. So many people sitting zazen all over America, even Europe. When he came, there was none of this. Many priests came before him. Even before this century, all kinds of priests in the Zen tradition came to America. We don't really know why, but until he came, no one started anything that lasted. After him, so much happened. That's what I most appreciate.

9

FORBIDDEN TIBET: WESTERN EXPLORATIONS AND FANTASIES

❖

Madame Blavatsky had spread the teachings of Buddhism through her tales of magical letters received from Himalayan Mahatmas. The next generation of Western students was, however, less inclined to rest content with mere rumors of Buddhist masters. One of the most resolute of that generation, the long-lived Alexandra David-Neel (1868–1969), was a member, in her early twenties, of Blavatsky's Theosophical Society. But David-Neel later took pains to deride both the society and its founder. In one of her most famous works, *Magic and Mystery in Tibet* (1929), she drew on her own real-life expeditions to Tibet to state emphatically that

> communications from mystic masters to their disciples through gross material means, such as letters falling from the ceiling or epistles one finds under one's pillow, are unknown in lamaist mystic circles. When questions regarding such facts are put to contemplative hermits, erudite lamas or high lamaist dignitaries, they can hardly believe that the inquirer is in earnest and not an irreverent joker.

Termed by the British novelist Lawrence Durrell "the most astonishing Frenchwoman of our time," she was born Alexandra David in 1868 in Paris but was raised in Brussels, as her Freemason father's liberal politics compelled the family to leave France. From earliest childhood, she was restless and unhappy both at home and in the Catholic convent school to which her parents sent her in vain hopes of keeping her in check. Twice in her teenage years, she ran away — the first time hiking across the Alps and on into the Italian Lake District, the second time bicycling from Brussels over the Ardennes. At age nineteen, she relocated to London, where she took up esoteric studies with both the Theosophical Society and a group known as the Supreme Gnosis. But David found herself more fundamentally drawn to the wisdom of the East. In 1891, she voyaged to India and studied there with a Brahman yoga master, Bashkarananda. She returned the following year to Paris, where she pursued a career as an opera singer, winning praise from the composer Jules Massenet for her portrayal of his famous coquette, Manon. All the while, however, due to her leftist and feminist sympathies, police dossiers were being opened on her both in Paris and in Brussels.

In 1900, at age thirty-two, David met the man with whom she would enjoy one of the strangest happy marriages on record. Philip Neel was a French engineer whom, after a four-year courtship, David agreed to marry. Immediately following the ceremony, she felt herself unpleasantly confined in spirit, and within days the couple ceased to live together. Even so, they remained devoted to each other for the next thirty-seven years (until Neel's death in 1941) — despite the fact that for most of that time, David-Neel was living half a world away in Tibet and other parts of central Asia. Through his lucrative profession, Neel financially supported her extensive travels and also served faithfully as her literary agent, seeing to the commercial publication of her classic works of travel, ethnography, and Buddhist studies — most notably, *My Journey to Lhasa* (1927), *Magic and Mystery in Tibet* (1929), and *Initiations and Initiates in Tibet* (1931). About his death, David-Neel wrote simply, "I had lost the best of husbands and my only friend."

From 1906 to 1911, David-Neel studied in Paris, Brussels, and London, obtaining a thorough academic grounding in Buddhist philosophy and the rudiments of Sanskrit and Tibetan. In 1906, while in London, she met Anagarika Dharmapala, whose influence on her was considerable. (Dharmapala, like David-Neel, had links to Theosophy, which he would later disown.) Her first book, *The Buddhism of the Buddha and Buddhist Modernism* (1911), praised the "modernist" reforms of the Maha Bodhi Society, which Dharmapala had founded in 1891. In this same period, she initiated a correspondence with D. T. Suzuki.

In 1911, David-Neel sailed for India, where she worked as a journalist and became, in 1912, the first Western woman ever to meet with — and interview — a Dalai Lama (the Thirteenth, who, like the current Fourteenth, was living in exile in India due to Chinese incursions on Tibetan soil). Her early impressions of him were strongly colored by her family background of anticlericalism: "I don't like popes. I don't like the kind of Buddhist Catholicism over which he presides. Everything about him is affected, he is neither cordial nor kind."

Some fifty years later, David-Neel came to reject those earlier views. In one of her last books, *Immortality and Reincarnation* (1961), she warned that

foreign writers commonly bestow titles such as "Living God," "Reincarnation of Buddha," "Spiritual Head of all Buddhists," and so forth on the Dalai Lama. A Dalai Lama is nothing of the sort. He is not a reincarnated god; and the Buddha, who has attained nirvana, doesn't reincarnate. No one among the Buddhists occupies a position similar to that of the pope in the Catholic Church. [. . .] Each Buddhist can adapt, according to his desire, the doctrines of whatever Buddhist sect seem best to him.

David-Neel's meeting with the Dalai Lama — which included a firm admonition from His Holiness that she learn Tibetan if she intended to progress in her Buddhist studies — inspired a quest that would fully absorb her for the next thirteen years. The ultimate goal was to become the first Western woman ever to reach Lhasa, the fabled capital of Tibet and the great center of Tibetan Buddhist teachings. But foreigners were forbidden access to Tibet by way of India unless they were on political or trade missions approved by the Raj. In this, the British were in accord with the wishes of the Thirteenth Dalai Lama, who had been restored to his rule in Lhasa in 1912. Notwithstanding his encouragement to David-Neel, His Holiness believed firmly that free access to Tibet by Westerners would only serve to weaken Tibetan Buddhism, which had long thrived in isolation.

David-Neel was undeterred. In 1914, she made her first crossing into Tibet — illegally, as Raj officials suspected her of spying on behalf of France. Nonetheless, she managed to find lodging in a monastery just inside the Tibetan border and spent the opening months of World War I deepening her knowledge of the Tibetan language. She then spent some months in a meditative cave hermitage in neighboring Sikkim before again passing illicitly into Tibet in 1915, when she succeeded in proceeding as far north as Shigatse. Her forays came to the attention of the British, who ordered her deportation. David-Neel was indignant: "What right had they to erect barriers around a country which was not even lawfully theirs?"

She was now compelled to approach Tibet by way of China. Following a circuitous route through Burma, Korea, and Japan (where she was the guest of D. T. Suzuki), during which she lived and studied in a variety of Buddhist monasteries, David-Neel, at age forty-nine, arrived in Peking in October 1917 and readied herself for the most difficult portion of her journey: a lengthy trek across the Chinese steppes to the eastern borderlands of Tibet. She recognized that her chances of success would be enhanced were she in the company of a native man of the region who could instruct her in the niceties of Tibetan language and customs, as well as deflect curiosity from a solitary woman. To this end, she struck an agreement with a young lama from Sikkim named Yongden. As in the case of her marriage, David-Neel came to form an utterly unconventional relationship with Lama Yongden, whom she originally hired as a servant and ultimately adopted as her legal son. They remained together for nearly forty years.

From Peking, they traveled — alone or as members of yak caravans — some two thousand miles across China while civil war raged in that nation. They lived on simple rations and carried minimal clothing and equipment, although David-Neel always kept with her a pistol, a camera, and a journal to record her observations. At last, they reached the great Tibetan monastery of Kumbum, where, despite the customary proscription of women, David-Neel and Yongden were allowed to remain for three years. David-Neel honed her skills in Tibetan and was given the name *Khadoma,* meaning a dakini, or feminine Buddhist deity.

In the winter of 1923, David-Neel and Yongden attempted to reach Lhasa, traveling in disguise as ragged Tibetan beggars on a sacred pilgrimage. David-Neel stained her skin with an admixture of charcoal, cocoa, and oil and dyed her brown hair black with Chinese ink. In October 1924, she attained her goal, a moment of which she wrote in *My Journey to Lhasa,* the book that would make her reputation: "The first white woman had entered forbidden Lhasa and shown the way. May others follow and open with loving hearts the gates of the wonderland, 'for the good, for the welfare of many,' as the Buddhist Scriptures say."

David-Neel's account of her journey was stylish and riveting, replete with encounters with brigands and the confidences of Tibetan lamas. But there were skeptics as well as admirers, given her matter-of-fact accounts of events, such as how she had warmed herself during a Tibetan snowstorm en route. Lama Yongden suggested that she employ the "thumo reskiang practice" of generating internal heat, which she had learned — "with great difficulties, showing an extreme perseverance in my desire to be initiated into the secret" — from her prior Tibetan teachers:

> I saw some hermits seated night after night, motionless in the snow, entirely naked, sunk in meditation, while the terrible winter blizzard whirled and hissed around them! I saw under the bright full moon the tent given to their disciples who, on the shore of a lake or a river in the heart of winter, dried on their bodies, as on a stove, a number of sheets dipped in the icy water! And I learned the means of performing these feats.

David-Neel was thus able to dry the moist and recalcitrant flint and steel so that she could start a fire to warm both Yongden and herself.

In 1991, Herbert Benson, a professor at Harvard Medical School, made a presentation at a symposium called "MindScience," sponsored by the Mind/Body Medical Institute of Harvard, New England Deaconess Hospital, and Tibet House New York. (Participants included the Fourteenth Dalai Lama, Howard Gardner, Daniel Goleman, and Robert A. F. Thurman.) The stimulus of Benson's presentation was the David-Neel account quoted above, from which Benson first learned of "*gTum-mo* yoga." With the cooperation of the Dalai Lama (an admirer of the works of David-Neel), Benson conducted studies on the technique among Tibetan monks living in northern India. One of his accounts reads as a virtual parallel to that of David-Neel:

> On a night considered to be the coldest of the year, the first full moon of that period, and in a room temperature of 40°F, just a few degrees above freezing, these monks dipped sheets into icy water and then taking these dripping wet sheets, which measured some 3 x 6 feet, wrapped

their essentially naked bodies in them. You and I would shiver uncontrollably and perhaps even die if we did this, but here, within three to five minutes the sheets started to steam and within forty-five minutes were completely dry. The monks repeated the process twice more before dawn. It was truly remarkable.

Benson stressed the need for further study of "the more subtle aspects of mind."

❖

David-Neel returned to France in 1925. Twelve years later, she commenced a new round of Asian travels through China and its borderlands with Tibet. During World War II, she received, through the French consulate in Chengtu, in western China, an annual stipend from the Vichy collaborationist government in return for unspecified services. The extent to which she supplied information to the Axis cause remains unclear, although she was suspected of this by the Chinese Nationalist government of Chiang Kai-shek, which sided with the Allied cause. John Blofeld, a Western Buddhist author of repute who was a British officer at the time, encountered David-Neel in Chengtu in the early 1940s. To David-Neel's biographers, Barbara and Michael Foster, Blofeld gave this account:

Jokingly, I asked why she chose this luxurious abode in preference to the exhilarating hardships of a lonely mountain cave. In reply she gave me a highly detailed description of a recent journey into Tibet, during which she had been robbed of her possessions and thus forced to return immediately to a city where she could obtain credit and hope to receive funds from France. Only later did I discover that the whole long story, doing much credit to her self-image, was pure fiction.

The biographers surmised convincingly that David-Neel did not wish to betray her Vichy affiliation.

In her later years, David-Neel received all the honors due her daring, persistence, and brilliance. The Geographical Society of Paris bestowed on her its Gold Medal. She became a Chevalier of the French Legion of Honor and was awarded the Insignia of the Chinese Order of the Brilliant Star. She was renowned as the ultimate expositor of the exotic mysteries of Tibet — no mean feat, given that the "Forbidden Tibet" genre was already a half century old when she first entered its ranks.

David-Neel lived in physical and psychological isolation in her final years, particularly so after the death of Lama Yongden in 1955. Yongden had not fared well in cultural exile in the West. He died at age fifty-six after years of protracted depression and alcoholism, accentuated perhaps by David-Neel's tendency to regard him foremost as a domestic servant rather than as an adopted son and literary collaborator. Indeed, four of David-Neel's lesser-known yet fascinating works — the novels *Mipam* (1935), *Tibetan Tale of Love and Magic* (1938), and *The Power of Nothingness* (1954), as well as the translations of Tibetan legends gathered as *The Superhuman Life of Gesar of Ling* (1934) — were written in tandem with Yongden, who was credited as coauthor of the last three works and, to David-Neel's credit, accorded sole authorship of *Mipam,* the first novel written from a Tibetan perspective for a Western audience. David-Neel had stylistically recast the novel in French after Yongden had fashioned its characters and plotline.

She ended her days in a Tibetan-style house she built in Digne, in the Basses-Alpes. She died in 1969, at age one hundred, having lived to see her books rediscovered by a new generation of "alternative" Western readers, including a young Allen Ginsberg, who later wrote, "Blakean imagery in Alexandra David-Neel's *Magic and Mystery in Tibet* magnetized me toward Buddhist meditation." In the sixties, City Lights Publishers, founded by Beat poet Lawrence Ferlinghetti, reissued her *Secret Oral Teachings in Tibetan Buddhist Sects* (first published in 1951) in paperback format, therein to enter the rucksacks of Western seekers who seldom wandered quite so far East as had David-Neel. Tibet, of course, was not an option during this period due to the policies of the Chinese Communists.

David-Neel's stance toward the postwar Chinese invasion of Tibet would have startled many of her adoring Western readers. In *Four Thousand Years of Chinese Expansion* (1964), she portrayed the Communist occupation as all but inevitable, given the backwardness of the Tibetans and their long-standing dependence on Chinese protection. She further contended that endemic poverty and the rights of women would be better addressed by Communist rule. The paradox — at once poignant and repugnant — is that her love for traditional Tibet never diminished. But a few months before her passing, David-Neel confided to a friend her grief at being so far from the only land in which she had felt herself at home: "I should have died there, among the immense grassy solitudes close to the Tibetan lakes; for a bed the earth, grass or snow, for a ceiling the canvas of my tent and the great starry sky. [. . .] That would have been a beautiful death . . . grand."

❖

Walter Yeeling Evans-Wentz (1878–1965) is the personification of a still prominent Western fantasy — a restless, mystical-minded scholarly wanderer who found, in grand Himalayan settings, a stirring confirmation of Buddhist wisdom.

Born in 1878 in Trenton, New Jersey, of an alcoholic German immigrant father and a Welsh English Quaker mother gifted in the telling of fairy tales, Evans-Wentz experienced, at age twelve, what he later described as an awakening to an expanded "consciousness of existence." Among his realizations: "I have been haunted with the conviction that this is not the first time that I have been possessed of a human body." By his late teens, he had discovered the teachings of the Theosophical Society. After taking bachelor's and master's degrees at Stanford, he pursued at Jesus College, Oxford, further studies that combined religion, folklore, and anthropology.

These culminated in Evans-Wentz's first book, *The Fairy-Faith in Celtic Countries* (1913). During the course of his research, Evans-Wentz had maintained friendships with two Irish poets deeply inspired by Celtic mythology, William Butler Yeats (a visiting professor at Stanford while Evans-Wentz was a student there) and Æ (George William Russell). Together with these poets, to whom he dedicated his book, Evans-Wentz argued that the testimony of the indigenous residents of Ireland and other Celtic lands in favor of the existence of faerie beings and realms ought to be accepted by scholars as evidence pointing toward a spiritual dimension beyond their academic confines. Evans-Wentz argued two further points — that the Celtic tales of faerie realms concealed an ongoing belief in reincarnation that had survived some fifteen hundred years of imposed Christian orthodoxy, and that the cloud-hidden mountains of Connemara, in western Ireland, provided an ideal setting for the experience of spiritual perceptions. Both of these points — the truth of reincarnation and the lure of remote peaks — would be vividly confirmed for him by his Himalayan adventures to come.

In 1917, Evans-Wentz journeyed to Asia to study Eastern religions firsthand. As he later wrote, "I spent more than five years in such research, wandering from the palm-wreathed shores of Ceylon, and thence through the wonder-land of the Hindus, to the glacier-clad heights of the Himalayan Ranges, seeking out the Wise Men of the East." His travels led him to Sikkim, where in 1919 he formed a translating partnership with the Lama Kazi Dawa-Samdup, who some years before had served as teacher and guide to another intrepid Western traveler, Alexandra David-Neel. An older man (who had at this point three years to live), the lama was deeply versed in Tibetan Buddhism and also possessed a working knowledge of English, as evidenced by his authorship of a Tibetan-English dictionary. Dawa-Samdup had a pronounced taste for alcohol and a proclivity for breaking off his daily tasks to disappear for extended periods of private study and contemplation. But his devotion to Buddhism was unquestioned. What the younger Evans-Wentz had to offer were his considerable analytical gifts, which enabled him to follow patiently the recondite arguments of Tibetan Buddhist texts, and his willingness to serve as what the lama affectionately called his living "English dictionary." Evans-Wentz not only translated Tibetan texts by means of the lama's interpretive guidance, but he also became a "disciple" (Evans-Wentz's term) of the lama. The Oxford scholar turned Buddhist neophyte lived on a simplified diet of Quaker Oats, butter tea, rice, and, rarely, fresh vegetables. He wore embroidered robes of yak wool and a round woven cap of the type donned by Tibetan Buddhist scholars.

The first product of their collaboration proved to be, without question, the single most influential translation of a Buddhist text in the twentieth century. The *Bardo Thödol* first came to light as a text in the fourteenth century. According to Tibetan tradition, the teaching had been composed orally by Padmasambhava and transcribed by his consort and inspiration, Yeshe Tsogyal, in the eighth century, then buried in the Gampo hill country of central Tibet. There it was rediscovered six hundred years later as a *terma,* or hidden Dharma treasure, by Karma Lingpa, an incarnation of a disciple of Padmasambhava. Evans-Wentz grandly titled the text *The Tibetan Book of the Dead; or, The After-Death Experiences on the Bardo Plane.* This title drew its inspiration from the popularity of a text commonly known as *The Egyptian Book of the Dead,* translated by Sir E. A. Wallis Budge in 1917. The title fulfilled its proper task of attracting readers to a remarkable text. The three subsequent English translations — by Francesca Fremantle and Chögyam Trungpa (1975), Robert A. F. Thurman (1994), and Stephen Hodge with Martin Boord (1999) — have all retained *The Tibetan Book of the Dead* as the title because of its enduring fame. Nonetheless, the objection made to it by Trungpa is an important one: "The approach of comparing it with *The Egyptian Book of the Dead* in terms of mythology and lore of the dead person seems to miss the point, which is the fundamental principle of birth and death recurring constantly in this life. One could refer to this book as 'The Tibetan Book of Birth.'"

Published by Oxford University Press in 1927, the first *Tibetan Book of the Dead* gave credit, on its title page, to Lama Dawa-Samdup as translator and Evans-Wentz as compiler and editor. Subsequent recognition of the considerable faults of this translation — faults acknowledged by Evans-Wentz himself — should not obscure its genuine achievements. The account given of the *bardo,* or postdeath realm, in which the human spirit chose — or was lured into, depending on the Buddhistic acumen of the chooser — its next rebirth, was true terra incognita for even the most learned Western readers. It was one thing to acknowledge that rebirth was a belief held by Buddhism and other Eastern religions. It was another to be confronted by a translation of a text so meticulous in detail and visionary in content regarding the precise nature of the perils and illuminations of rebirths low and high. The possibility of access to this new form of knowledge — at root, a new form of consciousness — seemed to many Western thinkers to parallel, from a Buddhist perspective, the discovery of the unconscious proclaimed by the new science of psychoanalysis.

❖

Small wonder that Carl Gustav Jung, who eventually composed an extended essay on *The Tibetan Book of the Dead,* declared that the book became "my constant companion" from the time of its publication and that "to it I owe not only many stimulating ideas and discoveries, but also many fundamental insights." First and foremost, Jung insisted that the postdeath Tibetan rituals closely paralleled, in psychological impact, the process of analysis undergone by Jung's own patients. But Jung did allow himself, briefly, to ponder aloud whether the Tibetan teachings indeed offered truths unimagined by the West: "They are so detailed and thoroughly adapted to the apparent changes in the dead man's condition that every serious-minded reader must ask himself whether these wise old *lamas* might not, after all, have caught a glimpse of the fourth dimension and twitched the veil from the greatest of life's secrets." But Jung declined to take a position on whether the *bardo* realm was a reality or an insightful psychological portrayal of the death experience.

Such equivocations by Jung, with their implicit nods to the superior scientific objectivity of Western psychology, drew the ire of a friend of Evans-Wentz, Lama Anagarika Govinda (1898–1985) — born Ernst Hoffmann, of German origin, a painter and independent scholar who, through some twenty years of study in the Kagyu lineage of Tibetan Buddhism, had attained the rank of lama. His writings included *Foundations of Tibetan Mysticism* (1960), an overview of the philosophical underpinnings of Tibetan practice, and *The Way of the White Clouds* (1966), a memoir of religious life in Tibet prior to the Chinese military occupation. He also contributed a foreword to the Evans-Wentz edition of *The Tibetan Book of the Dead*. Govinda came to the view that Jung portrayed Buddhist wisdom as a mere exotic species of Western psychological insight and hence "brings down these experiences to a plane where they lose their meaning and thus deprives them of their only value." The essence of the issue raised here — one that fostered much discussion in the midcentury West — was whether Buddhism was a religion with universal spiritual claims, as Evans-Wentz and Govinda believed, or a storehouse of alien knowledge from which the West should draw selectively, even cautiously.

Jung was the most fervent spokesperson for the latter view. It is striking that, at the height of his fame, he saw fit to write commentaries on both *The Tibetan Book of the Dead* and *The Tibetan Book of the Great Liberation,* a text on the yogic method of attaining enlightenment. (Two further volumes, without contributions from Jung, emerged from the joint labors of Evans-Wentz and Lama Dawa-Samdup — *Tibet's Great Yogi*

Milarepa [1928] and *Tibetan Yoga and Secret Doctrines* [1935].) In his 1954 commentary, Jung was careful not only to praise Buddhism but also to utter a fierce warning to Western readers drawn to Buddhist practice:

> If the European could turn himself inside out and live as an Oriental, with all the social, moral, religious, intellectual, and aesthetic obligations which such a course would involve, he might be able to benefit by these teachings. But you cannot be a good Christian, either in your faith or in your morality or in your intellectual make-up, and practice genuine *yoga* at the same time. [. . .] History, one might say, is written in the blood. I would not advise anyone to touch *yoga* without a careful analysis of his unconscious reactions. [. . .] If you can afford to seat yourself on a gazelle skin under a Bo-tree or in the cell of a *gompa* [Buddhist monk] for the rest of your life without being troubled by politics or the collapse of your securities, I will look favorably on your case. But *yoga* in Mayfair or Fifth Avenue, or in any other place which is on the telephone, is a spiritual fake.

Jung was making three separate, albeit tangled, arguments here. The first is that "blood," or racial heritage, affects the deepest spiritual urges of what Jung termed the collective unconscious. Westerners and Easterners are fundamentally different as a matter both of genetics and of culture, as Jung would have it. The second argument is that only complete isolation, individual or monastic, can lead to Buddhist enlightenment. The third is that any industrialized setting precludes the true pursuit of the Buddhist path, as it not only prevents isolation (argument two) but links us all the more strongly to society and its shrilly insistent political and material claims on our attention. All three arguments, made by Jung just in advance of the so-called Buddhism boom of the Beat and hippie eras, have since been rejected en masse by current-day Western students of Buddhism, many of whom have declared an indebtedness to Jung.

That Jung should have insisted that genuine understanding of Buddhism was all but impossible in the West indicates how much of a theologian — on behalf of the spiritual potential of his own psychology — he was in his writings on Eastern religion. The circumambulations of his rhetoric — praising Buddhist wisdom while setting forth impassable barriers to it — indicate that perhaps he was not convincing even to himself. For after all, Jung embraced the opportunity to comment on the works of Evans-Wentz and D. T. Suzuki, and the Jungian imprimatur fueled their popularity with midcentury Western readers. This Jung surely knew. But in his position as gatekeeper and interpreter, Jung sought to cast Buddhist teachings as aspects of the Western path of therapeutic enlightenment, which Jung believed himself largely to have created. This was appropriation in as grand a style as has yet been attempted by a Western thinker on Buddhism.

❖

As for Evans-Wentz, he continued to devote himself to comparative religious studies until his death. In 1935, he met with Sri Ramana Maharshi at the ashram of the famed Hindu sage in Tiruvannamalai, in southern India. Their encounter was later recorded in *Talks with Sri Ramana Maharshi* (1955). Ironically, Evans-Wentz only once ventured into Tibet, the country with which his name remains most closely associated, and that only for a single day. He resolved to make his home in India, purchasing, in the Himalayan foothills, a property named Kasar Devi, consisting of a cottage surrounded by wilderness in which panthers and leopards were known to roam. The outbreak of World War II impelled him to return to the United States, where he lived out the last twenty-three years of his life in the Keystone Hotel, a small brick way station for transients and the elderly in downtown San Diego. The rentals from his commercial properties in the city sustained him. Evans-Wentz was an ecumenist who offered financial support to the Buddhist Maha Bodhi Society, the Self-Realization Fellowship of the Indian yogi Paramahansa Yogananda, and the Theosophical Society, among numerous other organizations. In his final years, his books began to draw a wide younger readership, but in no wise did he make himself a public person. At his funeral, there was a reading from his translation of *The Tibetan Book of the Dead*.

❖

Two British writers with quite disparate intentions profoundly reshaped Western fantasies concerning Tibet. They were James Hilton (1900–1954), a fiction writer, and T. Lobsang Rampa (1911–1981), a self-convinced reincarnation of a Tibetan lama.

Hilton, a writer of no critical reputation, contrived to write two novels, both published in 1933, that endure — in part, certainly, due to their cinematic adaptations — in the popular imagination. The first, the lachrymose *Goodbye, Mr. Chips,* does not concern us here. The second, *Lost Horizon,* clearly does. The basic plot will be familiar to many: a party of Western travelers whose airplane is downed in the Himalayas discovers the hidden land of Shangri-La, where serenity reigns and longevity has expanded so as to enable the wise to enjoy fully the bliss of their enclave, even as the outer world hurtles toward yet another war to end all wars.

Hilton was concerned first and foremost about telling a good story, and he saw that recent accounts of Tibet by Western travelers and scholars — such as David-Neel and Evans-Wentz — had intrigued the public. A graduate of Cambridge University in history and literature, Hilton researched the history of past Western encounters with Tibet in the British Museum prior to writing the novel. Thus it is, for example, that a rare seventeenth-century work by the Catholic emissary Antonio de Andrade should appear in *Lost Horizon* as a title in the Shangri-La monastic library.

Hilton was not seriously interested in Buddhism. He spent the final years of his writing career in California producing hackneyed Hollywood screenplays. His High Lama of Shangri-La was deftly created to make the most of Hilton's cultural limitations, for, as the novel explains, the High Lama first came to Shangri-La by accident in 1719. At the time, he was Father Perrault, a Capuchin monk who has since converted to the hazy Shangri-La amalgam of Buddhist, Daoist, and Confucian wisdom. (This apostasy by a priest is finessed in the narrative.) Through this High Lama, Hilton could hint at the wonders of the East by means of what was in essence a Western voice. Indeed, the ultimate future hope offered by the High Lama is that "when the strong have devoured each other, the Christian ethic may at last be fulfilled, and the meek shall inherit the earth." Here was a Tibetan fantasy that was suitably exotic while approachably Buddhist-lite.

It worked. *Lost Horizon* became a best seller, a successful 1937 Hollywood film directed by Frank Capra, and the first ever mass-market pocket-size paperback. And, as the British writer Charles Allen observed, the very name "Shangri-La" has "entered the English language as a synonym for the ultimate haven. Today it has international currency.

In Kathmandu alone half a page in the telephone directory is given over to Shangri-Las of one kind or another, from hotels and restaurants to laundry services and magazine titles."

❖

If ever there was a figure who encompassed the fantasy, confusion, and longing that the West brought to its meeting with the Buddhist East, it was the self-styled Dr. T. (for Tuesday) Lobsang Rampa. Rampa's twenty-three-year writing career began with his first best-selling book, *The Third Eye* (1956), and ended with eighteen volumes and total sales in excess of 3.5 million copies, consumed by devoted and merely curious readers around the world. His influence was considerable, even among readers who later emerged as respectable adult intellectuals. As the American scholar Donald S. Lopez acknowledged,

> When I was discussing Rampa with Tibetologists and Buddhologists in Europe, many confessed that *The Third Eye* was the first book about Tibet that they had ever read; for some it was a fascination with the world Rampa described that had led them to become professional scholars of Tibet. Thus, some said, despite the fact that Rampa was a fraud, he had "a good effect."

The "good effect" was not limited to Western readers, as is commonly supposed. Consider this account by Chatsumarn Kabilsingh, born into a Thai Buddhist family:

> In the 1960s, as a teenager studying in India, I came across a book *The Third Eye* by Lobsang Rampa which ignited my interest in the Tibetan people. I attempted its translation which was serialised in a monthly magazine for three years. I was particularly impressed by the warm relationship between Lobsang Rampa and his Lama, which I found lacking in my own tradition (Theravada).

It was not until the 1980s, however, that Kabilsingh actually met with Tibetan Buddhists: "By that time I started to wonder what kind of quality their teacher must have in order to produce such kind-hearted and compassionate people. I was granted audience and met His Holiness the

Dalai Lama in 1983 only to be awakened, and realised the trait of compassion as embodied in His Holiness the Dalai Lama." There is no hint of irony or transgression as to his spiritual passage from Lobsang Rampa on to the Dalai Lama.

Rampa claimed to be a fully initiated Tibetan lama with medical training, who had been sent to the West to disseminate the wisdom of the ages. Despite ample evidence to the contrary, he insisted vehemently on this truth in each of his many books. To this day, there are enthralled readers who accept Rampa's claims, as well as his accounts of Tibetan Buddhist practice, as genuine. To the skeptic, Rampa must stand as one of the most perplexing literary frauds of the twentieth century — although I apply the term "fraud" with some reluctance to an author who plainly believed in the truth of what he said, out of a conviction based on mental illness or spiritual vision, as you like.

Without question, Rampa's books led millions of readers to conclude that they had for the first time encountered Tibetan Buddhism in a compulsively readable form. Alexandra David-Neel earned the respect of the cognoscenti, but it was Rampa who could be found on the book racks of the train stations and drugstores of the West in the 1950s and 1960s. Their eerie pulp-style covers usually portrayed, in graphic arts form, a bearded, bald, gnomic, Caucasian man with deep-set eyes and a look of impassioned realization. Once inside the narrative, the reader found in Rampa an enthralling guide to Tibetan mysteries that were reassuringly benevolent yet lavishly laced with the supernatural. Rampa never again matched the verve of *The Third Eye.* Although his writing showed a steady decline virtually volume by volume, his readership never wholly abandoned him.

Rampa's unlikely authorial success was initiated by his visit to the London publishing offices of Secker & Warburg in 1955. He was there to submit his manuscript of *The Third Eye,* which had already been rejected by several other houses. Rampa met with Frederick Warburg and assured him that, appearances aside, he was a Tibetan lama and an accredited surgeon. To establish the latter claim, Rampa produced a putative diploma from Chungking University. Warburg later recalled having been puzzled as to why the Chinese diploma was in English, but he did not at the time press this point. Rampa did score a redemptive coup by making a chiromantic scrutiny of Warburg's hand, which revealed Warburg's age and his recent involvement in major litigation, both matters of public record. The performance did not go amiss, however, and Rampa left with a promise that his manuscript would be reviewed.

The subsequent in-house responses of Warburg and his editors were strongly positive. The manuscript told of how Rampa had been born into a noble family in the vicinity of Lhasa. At age seven, by decree of astrologers of the court of the Thirteenth Dalai Lama, Rampa was placed in a monastery, where he pursued an extraordinarily rigorous course of Tantric, medical, and occult studies. All the while, Rampa wove in convincing details of life in Tibet, such as hearths fueled by yak dung; meals of buttered tea, barley tsampa, and vegetables; and the lightly etched comings and goings of a genuine historical figure, the British diplomat Sir Charles Bell. These details — which could easily have been obtained from extant works on Tibet by Bell, Heinrich Harrer, Evans-Wentz, and others — were blended with more idiosyncratic accounts of flying aloft over Lhasa in winged kites designed to carry worthy adepts, as well as encounters with his guru, the Lama Mingyar Dondup, and with a fatherlike Dalai Lama.

Without question, the most startling scene in *The Third Eye* was Rampa's account of how he came, at age eight, to the knowledge and power of that eye. Contrary to the reader's expectation of purely spiritual training, Rampa described an excruciating surgical probe directly into his own forehead, conducted without anesthetic by Tibetan doctors by means of a serrated auger. There followed the insertion into Rampa's brain of a sterilized sliver of wood. That sliver was the trigger that opened the newly realized eye of spiritual vision:

> Suddenly, there was a blinding flash, and in that instant the Lama Mingyar Dondup said *"Stop!"* For a moment, the pain was intense, like a searing white flame. [. . .] As the projecting sliver was being bound in place so that it could not move, the Lama Mingyar Dondup turned to me and said: "You are one of us, Lobsang. For the rest of your life you will see people as they are and not as they pretend to be."

Tales such as this made the book enticing to Secker & Warburg, but the exceeding strangeness of these tales also aroused suspicions. Frederick Warburg had the manuscript sent to about twenty Western readers, including Heinrich Harrer, who had some degree of expertise on Tibet. As Warburg later wrote, "Their opinions were so contradictory that no positive result emerged. Some questioned the accuracy of one section, some of another; what was doubted by one expert was accepted unquestioningly by another." Warburg also conducted some truth-finding methods of his own. He placed a new lure before Rampa — a promise to publish *The Third Eye* as compelling fiction if Rampa would simply admit that it was that. Rampa refused. Warburg also obtained from one of his experts a phoneticized version of a simple Tibetan phrase, which, when Warburg tried it on Rampa, so baffled the lama-author that he dropped to the floor of the publisher's office, clutching his head and moaning. Upon recovery, he explained that after leaving Tibet during World War II at the bidding of his teachers — who wished him to bring their wisdom to the West — Rampa had, while serving as a medical pilot for the Chinese army (his kite-flying training had served him in good stead), been taken prisoner by the Japanese, who had tortured him to obtain strategic secrets that could affect the security of Tibet. To prevent any such disclosures, Rampa employed his psychic powers to erase his own knowledge of the Tibetan language. Alas, that loss had proven permanent.

Warburg suspected theatrics but resolved that the narrative strength of the manuscript merited publication. And the world agreed, resoundingly. *The Third Eye* had been intended for a fringe-spiritual readership, but the British mainstream press — including the *Times Literary Supplement* ("It comes near to being a work of art") — praised the book lavishly. *The Third Eye* ultimately made the best-seller lists of twelve countries. But the experts whose critiques had been ignored by Warburg remained outraged. A review of the book by Harrer, for example, was sufficiently vitriolic for Rampa's German publisher to threaten a libel action. The experts hired a private investigator, who delivered evidence that the so-called Dr. T. Lobsang Rampa had been born in Plympton, Devon; that his real name was Cyril Henry Hoskin; and that, prior to writing *The Third Eye,* he had worked as a lowly clerk and a freelance photographer of criminal scenes.

Both the British and the American press avidly took up the Rampa/Hoskin story. Gravely embarrassed, Secker & Warburg refused to publish further titles by Rampa and appended a formal disclaimer to its paperback edition of *The Third Eye*. But Rampa found other willing publishers and, in *Doctor from Lhasa* (1959) and *The Rampa Story* (1960), explained the alleged untruths. Yes, he was now, in physical form, the undistinguished Hoskin. But that was because his Tibetan physical body had suffered a premature death. To complete his life's mission, he had obtained spiritual permission from Hoskin to release the Englishman's soul from his body — from whence it departed to a more favorable incarnation — while Rampa's soul assumed Hoskin's body. The switch occurred when Hoskin fell off a ladder while photographing an owl and received a severe blow to the head. Hoskin's English wife was perplexed at first but soon accepted the identity change.

To the end of his life, Rampa insisted that he was telling the truth. His final home was Calgary, Alberta — far from the sneering media Rampa detested — where he led a small-scale ashram. His last work, published posthumously, was *My Visit to Venus* (1988), which began, "Flying saucers? Of course there are flying saucers! I have been for a trip in one." Prior to his death, Rampa directed that any royalties from the book were to be donated "to The Save A Cat League" of New York City, "because poor little cats have a miserable time in this hard world."

10

BUDDHISM TAKES ROOT IN THE WEST: THE CHRISTIAN RESPONSE AND A HESITANT ECUMENISM

❖

The first Western Buddhist to missionize in the West was an English convert to Theravada Buddhism who had the temerity to lash back at the Christian portrayal of Buddhism as navel-gazing nihilism. Allan Bennett (1872–1923) came from an impoverished family. His father died when the boy was young, and the devout Catholicism of his mother offered no solace. In his early twenties, he joined and soon became an esteemed member of the Hermetic Order of the Golden Dawn, the most famous occult society of the day, the rolls of which also included William Butler Yeats and Aleister Crowley. Bennett was devoted to the leader of this order, S. L. MacGregor Mathers, who, Bennett testified, possessed genuine magical powers of evocation. Bennett was a worthy student, according to Crowley, who recorded this instance of his prowess: Bennett had fashioned a magical wand from a glass prism. "One day, a party of theosophists were chatting skeptically about the power of the 'blasting rod.' Allan promptly produced his and blasted one of them. It took fourteen hours to restore the incredulous individual to the use of his mind and his muscles."

It was Crowley's view that, as a result of his lifelong asthma, Bennett "regarded the pleasures of living (and, above all, those of physical love) as diabolical illusions devised by the enemy of mankind in order to trick souls into accepting the curse of existence." For whatever temperamental reasons, Bennett had already, in his youth, read extensively both on Hinduism and Buddhism. He was particularly affected, at age eighteen, by Edwin Arnold's *Light of Asia*. In 1900, Bennett forswore further practice of Western magic and boarded a ship for Sri Lanka, where the climate benefited his asthma while he studied the Pali language and Hindu yogic practices. The Pali Buddhist teachings at last took full hold, and he journeyed to Burma, where in December 1901 he took vows as a Theravada novice, becoming the Venerable Ananda Metteyya. In May 1902, Metteyya became only the second European to be ordained as a Buddhist *bhikkhu,* or monk.

During subsequent years of monastic practice, Metteyya simultaneously carried out his ambition of bringing Theravada Buddhism to the West. In 1903, he founded the Buddhasasana Samagama, or International Buddhist Society, which included representatives from Austria, China, Germany, Italy, and the United States. The journal *Buddhism,* also founded in 1903 and edited (and frequently contributed to) by Metteyya, won an influential readership during its five years and six issues of existence. In part this was due to Metteyya's marketing savvy — free subscriptions were provided to some six hundred European libraries, with the stipulation that they be kept on prominent display.

In his essays for the journal, Metteyya jousted with the Christian conception of Buddhism as a creed of emptiness and despair. On the contrary, he argued, the key to a genuine salvation of the world lay within daily Buddhist practice:

> If you aspire to lighten the burden of the world, to bring humanity a little nearer to the Peace it craves: — start right at home, and strive to free, to ennoble, to purify yourself [. . .] And why? Because each man is an integral portion of humanity. [. . .] All life is one in very truth, — the ant, and man, glory of sun and star, and the vast gulfs of space are one, one and no other, save that the darkness of our vain self-hood hides.

Metteyya believed that a purified humanity would ultimately refuse to participate in the carnages of world civilization: "It is the Wrong View: 'I am English; glorious English nationality is mine,' so it behooves me to fight against persons who have another sort of Self-Theory, and say: 'No, but a Teuton I.' It is that Wrong View which now makes necessary that the bulk of the resources of every branch of the West-Aryan race is wasted on armaments of war."

Metteyya led the first Buddhist mission to the West when he and three fellow Burmese Buddhists arrived in England in 1908 for a one-year stay. Although the mission spurred the creation of the Buddhist Society of Great Britain and Ireland, it scarcely reached the broader British public. Metteyya was not a gifted public speaker or public figure; his teachings were best exemplified in his daily life practice and his writings. Metteyya rejoined his Burmese *sangha* in 1909, but by 1914 physicians warned him that monastic austerities were too much for a man of his condition. He was compelled to return to lay life and to England, where he was provided for by family, friends, and Buddhist supporters for the final decade of his life. The British dramatist Clifford Bax, a friend of Metteyya, noted the paradox that

> as a Buddhist, he was an alert and powerful personality: as Allan Bennett, a poor man, dwelling unknown in London, he was a sick creature prematurely old. As he was putting on his overcoat, I heard Meena Gunn [a friend] saying, "Why it's riddled with moths," and Bennett responding, "They're such pretty little things," and Meena continuing, "Some day we must get you a new one: this coat is too full of holes," and Bennett answering, shy of his pun, "But, you see, I'm supposed to be a holy man."

❖

By the time of his death in 1923, Bennett was acknowledged as a leading teacher of Theravada Buddhism in the West. But he was far from alone. Within Germany and central Europe, there emerged a Theravada lineage of distinction. Its founder was an acclaimed German musician, Anton W. F. Gueth, who in 1903 voyaged to Burma to take monastic vows as the Venerable Nyanatiloka. By 1905, he had made contact with Metteyya, who arranged for Nyanatiloka to study Pali in Sri Lanka, where Nyanatiloka spent nearly all of his long monastic life. Such was his devotion and scholarship that on his death in 1957, he received a state funeral. Nyanatiloka believed that Buddhist teaching possessed a universalist quality lacking in the Western revealed religions. During the same period that Jung was insisting on the incommensurate gulf between the European Christian and the Eastern Buddhist psyches, Nyanatiloka blithely proposed, in a 1933 lecture broadcast on Colombo radio, that as one who had made the crossing, he could set minds to rest as to the existence of archetypal, cultural, or other barriers — for there were none to speak of: "The teaching of the Buddha is perhaps the only religious teaching that requires *no belief in traditions,* or in certain historical events. [. . .] The universal laws of morality hold good without variation everywhere and at all times, whether one may call oneself a Buddhist, Hindu, Christian or Mohammedan, or by any other name."

One who followed in Nyanatiloka's path was the renowned Nyanaponika Thera, born Siegmund Feniger of Jewish parents in pre-Nazi Germany. Nyanaponika trained as a *bhikkhu* in Sri Lanka, but returned to Germany in 1933 because he saw it as his Dharma calling to extend whatever help he could to the terrorized Jewish community there. He would often recite this quotation from the Buddha in the *Satipatthana Sutta:* "Protecting oneself, one protects others; protecting others, one protects oneself." Nyanaponika became a key member of the Central Jewish Committee for Reconstruction and Aid, which operated until 1936, when Nazi persecution ended its work and compelled him to return to Sri Lanka. Nyanaponika is now regarded as one of the founders of modern-day Engaged Buddhism.

Nyanaponika exercised considerable influence on a fellow German-born Jew, Ayya Khema, who as a young woman was forced to flee Nazi Germany with her family. In her memoir, *I Give You My Life* (1997), she addressed the issue of why a proportionately large number of modern-day Jews have been drawn to Buddhism. Khema had read *The Jew in the Lotus* (1994) by Rodger Kamenetz, which described an interfaith conference in Dharamsala between the Dalai Lama and Jewish rabbis and leaders. Khema, who earlier in her life had attempted to find teachers to guide her in the study of kabbalah, wrote of Kamenetz's book:

> What particularly touched me was the description of the meeting that took place between these conference participants and dozens of people of Jewish extraction who had been ordained as monks and nuns in the Tibetan tradition. [. . .] All of them had the same story to tell as I did. They had searched for the deeper, mystical aspect of their own religion, and then, when they found no way to make a connection with it, they had turned, full of faith, to Buddhism.

It is estimated that 33 percent of current Western Buddhist leaders come from Jewish roots, and further estimated that an astonishing 75 percent of Western students now in residence in Dharamsala (where the Dalai Lama has established a center for the study of Tibetan Buddhism) are Jews by birth. I would submit that, along with the factors discussed by Khema, a further reason for this powerful attraction is that Jews, whose conversion has long been sought by Christians and Muslims, tended to see these as taboo competing faiths, the embrace of which would demean their heritage and shock their families. Prior to the coming of Buddhism to the West, Jews seldom formally converted to other religions, although they did frequently intermarry and assimilate in a secular manner. Offered the "clean" alternative of Buddhism, which views Judaism and other religions with respect, the readiness of many Jews of keen spiritual intent to leave their theistic religious tradition behind has been striking.

Khema was ordained in Sri Lanka as a Buddhist nun in 1979, with Nyanaponika presiding over the ceremony. In 1987, she was a key organizer of the first International Conference on Buddhist Nuns, held in Bodh Gaya, India. One result of that conference was the founding, again with Khema's active involvement, of Sakyadhita (Daughters of the Buddha), an international society for Buddhist nuns and laywomen practitioners. In 1989, she returned to Germany, where she remained until her death in 1997, authoring widely read books on Buddhist teachings, such as *Being Nobody, Going Nowhere,* and founding the Buddha-Haus im Allgau, as well as the first Buddhist forest monastery in Germany, Metta Vihara (Pali for "residence of unconditional love").

❖

To the midcentury German Catholic theologian Hans Urs von Balthasar goes the distinction of being the first Christian thinker not merely to perceive the increased strength of Buddhism but also to recognize its import. Balthasar argued that the encounter between Christianity and Buddhism would prove of greater long-term significance for Christianity than even its early encounter with Greek culture and philosophy, which so decisively shaped the thought of Church Fathers such as Saint Paul and Saint Augustine. Through their efforts, the Church succeeded in reconciling faith and reason. But how could Christianity, the ultimate religion of the Logos — the Word — of Christ, reconcile itself with the wordless silence of Buddhism?

Balthasar allowed that "dialogue is possible." But his cautious concessions as to the spiritual value of Buddhism were typical of Western religionists of the time. As a "natural mysticism" — that is, one based on human aspiration and experiment, but without the aid of divine grace — Buddhism possessed remarkable techniques of spiritual practice, which, however, could offer no more than a sophisticated "world flight" that led to an annihilating "Nothing" in which the love of God for his creation had no place. As for the Buddhist doctrine of compassion, Balthasar viewed it as a mere principle that could not — as could Christ — inspire love.

Within Protestant theological circles, there were, in the 1950s, two leading voices who called for respectful relations with Buddhism. Arnold Toynbee (1889–1975) was first and foremost a historian, but in his writings he argued for religion as the central force behind all great civilizations. He further believed that the dialogic encounter between Christianity and Buddhism was the most significant event of the twentieth century. In the mid-1950s, Toynbee delivered, in the self-avowed dual voices of a historian and a born-and-raised Anglican believer, lectures at three American schools of theology, later published as *Christianity Among the Religions of the World* (1957). In those lectures, Toynbee posed a number of suggestions for peaceful tolerance. One was particularly startling in its breadth:

> We ought also, I should say, to try to purge our Christianity of the traditional Christian belief that Christianity is unique. This is not just a Western Christian belief; it is intrinsic to Christianity itself. All the same, I suggest that we have to do this if we are to purge Christianity of the exclusive-mindedness and intolerance that follows from a belief in Christianity's uniqueness.

The German Protestant Paul Tillich (1886–1965) was among the preeminent theologians of the twentieth century. Like Toynbee, he believed in the separate but equal status of all world religions. Tillich recognized the need for dialogue between Christianity and Buddhism, but he was also well aware that at stake in the dialogue was the long-unchallenged

Christian prominence in the West. In his *Christianity and the Encounter of the World Religions* (1963), Tillich acknowledged the success of D. T. Suzuki when he wrote of "the missionary attack of Japanese Zen Buddhism on the Western educated classes, both Christian and humanist." Tillich was frank in his comparative assessment of the Buddhist and Christian spiritual outlooks:

> In the depth of each living religion there is a point at which the religion itself loses its importance, and that to which it points breaks through its particularity, elevating it to spiritual freedom and with it to a vision of the spiritual presence in other expressions of the ultimate meaning of man's existence. This is what Christianity must see in the present encounter of the world religions.

Here was a soundly argued, badly needed abstract basis for tolerant dialogue. But what Tillich failed to foresee was that the Buddhist "attack" might involve not merely a competition for believers but also a transformation of Christian practice for those who pursued with passion the dialogue with Buddhism.

Such a one was Thomas Merton (1915–1968), surely the most influential American Catholic monk of the twentieth century — not only as a theologian but also as a poet and a sympathetic interpreter of Buddhist and Daoist thought to the Christian West. For the final twenty-seven years of his life, Merton lived in the most rigorous of monastic orders, that of the Cistercians of the Strict Observance, better known as the Trappists.

Merton first encountered Buddhism as a student at Columbia University in 1937, through mentions of Buddhist teachings in a just-published book of spiritual philosophy, *Ends and Means* by Aldous Huxley. The impact — far more distracting than helpful — was recounted in an acidly patronizing tone, utterly contrary to Merton's later views but in keeping with the Catholic outlook of the times, in his well-known memoir, *The Seven Storey Mountain* (1948). Merton wrote that he began

> ransacking the university library for books on Oriental mysticism. [. . .] I have forgotten the titles, even the authors, and I never understood a word of what they said in the first place. [. . .] The only practical thing I got out of it was a system for going to sleep at night, when you couldn't

sleep. [. . .] I suppose it was a variety of auto-suggestion, a kind of hypnotism, or else simply muscular relaxation, with the help of a little work on the part of an active fancy. Ultimately, I suppose all Oriental mysticism can be reduced to techniques that do the same thing, but in a far more subtle and advanced fashion: and if that is true, it is not mysticism at all. It remains purely in the natural order. That does not make it evil, *per se,* according to Christian standards: but it does not make it good, in relation to the supernatural. It is simply more or less useless, except when it is mixed up with elements that are strictly diabolical.

By the mid-1950s, Merton had become an eminent writer of devotional Catholic works. But in the second half of that decade, the works of D. T. Suzuki, in particular, began to make an impression. The assiduous caution with which Merton approached the question of comparative Buddhist and Christian mysticism reflected his desire to pursue his mature fascination with Eastern thought while avoiding heresy outright. In his essay "Zen Buddhist Monasticism," written in the early 1960s, Merton employed the device of an unanswered hypothetical query to broach the possibility that Zen enlightenment was equivalent to Christian salvation: "In Christian terms, one can hardly help feeling that the illumination of the genuine Zen experience seems to open out into an unconscious demand for grace — a demand that is perhaps answered without being understood. Is it perhaps already grace?"

Some interpreters of Merton assert that, by the time of his death, he longed to cross over into Buddhist practice. The basis for this viewpoint lies not in Merton's essays, but rather in certain encounters and informal writings of the five years preceding his death. In particular, Merton's endorsement of the Vietnamese Zen teacher Thich Nhat Hanh and his peace efforts during the Vietnam War included a movingly personal statement on Buddhism, albeit a statement most revelatory in what is left unsaid:

I have said that Nhat Hanh is my brother, and it is true. We are both monks, and we have lived the monastic life about the same number of years. We are both poets, both existentialists. I have far more in common with Nhat Hanh than I have with many Americans, and I do not hesitate to say it. It is vitally important that such bonds be admitted. They are the bonds of a new solidarity and a new brotherhood which is beginning to be evident. [. . .] This unity of the young is the only hope of the world. In its name I appeal for Nhat Hanh. Do what you can for him. If I mean something to you, then let me put it this way: do for Nhat Hanh whatever you would do for me if I were in his position. In many ways I wish I were.

In his letters of November 1968, chronicling the commencement of a journey to Asia that was cut short by his death, Merton wrote with evident delight of his encounters with the Dalai Lama and other Tibetan lamas in Dharamsala: "With all of them I have had really delightful and fruitful conversations (with a good interpreter) and it has been an amazing experience — like meeting monks of the time of St. Bernard." As for the Dalai Lama himself, Merton wrote:

I have seldom met anyone with whom I clicked so well and I feel that we have become good friends. He asked me a lot of questions about Western monasticism and they all had to do with "attainment" or, in other words, whether or not the monks were reaching the higher degrees of the mystical life, and what we did to help them make it. He talked a lot about Tibetan methods of *samadhi* [. . .] and he gave me some very good suggestions, so that I am going to study the philosophical groundwork which underlies both Tibetan meditation and Zen. This is Madhyamika [Middle Way] philosophy, which is not speculative and abstract but very concrete. [. . .] You will be happy to know that when we parted the DL called me a "Geyshe," which is for his group the highest praise, meaning one who is completely learned and proficient in spiritual things. Someone who was with me said the DL had never before said any such thing of a Westerner.

While in Sri Lanka, Merton paid a visit to the caves of Polonnaruwa, in which large-scale Buddhist sculptures and frescoes abound. Merton's response to the setting was extraordinary:

Looking at these figures I was suddenly, almost forcibly, jerked clean out of the habitual, half-tied vision of things, and an inner clearness, clarity, as if exploding from the rocks themselves, became evident and obvious. [. . .] The thing about all this is that there is no puzzle, no problem, and really no "mystery." All problems are resolved and everything is clear, simply because what matters is clear. The rock, all matter, all life, is charged with dharmakaya . . . everything is emptiness and everything is compassion. I don't know when in my life I have ever had such a sense of beauty and spiritual validity running together in one aesthetic illumination.

Merton died in December 1968, accidentally electrocuted as he turned on the fan in his hotel room in Bangkok, where he was attending a conference on monasticism. There is no evidence whatsoever that Merton, in his final years or months or weeks, "turned" Buddhist. But there is every evidence that he felt he had much to learn from Buddhist teachings. The passion Merton felt for interfaith exchange has had a lasting effect on both Buddhist and Christian monastic communities. In July 1996, some fifty monks from both traditions gathered at the monastery in which Merton had lived for more than twenty years before departing for Asia — the Abbey of Gethsemani in Trappist, Kentucky. The five-day gathering included the Dalai Lama, who spoke of Merton: "He had the complete qualities of hearing — which means study, contemplating, thinking on the teachings — and of meditation. He also had the qualities of being learned, disciplined and having a good heart. [. . .] And so for the rest of my life, the impact of meeting him will remain until my last breath."

◈

Merton was not alone among Catholics of his era in being drawn to Buddhist contemplative practice. Indeed, there was a kind of Catholic boomlet of interest during that time, encouraged by the ecumenical initiatives of Pope John XXIII.

The stance of the Second Vatican Council (1962–1965) toward Buddhism, in particular, avoided the dominant prior approach in Catholic theology of regarding Buddhism as a nihilistic creed that had by some mysterious means acquired a mass following. By contrast, the Buddhism acknowledged by Vatican II was a radiant faith: "Buddhism in its multiple forms acknowledges the radical insufficiency of this shifting world. It teaches a path by which men, in a devout and confident spirit, can either reach a state of absolute freedom or attain supreme enlightenment by their own efforts or by higher assistance."

As for the proper approach of believing Catholics to teachings of Buddhism, the view of the Church could perhaps be paraphrased as permission to engage in heavy petting without becoming unduly aroused: "The Church therefore has this exhortation for her sons: prudently and lovingly, through dialogue and collaboration with the followers of other religions, and in witness of Christian faith and life, acknowledge, preserve, and promote the spiritual and moral goods found among these men, as well as the values in their society and culture." Dom Aelred Graham, author of *Zen Catholicism* (1963), described the boundary of permitted Catholic-Buddhist relations with more delicacy than I have above, while retaining an erotic subtext: "Provided it be judiciously administered, perhaps none of us will take any harm from at least 'a tongue-tip taste of Zen.'"

The forerunner of the midcentury Catholic contemplatives fascinated with Buddhism was the German Jesuit Hugo Enomiya-Lassalle (1898–1990), who studied Zen in Japan for more than twenty years. There he worked with the poor in Tokyo and founded the Church of World Peace in Hiroshima. In 1968, Lassalle returned to Germany, where he lectured and offered courses on "Zen Meditation for Christians," which drew a wide public audience.

William Johnston, an Irish Jesuit missionary to Japan and a longtime professor of religion at Sophia University in Tokyo, has been in many ways Lassalle's successor. For Johnston, the fourteenth-century classic Christian mystical text *The Cloud of Unknowing,* written in Middle English by an unknown author, represented a prime example of the Christian contemplative tradition, vitiated in the modern day, that could stand comparison with the paradox-laden meditational approach of Zen. The author of *Cloud* was resolute in insisting that all personal selfhood conceptions had to be abandoned before one could encounter the divine hidden away in a seeming cloud of unknowing. Johnston founded a Catholic center in Tokyo where Japanese Christians could both attend mass and practice meditative prayer. In 2000, after decades of service, Johnston remained convinced that *Cloud* could serve a vital role in creating a truly Asian Catholic worship: "Those of us who live in Asia know that the future of Christianity (and, indeed, the future of the world) belongs to the teeming millions who inhabit this vast continent and have created its rich culture. Dialogue with the mystical tradition of Asia is surely the way of theology in the twenty-first century."

❖

Theology has its formative power. But far more influential an impact was made on the Western public by the European visual artists, composers, and writers who encountered and responded to Buddhist teachings. Two authors in particular engaged with Buddhist themes in depth: the Swiss Nobel Prize winner Hermann Hesse (1877–1962), whose novel *Siddhartha* (1922) has sold more than four million copies in the United States alone since the first English-language translation was published by New Directions in 1951; and the Greek author Nikos Kazantzakis (1885–1957), who addressed this topic in numerous works, including the little-known dramatic play *Buddha* (1956).

Hesse, whose father and grandfather had been Christian missionaries to India, himself made a pilgrimage to India in 1911 in homage both to his family legacy and to the Indian religions — Buddhism and Hinduism — which fascinated him throughout his life. Hesse was never a doctrinal follower of any religion, Eastern or Western, but he did practice Buddhist meditation for a time before writing *Siddhartha*. The depth — and the ambivalence — of his response to Buddhism is borne out in that novel, in which the protagonist, Siddhartha, encounters the historical Gotama Buddha, responds with reverence to the teachings and the teacher, yet goes on to find his own path to awakening. The Buddhism of the novel is that of the Theravada tradition, although it is not labeled as such. As the novel depicts the living Gotama Buddha, it is not surprising that Hesse modeled him after the Pali texts. Siddhartha's path, while distinct, is yet Buddhist in spirit: "I know that I am at one with Gotama. [. . .] Not in speech or thought do I regard him as a great man, but in his deeds and life."

Hesse was so widely read and discussed in the West in the 1960s that his work has been largely dismissed by academic critics ever since. Nonetheless, the best of it remains in print and popular. *Siddhartha*, which might be viewed as Hesse's fantasy of a Buddhist heresy, is a subtle and eloquent novel. Not the least of its stylistic virtues is its capacity to be read raptly by the young, and thus the book has served as an early imaginative entry into Buddhism for many Western readers, long ago superseding the role once held by Arnold's *Light of Asia*.

Kazantzakis is best known for his *Last Temptation of Christ* (1960), a novel in which the speculation that there were Buddhists in the Palestine of Jesus's era is briefly and subtly woven into the narrative. In an early scene, as Jesus waits in the anteroom of Magdalene's brothel for an opportunity to beg her forgiveness for having driven her into such a life, there sits nearby a meditative nobleman from India, who is questioned by a fellow john-in-waiting as to his religious beliefs: " 'Prince of India, what does your God have to say about all this?' The youth opened his eyes. 'All what?' he asked. 'Here: in front of you: men, women, crabs, love.' 'That everything is a dream.' " This is both a Buddhist and a Hindu conception, but the choice of a young Indian prince seems intended to echo the Buddha. As the spiritual atmosphere of the brothel becomes increasingly oppressive to Jesus, he wonders: "Could the Indian nobleman really be right? Could all this — yard, pomegranate, grate, partridge, men — be a dream?" Jesus concludes that life is other than a dream, and that realization enables him to overcome the last temptation of the narrative. But his brief encounter with Buddhist metaphysics was a typical touch by Kazantzakis, who drank deeply from both the Christian and the Buddhist traditions.

For a time, while living in Vienna in the early 1920s, Kazantzakis came to regard himself as a passionate self-convert to Buddhism. In the verse play *Buddha,* begun at this time but not completed until the early 1940s, Kazantzakis developed his vision of the Buddha as a teacher who, above all, emphasized spiritual freedom of so radical a kind that death itself was shorn of its terror. In his memoir *Report to Greco* (1961), Kazantzakis described his state of mind at the time he commenced writing the play: "Only now did I realize that Buddha urges man to give consent to death, to love the ineluctable, to harmonize his heart with universal flux, and, seeing matter and mind pursue each other, unite, beget, and vanish, to say, 'That is what I want.' "

Kazantzakis came to see the Buddhist infatuation of his earlier days as a retreat from the beauties and realities of life. In *Zorba the Greek* (1952), the timid first-person narrator — a man of letters who is writing a play on the Buddha and who becomes the unlikely "Boss" to Zorba — is a veiled portrait of the younger Kazantzakis. The narrator comes to realize, through his friendship with the charismatic Zorba, that Buddhism is no more than a pathetic evasion of experience — in his own case, in particular, of erotic experience: "'Come! Come!' she cried. 'Life passes in a flash. Come quickly, come, come, before it is too late!' I was well aware that it was Mara, the spirit of the Evil One, in the shape of a woman with powerful thighs and buttocks. I fought against him. I applied myself to writing *Buddha*."

Although Kazantzakis visited the Buddhist lands of Japan and China, his understanding of Buddhism never progressed beyond a sense of the seductiveness of its embrace of nothingness, the abyss. He was, in essence, a follower of the Orientalists, parting from them only in his deep admiration for Buddhist courage in the face of extinction. But for Kazantzakis, the full embrace of the spirit was that of the earthy Zorba and the ascetic Jesus, both of whom remained rooted in life.

❖

The limitations that Kazantzakis found in Buddhism were rooted in some measure in his limited knowledge of the breadth of the teachings of Buddhism. For all the research of the Western scholars, for all the contributions of D. T. Suzuki and other Asian Buddhist writers, there remained in the West an unclear understanding of the place of social and political engagement within Buddhist tradition.

The person most responsible for bringing this aspect of Buddhist practice to Western awareness is unquestionably Thich Nhat Hanh (b. 1926; Nhat Hanh means "one action"), a Vietnamese Zen monk in the lineage of the Chinese master Lin-chi, whose life and spiritual development have intertwined dramatically with the past four decades of American history.

In 1942, at age sixteen, Nhat Hanh entered the Tu Hieu monastery in central Vietnam as a novice. By age twenty-three, he had received full priestly ordination. Nhat Hanh early on reached the conviction that "monasteries are only a kind of laboratory to spend time in, in order to discover something. They are not an end, they are a means. You get training and practice of the spiritual life so you can go elsewhere and be with other people." This was not an isolated viewpoint within the tradition of Vietnamese Buddhism, in which social engagement by Buddhist monks and clergy had been prominent since the late nineteenth century. But Nhat Hanh pushed it further still. Even while a mere novice, he challenged his monastic elders by advocating that training for monks include philosophy, the arts, and foreign languages. In the 1950s and early 1960s, Nhat Hanh took it on himself to pursue such studies, first at Saigon University, then for several years in the United States as a student of comparative religion at Princeton and a lecturer on Buddhism at Columbia. His career as a respected exponent of Buddhism seemed assured.

With the onset of the Vietnam War in the early 1960s, Nhat Hanh recognized that his life of personal meditation and study had come to an end. He returned to Vietnam and there founded the School of Youth for Social Service, a deceptively bland nomenclature that little indicated the innovations in Buddhist practice that he was now creating. The school consisted of unpaid volunteers only, including Nhat Hanh himself. Volunteers were trained to do everything in their power to alleviate the immense suffering caused by the war. Nhat Hanh and his students remained steadfastly neutral, extending their aid to all individuals and urging both sides of the conflict to reconcile. For this, they earned at times the hatred of both. Several volunteers were killed, and Nhat Hanh was the target of assassination attempts.

Among the writings prepared by Nhat Hanh expressly for his students at this time was this credo of radical compassion:

> Our enemy is our anger, hatred, greed, fanaticism, and discrimination against people. If you die because of violence, you must meditate on compassion in order to forgive those who kill you. When you die realizing this state of compassion, you are truly a child of the Awakened One. Even if you are dying in oppression, shame, and violence, if you can smile with forgiveness, you have great power.

Two School of Youth teachers chose to immolate themselves — sitting calmly as flames licked their bodies — to exemplify the possibility of peace even in the extremity of suffering. "Sometimes," Nhat Hanh later explained, "we had to burn ourselves alive to get the message across."

By 1965, Nhat Hanh recognized the need to travel again to the United States in hopes of influencing both American policymakers and the American public. Thomas Merton championed his cause, as previously discussed. But perhaps the most far-reaching influence Nhat Hanh had was on Martin Luther King Jr., the eloquent champion of nonviolence as a means to lasting social change. King had for some time refrained from speaking out against the Vietnam War because he feared that the issue would polarize support for his civil rights movement. But as King's close associate Andrew Young later affirmed, the "spiritual inspiration" afforded by Nhat Hanh led King to recognize that one could oppose the war without seeming to side with communism. In 1967, King nominated Nhat Hanh for the Nobel Peace Prize: "This gentle Buddhist monk from Vietnam is a scholar of immense intellectual capacity. His ideas for peace, if applied, would build a monument to ecumenism, to world brotherhood, to humanity."

In 1966, Nhat Hanh was warned by his friends in Vietnam not to return due to the risk of assassination. When at last the war came to an end in 1975, the Communist regime declared Nhat Hanh a traitor. After years of teaching throughout the West, he established two monastic Zen communities — Plum Village in France in 1982, and the Maple Forest Monastery in Vermont in 1997. His Order of Interbeing, founded during the war and now with members throughout the world, holds as a fundamental principle of training that Buddhist practice must encompass all aspects of life, from family to livelihood to public peace and justice. Among the projects that Nhat Hanh pursued was a series of healing retreats for American Vietnam veterans in 1989. He also worked with alcoholic treatment groups and praised 12-step programs as a kind of "American dharma." His support for cooperative learning between Buddhism and Western psychotherapy has been in keeping with his own Engaged Buddhist outlook.

Nhat Hanh achieved best-seller status in 1995 with *Living Buddha, Living Christ,* which elucidated the essential agreement between Buddhist and Christian teachings on peace, love, and compassion. But the author also took the opportunity to chide Pope John Paul II, who had written in *Crossing the Threshold of Hope* that Christ "is the one mediator between God and humanity." Nhat Hanh's response to what is, after all, a perfectly standard statement of Christian belief, was calmly to request a change. The pope's view, he countered, does not seem to reflect the deep mystery of the oneness of the Trinity. . . . Of course Christ is unique. But who is not unique? Socrates, Muhammed, the Buddha, you, and I are all unique. The idea behind the statement, however, is the notion that Christianity provides the only way of salvation and all other religious traditions are of no use. This attitude excludes dialogue and fosters religious intolerance and discrimination. It does not help.

Vatican concern over the Western inroads of Buddhism was first plainly manifested in 1989, when Cardinal Joseph Ratzinger — the future Pope Benedict XVI — issued a position paper forbidding Eastern-inspired meditation practices for Catholics. Such concern could only have been heightened by a Church-sponsored study of the same period, which indicated that the potential existed for large numbers of European Catholics to convert to Buddhism. Italy, the homeland of the papacy, was itself susceptible: "Nearly 10,000 Italian Catholics have converted to Buddhism. But Rome fears that one quarter of all Italians share Buddhist beliefs such as reincarnation and others incompatible with the Catholic faith."

Not only did Nhat Hanh correct the pope on matters of Christian doctrine, but he did so to applause in at least some Christian circles. *Living Buddha, Living Christ* featured both a glowing foreword by Brother David Steindl-Rast, OSB, and an introduction by Elaine Pagels, a scholar of early Christianity, who declared Nhat Hanh to be an exemplar of the wisdom found not only in Buddhist teachings but also in those of the early Gnostic Christians — teachings that were suppressed and destroyed by the Church. It is one of the most pointed ironies of religious history that the "lost" Gnostic cause may be viewed, some 1,700 years later, as having been taken up by a Vietnamese Zen master whose aim was to reduce the importance of the distinction we draw between "Buddhist" and "Christian."

❖

The bridge building, and the hostilities, between Christianity and Buddhism will continue. Nhat Hanh, in a later work, *Going Home: Jesus and Buddha as Brothers* (1999), spoke on behalf of Christ in a manner that few devout Christians would accept:

The Buddha comes to Europe and America every day. The Buddha is saying to Jesus, "I am new to this land. Do you think I should stay here or should I go back to Asia?" [. . .] Can you imagine that Jesus would tell him, "No, in Europe we already have Christianity, and it is not nice for you to try to propagate a new faith in this new land." We can imagine all kinds of proposals, we can imagine all kinds of reactions.

The central purpose of this book has been to examine the "proposals" and "reactions" of the past two millennia in sufficient detail that their consequences may be understood. My conclusions need not be the readers' conclusions, for historical narratives have a strange tendency to speak for themselves. I would suggest, however, that any attempt to restrict the spiritual freedom of humankind is futile, at the very best, and genocidal, at the very worst.

11

BEAT ZEN AND CRAZY WISDOM

❖

Of all the twentieth-century Western explicators of Buddhism, none achieved the charismatic adulation enjoyed by the Englishman turned American Alan Watts (1915–1973). Born into a pious Evangelical family, Watts proved himself, at the King's School, Canterbury, to be a brilliant maverick resolved to steer clear of the typical Oxbridge career path. The schoolboy further unsettled his family by announcing that he had become a Buddhist after reading Lafcadio Hearn on Japanese Buddhism. As the fifteen-year-old explained in a letter home, the Christian God was constantly "telling you off," whereas in Buddhism "one's own self and being are ultimately identical for always and always."

Watts here resembled many of his later readers: authority-resistant Westerners who would see in Buddhism precisely the haven of freedom Watts believed it to be. He found an agreeable mentor in Christmas (Toby) Humphreys (1901–1983), an eminent London barrister who served as a prosecutor (and later judge) in the Old Bailey criminal courts. Watts had precociously begun a correspondence with the older man promptly after his conversion to Buddhism. Humphreys was sympathetic, for he, like Watts, had first read of Buddhism while a schoolboy and became a Buddhist while studying law at Cambridge. In 1924, Humphreys founded the Buddhist Lodge, later the Buddhist Society, a lay nonsectarian organization that published the influential journal the *Middle Way,* to which he was a frequent contributor. Humphreys also wrote numerous books, such as *Karma and Rebirth* (1959), that served, alongside those of Watts, as popular Western expositions of Buddhism. Humphreys was not a profound thinker, but he was, for Watts and others of his generation, an exemplar of an educated Westerner who had adapted Buddhist teachings, including Right Livelihood, to the demands of a public career. Humphreys preferred prosecutorial to defense work because, as the American legal scholar Damien P. Horigan noted, he "believed that witnesses for the prosecution were far more likely to tell the truth or to attempt to do so, than witnesses for the defense. [. . .] To Humphreys, it was karma that made him a prosecutor just as it was karma that had led criminals to commit crimes." Like his German contemporary George Grimm, a Buddhist jurist of the Weimar period, Humphreys became known, once he took the bench, as a lenient sentencer. Indeed, he insisted that his acceptance of an Old Bailey judgeship in 1968 was made possible by broad restrictions on the death penalty in England.

Watts became a regular visitor to Humphreys's flat, and it was through the latter's graces that Watts, in 1936, met personally with D. T. Suzuki, who seemed to the teenager to be the living master he had longed for. Watts never studied formally with Suzuki, but the immediate influence was so great that Watts at once decided to write his own introduction to Zen. Over the summer of his nineteenth year, Watts completed a short book, *The Spirit of Zen* (1935), dedicated to Humphreys and with a preface offering effusive thanks to Suzuki. The book has remained in print ever since. It was a prodigious feat by a Western neophyte and displayed the talents that served Watts so well in the decades to come: a light, epigrammatic style with flashes of brilliance and humor; a connoisseur's appreciation for the beauties and pleasures of Zen painting and literature; and an underlying lucidity that made Watts difficult to discount as a thinker, even as he sought to appeal to a popular readership. Shortly after this authorial success, he briefly became a student of the Japanese Zen master Sokei-an in New York City, a turbulent relationship recounted in chapter 8.

Gary Snyder, the Pulitzer Prize–winning American Buddhist poet, was a student of Watts in the mid-1950s at the American Academy of Asian Studies in San Francisco. By that time, Watts had passed through a transformative decade that saw him return to Christianity, complete seminary studies (having obtained a waiver of the bachelor's degree prerequisite), take Episcopal priestly orders, and serve as chaplain at North-western University — then renounce the priesthood as he divorced his first wife and moved to the West Coast. Despite this seeming turmoil, Snyder found in Watts a gifted teacher of Zen:

He blazed out the new path for all of us and came back and made it clear. Explored the side canyons and deer trails, and investigated cliffs and thickets. Many guides would have us travel single file, like mules in a pack train, and never leave the trail. Alan taught us to move forward like the breeze, tasting the berries, greeting the blue jays, learning and loving the whole terrain.

Tall, slim, and finely featured, with a faint British accent that somehow blended well with his taste for austere silk robes, Watts found success as a teacher and writer in America. Titles such as *The Way of Zen* (1957), *This Is It, and Other Essays on Zen and Spiritual Experience* (1960), and *Psychotherapy East and West* (1961) sold well and, in many cases, served to introduce young readers of the 1960s to Buddhist vocabulary ("nirvana," "karma," "satori") and to a "Zen" attitude of openness without answers. His widely read 1956 essay, "Beat Zen, Square Zen, and Zen," laid out a catchy jargon for distinguishing between the "too self-conscious, too subjective and too strident" Buddhism of the Beats, the snobbish back-to-the-Orient monastic purity of Square Zen proponents, and the free-form, spontaneous "experience of awakening which truly constitutes Zen." Watts placed himself in this third category while insisting that "I do not even style myself a Zen Buddhist. For the aspect of Zen in which I am personally interested is nothing that can be organized, taught, transmitted, certified or wrapped up in any kind of system. It can't even be followed, for everyone has to find it for himself."

One of the overlooked ironies of Watts's career is that, influential as he was as an interpreter of Buddhism, he was utterly unheeded in his writings on the Christian tradition. Even after he left the Episcopal priesthood, he devoted some years to a series of books — *Behold the Spirit* (1947), *The Supreme Identity* (1950), and *Myth and Ritual in Christianity* (1953) — which, as Watts later described them, attempted a "synthesis between traditional Christianity and the unitive mysticism of Hinduism and Buddhism." To this end, Watts treated Christianity as akin to the two Eastern paths in core outlook, despite dogmatic differences. But a decade later, in *Beyond Theology: The Art of Godmanship* (1964), he broke vehemently with that approach:

> There is not a scrap of evidence that the Christian hierarchy was ever aware of itself as one among several lines of transmission for a universal tradition. Christians, whether of the right wing of the Catholics or the left wing of the Protestants, do not take at all kindly to ideas that even begin to question the unique and supreme importance of the historical Jesus. [. . .] My previous discussions did not take proper account of that whole aspect of Christianity which is uncompromising, ornery, militant, rigorous, imperious, and invincibly self-righteous. They did not give sufficient weight to the Church's disagreeable insistence on the reality of the totally malignant spirit of cosmic evil, on everlasting damnation, and on the absolute distinction between the Creator and the creature.

Watts now declared both Buddhism and Hinduism to be examples of a "superior religion" that "goes beyond theology" to "*identity* with existence itself."

Beyond Theology was published in the midst of the Vatican II proceedings. At the same time that Merton and other Christian thinkers sought to bridge differences with Buddhism, Watts — who had tilled that field in relative isolation for some twenty years — left off his efforts with a kind of relief. For the final decade of his life, he focused on Eastern thought and its applications — psychological, sexual, and spiritual — to Western life.

Having been married three times and fathered seven children, Watts became, by the 1960s, a public advocate of respectful free love. From the Buddhist perspective, he argued that the lesser emphasis on abstinence in traditional Zen training constituted a higher spiritual ground than the forced celibacy of the Western monastic tradition. He also came out as a qualified supporter of LSD use, based on his own experimentation with the drug, which had given him

> an undeniably mystical state of consciousness. [. . .] But [. . .] the injudicious use of LSD (often mixed with strychnine or belladonna or quite dangerous psychedelics) has afflicted uncounted young people with para-

noid, megalomaniac, and schizoid symptoms. [. . .] My retrospective attitude to LSD is that when one has received the message, one hangs up the phone. I think I have learned from it as much as I can, and, for my own sake, would not be sorry if I could never use it again.

Even so, Watts took some years before hanging up the phone and personally provided LSD to several of his children when they turned eighteen, remaining on hand to provide guidance throughout their experience.

Watts had always shied away from formal Zen training and found the concept of monastic life anathema to his own preferred approach of perceiving the Zen quality in untrammeled daily life encounters. This approach could be parodied, as it was by Kerouac in *The Dharma Bums* (1958), in which Watts appears briefly as Arthur Whane at a chic San Francisco gathering

having a perfectly serious discussion about world affairs with two naked men. "Well, what is Buddhism?" someone asks him. "Is it fantastic imagination, magic of the lightning flash, is it plays, dreams, not even plays, dreams?" "No, to me Buddhism is getting to know as many people as possible." And there he was going round the party real affable shaking hands with everybody and chatting, a regular cocktail party.

Indeed it was. Watts had criticized Beat Zen enthusiasts for their depressive overuse of marijuana. But this was in dubious contrast to Watts's own chain-smoking and heavy drinking, which he justified on the grounds that it made his intensive teaching schedule bearable. Like Kerouac, Watts used alcohol to fuel himself in social situations that could otherwise seem invasive and terrifying. By the late 1960s, Watts was a best-selling author in both Europe and America; he had purchased a house on Mount Tamalpais, overlooking San Francisco Bay, and lived out the role of a lionized star of the counterculture. But by then he was consuming a bottle or more of vodka per day. There were financial strains in his life — he had numerous dependents and friends whom he supported by seminars and speeches, which he often gave while drunk, usually unbeknownst to his audience. His oldest son, Mark, concerned over his drinking, asked, "Dad, don't you want to live?" Watts replied, "Yes, but it's not worth holding onto."

Despite his counterculture status in the 1960s, Watts always steered clear of political issues such as civil rights and the Vietnam War. For all his playful innovations in presenting Zen to the West, Watts never viewed it as other than the way it existed in Japan and China — as a quietist approach to enlightenment. That there might emerge, outside the walls of monastic seclusion, an activist Zen, an Engaged Western Buddhism, Watts, the Zen aesthete with the popular touch, did not anticipate.

❖

Watts might disparage the Beats, but most of his young readers did not. To their minds, the publicity explosion that was Zen had its full artistic expression in the writings of the Beat generation — in particular, the work of Gary Snyder, Jack Kerouac, and Allen Ginsberg.

Snyder (b. 1930), while an undergraduate at Reed College, became housemates with two fellow students, Lew Welch and Philip Whalen, who, like Snyder, went on to become poets and Buddhists. Snyder briefly pursued graduate studies in linguistics and anthropology at Indiana University, but he dropped his academic studies in favor of Zen training largely as a result of his dedicated study of a book he had purchased in an out-of-the-way metaphysical bookstore in San Francisco in the spring of 1951. *Essays in Zen Buddhism (First Series)* by D. T. Suzuki was in Snyder's backpack as he hitchhiked that summer to Indiana to begin graduate school. On a Nevada desert roadside, in the absence of traffic, Snyder read Suzuki. John Suiter, a biographer of Snyder, wrote: "In that clear-aired Nevada landscape [. . .] Suzuki's Zen was profoundly magnified. 'It catapulted me into an even larger space,' Gary would remember several years later. [. . .] In a road-shoulder revelation — 'a practical epiphany,' in Snyder's phrase — suddenly it hit him: Route 40 was equally empty both East and West. He was free to go either way."

By the spring of 1952, Snyder was back in San Francisco, sharing a cheap North Beach apartment with Whalen. During the next few years, first Snyder, then Whalen, and eventually their new friend Jack Kerouac spent summers as fire lookouts in small cabins on the top of remote peaks of the Cascade Range in Washington State. Snyder and Kerouac practiced *zazen* in the long weeks of isolation. Whalen, a sporadic *zazen* practitioner since 1946, was not at the time as drawn to Buddhism as were his two friends, and he would not begin serious Zen study until the late 1960s. The influence of those summers shows itself in the writings of all three men.

Snyder felt capable of disciplined *zazen,* but he also recognized his need for more formal Zen training. In the autumn of 1952, after his first summer in the Cascade Range, Snyder wrote both to Nyogen Senzaki in Los Angeles, from whom he received no response, and to the First Zen Institute in New York, which was, under the leadership of Ruth Faller Sasaki, still in search of a Zen teacher to replace her late husband, Sokei-an. In a June 1953 letter to Snyder, Sasaki, who had spent considerable time in Japan, afforded the young aspirant some canny advice on the realities of studying Zen in Japan as an American. Mastering the language was essential, of course, but the difficulties for a Westerner went deeper:

> He must be prepared to endure extreme heat and extreme cold. He must also be prepared to adapt himself physically and mentally to a culture which, though charming and containing many real values, is alien to himself and at times difficult to understand, and he must, last of all, be prepared to have swept away every illusion he has ever held about Buddhism and about Zen. For such a person it is not impossible to study Zen in Japan.

In the fall of 1953, at the University of California at Berkeley, Snyder began his preparations for such a trip by studying the Japanese and Chinese languages, as well as the *sumi* ink-brush technique and the poetics of the T'ang dynasty poets. His encounter with eastern Asian art traditions during this period led him to a hand scroll titled *Mountains and Rivers Without End.* Snyder chose the title for his major work, a long poem begun in 1956 and published in its entirety forty years later, which Snyder described "as a sort of sutra — an extended poetic, philosophic, and mythic narrative of the female Buddha Tara."

Snyder also produced distinguished translations of both Chinese and Japanese verse, most notably of the T'ang dynasty poet Han-shan ("Cold Mountain"), an enlightened hermit whose poems express a self-forged synthesis of Buddhist and Daoist wisdom. Those translations first appeared in 1958 in the *Evergreen Review,* the most prominent avant-garde quarterly of the era. Here was a practicing American Buddhist poet aptly rendering a wild-haired Chinese trickster-poet embraced by both the Chinese and Japanese Buddhist traditions. Snyder's directness of tone is conveyed in this stanza from an untitled poem written by Han-shan on the way to Cold Mountain, the hermitage from which the poet took his name:

> *How did I make it?*
> *My heart's not the same as yours.*
> *If your heart was like mine*
> *You'd get it and be right here.*

In May 1956, Snyder sailed to Japan, where he remained for most of the next decade. Ruth Fuller Sasaki proved of great assistance in helping to arrange this trip, battling on Snyder's behalf in his prolonged effort to obtain a passport from the State Department, which falsely suspected him, due to his pacifism and labor movement sympathies, of being a Communist. He began his Rinzai Zen studies at Shokoku-ji under Miura Isshu Roshi. At Miura's suggestion, he continued his training at Daitoku-ji under Oda Sesso Roshi, whom Snyder considered "an extremely subtle man, by far the subtlest mind I've ever been in contact with, and a marvelous teacher whose teaching capacity I would never have recognized if I hadn't stayed with it, because it was only after five or six years that I began to realize that he had been teaching me all along."

In 1962, with his wife, the poet Joanne Kyger, Snyder interrupted his Zen studies in Japan to pay a six-month visit to India, in order, as he later wrote, "to see the hearth-land of the Buddhist teachings." While there, the two met up for a time with fellow travelers Allen Ginsberg and Peter Orlovsky. Together, they made their way to Dharamsala, where, with considerable ease, they arranged to meet with the Fourteenth Dalai Lama. The exchange, as recorded by Snyder, offers a frank and candid snapshot of the Dalai Lama as a young man in his twenties, still subject to a strict study schedule set by his elder Tibetan teachers, but already evincing a capacity for untrammeled and respectful dialogue with Western seekers.

In something of an irony, given the persistent Western fantasy of posing grand spiritual questions to the Dalai Lama, it was the latter who earnestly queried Snyder on the Zen meditation techniques the American had learned in Japan. Snyder wrote:

> The Dalai Lama is big and rather handsome. He looks like he needs more exercise. Although he understands a lot of English, he always keeps an interpreter by when talking to guests. Allen and Peter asked him at some length about drugs and drug experiences, and their relationship to the spiritual states of meditation. The Dalai Lama gave the same answer everyone else did: drug states are real psychic states, but they aren't ultimately useful to you because you didn't get them on your own will and effort. [. . .] But he [the Dalai Lama] said he'd be interested in trying psilocybin, the mushroom derivative, just to see what Westerners are so excited about. Allen promised to try and put Harvard onto it, and have this professor Dr. Tim Leary send him some.

There is no evidence that the Dalai Lama ever scored psilocybin through the soon-to-be-famous (and no longer with Harvard) Timothy Leary. Quite without aid from or participation by the Dalai Lama, two years later Leary, with coauthors Ralph Metzner and Richard Alpert (later Baba Ram Dass) published *The Psychedelic Experience: A Manual Based on the Tibetan Book of the Dead* (1964). Inspired far more by Western psychology than Tibetan Buddhism, the book nonetheless included special tributes to W. Y. Evans-Wentz and Lama Anagarika Govinda.

Leary's manual was never widely used, but its optimism as to the benefits of drug experiences as a means of making sense of Buddhist teachings was widespread. A sizable percentage of Americans and Europeans who were drawn seriously to Buddhism during this decade experimented with psychoactive substances (for which the modern general term is "entheogens"). Intense debate — without signs of resolution — continues to this day among Western Buddhists as to whether the drug experimentation of the era served to foster or hamper the acceptance of Buddhism. The American historian of religions Huston Smith recently offered this highly speculative and provocative perspective:

> Medical anthropologists have discovered that brain changes that result from taking entheogens are very much like those that are produced by physical exhaustion from prolonged fasting and other ordeals of the sort

the Buddha undertook before he assumed his seat under the Bodhi Tree. This being the case, it may be one of the great paradoxes of history that one of its greatest religions was launched (chemically speaking) by a state of mind that is virtually indistinguishable from ones that are produced by fudging the fifth of the Five Precepts in the Eightfold Path that the Buddha prescribed as leading to enlightenment, the one that proscribes the taking of intoxicants.

Neither in Japan nor subsequently in America, where he was for a time a student of Robert Aitkin Roshi, did Snyder ever take monastic vows. But he did go on to found, in the 1970s, the Ring of Bone Zendo (the name comes from the title of the collected poems of his late friend Lew Welch) in the Sierra Nevada of California. The *zendo* drew practitioners from the surrounding lay community and ultimately obtained a Zen teacher in residence.

❖

Jack Kerouac became a dedicated student of Buddhist scriptures in the mid-1950s, and his writings produced in that period have exercised a considerable influence on American Buddhism. In 1953, having completed the manuscript of *On the Road* (ultimately published in 1957), with its "spontaneous prose" style, Kerouac became fascinated with the affinities between his aesthetic and spiritual aims as a writer and the teachings of Buddhism. Another motivating force was his despair over making his love relationships work, having endured a painful breakup in the autumn of that year with Alene Lee, the model for Mardou Fox in Kerouac's novel *The Subterraneans* (1958).

His earliest readings on Buddhism included a Sacred Books of the East translation of *The Life of Buddha* by Ashvaghosha and various essays on Zen by D. T. Suzuki, as well as essays and translations of Japanese haiku by the British writer R. H. Blyth (1898–1964). But the most formative impact was produced by the *Buddhist Bible,* edited by Dwight Goddard, which Kerouac checked out from the San Jose Public Library in 1954. Presented in admirably nonsectarian form were teachings from the Theravada, Mahayana, and Vajrayana traditions. Kerouac became so immersed in the book that he never returned it, but rather had it bound in leather so as to withstand his rucksack travels. Buddhist teachings and metaphors effloresce in his poetry of the period, most famously in the "239th Chorus" of *Mexico City Blues* (1959), in which Kerouac melds the wisdom of the East with the emergent creative energy of the West in the form of the greatest American musician of the time, Charlie Parker, whose expression

> *Was as calm, beautiful, and profound*
> *As the image of the Buddha*
> *Represented in the East, the lidded eyes,*
> *The expression that says "All is Well"*
> *— This was what Charley Parker*
> *Said when he played, All is Well.*

Kerouac's massive work *Some of the Dharma* (posthumously published in 1997) was composed between 1953 and 1956 and consists of an intricate array of haiku and other free verse, study notes, journal riffs, prayers, letters, and reflections — all inspired by the spirit of Buddhism. The *Diamond Sutra* was Kerouac's particular favorite, with its Middle Way teaching that suffering and selfhood were illusions underlain by the primordial purity of the Dharma. In May 1954, Kerouac wrote to his friend Allen Ginsberg of his

> discovery and espousal of sweet Buddha. . . . I always did suspect that life was a dream, now I am assured by the most brilliant man who ever lived, that it is indeed so. . . . I will and would go to El Paso Texas at first, to wash dishes and live across the river in $4 a month adobe cottage where with my Buddha Bibles and bean stews I would live life of mendicant thinker in this humble earth dream.

It was by reason of letters such as this that Ginsberg, on the dedication page of his *Howl and Other Poems* (1956), offered a paean to "Jack Kerouac new Buddha of American prose." Nor was this entirely hyperbole, if one considers Kerouac's intentions of the time: "I dont really want to write systematic books of literature any more, just these private memorial notes. [. . .] I'd like to bone myself now down to purity of Tao, go deeper into Buddhahood, give up individuality and the 'I,' that awful abstract 'I' of writing — give up letters, for 'virtue evaporates into desire for fame.'"

In 1956, while living in an unfinished cabin in Mill Valley, California, Kerouac wrote *The Scripture of the Golden Eternity* (1960), the only one of his prose works centered on Buddhist teachings to be published in his lifetime. But *Scripture* is better described as a work of prose poetry. In it, Kerouac demonstrated a gift for vivid jazz-rhythm American versions of abstract Buddhist conceptions, such as awakening from the illusion of a self:

> We know what we're doing: we're not disturbed: because we're like the golden eternity pretending at playing the magic cardgame and making believe it's real, it's a big dream, a joyous ecstasy of words and ideas and flesh, an ethereal flower unfolding and folding back, a movie, an exuberant bunch of lines bounding emptiness, the womb of Avalokitesvara, a vast secret silence, springtime in the Void, happy young gods talking and drinking on a cloud.

The Dharma Bums, discussed in chapter 8 in connection with Kerouac's 1958 encounter with D. T. Suzuki, was a disappointment to Gary Snyder in terms of its portrayal of Buddhism. Snyder acknowledged the kindness and artistry of Kerouac's portrait of Japhy Ryder, but objected to the views on sex expressed in the novel that Snyder believed were alien to Buddhist teachings. In a March 1959 letter to Kerouac, Snyder made his point emphatically: "Nobody ever said anything against love or entanglement with women but you." But during his own private Buddhist studies prior to meeting Snyder, Kerouac had reached a different conclusion. In early January 1955, for example, Kerouac wrote: "Sexuality, the most powerful force in all nature because of its sometimes fabulous delight, is the very incarnation of ignorance. [. . .] Lust is no different from killing — the squeal of the murdered pig, the hoarse panting of the sexers, it's all vicious, fleshy, and blind, and subject of the devouring worm." The broad history of Buddhist doctrine and practice includes the views of both Snyder and Kerouac. In terms of the emergence of Western Buddhism, Snyder's view has very strongly prevailed.

By the end of 1958, in the aftermath of the personal and critical rebuffs he had received for *The Dharma Bums*, Kerouac confessed to a declining commitment to Buddhism. And in the last years of his life, the Catholicism of his youth fully reasserted itself. His explanation of the sea change within him was, in substance, typical of many Western persons who have found the Buddhist path lacking in ultimate solace. In a letter to Philip Whalen, Kerouac (a recent father) wrote:

> Myself, the dharma is slipping away from my consciousness and I can't think of anything to say about it any more. I still read the Diamond Sutra, but as in a dream now. Don't know what to do. Can't see the purpose of human or terrestrial or any kinda life without heaven to reward the poor suffering fucks. The Buddhist notion that Ignorance caused the world leaves me cold now, because I feel the presence of angels. Maybe rebirth is simply HAVING KIDS.

❖

Even if one sets aside the Beats and their lineage, the influence of Buddhism on the American literature of the second half of the twentieth century has been more profound than is commonly acknowledged. Jim Harrison, bell hooks, Charles Johnson, and Peter Matthiessen are among the contemporary authors who have acknowledged their indebtedness to Buddhist teachings. John Cage (1912–1992), the composer and writer, attended postwar lectures on Zen Buddhism given by D. T. Suzuki at Columbia University. Cage credited Zen with a decisive influence on his experimental music, with its elements of spontaneity and simplicity — at times, extreme simplicity, as in his 1952 composition *4'33"*, throughout which a pianist sits motionless before a keyboard. The aim of art, as of Zen, was, in Cage's words, to inspire "waking up to the very life we're living." Visual artists of the period, such as Ad Reinhardt, Robert Motherwell, and Mark Tobey, were drawn — in part through the influence of Cage — to explore Zen themes in their own works.

But the depth of Kerouac's impact on the evolution of Western Buddhism is beyond question. *The Dharma Bums,* in particular, has served as an introduction — evocative and idealized — to the American Buddhist life of the open road and open mind for a half century of young readers. Kerouac also exercised an influence on the Tibetan Buddhist teacher Chögyam Trungpa. Ginsberg, who became Trungpa's student in the early 1970s, offered this account of the intertwined Western lineage of poetics and Buddhist awakening:

Poetry can be "writing the mind," the Ven. Chögyam Trungpa phrased it, corollary to his slogan "First thought, best thought," itself parallel to Kerouac's formulation "Mind is shapely, Art is shapely." Reading *Mexico City Blues* to that great Buddhist teacher from the front carseat on a long drive [. . .] Trungpa laughed all the way as he listened. [. . .] The next day he told me, *I kept hearing Kerouac's voice all night, or yours and Anne Waldman's* [a fellow poet]. . . . It'd given him a new idea of American poetry, for his own poetry. [. . .] Thus two years later the "Jack Kerouac School of Disembodied Poetics" was founded with Naropa Institute, certainly a center for meeting of classical Eastern wisdom meditative practice with Western alert spontaneous candid thought, healthy synthesis of Eastern and Western Mind, at last these twain've met forever Hallelujah Svaha!

❖

Of all the teachers who have come from East to West in the twentieth century, none poses so perplexing a legacy as Chögyam Trungpa Rinpoche (1939–1987).

Trungpa was born in a cowshed on the high steppes of eastern Tibet, the son of a shepherding family. While still an infant he was tested and declared to be the eleventh tulku (reincarnated lama) of the revered Trungpa teaching lineage. Taken away from his family by his new guardian monks, he was ritually enthroned, at age thirteen months, as chief abbot of the Surmang monasteries and given the name Chokyi Gyatso ("Ocean of Dharma") and the honorific title Rinpoche ("Precious One"). His Buddhist spiritual development was overseen by some of the most esteemed lamas in all of Tibet. But in 1959, like the Fourteenth Dalai Lama, Trungpa was forced by the brutality of the Chinese occupation to flee Tibet by stealth. Trungpa escaped with some three hundred Tibetan refugees to India, where he was appointed by the Dalai Lama as a spiritual adviser to the Young Lamas Home School in Dalhousie.

All of these events are described in Trungpa's *Born in Tibet* (1966), published in Britain and the United States to both scholarly and popular acclaim. The book came about because Trungpa had grown restive with his teaching role in India and, in 1963, traveled to England, where he became the first Tibetan to be accepted at Oxford University. There he studied Western philosophy and religion as well as the English language, at which he quickly became proficient. He soon attracted a small but growing number of Western students interested in studying the vaunted mysteries of Tibetan Buddhism. Trungpa proceeded to establish, on donated land in Dumfriesshire, Scotland, Samye Ling, one of the earliest Tibetan Buddhist meditation centers in the West. He also applied for and was granted British citizenship.

Thus far, Trungpa had pursued a Buddhist career path of austere respectability. By virtue of his first book and his charismatic teaching style — which included a remarkable knack for grasping the problems of beginning Western students — Trungpa was poised for a public role similar to that achieved by the Dalai Lama some fifteen years later. But Trungpa was as interested in exploring life's possibilities in the West as he was in transmitting the wisdom of the East. While continuing to wear the robes of a Tibetan monk, he pursued clandestine affairs with women and consumed large quantities of alcohol, keeping both of these activities a secret from his students.

In 1968, upon the invitation of the royal family of Bhutan — whose princely heir Trungpa had tutored at Oxford — Trungpa visited Bhutan and spent ten days in meditational retreat at Taktsang, a sacred site in the Tibetan tradition. As Trungpa explained, Padmasambhava had manifested there "in the wrathful form of Dorje Trollo and subjugated forces before entering Tibet." Padmasambhava (Guru Rinpoche) was then in a position very similar to that of Trungpa in the West — preparing himself for the bringing of the Dharma into a new and challenging cultural realm. For Trungpa, the impact in terms of teaching approach was formative:

During my retreat there I was able to reflect on my life and particularly on how to propagate the Dharma in the West. I invoked Guru Rinpoche and the Ka-gyu forefathers to provide vision for the future. [. . .] The message that I had received from my supplication was that one must try to expose spiritual materialism and all its trappings, otherwise true spirituality could not develop. I began to realize that I would have to take daring steps in my life.

It was during this period that Thomas Merton met Trungpa in Calcutta, a city both were visiting on their disparate travels. The rapport between the two was immediate. Trungpa later described Merton as "an open, unguarded and deep person," while Merton, in his journal, extolled Trungpa as "a completely marvelous person. Young, natural, without front or artifice, deep, awake, wise." The two discussed the possibility of working together on an anthology of Vajrayana and Catholic teachings. It is fascinating, in light of Trungpa's future innovations as a teacher in the West, that Merton recorded their shared concern over tampering with monastic tradition: "He has the same problems we have with 'progressive' monks whose idea of modernization is to go noncontemplative, to be 'productive' and academic." But Trungpa never went "noncontemplative" — his emphasis on rigorous meditation training was a constant with his Western students.

In May 1969, after his return to England, Trungpa blacked out while driving a car in which one of his lovers was a passenger. The only person injured in the crash was Trungpa, who suffered permanent paralysis on his left side. The experience was transformative on a spiritual level. As Trungpa later explained, the crash led him to abandon his status as a monk:

> When plunging completely and genuinely into the teachings, one is not allowed to bring along one's deceptions. I realized that I could no longer attempt to preserve any privacy for myself, any special identity or legitimacy. I should not hide behind the robes of a monk, creating an impression of inscrutability which, for me, turned out to be only an obstacle. With a sense of further involving myself with the sangha, I determined to give up my monastic vows. More than ever I felt myself given over to serving the cause of Buddhism.

Not only did Trungpa abandon his robes, but he also abandoned his habit of secrecy in matters of sex and intoxication. Henceforth, as a self-declared lay teacher of Buddhism — although he was always treated by his Western students as a revered tulku — he would challenge all who would learn from him to confront him as he was. That the renunciation of monastic vows should heighten his devotion to the Dharma was a remarkable instance of Trungpa's capacity not only to adapt to but also to embrace the possibilities of change in the West. The love of women, for example, offered a radiant fulfillment of the Vajrayana teachings on the union of male and female energies. In "The Perfect Love Poem," written near the time of his marriage to sixteen-year-old Diana Judith Pybus, of upper-class British upbringing, Trungpa declared, with a hint of defiance at the strictures of Christian theology: "This loving is the pattern of Mahamudra, universal love. / [. . .] And I will dance bearing the burden of the cross. / No one has forsaken me. It is such a joyous love dance, my partner and I united."

Not only was the bride's family opposed to the marriage, but so too were some of Trungpa's Tibetan lama peers, as well as his Western students at Samye Ling. So fierce were the tensions at Samye Ling that Trungpa and his wife, now Diana Mukpo, moved to North America. The depth of the pain and resentment that Trungpa experienced during this period is confirmed in a recent memoir account by Mukpo:

> The time from Rinpoche's accident until we married and left for America a year later was one of the darkest periods in his life. Rinpoche was often in the depths of depression. He was sick with pleurisy and pneumonia, his Tibetan compatriots were trying to control him, and many of his students had left him. He felt that his only reason for existence was to present the Buddhist teachings, and at this point he couldn't. [. . .] That night in the hotel, Rinpoche had a big jar of Seconals, which are sleeping medications. I don't know where he had got them. At one point that night, he turned to me and said, "Let's take all these pills. Let's just do it." I grabbed the bottle out of his hand and threw the pills out of the hotel window, saying, "We're not going to do that. There's a future for us." Then we went to bed.

There was indeed a future. In 1970, Trungpa established Tail of the Tiger, a rural meditation center in Barnet, Vermont. Shortly thereafter, he founded what would become his most famous contribution to American culture — the Naropa Institute in Boulder, Colorado, which by the 1980s had evolved into the first accredited Buddhist university in the United States. Most of Trungpa's early American students were shaggy-haired hippies who were startled and pleased to find that their Tibetan teacher relished, at times, wildly uninhibited parties with hundreds of guests. Not coincidentally, Naropa began to draw famous faculty names who wanted to explore firsthand what all the rumors were about. Teachers at Naropa in its early years included Allen Ginsberg, Gregory Bateson, William Burroughs, John Cage, Baba Ram Dass, Anne Waldman, and Trungpa himself. Harvey Cox, a noted Christian theologian from Harvard Divinity School who attended courses at Naropa, later wrote that "studying with Trungpa was one of the most memorable intellectual and spiritual adventures of my life."

Trungpa's willingness to employ direct and startling means to awaken his American students became a hallmark. During meditation sessions, for example, he might suddenly pull out a water pistol and squirt inattentive sitters. On his own, Trungpa pursued a specific Vajrayana Tantric discipline that he allowed was "dangerous" and fit only for the very few. Termed "swallowing the poisons," it consisted of the open but nonattached embrace of all the seeming "poisons," or dangers, of the illusory world of samsara — greed, lust, and power. This embrace, the counterpart to the path of ascetic avoidance, transmuted the supposed evils of human passions into means for more fully realizing the dancing impermanence of all existence. So, while maintaining his marriage, Trungpa had open affairs. He also drank to excess, sometimes even staggering as he delivered talks on Buddhist practice.

Trungpa early on formed a close relationship with Shunryu Suzuki, who paid the younger man the singular homage of inviting him to lecture frequently at Suzuki's Page Street *zendo* in San Francisco. As Suzuki's biographer David Chadwick observed,

> Suzuki had no relationship like this with any other teacher. They talked about the loneliness of being a teacher. Trungpa called him his new spiritual father, and Suzuki told him, "You are like my son." Suzuki's relationship with Trungpa disturbed some people, maybe because Trungpa, in addition to being a brilliant, inspiring speaker and the beloved teacher of many disciples, was also an outrageous alcoholic who slept with some of his female students.

In a 1971 lecture to his students, Suzuki defended Trungpa as a teacher who was helping to preserve the nascent Buddhist *sangha* in the West:

> That is why I respect Trungpa Rinpoche. He is supporting us. You may criticize him because he drinks alcohol like I drink water, but that is a minor problem. He trusts you completely. He knows that if he is always supporting you in a true sense, you will not criticize him, whatever he does. And he doesn't mind whatever you say. That is not the point, you know. This kind of big spirit, without clinging to some special religion or form of practice, is necessary for human beings.

During his first two years in America, Trungpa formulated two key introductory conceptions for the benefit of his Western students who had not yet, due to Trungpa's caution in that regard, commenced formal Vajrayana training. The success of these two conceptions — "spiritual materialism" and "crazy wisdom" — may be gauged by their ongoing presence as catchphrases in our language. By "spiritual materialism" he meant the panoply of devices by which religious seekers subtly flatter and deceive themselves through their obsessive quest of "attainments" that fuel ego fantasies of ultimate attainment: "Ego is able to convert everything to its own use, even spirituality. [. . .] When we have learned all the tricks and answers of the spiritual game, we automatically try to imitate spirituality, since real involvement would require the complete elimination of ego, and actually the last thing we want to do is to give up the ego completely."

The linkage between "spiritual materialism" and "crazy wisdom" was that the former was "trying to live up to what you would *like* to be" while the latter meant "trying to live what you are." The embrace of crazy wisdom necessitated abandoning all illusions of doctrinal solace and personal virtue:

> The process is one of going further in and in and in without any reference point of spirituality, without any reference point of a savior, without any reference point of goodness or badness — without any reference points whatsoever! [. . .] This process of going deeper and deeper is the process of crazy wisdom, and it is what characterizes a saint in the Buddhist tradition.

Crazy wisdom insisted on recognizing that pain was part of life, that suffering as well as joy offered necessary teachings. One did not practice Buddhism to evade the realities of human existence. A revered patriarch in the Trungpa Kagyu lineage, Marpa the Translator, the teacher of Milarepa, employed emotional and physical extremes in his training of his great student. Trungpa was heir to these methods of teaching, and they coincided with his crazy wisdom. The lasting beneficial impact he left on many of his students is confirmed by their own testimonies.

The risks of the method in terms of Western public perception — a new factor in the practice of Vajrayana training — showed themselves in what the American poet Tom Clark came to term "The Great Naropa Poetry Wars." In the fall of 1975, the poets W. S. Merwin and Dana Naone, then a couple, sought and received permission from Trungpa to participate in his autumn Vajrayana seminar in Snowmass, Colorado, intended for advanced students, which Merwin and Naone were not. During a Halloween party held to inaugurate the final stage of the training, Trungpa and several students doffed their clothing. Merwin and Naone, who had chosen not to attend the party, were brought down from their room by force by their fellow students on Trungpa's order. They were then, in front of Trungpa, compelled to strip naked.

The next day, after an interview with Trungpa in which no apology was offered, the two poets requested to remain for three more weeks of training, after which they departed. In a letter distributed to all students the day after the party, Trungpa, by way of explanation, emphasized the uniqueness of Vajrayana practice: "You must offer your neuroses as a feast to celebrate your entrance into the vajra teachings. Those of you who wish to leave will not be given a refund, but your Karmic debt will continue as the vividness of your memory cannot be forgotten."

Allen Ginsberg was not present for these events, but his views were sought out, as he was the leading presence in the Naropa Institute poetry community, as well as a student of Trungpa — with whom, as an added wrinkle of complexity, Ginsberg had fallen romantically in love. In an interview with Clark some four months after the Halloween party, Ginsberg responded to the report that Naone had cried out futilely "call the police!" while being stripped: "In the middle of that scene, to yell 'call the police!' — do you realize how *vulgar* that was? The Wisdom of the East was being unveiled, and she's going, 'call the police!' I mean,

shit! Fuck that shit! Strip 'em naked, break down the door! Anything —
symbolically. I mentioned privacy before — the entrance into Vajrayana
is the abandonment of all privacy."

There was, at the time of its first publication, considerable outrage
over this statement by Ginsberg, for obvious reasons pertaining to the legal and ethical ramifications of physical, sexual, and psychological assault. There is also some justification for Ginsberg's views if one sees the
entirety of the events within the framework of Vajrayana teaching. In
Born in Tibet, Trungpa chronicled how, at an early age, he was asked to
remove his clothes before his own teacher, an unthinkable action within
the norms of Tibetan culture. Vajrayana uses and transforms all manner
of psychological energies — including fear, anger, and arousal — in its
committed efforts to vanquish the neuroses. But the students must be
willing.

In his journal, Ginsberg testified to the uncertainties and fears that
endured within him as a result of the Naropa controversy: "As time's
gone on the last two years, the conflict's crossed my mind every morning on waking, and I've had difficulty knowing whether I'm lying to
cover Trungpa's Hierarchical secrecy, or lying to Clark in not openly and
continuously confronting him in his journalistic spitefulness and in-
trigue." Just how anguished his self-examination became is evidenced by
this further journal entry: "I used to boast no identity! Now why am I
stuck with the accusation of a fixed identity as Trungpa's sucker? Am I?
If so, where else could I go in sincerity if I want meditation?" As this final sentence confirms, Ginsberg was not only in love with his teacher
but convinced of his unique value as a spiritual mentor. Ginsberg's loy-
alty to Trungpa held through the crisis.

❖

In 1976, Trungpa founded a pointedly secular system of training called
Shambhala, after the Buddhist kingdom of Tibetan legend in which
peace and harmony always reigned. Trungpa acknowledged that while
Shambhala was

> founded on the sanity and gentleness of the Buddhist tradition, at the
> same time, it has its own independent basis, which is directly cultivating
> who and what we are as human beings. With the great problems now

facing human society, it seems increasingly important to find simple and nonsectarian ways to work with ourselves and to share our understanding with others.

The guiding ideal of the Shambhala warrior, female or male, was that of service to others. In one of his Shambhala lectures on compassionate human behavior, Trungpa addressed subtly the differences he felt between himself and other religionists who had sex with their followers:

> Passion has been undermined so much, particularly by religiosity, by just a simple remark like "Sex is bad." We are not saying here that sex is the best, either. Rather, we are talking about human nature and the human virtue, or goodness, of helping others. How to help others, how to like somebody, or how to love somebody are often so mixed up. We hear dreadful stories, such as the stories about priests making it with their parishioners. There is all that garbage that goes on, all those human stories. We might discuss warped love later, but here we are talking about fresh love.

In the early 1970s, Trungpa had begun the creation of a network of Dharmadhatu ("space of Dharma") meditation centers in the United States and Canada, with a central organization, Vajradhatu, coordinating their efforts. He ultimately moved the headquarters for all of his teaching networks from Boulder to Halifax, Nova Scotia. Trungpa died in Halifax in 1987, at age forty-seven, his life foreshortened by alcohol excess.

In light of the emphasis Trungpa placed on his lineage with the renowned nineteenth-century Tibetan sage Jamgon Kongtrul, it is useful to consult the latter's treatise, *Buddhist Ethics,* for perspective on the relationship between vajra masters and their students. Kongtrul emphasized that such masters were required to conform to traditional Buddhist teachings. At the same time, he urged students to recognize the humanity of their teachers:

> Because we are living in a [degenerate] age, we very rarely meet a teacher endowed with all of the necessary qualifications. Since we may never meet such a teacher, we should accept a master who has many good

qualities and very few weaknesses. [Pundarika's] *Ultimate Familiarization* states:

> *"In this age of conflict, spiritual masters will exhibit both*
> *faults and virtues;*
> *Not one is absolutely irreproachable.*
> *Therefore, examine well even those who excel in virtue*
> *Before beginning to study with them."*

❖

In 1976, eleven years before his death, Trungpa appointed Ösel Tendzin as his Dharma heir and regent and his ultimate successor in leadership. In his foreword to *Buddha in the Palm of Your Hand* (1982), the debut book of Tendzin, Trungpa offered this vibrant endorsement:

Many Oriental advisors have said to me, "Do not make an Occidental your successor; they are not trustworthy." With the blessing of His Holiness the 16th Gwalya Karmapa, and through working with Ösel Tendzin as my Regent, I have come to the conclusion that anybody who possesses tathagatagarbha [Buddha-nature, possessed by all beings] is worthy of experiencing enlightenment. [. . .] I have worked arduously in training him as my best student and foremost leader, and His Holiness Karmapa [during his second visit to the United States] has confirmed his Regency. With His Holiness' blessing, Ösel Tendzin should hold his title and the sanity of the enlightened lineage. He is absolutely capable of imparting the message of buddhadharma to the rest of the world.

This passage is of especial historical interest, as it documents precisely the same sorts of hesitancies, racial and cultural in nature, on the part of Asian Buddhists as were felt centuries before by early European Christian missionaries when it came to the priestly ordination of Asian-born converts. It also, of course, documents a colossal error of judgment on the part of Trungpa, a highly attained Tibetan Buddhist master. Some apologists for Trungpa have attempted to find a species of "crazy wisdom" in his choice of a regent, although none have been able convincingly to discern any wisdom in so great a disregard for the Buddhist values of compassion and skillful means. It is all the more ironic that

Trungpa himself should have stressed that Tendzin would uphold "the sanity of the enlightened lineage."

If there was one pronounced behavior trait in Trungpa, it was defiant openness. If a student was offended by his master's drunkenness or sexual activity, the student could go elsewhere. But Trungpa's appointed Dharma heir reverted to shameless concealment. In December 1988, the Vajradhatu administration made an announcement to its membership that the sexually active Tendzin was a carrier of the AIDS virus but had neither protected his partners nor informed them of his condition. Two persons were now infected with the virus as a result.

Rick Fields, the author of the first and finest full-scale history of Buddhism in America, *How the Swans Came to the Lake* (1981 and later expanded editions), recounted therein a conversation he had with Tendzin shortly after all this became public. Fields was himself a committed member of the Vajradhatu community, lending the occasion all the more drama: "I asked, 'So what happened?' His answer was direct and spontaneous: 'I was fooling myself,' he told me. [. . .] 'Thinking I had some extraordinary means of protection, I went ahead with my business as if something would take care of it for me.'"

Tendzin refused to resign. Ultimately, the verdict of Tibetan elders in Nepal and India who had been consulted on the matter was a venerable course of action in the case of difficult lamas: it was suggested that the regent undertake a long-term meditational retreat. After some protracted resistance, Tendzin consented. In August 1991, Tendzin died in a San Francisco hospital, a victim of AIDS. Two days later, Ösel Mukpo, the twenty-seven-year-old eldest son of Chögyam Trungpa, was formally installed as the new spiritual head of Vajradhatu.

❖

There is a discomfiting parallel between Tendzin's blatant denial as to sexual choices and the attitude of Trungpa toward his own constant drinking. Ginsberg biographer Michael Schumacher, who interviewed the poet, offered this summary of a 1971 discussion between Ginsberg and Trungpa:

Fully aware of the fate Kerouac suffered as a result of his alcoholism, Allen again asked Trungpa why he drank so much. Trungpa explained he hoped to determine the illumination of American drunkenness. In the United States, he said, alcohol was the main drug, and he wanted to use his acquired knowledge of drunkenness as a source of wisdom, as a means of using the energy of pain. This, too, reminded Allen of Kerouac.

There is nothing outside the possible realms of Vajrayana practice in Trungpa's explanation. But it is worth remembering that Taizan Maezumi Roshi, the founder of the Los Angeles Zen Center, ultimately confessed — after pressure from his students — to his alcoholism and entered treatment prior to his death in 1995. Maezumi Roshi was also alleged to have had affairs with students.

Realized Buddhists can also be alcoholics who make dicey choices. The experience of enlightenment does not produce perfect persons, who seem to be in short supply in all world religions. Prominent spiritual teachers of the present and the foreseeable future will be subject to an intensive scrutiny not imposed on the sages of the past. Legends of a saintly life and practice, so vital to conveying the spirit of a teaching, are, in our very public times, decidedly more difficult to create and sustain.

For many of his former Western students, Trungpa's sexual and drinking preferences are tangential to the meaning of his work. Judith Simmer-Brown, an Acharya, or senior teacher, in the lineage of Trungpa and also a professor at Naropa University, noted that "whereas Trungpa Rinpoche was best known to the public as unconventional in his lifestyle and teachings, with his students he was meticulous, generous, and exacting in his presentation of Tibetan tantra." She further praised Trungpa for his pioneering efforts in acknowledging the role of women in Tibetan Tantra:

> Tibetan Buddhism in its Asian and North American manifestations at that time had male teachers, strong hierarchical patterns, and neither sympathy for nor openness to feminism. [. . .] [Trungpa] presented this material in a completely unique way for a Tibetan lama, couching traditional and fundamental insights of tantra in language accessible to citizens of the late twentieth century influenced by feminism.

Among the women who studied with Trungpa and became strong voices within Western Buddhism are the author Francesca Fremantle, the scholar Rita Gross, and the Tibetan Buddhist nun Pema Chödrön, who in the 1990s wrote three highly successful books on Buddhist teachings directed to Western readers — *The Wisdom of No Escape* (1991), *Start Where You Are* (1994), and *When Things Fall Apart* (1997).

Even with such grateful testimony, an awkward question remains: if the teachings of Trungpa were masterly and efficacious, why the lingering discomfort among so many Western Buddhists? Perhaps the answer lies in the seeming conflicts between the assumptions of Western psychotherapy and the contextual Vajrayana training offered by Trungpa. Stephen T. Butterfield, a onetime student of Trungpa, observed:

> To be part of Trungpa's inner circle, you had to take a vow never to reveal or even discuss some of the things he did. This personal secrecy is common with gurus, especially in Vajrayana Buddhism. It is also common in the dysfunctional family systems of alcoholics and sexual abusers. This inner circle secrecy puts up an almost insurmountable barrier to a healthily skeptical mind.

Butterfield is pointing to a genuine danger that can and does arise in all religious frameworks; "inner circle secrecy" has served, for example, to protect sexually abusive clergy in the Catholic Church.

But there is also no question that Vajrayana Buddhism has, during its long history in Tibet, accorded its venerated teachers an untrammeled freedom of method, which is to say that it has accorded them untrammeled lives. Democracy, as Trungpa often emphasized in his talks to American students, was not a valuable means by which to penetrate the truths of the Vajrayana; for that, one needed a master of crazy wisdom. It remains to be seen if the West will accommodate such masters in the future. They do not seem to be afoot at present.

12

THE DALAI LAMA AND THE
TRANSFORMATION OF
BUDDHISM IN THE WEST

❖

The Fourteenth Dalai Lama (b. 1935) is a difficult figure to assess historically, for his career as a political leader, Buddhist teacher, and ecumenical world spokesman may well, as of the time of this writing, be far from
completed. It would be as rash to summarize his achievements and influence — even as he enters his seventies — as it would have been in the
case of a very different personage, Winston Churchill, at that same time
of life. The uncertainty of the situation in Tibet under Chinese rule im-
poses caution in this regard.

Because the life of the Dalai Lama, the circumstances of his escape
from Tibet in 1959, the genocidal toll of 1.2 million Tibetans killed by
the Chinese military occupiers, and the systematic destruction of Tibetan
Buddhist monasteries all have been well documented, there is no need to
revisit these matters in detail here. In the aftermath of the Cultural Revolution, Tibetan Buddhist practice of a limited order has been gradually
authorized by the Chinese government. This is particularly true in the far
western Chinese province of Qinghai — as well as parts of the neighboring provinces of Sichuan, Yunnan, and Gansu, which contain a substantial ethnic Tibetan Buddhist population. This Himalayan region, known
as Greater Tibet, was not historically a part of Tibet, and hence the current Chinese regime has been less disinclined to grant its people freedom
of worship. But within Tibet proper, and particularly in the Buddhist centers of Lhasa and Shigatse, concern over the ongoing popularity of the
Dalai Lama and its relation to hopes of independence have led to contin-

ued repression by the Chinese. Since 2002, largely secret discussions between the Chinese and representatives of the Dalai Lama have taken place, with the Dalai Lama proposing (as he has since the 1970s) what he has termed a "middle way" approach of autonomy — as opposed to full political independence — both for Tibet and Greater Tibet. The Chinese have asserted in turn that such autonomy would violate their constitution and that Greater Tibet is none of the Dalai Lama's affair.

Some political analysts suggest that the recent willingness of China to negotiate to any extent with the Dalai Lama is due to its fears of unrest among its Tibetan population should the revered leader die in exile. For his part, the Dalai Lama announced in 2003 that he would be reborn as the Fifteenth Dalai Lama to a Tibetan family living not in China but in a politically free country, so that his present work on behalf of Tibet could continue. The role that the Dalai Lama can play in the unfolding of Chinese policy remains unclear.

What may safely be said is that the Dalai Lama has achieved the widest Western audience — a disparate one, of readers, listeners, religious followers, and sympathizers at a distance — of any Asian Buddhist teacher in history. Indeed, it may be the case that the Dalai Lama, by virtue of his title and lineage, will be the last Asian Buddhist teacher whose public appeal draws on Western fantasies of an "exotic" East — for the Dalai Lama, by his plainspokenness, has done much to expel the lingering exoticism associated with Buddhist teachings. Further, it seems that certain of his writings and outlooks will enter the Western academic canon: the Fourteenth Dalai Lama will be taught as a "great thinker" and a "great religious leader" for generations to come, in the same manner that Gandhi and Martin Luther King Jr. are currently taught. And finally, one may accord the Dalai Lama four signal successes in his role as a religious leader: the preservation, to the extent possible, of Tibetan Buddhist culture and practice in Dharamsala and in the exiled Tibetan communities of the West; the lucid and empathetic dissemination of Tibetan Buddhist teachings for Western Buddhist practitioners; the strengthening of the alliance between Buddhism and the Western scientific community; and the fostering of changes in outlook and practice in order that the Dharma take root in the West.

❖

The Dalai Lama did not emerge as a major spokesman for Buddhism in the West until the mid-1980s. His principal focus until then had been on the establishment of a Tibetan teaching and population center in Dharamsala, India. The groundswell of Western interest in Buddhism that he encountered, and magnified, had been cultivated by other hands, and certain of those prior efforts deserve emphasis.

In the 1970s and 1980s, Tibetan Buddhist centers emerged in the United States, Canada, Great Britain, France, and Switzerland under the leadership of exiled Tibetan teachers and authors such as Chögyam Trungpa, Tarthang Tulku, Geshe Wangyal, Geshe Rabten, and Kalu Rinpoche. Meanwhile, the Western Zen communities of that period were changing in two key respects. First, a number of American-born roshis received Dharma transmission from their Japanese teachers and became the new leaders of the proliferating Zen centers. Second, a significant number of those roshis were women, including Jiyu Kennett, Joanna Macy, Toni Packer, and Maureen Stuart. As Gary Snyder said in a 1977 interview, "The single most revolutionary aspect of Buddhist practice in the United States is the fact that women are participating in it." This gender equality soon extended to Tibetan Buddhist centers as well.

The presence of women as both teachers and students has encouraged the emergence of values and practices that distance Western Buddhism all the more from the monastic frameworks of the Asian tradition. Families are welcomed into many Buddhist *sanghas,* with day care provided while parents meditate. Women have also emerged with vigor in the traditional male realm of Western academic Buddhology. An acknowledged pioneer of postmodern Buddhist feminist scholarship is Rita Gross, whose *Buddhism After Patriarchy* (1993) is a provocative inquiry into Buddhist misogyny. Gross began by detailing the failure of the Buddha to show adequate compassion to his own family:

> Siddartha Gautama, the Buddha, abandoned his wife and new-born infant because he was convinced that they were an obstacle to his own spiritual development. Nevertheless, he resisted women's attempts to abandon their domestic responsibilities and to seek their own spiritual development and liberation. Can a religion founded by such a man possibly serve women's interests and needs?

Gross concluded that it could, but only if women accepted the challenge to rid Buddhism of its lingering elements of patriarchy.

During this same period, the Theravada school of Buddhist meditation found two key American exponents, Joseph Goldstein and Jack Kornfeld, who melded Vipassana mindfulness teachings with the wisdom teachings of all the Buddhist schools, as well as with Western psychotherapy. Goldstein and Kornfeld were not alone in their Buddhist ecumenism, but they were among its most effective proponents, as their seminars and writings encouraged the fertile intersection of the Dharma and the human-care professions. Both men continue their teaching and writing.

❖

The awarding of the 1989 Nobel Peace Prize to the Dalai Lama brought the "Free Tibet" movement to great public prominence. Both as a prolific author and a compelling speaker, the Dalai Lama has since become the leading Buddhist teacher in the West, even as he seeks to ensure that the exiled Tibetan Buddhist teachings can themselves survive, in their essence, the onslaught of Western culture. Indeed, he draws a sharp distinction between cultural trappings and essential teachings, as evidenced in an overview he once offered on Buddhist history and transformation:

> Now you know Buddhism originally comes from India and then spread into different countries. Eventually it took on local conditions and the local cultural heritage. Buddhism eventually developed certain outwardly new forms, because it combined with local conditions. Therefore, in any religion I think there are two aspects, the cultural and the religious. Therefore, as Buddhism has begun to flourish in new places and areas such as the European continent or America or South America, I think if people from these areas try to adopt the same way or manner which is practiced by the Tibetan or Thai or Sri Lankan or any other Asian Buddhist individual, it is not so good. So taking the essence, such as the Four Noble Truths or the Eightfold Path, and at the same time taking into consideration the local conditions, then there will be some kind of synthesis.

Nonviolence has remained at the heart of his outlook, not only with respect to obtaining Tibetan freedom but also in regard to the broader issue of human survival. In his view, violence caused by anger or adopted to force social change inevitably spurs further killing, further suffering. In a 1993 interview conducted on Thai television, the Dalai Lama reflected on the military heritage of Tibet:

> As a Buddhist naturally you have to oppose any kind of warfare or any form of military establishment. Tibet is a Buddhist country, yet at the same time in the past we have also had some limited military forces because of necessity. The border problems, particularly with China, compelled the Tibetan government to keep some Tibetan forces; however, as a Buddhist nation we have very much neglected that field. I think now we have to try to completely eliminate all these things and to create a genuine zone of peace. This is I feel very important.

Within the small sphere of temporal operations, primarily in Dharamsala, that is the Tibetan government-in-exile, the Dalai Lama functions as a temporal as well as a spiritual leader of Tibetan Buddhism. In 1986, he banned the worship of Dorje Shugden in state-owned monasteries and workplaces. This was not the first time that a Dalai Lama had so decreed. The Fifth Dalai Lama forbade such worship just after it first arose in 1655, when Shugden, a Tibetan Buddhist abbot, died in his own palace under circumstances that aroused suspicion. The Fifth Dalai Lama declared that the spirit of Shugden was evil, but Shugden's followers in Tibet and the West — the latter known as the New Kadampa Tradition (NKT) — still worship him in the form of Dorje Shugden, a wrathful deity of great efficacy. The current NKT leader is the Tibetan-born Geshe Kelsang Gyatso, a Tibetan Buddhist author and teacher and an opponent of the policies of the Fourteenth Dalai Lama. The Geshe established a center for Tibetan Buddhist studies, called the Manjushri Centre, in Cumbria, England.

In accordance with the view that one's enemy's enemy is one's friend, the Chinese government has exploited the Shugden dispute by making a priority of rebuilding Shugden monasteries within Tibet and granting more ready approval of exit visas for Shugden sect members. When asked in a 1998 interview what had led him to forbid public Shugden worship, the Dalai Lama explained: "I took this decision as a matter of principle in the larger interest. There is a danger that the great Tibetan tradition will degenerate into spirit worship. It is my responsibility to make people aware of the consequences of worshipping Dorje Shugden. But whether they listen or not is up to the individual. Right from the beginning that's my position."

The Dalai Lama has observed on many occasions that his own office of Dalai Lama is not necessarily one that should be preserved into the distant future. In a 1995 interview, he expressed approval of the American principle of separation of church and state and indicated that it might be of future use for the Tibetan people: "The title itself, the institution of the Dalai Lama, could disappear overnight. It wasn't established forever by some force outside human beings and the earth. There's no contradiction between Buddhism and democracy."

But there are contradictions, the Dalai Lama has allowed, between Buddhist teachings and the doctrines of Western theistic religions. In this, the Dalai Lama has not followed the lead of Thich Nhat Hanh, who has stressed the essential likeness of the Christian and Buddhist religious outlooks. In his *Ethics for the New Millennium* (1999), the Dalai Lama insisted on the genuine differences, so as to form a basis for knowing and respectful tolerance:

> There are compelling similarities between the Mahayana Buddhist concept of *Dharmakaya, Sambogakaya,* and *Nirmanakaya* and the Christian trinity of God as Father, Son, and Holy Spirit. But to say, on the basis of this, that Buddhism and Christianity are ultimately the same is to go a bit far, I think! As an old Tibetan saying goes, we must beware of trying to put a yak's head on a sheep's body — or vice versa. What is required instead is that we develop a genuine sense of religious pluralism in spite of the different claims of different faith traditions.

But for all his insistence on difference, the Dalai Lama did affirm the existence of underlying core values common to all religions, which, paradoxically, are independent of religion: "I have come to the conclusion that whether or not a person is a religious believer does not matter much. Far more important is that they be a good human being." As for the nature of human goodness, the Dalai Lama has often stated that compassion for one's fellow living beings is a matter not of religious doctrine but of common sense, given that such compassion is the surest road to happiness.

If there is a faint latent tension here between right Buddhist outlook and free Buddhist outlook, there is a similar flutter when it comes to the global economic vision of the Dalai Lama, which is rooted in compassion and detachment, but which can challenge Western readers accustomed to dichotomizing the outlooks of Ronald Reagan and Karl Marx. The Dalai Lama can at times sound like the former, as in a 1997 interview in which he observed that "not so long ago people believed in ideologies, systems, and institutions to save all societies. Today, they have given up such hopes and have returned to relying on the individual, on individual freedom, individual initiative, individual creativity." But he has also expressed his support for the ethical aims — though not the political methods — of Marxism. In a 1999 interview, he offered an overview on socialism and freedom and their need to merge: "Personally, I still believe that the idea of socialism is valid. Even Marxism wasn't completely wrong. The recent collapse of the former Soviet Union was not the collapse of Marxism but of a totalitarian Marxist system. The main defect of the totalitarian system is that it instigates anger and hatred as forces of change." It is worth recalling that this defense of the Marxist outlook came from one who had witnessed personally the Communist abuses in Tibet.

The ability of the Dalai Lama to communicate with Western audiences did not come easily. It took years for him to be able to express himself effectively in spoken and spontaneous English and other Western languages. Over time, he transformed what had been, at the outset, a highly analytical style of public speaking, reflecting his monastic training, into a voice capable of simplicity, nuance, and heart. The Dalai Lama came also to write directly about Buddhist teachings and their ability to enhance life and to sustain hope. Like Thich Nhat Hanh, he is a forceful advocate of the alliance between Buddhist teachings and the Western study of mental health. In his foreword to *Thoughts Without a Thinker: Psychotherapy from a Buddhist Perspective* (1995) by Mark Epstein, a Harvard Medical School graduate, the Dalai Lama offered a Buddhist outlook that would have shocked the old-time Orientalists:

The purpose of life is to be happy. As a Buddhist I have found that one's mental attitude is the most influential factor in working toward that goal. [. . .] Recently, psychotherapists, with their background in science and medicine, have begun to explore the possibilities of employing Buddhist techniques in a therapeutic context. I feel this is entirely consistent with the aim of overcoming suffering and improving the welfare of all sentient beings.

The Dalai Lama has also committed himself — quite apart from his dialogue with Western psychotherapy — to preserving Tibetan Buddhist practice in the West in its traditional forms. In 1981, in Madison, Wisconsin, he conducted the first Kalachakra initiation on Western soil. A detailed text of the ritual and the Dalai Lama's commentaries was later published. There he stressed the preeminent value of Tantric practice — for example, visualization of oneself as a buddha — for the dedicated practitioner:

> To become fully enlightened as a Buddha, it is necessary to practice Mantra and, within Mantra, Highest Yoga Mantra; otherwise, it is not possible to attain Buddhahood. The reason for this is that to actualize the effect state of the two bodies of a Buddha — Form Body and Truth Body — it is necessary meditatively to cultivate a path that accords in aspect with those two bodies.

The Dalai Lama collected his teachings on this ultimate vehicle of Tibetan Buddhism, as offered to European and American audiences in the 1980s, in *Dzogchen: The Heart Essence of the Great Perfection* (2000). For all his ecumenism, he has taken care to honor and extend the Vajrayana lineage.

❖

It is inevitable, even given the guidance of teachers such as the Dalai Lama, that the traditions of Buddhism will bend to the needs and obsessions of Western students. And surely one of the most significant differences between Eastern and Western Buddhism is the attention paid to sexual desire.

Consider this dialogue with a Chinese Buddhist teacher recorded by John Blofeld — a British-born expatriate who studied for years in China and Tibet — in his memoir *The Wheel of Life* (1959). Blofeld, a young man at the time, had blushingly revealed to his teacher that he had from time to time visited the "flower-houses" of Peking to relieve certain persistent urges. His teacher, an ordained Buddhist abbot, replied, "What of it? Young men usually do. I did." Blofeld persisted, explaining that he knew Buddhism did not regard sexual relations as a sin, but surely it was a "powerful barrier" to spiritual achievement?

Here the abbot intervened to instruct Blofeld as to the nature of all so-called barriers:

> "You see," the Abbot began, "so long as you live on the level of the senses, however scholarly or aesthetic your approach, you will make no progress in the Buddhist path. You are very fond of people, books, travel, experiences and observation. All of these are sensual in nature. But now, perhaps because of your Christian upbringing, you single out one of these activities — sex — for special blame. Yet to fight against what appeals to you so strongly would be to tie your bowels into knots, from which no good at all could come. As you are so young and life-hungry, take life with both hands. Take all it has to offer, from the scent of flowers in a garden to the ecstasy bestowed by that secret flower. Keep always in your mind the Buddha-truth that life and suffering are indivisible. Flee life only when you see it for something no longer to be borne."
>
> "And if I never do come to see it that way?"
>
> "You will, you will," the Abbot laughed.

❖

Sexuality does not constitute an exceptional breach of morality under Buddhist training precepts (vinaya), which address all forms of undue attachment — all, at root, one's egoistic self — with equal concern. Buddhist doctrine does not follow Saint Paul in espousing marriage as the sole lawful means to channel the sinful heat of human passion. In principle, a Buddhist monk is to overcome lust; in practice, assuagements have been allowed so that lust might not become a lingering barrier to attainment. We do not know much about the real-life sexual practices of Buddhist teachers and monks of the past 2,500 years. We may safely assume, however, human nature being what it is (and with the history of Christian holy orders offering a rough analogue) that there would be ample examples of forbidden affairs — some consensual and passionate, others rank and abusive. Few Buddhist chroniclers thought fit to record such behavior, as it was deemed neither important nor conducive to the transmission of the Dharma.

The heated vigilance and obsession with which the modern West approaches all sexual matters has had an impact on Western Buddhism. Hence the sexual activities of Buddhist teachers in the West over the past four decades have been relatively well documented. A good many of them have had affairs with their students. Unsurprisingly, Western Buddhists have brought their own sexual desires and struggles into their newborn *sanghas.*

❖

The story of the rise and fall of Zentatsu Richard Baker, onetime chief abbot of the San Francisco Zen Center, could readily fit the format of a rock documentary.

During his time as chief abbot, Baker created — by way of fundraising and astute real estate purchases — $25 million in assets for the Zen Center. These assets produced an annual $4 million in gross income and provided for the employment of dozens of its students. (The annual budget for the entire center had been $6,000 when Baker first took office.) Two of the center's San Francisco–based businesses, the Tassajara Bread Bakery and Greens restaurant, were so prosperous that they seemed to many observers to confirm an unanticipated sympathy between Zen awareness and the Protestant work ethic.

At a time when Zen Buddhism still had a "flaky" image in the minds of most mainstream Americans, Baker — a Harvard dropout who was chosen Dharma successor to the late Shunryu Suzuki — provided reassurance. Under his leadership, the San Francisco Zen Center hosted speeches by esteemed intellectuals and multifaith religious dialogues. The center also addressed the concerns of the everyday world. Baker became part of the inner advisory circle of California governor Jerry Brown and hobnobbed with members of the New Age spiritual elite, such as Esalen Institute founder Michael Murphy and *Whole Earth Catalog* creator Stewart Brand. He maintained homes at each of the three locations of the Zen Center — Page Street in San Francisco, the Tassajara Zen Mountain Center in the Carmel Valley, and the Green Gulch Farm in Marin County. His extensive personal library was triplicated to afford him ready access at whichever home he chose to stay. The Zen Center further provided him with a BMW and a generous expense account. Of the 250-some resident students at the Zen Center, nine were employed as his personal aides and attendants.

In April 1983, all of that came to an end. Paul Hawken, cofounder of the highly successful Smith & Hawken catalog retail company and a member of the San Francisco Zen Center, had formed a close relationship with Baker, who in turn had often publicly referred to Hawken as his best friend. Now Hawken announced to the press that Baker, who was married, had been having a secret affair with Hawken's wife, Anna. It was also reported that Hawken had privately confided to friends that he was considering suicide.

Hawken's announcement received major media coverage across the United States. In its aftermath, the San Francisco Zen Center *sangha* went through bouts of rage and grief. Like a kind of karmic contagion, word leaked out about other secret affairs between Baker and his students. Anger that many *sangha* members had long harbored about Baker's aloofness, his lavishly maintained lifestyle (as compared to the barebones lifestyles of Zen Center workers), and his seeming preference for celebrities over mere students now peaked in public confrontations between Baker and the members. One American Zen priest who had been ordained by Baker told his former master that he was a "pile of shit."

Baker had a good number of supporters, however, and he defended himself adamantly on the grounds that Japanese Zen practice contained no sexual ethic that he, as chief abbot, was bound to maintain. But some seven years earlier, while attending a conference on world religions in Colorado, Baker had in fact addressed the issue — in words that many of his former students now flung back at him:

> The two most important rules of the Sangha community are "do not hurt others" and "do not deceive others." These are especially important in guiding members of the community in love and sexual relationships. You must be able to place the general community's good above your own personal satisfactions. In a community it usually becomes very clear that when the price of personal satisfaction is deception and pain, it is not worth it.

Baker ultimately lost the support of the Zen Center's board of directors and submitted his resignation in December 1983. In the intervening months, he ended the affair with Anna Hawken but continued to insist that she was the love of his life. After his departure, Baker gave numerous interviews in which he insisted that there had been no impropriety: "The accusation of a teacher sleeping with students is generally meant to imply someone who is using his power with women who are very young or where there is a misuse of his authority. I have not done that." As for his expenditures, Baker declared:

> If I spent $6,000 a year taking people out to dinner, I could get that with a phone call. But the students don't think of it that way. [. . .] I saw the abbot-platform as a way of presenting Buddhism, not myself. And it is true that I used the students as part of that platform. But I did not think I was using them for personal gain, and I thought they shared my goal.

In 1984, with six followers from the San Francisco Zen Center and ample funding from wealthy supporters, Baker established a new Dharma *sangha* on an expansive ranch site in Santa Fe, New Mexico. Since then, he has founded the Crestone Mountain Zen Center in California and the Buddhistisches Studienzentrum in the Black Forest region of Germany. Throughout Europe, he is a popular speaker at spirituality seminars, but his standing within the American Buddhist community has never been restored. A recent work by the American writer Michael Downing, *Shoes Outside the Door* (2001), chronicled the efforts at healing that continue, some two decades later, within the San Francisco Zen Center.

❖

Buddhist *sanghas* and meditation centers throughout the West have paid great heed to the fate of Baker and have attempted, with varying success, to apply the seeming lessons offered. But the first fact they had to confront was that the Baker case was anything but unique.

In 1985, Jack Kornfeld, a well-known Western Buddhist teacher, conducted and published an informal survey he wryly titled "Sex Life of the Gurus." Kornfeld interviewed Buddhist, Hindu, and Jain teachers working in the United States, some of Asian descent, some American-born. Only fifteen of the teachers declared themselves celibate. Thirty-four out of fifty-four — 63 percent — said that they had engaged in sex with one or more students.

As Kornfeld's research indicated, the sexual pursuits of many Asian-born Buddhist teachers are every bit as wide-ranging as those of their Western-born peers. Consider the information that emerged in the years following Kornfeld's survey. The Korean-born Zen master Seung Sahn, who had for decades portrayed himself as a celibate to his American students, at last disclosed, in the late 1980s, long-term affairs with two of his female students. As discussed in chapter 11, Taizan Maezumi Roshi, founder of the Los Angeles Zen Center, was alleged to have had affairs with several of his students; he also entered an alcohol treatment program. Nonetheless, he continued on as roshi until his passing in 1995, as his virtues as a teacher were deemed greater than his failings as a human being.

❖

Over the millennia, Buddhist teaching on homosexuality largely conformed to prevailing custom in Asia: the matter was little discussed, broadly disapproved, and publicly forbidden. The first-century Indian Buddhist scholar Ashvaghosha defined sexual misconduct for monks as arising from "inappropriate partner, organ, time and place." Among the "inappropriate" partners were those of the same sex, while the "inappropriate" organs included the anus and the mouth. The current Dalai Lama has raised hackles within Western gay communities by adhering to the traditional teachings of Ashvaghosha, while at the same time publicly denouncing all forms of discrimination against gays. In this, as in many other matters, the Dalai Lama has attempted both to uphold the values of the Tibetan monastic tradition and to adapt Buddhist teachings to Western needs.

Issan Dorsey, the first openly gay Zen master in the West, emerged as a teacher and leader in the 1980s — the precise time when AIDS transformed the San Francisco gay community. Dorsey, a onetime star transvestite performer in underground gay clubs during the 1950s, exemplified just how unbounded were the possibilities for Buddhist compassion in the West. Gay teachers such as Dorsey have transformed the parameters of Buddhist practice.

Dorsey's life prior to his commitment to Zen in the 1970s is as remarkable as that of any Zen teacher known to us. Born Thomas Dorsey in 1933, the charismatic and handsome young man became a successful drag queen entertainer (under the name "Tommy Dee") in 1950s San Francisco, then fell victim to heroin addiction and supported his habit by becoming a male prostitute. Dorsey frequently mixed junk with LSD, so he took notice when the San Francisco Zen Center held a seminar on the potential relationship between the LSD experience and Zen enlightenment.

Dorsey always acknowledged the positive impact that LSD had on him — by opening, at a low point in his life, the possibility of genuine spiritual change. Dorsey was also frank about being gay, despite the fact that it unsettled some students at the San Francisco Zen Center, where Dorsey began to meditate daily. To foster mutual support, Dorsey created the Gay Buddhist Club, the first such group in history. As Dorsey later recalled, "At first we'd just sit around and smoke cigarettes and complain about how hard it was to practice and be gay. Gradually, we began to meditate for a while before our discussions, and pretty soon there was a Buddha and incense and flowers."

Through all the public turmoil over Richard Baker's sexual affairs, Dorsey remained an unfazed supporter, perhaps in part due to sympathy for anyone whose sexual particulars led to public scrutiny and scandal. But Dorsey's primary concern was the creation of a Zen-inspired AIDS hospice in San Francisco's Castro district. Called Maitri (Sanskrit for compassionate friendship), it accepted patients regardless of religious affiliation and earned national attention. Dorsey died from AIDS in 1990, but his Dharma students continue the hospice movement he inspired.

❖

The Buddhist social engagement exemplified by Dorsey has found its modern-day American spokesperson in Bernard Glassman (b. 1939), the son of eastern European Jewish immigrants with socialist sympathies. He grew up in Brighton Beach, New York; earned a Ph.D. in applied mathematics at UCLA; and became a high-ranking executive at Mc-Donnell Douglas, where, in the late 1960s, he headed its Earth-Mars shuttle design team. All the while, Glassman was also studying Zen in both the United States and Japan. He ultimately became — after years of discipleship under Taizan Maezumi Roshi, Yasutani Haku'un Roshi, and Osaka Koryu Roshi — the first American to receive Dharma transmission in the Japanese Soto Zen lineage.

Glassman's first *kensho* (great spiritual opening) took place in Japan while he was studying under Koryu Roshi. The experience revealed to him the absence of any true distinction between self and world: "Tears were pouring down my face as I served Koryu Roshi, and afterwards, when I went out of the zendo, there was a tree there, and looking at the tree . . . I felt the wind on me, I felt the birds on me, all separation was completely gone."

While carpooling with fellow McDonnell Douglas executives, Glassman experienced a second and still more powerful *kensho,* this one spurred by meditation on the koan *Mu:* "I couldn't stop laughing or crying, both at once, and the people in the car were very upset and concerned, they didn't have any idea what was happening, and I kept telling them that there was nothing to worry about! Luckily I was an executive and had my own office, but I just couldn't stop laughing and crying, and finally I had to go home." Shortly thereafter, Glassman left McDonnell Douglas to pursue the path revealed by his *kensho:* "That opening brought with it a tremendous feeling about the suffering in the world. I saw the importance of spreading the Dharma, developing a Dharma training in America that would help many people. I wanted to work with greater numbers because I saw the 'crying out' of all of us, even those who do not feel they are crying out."

In 1976, Glassman was the first of Maezumi's American students to receive Dharma transmission. Maezumi, Glassman later wrote, understood the need to transform traditional Japanese Zen training methods into living American forms:

"Taste as much of this as you can," he told us. "Swallow what you need and spit out the rest." He was better aware than anyone of the difference in cultural contexts and that certain mores which made sense in Japan could not pass muster in the West. Already during his lifetime he witnessed his successors experiment with new forms and practices that he probably never dreamed of seeing in a Zen center.

In the early 1980s, Glassman, as abbot of the Zen Community of New York, created the Greyston Mandala (the name came from a donated mansion that housed operations) — a network of Buddhist social services in Yonkers, where unemployment and ethnic conflict were particularly severe. Glassman's approach was to use for-profit enterprises, including a bakery, to fund nonprofit organizations that provided affordable housing, child care, and job opportunities. His Zen students were expected both to practice *zazen* and to devote considerable time to service projects. But some critics, including former students, complained that however compassionate such projects were, they did not comprise a true training in Zen such as Glassman himself had received. Glassman's response was that working in a bakery could be analogous to solving a koan:

> On the outside the bakery may not look different from other bakeries, but actually I think that even on the outside it would look different, feel different. Because at the same time that all this work is going on there is also a release of the ego-structure, a letting go of the self. [. . .] We have to get it all together, but getting it all together is the teaching. That's a hard one for people to grasp.

But Glassman acknowledged the centrality of *zazen:* "If we didn't have work practice, we could still be a Zen community. If we didn't have *zazen,* we could not."

In 1996, with his wife Jishu Holmes, Glassman founded the Zen Peacemaker Order, which has drawn an international membership committed to peacekeeping activity on the basis of the Three Tenets drawn by Glassman from Buddhist teachings: to penetrate the unknown, to bear witness both to suffering and joy, and to heal oneself and others. The fundamental process of healing is the recognition of a oneness unifying all beings. But the methods of peacemaking are always influenced by the first of the tenets — the lack of any illusions that there are easy answers, or answers at all. Glassman wrote: "As peacemakers, the action we take in any situation will reflect our understanding of the different aspects of that situation, the extent to which we're able to bear witness to them, and consequently, who we are. If we truly believe that we are all one body, if we truly bear witness to that one body, then we won't neglect anyone."

The efforts of Glassman and the Zen Peacemaker Order have included bearing witness at Auschwitz-Birkenau and working with the inner-city poor of Yonkers and with drug addicts in the needle parks of Zurich. When asked why he was drawn to places of great suffering, Glassman replied, "I don't know. The words that come to me are *the desire to learn.* It generally involves suffering. When I enter a situation that is too much for me and that I don't understand — I have a desire to sit there, to stay a while."

❖

The societal engagement stressed by Glassman is, of course, not unique to him. The term "Engaged Buddhism" has become ubiquitous in discussions of Western Buddhism, and it has been argued that Engaged Buddhism — with its roots in the East and its present efflorescence in the West — represents a fourth great *yana,* or vehicle, in the history of Buddhist thought and practice. The issues that require engagement exist not only in the geopolitical realm but also in the practicalities of daily life. Right Livelihood is, after all, a component of the Eightfold Noble Path common to all Buddhist schools, and Right Mindfulness, another component, certainly pertains to the seductions of consumerism.

It was the British economist E. F. Schumacher, in his widely read work *Small Is Beautiful* (1973), who was instrumental in focusing the attention of Western Buddhists on the vital interrelationship of mindfulness and livelihood by devoting a chapter in that book to "Buddhist economics." Schumacher was not a Buddhist, but rather a thinker sympathetic to certain spiritual insights that he found confirmed in a broad range of world religions. Schumacher made the subtly startling point, in response to the avidity of Westerners for Buddhist teachings, that "no one seems to think that a Buddhist way of life would call for a Buddhist economics." Schumacher called for an economic approach that placed human spiritual needs above productivity needs. In his view, rampant greed led to environmental havoc and the breakdown of human communities, while a heightened spiritual awareness could lead to harmonious societal balance without sacrifice of the essentials of survival.

One of the prominent modern teachers of Western Buddhism, Urgyen Sangharakshita, has placed Right Livelihood at the center of the training provided by the Friends of the Western Buddhist Order (FWBO), an organization he founded in 1967. Born in 1925 and raised in a working-class London family, Dennis Lingwood realized at the age of sixteen, upon studying the teachings of Madame Blavatsky, that he was a Buddhist. Drafted by the British army for service in World War II, he was stationed in India and remained there after the war for some two decades, during which he pursued Buddhist study and practice under both Theravada and Tibetan teachers. He was ultimately ordained a monk in Burma.

The diverse range of his Buddhist studies fostered an independent out-

look, which showed itself in the FWBO, established subsequent to his return to England in 1964, which included teachings from a variety of Buddhist perspectives, as well as ideas drawn from Western spiritual thinkers
such as Goethe and William Blake. The original, and ongoing, goal of the
FWBO was a fundamental transformation of the economic parameters of
Western society. The order created an intensive community by means of
its tripartite structure — friends (supporters of the FWBO), *mitras* (committed Buddhist practitioners), and members (those who met the criteria
of long-term practice, approval by FWBO leaders, and ordination). Centers were established for worship and meditation practice, as were com-
munal single-sex male and female residences. FWBO businesses were
launched and managed according to Right Livelihood principles.

Estimates are that the FWBO currently numbers some 100,000 friends
worldwide, the bulk of them residing in India as a result of intensive
work, since 1978, with the Buddhist conversion movement established
by Dr. Bhimrao Ranji Ambedkar in 1956 as a means of alleviating the
social and economic injustices of the Hindu caste system. The inner-
core number of members is roughly eight hundred. The largest number
of FWBO centers and businesses are located in Great Britain.

There have been two principal critiques of the FWBO by other Western Buddhists. The first is that the order is separatist — a charge answered
by Subhuti, a senior FWBO member, who has noted that Sangharakshita's
early attempts at cooperation with other Western Buddhist teachers led to
their attempting to steal his students. The second critique is that the
FWBO puts forth a misogynist version of Buddhist teachings. This is
patently true, as evidenced by the texts produced by FWBO leaders. As
James William Coleman, an American sociologist, noted, Sangharakshita
"has expressed the view in many of his writings that women are less spiritually capable than men. His head disciple, Subhuti, made this view quite
explicit in his 1995 book, *Women, Men, and Angels,* in which he posits that
there are five stages of evolution from Animal, which is the lowest, to
Woman, Man, Artist, and finally to Angel, which is the highest."

The history of Buddhism is replete with patriarchal assumptions and
fears. But as the Buddha, by authorizing an order of nuns during his lifetime, clearly acknowledged the capacity of women to achieve enlightenment, the credit for this particular misogynist hierarchy must go to the
FWBO.

❖

Buddhism Without Beliefs (1997) is one of the most challenging texts produced by a Western Buddhist to date. Its author, the British Buddhist Stephen Batchelor, was born in Scotland and never attended a university, but rather journeyed to India in the early 1970s to study Tibetan Buddhism in Dharamsala. At age nineteen, he became a monk in the Gelukpa tradition. He continued his Buddhist studies under Geshe Rabten, who established a Tibetan Buddhist monastery in Switzerland. Batchelor thereafter spent four years in training at a Korean Zen monastery, then resumed a secular life and married. In 1985, he returned to England, where he founded Sharpham College for Buddhist Studies and Contemporary Inquiry.

In *Buddhism Without Beliefs,* Batchelor interpreted the teachings of the Buddha as an impassioned agnosticism, which sought to alleviate suffering rather than to found a religion. The Dharma of the Buddha, Batchelor argued, focused on daily behavior: "First and foremost the Buddha taught a method ('dharma *practice*') rather than another '-ism.' The dharma is not something to believe in but something to do. [. . .] Dharma practice has become a creed ('Buddhism') much in the same way scientific method has degraded into the creed of 'Scientism.'" As this quotation shows, Batchelor's view of organized religion is a dim one. Despite the title of his book, certain beliefs do permeate his outlook. For example, he believes that when Buddhism became a doctrinal creed, the purity of the original teachings was degraded. He also believes that only experiences of a transcendental divinity, or an ultimate cosmological realization, may properly be termed mystical, thus negating the validity of the Buddhist mystical tradition: "The Buddha was not a mystic. His awakening was not a shattering insight into a transcendent Truth that revealed to him the mysteries of God. He did not claim to have had an experience that granted him privileged, esoteric knowledge of how the universe ticks. Only as Buddhism became more and more of a religion were such grandiose claims imputed to his awakening."

There is strong evidence that the Buddha himself believed that he was founding a religion, albeit of a nontheistic nature, as he authorized the establishment of monastic orders. But Batchelor insists that the Buddha's own emphasis on personal experience as the only true source of valida-

tion of his teachings has left subsequent Dharma practitioners free to decide for themselves on questions of practice — or even to acknowledge
that they simply do not know. This approach allows for the teachings of
the Dharma to be practiced as a secular path of compassion and commitment — an approach echoed by Chögyam Trungpa (in his creation
of the Shambhala teachings) and by the Dalai Lama (most notably in his
Ethics for the New Millennium [1999]).

The question remains whether Buddhism requires a religious form
for long-term survival. Consider, by way of comparison, the fate of two
nineteenth-century schools of Western thought that began as impassioned life philosophies and are now mere trickles of cultural influence:
transcendentalism and utilitarianism. The convictions of religion have
their place among the existential needs of large numbers of human beings. Buddhism, for example, has, for more than two millennia, drawn
upon the motivational power of belief in rebirth. But in his book,
Batchelor held to uncertainty on this score as well: "The Tibetan tradition claims to have proof and reasons why one has to believe this, but I
never found any of them convincing. The turning point came for me
one day when I woke up and realized that even if it turns out that after
death there is a big, blank void it wouldn't make the slightest bit of difference to my commitment to the practice now."

❖

In the West, there has long been a resistance — among academics and
Buddhist practitioners alike — to come to terms with Pure Land Buddhism in its multifold variations. The American scholar Galen Amstutz described this resistance in terms of a modern-day Orientalist
consumerism — in essence, what the West wanted from Buddhism was
not what Pure Land Buddhism had to offer, hence it was marginalized.
As Amstutz wrote of Japanese Shin Buddhism, which has its origins in
Chinese Pure Land teachings,

> Shin failed to capture the interests of Western existential seekers, reli-
> gious studies scholars, Buddhologists or social scientists. [. . .] Since the
> beginning of the Western encounter with Shin, its most sympathetic
> outside observers have been Western Christian missionaries, who recog-
> nized that although its philosophical and even institutional similarities

with Christianity were somewhat superficial, Shin was closer to Christianity (especially Protestantism) in its social and political performance than any other world religion. However, these similarities appear to have blocked rather than encouraged subsequent investigations by others, for European iconoclasts and post-orientalists are still enmeshed in rejection of Christianity, and [. . .] in locating "interesting" Buddhism as an overtly non-Christian phenomenon.

The founder of Shin Buddhism was Nichiren Daishonin (1222–1282), a Japanese monk who challenged the prevailing Pure Land doctrine that salvation depended on the mercy of Amitabha Buddha in admitting one, after one's death, into the Pure Land realm. By contrast, Nichiren taught that the Pure Land was no distant aspiration, but rather a transformed vision of oneself and one's society that could be attained — as could spiritual and material blessings of all sorts — through the chanting of *"Nam-myoho-renge-kyo,"* drawn from the Japanese title of the *Lotus Sutra*. As the American scholar Jane Hurst explained,

Nam represents dedication of one's whole life to the law of the universe, or *Myoho-renge-kyo. Myoho* is the mystic law of the universe, the underlying principle of duality which is the basis of human life. *Renge* is the lotus flower, which can be understood as a metaphor for the simultaneity of cause and effect (karma) and the pure flower which blooms in a swamp. *Kyo* is the sound or vibration one creates in chanting which attunes the individual to the law of the universe.

It was the Jodo Shinshu (True Pure Land) Buddhist missionaries of the Buddhist Churches of America (BCA) who were the first to bring the teachings of Nichiren to the West. (Their efforts were discussed in chapter 7.) By the late twentieth century, the scope of the BCA's efforts had dwindled, and its total American membership was estimated at about 20,000.

Soka Gakkai, the most powerful modern Shin Buddhist movement, was founded as a lay Buddhist educational sect in 1930 by Tsunesaburo Makiguchi, a Japanese school principal. Soka Gakkai soon affiliated with the Nichiren Shoshu sect and long operated under the name Nichiren Shoshu of America. But in 1991, Nichiren Shoshu, with six American temples, separated from Soka Gakkai, which took the new name Soka Gakkai International (SGI). Through the leadership of Daisaku Ikeda (b. 1928), SGI now has millions of members in Japan and hundreds of thousands of members throughout the rest of the world, including a strong presence in both the United States and Britain.

Ikeda first visited the United States in 1960, but the main organizational work in America was accomplished by a Korean-born Soka Gakkai leader named Masayasu Sadanaga, who changed his legal name to George M. Williams so as to underscore his commitment to full integration with American culture. SGI-USA membership is estimated at 50,000 to 150,000, which approaches 10 percent of the current estimate of all American Buddhists (about 2 million). Its success in drawing a diverse membership is, according to the American scholar David W. Chappell, a by-product of an outlook that stresses compassion:

> Racial diversity has never been a goal of Soka Gakkai, and Ikeda has attacked the very concept of race as a false social construct. [. . .] The political fight for equal rights and economic justice, or practical relief for the dying, homeless, imprisoned, or sick, is encouraged among its members but not institutionalized within SGI-USA. It is fair to say in 1998, however, that with its large diversity of local leaders, its emphasis on dialogue by its national director, Fred Zaitsu, and the socially engaged educational institutions established by its international leader, Daisaku Ikeda, Soka Gakkai in America has committed more resources, has impacted more lives, and has created more substantial institutions to implement programs in social and cultural improvement than any other American Buddhist organization.

Charles Johnson, who won the 1990 National Book Award for his novel *Middle Passage,* is a preeminent African American writer and a practicing Buddhist. Johnson is not a member of Soka Gakkai, but he recounted why friends and family were drawn to it:

> They discovered that through chanting they could transform their lives and, in fact, that they alone were the architects of their own suffering and happiness. For my sister-in-law, raised Baptist and impoverished in a housing project on Chicago's South Side, the black church with its white Jesus

had always been an unsatisfying experience. [. . .] For me, Soka Gakkai is but one branch on the Bodhi tree. Yet its success in recruiting black Americans indicates that people of color find in Buddhism the depths of their long-denied humanity; centuries-old methods of meditation — very empirical — for clearing the mind of socially manufactured illusions (as well as personally created ones); an ancient phenomenology of suffering, desire, and the self; and a path (the Eightfold Path) for a moral and civilized way of life.

There were, of course, Buddhist teachers in traditions other than Soka Gakkai who proffered this support effectively. Jan Willis, an African American scholar and practitioner of Tibetan Buddhism, recalled in her memoir, *Dreaming Me* (2001), the kindness shown by her Tibetan teacher Lama Yeshe (1935–1984):

> As a child, I had been shown off because I was smart; but when Lama Yeshe showed me off it was a loving way of helping me to heal a long list of old wounds: my mother calling me evil, the white superintendents' amazement at a black child's intelligence, [. . .] going to college amid Klan threats, and the bogus idea that universities were lowering their standards in order to let in black students. It was as if Lama Yeshe were saying, "Let the old wounds go, daughter. Let them all go."

❖

In 2001, BMW produced an arty commercial titled *Chosen* and directed by the world-renowned Ang Lee. It depicted the rescue of a young Tibetan tulku — the reincarnation of a recently deceased Buddhist master — by a chiseled and masterful white male driver of a BMW sedan that outperformed, in a beautifully choreographed car chase, the Jeep Cherokees driven by the "bad guys" seeking to abduct the boy. The story line was plainly inspired by the plight of the young Panchen Lama of Tibet, who, at age six, was abducted by the Chinese Communists in 1995 and has not been heard from since. In the commercial, however, so as not to offend potential customers, the pursuers were shown as Caucasian, not Chinese. But the key marketing point was clear: sometimes even an incarnate Buddhist master can use the ultimate in automotive speed and handling.

Fantasy upon fantasy. The West will have its Buddhism in the forms it can digest. But its freewheeling appropriations have not been limited to the realm of popular culture. Until very recently, it was taken for granted in academia that the study of Buddhism was the study of a religion rooted in Asian culture. Doctoral candidates were required to master one or more Asian languages and perhaps to translate a canonical Asian Buddhist text. Those expectations have now been questioned by younger scholars and upcoming students, who insist that the study of Western Buddhism be granted academic respect. Further, many current Western Buddhist scholars, deeply versed as they are in postmodern textual criticism, no longer find it useful to regard the Buddhist teaching tradition as sacred or stable.

❖

There has been a dramatic increase (from a former level, some fifty years ago, of zero) in the number of North American and European reincarnations of Tibetan Buddhist holy persons (tulkus). Estimates differ, as some claims are in dispute, but the total is perhaps five or six. One or two of these rebirths have taken place in female form — an exceedingly rare event in Buddhist history. When I have questioned Tibetans of my acquaintance about this, they have been calm and accepting of the situation. From their perspective, a great lama is able to use the postdeath *bardo* realm to choose the form of rebirth most beneficial to others. As there are Western men and women drawn to Tibetan Buddhism, enlightened incarnations in those forms are clearly needed.

The 1993 Bernardo Bertolucci film *Little Buddha* depicted the rebirth of a Tibetan lama in the form of an American boy in Seattle. Since then, reality has mirrored art. A recent case involved Jack Churchward, a Florida resident who was identified at age seven as the sixth incarnation of the Tibetan lama Tradak Tulku, formerly the chief abbot of a monastery near Lhasa. An examination conducted in the Churchward home by Chetsang Rinpoche, the leader of the Drikung Kagyu lineage, established the boy as a tulku. His mother, Cindy Churchward, who along with her husband is a Western student of Buddhism, insisted that she was not surprised, as she had long observed in her son a high level of compassion. She pointed, in particular, to an incident when Jack was four: "He was chucking his burnt french fries out the car window. I asked, 'Jack, why are you throwing them in the grass?' He answered, 'Because if I throw them on the street and the ants come out to eat them, they'll get run over.'"

But Jack did not go through his early teens as a perfect child. School was difficult for him, and he was diagnosed as having attention deficit disorder. During the ninth grade, he stopped attending classes altogether. At age fifteen, Jack was caught shoplifting; the community-service sentence required him to work on the construction of a Buddhist meditation center founded by his parents.

But at age seventeen, Jack abruptly reexamined his life. Repeatedly, over the ten years since Jack had first been declared a tulku, he had been invited by Chetsang Rinpoche to come to India for training and formal enthronement. Jack was at last ready to accept and spent two months in India with the Drikung order: "They told me I died seventy to ninety years ago, and they were searching for me all this time."

He thereafter returned to Florida, uncertain as to the precise nature of his future role. Unlike Tibetan tulkus of the past, Jack had spent his childhood not in monastic seclusion, but on the streets of the Miami urban sprawl. He now wished to retain both his American and his Tibetan heritages.

❖

History has no predictive capacity, as history itself demonstrates. The primary directions that Western Buddhism will take through the twenty-first century may depend quite as much on political developments as on gifted Dharma teachers. Certainly that much can be said of the twentieth century, which witnessed the exodus of teachers from Tibet to the West. The growth of Western Buddhism must stem to some extent — as it has in Asia for more than two millennia — from Western Buddhist families raising Western Buddhist children in Western Buddhist schools and communities, for it is unlikely that Buddhism in the West can re-create itself every generation strictly by drawing new believers from without. Such growth will require ongoing religious tolerance by the Western nations, which cannot be regarded as a certainty.

But the Dharma has survived all manner of regimes and climes. It may just survive the West as well.

ACKNOWLEDGMENTS

❖

Writing this book was both a challenge and a joy, and while I am grateful to the kindness of many people over the years for the assistance they gave me in approaching the history and teachings of Buddhism, the following deserve special thanks: Kate Borowske and the staff of the Bush Memorial Library at Hamline University; the staff of the Ames Library of the University of Minnesota, with its comprehensive southern Asia collection; the scholars Peter Harle and Jules Levinson, both of whom read an early version of the manuscript and made invaluable suggestions and criticisms; Mary Rockcastle, dean of the graduate liberal studies programs at Hamline University, who did much to facilitate the writing of this book; Avrom Schwartz, the library coordinator at the Arneson Methodist Library, who directed me to the recent medical literature on Buddhism; Nancy Barron and Rhesa Schwartz, booksellers extraordinaire, who assisted me in locating scarce reference works; Mary Caruso, who made available to me her extensive collection of modern-day American Buddhist periodicals; Jerry Cornelius, who provided materials relating to Ananda Metteyya; my editors at Little, Brown — Deborah Baker, Asya Muchnick, and Elizabeth Nagle; and my agent, Anna Ghosh, who most ably represented this book. My deepest thanks, of course, go to my family, and in particular to my wife and daughter, to whom this book is dedicated.

NOTES

<figure>❖</figure>

Book titles supplied for these notes are generally shortened versions. For fuller descriptions, see Sources Consulted.

Chapter One

1 "the recluse Gotama" *Assalayana Sutta,* in Ñanamoli and Bodhi, *The Middle Length Discourses of the Buddha,* p. 764.

1 "'What do you think'" Ibid., pp. 764–65.

2 "Except among the Greeks" Thapar, *Asoka and the Decline of the Mauryas,* p. 257.

4 "Now, if some men" Aristotle, *Politics* 7.13, in *The Basic Works of Aristotle,* ed. McKeon, p. 1296.

4 "We find in the fragments" Werner Jaeger, "Greeks and Jews," *Journal of Religion* (April 1938):128, quoted in Radhakrishnan, *Eastern Religions and Western Thought,* p. 151, n. 4.

4 "importance of Indian influence" Radhakrishnan, *Eastern Religions and Western Thought,* p. 151.

4 "tells the following story" Eusebius, *Praeparatio Evangelica,* 11.3, quoted ibid.

5 "Unfortunately, however" Kiriyama, *21st Century,* p. 110. While finding ample affinities between Greek and Buddhist thought, Kiriyama asserted no theory of actual contact between the two cultures. He did, however, note what he believed to be a lessening of such affinities in the subsequent Christian Scholasticism of the West: "I can't help thinking that such pure love of wisdom, this *philosophia,* may have in fact died with the ancient Greeks. For the medieval period is not an age of philosophy, but an age of theology" (p. 25). This is of interest as a muted dissent from the more prevalent modern view, expressed by Buddhist luminaries such as the Fourteenth Dalai Lama and Thich Nhat Hanh, that the essential similarities between Buddhism and Christianity are paramount. As Kiriyama founded the Agon sect of Buddhism in Japan in 1978 based on his belief in the primacy of early Theravada scriptures, his dissent may be based on differences in Theravada and Mahayana views of Christian doctrine.

5 "it will save us" Plato, *The Republic,* 10, in *Plato: The Collected Dialogues,* ed. Hamilton and Cairnes, p. 844.

5 "We shall hold ever" Ibid.

6 "It is true that no" Gomperz, *The Greek Thinkers,* vol. 1, p. 127.

6 "telepathic missionary" Mills, "The Buddhism in Heraclitus," p. 270.

6 "received the message" Ibid., p. 279.

7 "very arrogantly and roughly" Plutarch, "Alexander," in *Lives of the Noble Greeks*, p. 339.

8 "for otherwise they would not" Strabo, *Natural History* 15, quoted in McCrindle, *Ancient India as Described in Classical Literature*, p. 71.

8 "It is impossible" Strabo, *Natural History* 15.1.61, quoted in Vassiliades, *The Greeks in India*, p. 49.

9 "stirred not when" Plutarch, "Alexander," p. 342.

9 "The Seleucid empire was nothing" Tarn, *The Greeks in Bactria and India*, p. 4.

10 "were the *first* people" Abbay Kumar Singh, "The Indo-Greek Disposition," in *Graeco-Indica*, ed. Arora, p. 179.

10 "History testifies" Ibid., p. 181.

10 "un-Aryan" Ibid., pp. 179, 181.

11 "in many points their" Megasthenes, quoted in Radhakrishnan, *Eastern Religions and Western Thought*, p. 155.

12 "in Greece it is not done" Antiochus I, as quoted in Woodcock, *The Greeks in India*, p. 51.

13 "many times that number perished" Thapar, *Asoka and the Decline of the Mauryas*, p. 255.

13 "when an independent country" Ibid.

13 "The Beloved of the Gods believes" Dharmapal, *Asoka 2300*, p. 256.

13 "not because he completely" Thapar, *Asoka and the Decline of the Mauryas*, p. 168.

14 "He gave up a life" Rabindranath Tagore, "Asoka: The Great Emperor," in *Asoka 2300*, p. 9.

14 "amidst the tens of thousands" H. G. Wells, quoted in Gokhale, *Buddhism and Asoka*, p. 132.

14 "Ashoka's policy of tolerance" Hajime Nakamura, "The Mauryan Dynasty," in *Asoka 2300*, p. 28.

15 "to narrow the meaning" Romila Thapar, "Asoka and Buddhism as Reflected in the Asokan Edicts," in *Asoka 2300*, p. 78.

15 "It is difficult to say" T. W. Rhys Davids, quoted in Bhandarkar, *Asoka*, pp. 140–141.

16 "This would be charging" Bhandarkar, *Asoka*, p. 141.

16 "confessions, fasting" Ibid., p. 147.

16 "of its claim" Ibid., p. 148.

16 "includes the Greek kingdoms" Thapar, *Asoka and the Decline of the Mauryas*, pp. 167–168.

17 "the people in my part" Murray-Aynsley, *Symbolism of the East and West*, p. 177. Murray-Aynsley noted, in a different context, that in her view the architectural style of certain older Norwegian storehouses "might stand for an almost exact reproduction of certain superior native houses" in the Himalayan regions (p. 179).

18 "If the Greek king" Zimmer, *Philosophies of India*, p. 505.

20 "everything exists everywhere" A. C. Banerjee, "The Sarvastivada School of Buddhist Thought," in *Sarvastivada and Its Traditions*, ed. Sanghasen Singh, p. 10.

21 "remains a speculative" Pande, *Studies in Mahayana*, p. 13.

21 "The venerable symbols" Tadgell, *The History of Architecture in India*, p. 13.

22 "it seems probable" Coomaraswamy, *The Dance of Shiva*, p. 62.

22 "how great an exaggeration" Ibid., p. 63.

22 "It was not until 1852" Stanley K. Abe, "Inside the Wonder House," in *Curators of the Buddha*, ed. Lopez, p. 70.

22 "In Gandhara the translation" Rowland, *Art in Afghanistan*, p. 24.

23 "It has been suggested that Plotinus'" Halbfass, *India and Europe,* p. 17. One of the more interesting responses to the debate over Eastern influence on Plotinus was rendered by W. R. Inge, dean of St. Paul's, in his 1917–1918 Gifford Lectures on Plotinus at St. Andrews. Inge held it unlikely that such influence had occurred but added, "I do not wish to be too dogmatic about this. The contrast between Form and Matter is Greek, that between Light and Darkness is Oriental. Both are prominent in Plotinus" (*The Philosophy of Plotinus,* vol. 1, p. 82, n. 1). Inge further criticized the Neoplatonic outlook of Plotinus — presumably imbibed from his teacher Ammonius, under whom Plotinus studied for some twenty years — as lacking the element of compassion stressed in Buddhist teachings: "Even Buddhism learned this truth better than Neoplatonism. Buddha himself said that he would not enter Nirvana till he could bring all others with him. The sense of organic unity with our fellows ought to make it intolerable for us to reach the One alone. Perhaps it is even impossible to do so" (p. 192). Given the Christian critique — so dominant in the nineteenth and early twentieth centuries — of Buddhism as lacking in compassion, this "turnabout" by Inge is particularly remarkable. Decades later, the Italian historian Giovanni Filoramo, in *A History of Gnosticism,* drew parallels between the direct knowledge of Buddhist teachings and the doctrines of the second-century Middle Platonist philosopher Numenius, who held that the path to gnosis lay in emptying one's mind of all concepts and contents so as to allow for a merging with the unknown and unknowable God.

24 "knowledge of the divine" Merkur, *Gnosis,* p. 111.

24 "They say that God" Hippolytus, quoted in Pagels, *The Gnostic Gospels,* p. xxi.

24 "some, too, of the Indians" Clement of Alexandria, *Writings,* vol. 1, p. 399.

25 "neither inhabit cities" Ibid.

25 "the Indians who are called" Clement of Alexandria, quoted in Oulton and Chadwick, *Alexandrian Christianity,* p. 68.

25 "divine honours" Ibid.

25 "without women, sex" Pliny, *Natural History,* quoted in Wise, Abegg, and Cook, *The Dead Sea Scrolls,* p. 16.

25 "it was through the Jewish" Lillie, *India in Primitive Christianity,* p. 161.

25 "Buddhist Jews" Berry, *Christianity and Buddhism,* p. 120.

26 "The theologians and the historians" Jung, *Nietzsche's Zarathustra,* vol. 1, p. 41.

26 "The similarities are not" Borg, *Jesus and Buddha,* pp. xiii–xv.

26 "The office of Jesus" J. Kennedy, "Buddhist Gnosticism, the System of Basilides," p. 412.

27 "He adopts the Buddhist" Ibid., p. 388.

27 "to love everything" Basilides, quoted in Filoramo, *A History of Gnosticism,* p. 160.

27 "before I came into" Ibid., p. 129.

27 "deprived men of a salutary" Origen, *Commentary on St. Matthew* iii, quoted in J. Kennedy, "Buddhist Gnosticism, the System of Basilides," p. 390.

28 "the doctrines of the Druids" Origen, quoted in Batchelor, *The Awakening of the West,* p. 28.

29 "extra-conciliary" Prat, "Origen and Origenism," in *The Catholic Encyclopedia,* vol. 11, pp. 311–12. Prat's argument is further explored in Head and Cranston, *Reincarnation: The Phoenix Fire Mystery,* an anthology illustrating that belief in reincarnation has been ubiquitous in world religious thought — with the sole major exception of post-sixth-century Christian doctrine. Head and Cranston lament, in light of Prat's exculpatory argument (made on behalf of Origen's entire distinguished theological opus, with Prat

having carefully noted the "error and danger" of Origen's belief in reincarnation), that "probably many a good Christian would have another look at the whole subject if he were only aware of the foregoing facts" (p. 87).

29 "an actual ecumenical council" Prat, "Origen and Origenism," pp. 311–12.

29 "certain" Runciman, *The Medieval Manichee*, p. 172. Runciman offered only a single example of such a legend — that of Barlaam and Josaphat, which entered "Gnostic scripture" only by way of Manichaean writings of central Asia. As to the scriptures of the Gnostics of the Mediterranean region, there is no certainty offered by Runciman or any other scholar of a direct influence of Buddhist legend on surviving Gnostic texts.

29 "were absorbed" Ibid.

30 "second Ashoka" Fowden, *Empire to Commonwealth*, p. 84.

30 "state religion" Ibid.

31 "with the Lord in his" Saint Ephrem, quoted in Sharan, *The Myth of Saint Thomas and the Mylapore Shiva Temple*, p. 18.

31 "The sunburnt India" Saint Ephrem, quoted in Neill, *A History of Christianity in India*, p. 29.

32 "Remember, St. Thomas came" Prasad, quoted in Pothan, *The Syrian Christians of Kerala*, p. xiii.

32 "Could the title" Pagels, *The Gnostic Gospels*, p. xxi.

32 "Does Thich Nhat Hanh" Pagels, introduction to Nhat Hanh, *Living Buddha, Living Christ*, p. xxvii. Quite independently, the American scholar Joscelyn Godwin saw the same connection some twenty years earlier, observing of the heretical Gnostic Nag Hammadi texts (which include the *Gospel of Thomas*), "While their theology is as radical as any, the reader feels closer to Zen Buddhism than to modern Satanism when confronted with their *koan*-like paradoxes, and instructed by the true God: 'Do not be ignorant of me anywhere or at any time. Be on your guard!'" (*Mystery Religions in the Ancient World*, p. 86).

33 "Buddhist counterpart" Nakamura, *Buddhism in Comparative Light*, p. 128.

33 "most alluring" Latourette, *A History of Christian Missions in China*, p. 49.

33 "in many respects Christianity" Ibid.

33 "More than one curious" Eliade, *Yoga: Immortality and Freedom*, p. 202. Eliade's views here coincide with those of the pioneering Italian scholar of Vajrayana Buddhist art Giuseppe Tucci, who wrote of the "surprising simultaneity" between Tantric and Gnostic doctrines in terms of their "inwardly experienced psychological drama." See Tucci, *Tibetan Painted Scrolls*, pp. 210–13.

Chapter Two

36 "any intercourse with strangers" Bardesanes, quoted in Gillman and Klimkeit, *Christians in Asia Before 1500*, p. 208.

36 "One could almost speak" Ibid., p. 206.

37 "Buddha" *The Jesus Messiah Sutra*, quoted in Gillman and Klimkeit, *Christians in Asia Before 1500*, p. 276.

37 "In India, the twenty-seven" Red Pine, *The Zen Teaching of Bodhidharma*, pp. 41–43.

38 "The Persian monk A-lo-pen" Emperor T'ai-tsung, quoted in Gillman and Klimkeit, *Christians in Asia Before 1500*, p. 269.

39 "Let you who hold" *The Ta-ch'in Luminous Religious Sutra on the Origin of Origins*, quoted ibid., p. 280.

39 "Emptiness" Ibid., p. 270.

39 "Since at that time" Yuan-chao, quoted ibid., p. 283.

40 "faced Buddhism and wrestled" Baring-Gould, *Curious Myths of the Middle Ages*, p. 33.

40 "The most curious thing" G. N. Banerjee, *Hellenism in Ancient India*, p. 213.

41 "Was Barlaam truly Josaphat" Opening lines of the poem "Barlaam and Josaphat" by Israel Zangwill, quoted in Lang, *The Balavariani*, p. 7.

42 "the Messiah-Buddha" Klimkeit, *Gnosis on the Silk Road*, p. 18.

42 "advocacy of the ascetic" Lang, *The Balavariani*, p. 9.

43 "Christ taught by His example" Runciman, *The Medieval Manichee*, p. 149.

43 "both a Christian" Gillman and Klimkeit, *Christians in Asia Before 1500*, p. 255.

43 "ransom" Ibid., p. 260.

44 "Thus the idea" Ibid., p. 261.

44 "to confound the customs" *The Ta-ch'in Luminous Religious Sutra on the Origin of Origins*, quoted ibid., p. 283.

47 "John, Priest by the" Prester John to the emperor of Constantinople, quoted in Baring-Gould, *Curious Myths of the Middle Ages*, p. 29.

47 "In the three Indies" Ibid., pp. 29–31.

48 "from the persecution of Christians" Pope Innocent IV to Guyuk Khan, quoted in Witek, "Christianity and China," in *China and Christianity*, p. 15.

48 "Let these dogs destroy" Bishop of Winchester to King Henry III, quoted in Witek, "Christianity and China," p. 15.

49 "To these words, I answered" William of Rubruck, quoted in C. Dawson, *Mission to Asia*, p. 141.

50 "that in all their prayers" Ibid., p. 194.

50 "When this was finished" Ibid.

52 "Among these people" Polo, *The Travels of Marco Polo*, p. 177.

52 "The son of a king" Ibid., p. 245.

52 "has died eighty-four" Ibid., p. 246.

53 "The Lord Buddha gave" Prince Godan to Kunga Gyaltsen, quoted in Shakabpa, *Tibet: A Political History*, p. 62.

54 "The Prince has told me" Kunga Gyaltsen, letter, quoted in Shakabpa, *Tibet: A Political History*, p. 63.

55 "As a true believer" Khubilai Khan, letter of investiture, quoted in Shakabpa, *Tibet: A Political History*, p. 65.

55 "History informs us that" Huc, *Christianity in China, Tartary and Thibet*, p. 246.

56 "But return to your Pope" Polo, *The Travels of Marco Polo*, p. 126.

56 "The Egyptian capture" Witek, "Christianity in China," p. 16.

57 "the countries of the unbelievers" Odoric, *The Travels of Friar Odoric*, pp. 63–64.

57 "something worth seeing" Ibid., pp. 63–64.

57 "a multitude of animals" Ibid.

57 "So I, laughing heartily" Ibid., pp. 129–30.

57 "And say what I list" Ibid.

57 "great plenty of bread" Ibid., p. 152.

57 "chief and royal city" Ibid.

Chapter Three

60 "seeking and discovering" Ignatius, quoted in De Nicholas, *Powers of Imagining*, p. 105.

60 "Man is created to praise" Ibid., pp. 110–11.

61 "father of his soul" Schurhammer, *Francis Xavier, His Life and Times*, vol. 1, p. 224.

61 "only father" Ibid.

61 "whether they should send us" "Formula of the Institute," quoted in Correia-Afonso, *The Ignatian Vision of India*, p. 11.

61 "the pious Kings of Portugal" Papal Bull of Canonization of Ignatius, quoted in Correia-Afonso, *The Ignatian Vision of India*, p. 1.

63 "Neither for the present king" King Bhuvaneka Bahu VII of Ceylon, quoted in Schurhammer, *Francis Xavier: His Life and Times*, vol. 2, p. 424.

63 "The missionaries were not" Don Peter, *Francis Xavier, Teacher of Nations*, p. 12.

64 "Let the letters be" Francis Xavier, letter, June 1549, quoted in Cooper, *Rodrigues the Interpreter*, p. 164.

64 "What may be conceded" Ibid., p. 163.

64 "It is obvious" Donald F. Lach, *Asia in the Making of Europe*, vol. 1 (1965), bk. 2, p. 728, quoted in Kitagawa, *On Understanding Japanese Religion*, p. 287.

65 "Very early they formed" Steinmetz, *History of the Jesuits*, vol. 1, pp. 422–23.

66 "very austere in their manner" Ley, *Portuguese Voyages*, p. 101.

67 "*talapicor* [monk] of Lechuna" Ibid., p. 206.

67 "I do advise and enjoin" Ibid., pp. 206–7.

68 "a world of extravagancies" Ibid., p. 207.

68 "extreme devotion" Ibid., p. 208.

68 "*Taiximida*" Ibid.

68 "hearing the auditors" Ibid., pp. 206–8.

68 "the religion of these gentiles" Ibid.

69 "Xaca [Buddha] is there" Postel, quoted in Droit, *The Cult of Nothingness*, p. 16.

69 "because of his illusions" Schurhammer, *Francis Xavier, His Life and Times*, vol. 3, p. 221, n. 65.

69 "in 1544 he [Postel] joined" Ibid., vol. 1, p. 164, n. 131.

69 "the most wonderful religion" Postel, quoted in Lacouture, *Jesuits: A Multibiography*, p. 200.

70 "Observe [. . .] how religion" Postel, quoted in Levi, *The History of Magic*, pp. 253–54, 255.

70 "Two years after" Ibid., p. 254.

70 "Mad because he believed" Levi, ibid., p. 255. I have changed "William" to "Guillaume" Postel in this quotation in the interest of clarity.

72 "They read in the manner" Jorge Alvares to Francis Xavier, report, December 1547, quoted in Schurhammer, *Francis Xavier: His Life and Times*, vol. 3, pp. 279–80.

73 "First of all, the people" Francis Xavier, letter, November 5, 1549, quoted in Schurhammer, *Francis Xavier: His Life and Times*, vol. 4, p. 82.

73 "The people are all white" Valignano, quoted in Schirokauer, *A Brief History of Japanese Civilization*, p. 133.

73 "to relate some accounts" Francis Xavier, letter, November 5, 1549, p. 92.

74 "It will not take much" Ibid., pp. 92–93.

74 "The evil which comes" Ibid., pp. 90–91.

74 "Paul [Anjiro] is in" Ibid., p. 91.

74 "probably mistook the painting" Schurhammer, *Francis Xavier: His Life and Times*, vol. 4, p. 62, n. 93.

75 "the first step in" W. Hoffmann, quoted ibid. Hoffmann was a nineteenth-century German Protestant.

75 "Some of them are" Luis Frois, quoted in Schurhammer, *Francis Xavier: His Life and Times,* vol. 4, p. 74.

75 "If you saw a ship" Francis Xavier, quoted in Schurhammer, *Francis Xavier: His Life and Times,* vol. 4, p. 74.

75 "Father, I understand you" Ibid., p. 74.

75 "a 'Nothing'" Ibid., p. 75.

76 "This old man lived on" Frois, quoted in Schurhammer, *Francis Xavier: His Life and Times,* vol. 4, p. 132, n. 31.

76 "that he would tread" Almeida, quoted in Schurhammer, *Francis Xavier: His Life and Times,* vol. 4, p. 76, n. 70.

76 "he had read more" Ibid.

77 "with hands upraised" Ibid., p. 75, n. 69.

77 "the elements of Zen" Ibid.

77 "that if the prince" Ibid., p. 76, n. 70.

78 "as a personification" Yamasaki, *Shingon,* p. 63.

78 "as a metaphor" Ibid., p. 64.

79 "the Japanese worshipped" Schurhammer, *Francis Xavier: His Life and Times,* vol. 4, p. 108.

79 "Pure Substance" Xavier, quoted ibid., p. 223.

79 "Creator" Ibid.

79 "Pray to Dainichi!" Ibid., p. 225.

79 *"materia prima"* Ibid.

80 "an obscene meaning" Schurhammer, ibid., p. 226.

80 "We frequently tell" Francis Xavier, letter, November 5, 1549, p. 84.

81 "The preface of the brief" Schalow, "Kukai and the Tradition of Male Love in Japanese Buddhism," pp. 216–17.

81 "had not been men" Xavier, quoted in Schurhammer, *Francis Xavier: His Life and Times,* vol. 4, p. 227.

81 "proved indeed to be" Neill, *A History of Christian Missions,* pp. 154–55.

82 "Some later said of him" Frois, quoted in Schurhammer, ibid., p. 130, n. 22.

83 "that for several months" Cooper, *Rodrigues the Interpreter,* p. 50.

83 "How much they understood" Neill, *A History of Christian Missions,* p. 156.

84 "In Thee, O Lord" Francis Xavier, quoted in Schurhammer, *Francis Xavier: His Life and Times,* vol. 4, p. 643.

85 "preaches the absolute void" Fabian Fucan, quoted in Elison, *Deus Destroyed,* pp. 52–53.

85 "at an early age" Ibid., p. 259.

85 "a Zen recluse" Ibid., p. 260.

85 "Their religion expounds" Ibid., p. 302.

86 "wear rosaries of driftwood" Unidentified Jesuit missionary, quoted in Schirokauer, *A Brief History of Japanese Civilization,* p. 135.

87 "If Japanese were to go" Hideyoshi, quoted in Cooper, *Rodrigues the Interpreter,* p. 162.

87 "As usual, legend" Neill, ibid., pp. 161–62.

88 "a consummate torture" Elison, *Deus Destroyed,* p. 191.

88 "The inquisitors wanted the victim" Ibid.

90 "cultural accommodation" Valignano, quoted in Cameron, *Barbarians and Mandarins,* p. 154.

91 "since the Evil One" Valignano, quoted in Lacouture, *Jesuits: A Multibiography,* p. 201.

91 "that we are not priests" Ricci, letter, November 15, 1592, quoted in Spence, *The Memory Palace of Matteo Ricci,* p. 115.

92 "Now he has perfectly mastered" Li Chih, quoted in Franke, *China and the West*, pp. 38–39.

93 "could certainly become Christians" Ricci, quoted in Spence, *The Memory Palace of Matteo Ricci*, p. 210.

93 "a Babylon of doctrines" Ibid., p. 217.

93 "It was inevitable" Spence, *The Memory Palace of Matteo Ricci*, p. 250.

94 "by changing a few words" Ricci, quoted ibid., p. 252.

94 "in such a way" Yu, quoted in Spence, *The Memory Palace of Matteo Ricci*, pp. 252–53.

95 "Marriages between men and women" Zhuhong, quoted in Spence, *The Memory Palace of Matteo Ricci*, p. 253.

95 "battle prizes" Ricci, quoted in Spence, *The Memory Palace of Matteo Ricci*, p. 249.

95 "he was wont to boast" Ibid., p. 216.

97 "telling me that Heaven" K'ang-hsi, quoted in Spence, *Emperor of China*, pp. 79–80.

98 "It was all one dazzling" Antonio de Andrade, quoted in Caraman, *Tibet: The Jesuit Century*, p. 40.

98 "humid principle" Godwin, *Athanasius Kircher*, p. 52.

99 "confused image of" Ibid.

99 "sea-girt paradise" Blofeld, *Bodhisattva of Compassion*, p. 150. In a similar vein, the Canadian scholar David Kinsley noted: "Kuan-yin is often shown holding a slender vase. Sometimes she is shown pouring liquid from it. The liquid is magical water that bestows vitality and wakefulness on Kuan-yin's devotees" (Kinsley, *The Goddesses' Mirror*, p. 49).

99 "principal emblems" Blofeld, *Bodhisattva of Compassion*, p. 150.

99 "From him, as from" Kircher, *China Monumentis*, quoted in Allen, *The Search for the Buddha*, p. 33.

99 "this foolish People" Ibid., p. 34.

101 "the general merit" Sven Hedin, *Southern Tibet: Discoveries in Former Times Compared with My Own Researches* (Stockholm, 1917), quoted in Allen, *The Search for the Buddha*, pp. 105–6.

101 "to listen to what" Desideri, *An Account of Tibet*, p. 98.

101 "I made it a rule" Ibid., p. 94.

102 "finish at his leisure" Ibid.

102 "Their opinion was that" Ibid., p. 101.

103 "This the Thibettans" Ibid., p. 196.

103 "Above all I applied" Ibid., p. 104.

103 "the Doctor who had" Ibid., p. 105.

104 "I was often persuaded" Ibid., p. 177.

104 "Seeing that human aid" Ibid., p. 241.

104 "Having by my aforesaid" Ibid.

105 "nothing exists because" Ibid., p. 105.

105 "independent of any cause" Ibid., p. 106.

105 "Although I believe" Ibid., p. 300.

Chapter Four

109 "Our circumstances seem" Leibniz, quoted in Franke, *China and the West,* p. 62.

109 "It is in my view" Ibid., p. 63.

110 "A favorite device" Aiton, *Leibniz: A Biography,* p. 328.

110 "taught, like these Japanese" Bayle, quoted in Faure, *Chan Insights and Oversights,* p. 32.

111 "they meant roughly" Ibid., p. 33.

111 "They neglect the externals" Ibid. The bracketed material is supplied by Faure.

111 "the world is nothing" Diderot, quoted in Halbfass, *India and Europe*, pp. 59–60.

111 "could only attain" Hegel, quoted in Halbfass, *India and Europe*, p. 60.

112 "for having said" Voltaire, "An Indian Adventure," in *Candide, Zadig, and Selected Stories*, p. 253.

112 "the God Fo does not" Voltaire, *Philosophical Dictionary*, p. 87.

112 "natural law permits" Ibid., p. 88.

113 "What! A ferocious animal" Voltaire, quoted in Gay, *The Enlightenment*, p. 391.

113 "May this great God" Ibid., p. 392.

113 "it was raining bombs" Diderot, quoted in Gay, *The Enlightenment*, p. 372.

113 "the great prostitute" Ibid.

113 "reign of Anti-Christ" Ibid.

114 "the Chinese, when their" Hume, *The Natural History of Religion*, p. 33.

114 "the excessive penances" Ibid., p. 71.

115 "There is another great God" Knox, *An Historical Relation of Ceylon*, p. 115.

115 "These people do firmly" Ibid., p. 135.

115 *"That the cause or causes"* Hume, *Dialogues Concerning Natural Religion*, p. 93.

116 "If this proposition" Ibid.

116 "Celibacy, fasting, penance" Hume, *Enquiries Concerning Human Understanding and Concerning the Principles of Morals*, p. 270.

117 "I may venture to affirm" Hume, *Treatise of Human Nature*, quoted in Quinton, *Hume*, p. 32.

118 "Hume's philosophy" Russell, *A History of Western Philosophy*, p. 672.

118 "The growth of unreason" Ibid., p. 673.

119 "Mercury, who was" La Loubere, quoted in Droit, *The Cult of Nothingness*, p. 30.

119 "the followers of Brahma" Upham, quoted in Droit, *The Cult of Nothingness*, p. 32.

121 "When I was at sea" Jones, quoted in Chatterji, "Sir William Jones," p. 89.

122 "Oriental Renaissance" See Schwab, *The Oriental Renaissance*.

122 "The Sanscrit language" Jones, quoted in Chatterji, "Sir William Jones," p. 92.

123 "Bood-dha, the Author of Happiness" Wilkins, quoted in Allen, *The Search for the Buddha*, p. 60.

123 "Ethiopia and Hindustan" Jones, quoted in Allen, *The Search for the Buddha*, p. 67.

123 "The Hindu religion" Ibid.

124 "It is completely certain" Wilford, quoted in Droit, *The Cult of Nothingness*, p. 35.

125 "I am no Hindu" Jones, quoted in Arberry, *Asiatic Jones*, p. 37.

125 "As in the case" Chatterji, "Sir William Jones," p. 87.

127 "It is clear that" Hodgson, quoted in Allen, *The Search for the Buddha*, p. 155.

129 "despite the aura" Batchelor, *The Awakening of the West*, p. 237.

129 "Father of Tibetology" Donald S. Lopez Jr., "Foreigner at the Lama's Feet," in *Curators of the Buddha*, p. 258.

129 "a distinguished philosopher" Ozeray, quoted in Droit, *The Cult of Nothingness*, p. 39.

129 "The statement marks" Droit, *The Cult of Nothingness*, pp. 37, 39.

130 "One must not confuse" Ozeray, quoted ibid., p. 38.

132 "simple" Burnouf, *Introduction to the History of Buddhism*, quoted in F. M. Müller, *Chips from a German Workshop*, vol. 5, p. 233.

132 "developed" Ibid.

132 "the production of the successive" Burnouf, *Le Lotus de la Bonne Loi*, vol. 2, p. 532. Translations from the French are by the author.

132 "As for the notion" Ibid.

132 "a disappearance of individuality" Burnouf, quoted in Tuck, *Comparative Philosophy and the Philosophy of Scholarship*, pp. 32–33.

133 "For some time past" Saint-Hilaire, *The Buddha and His Religion*, p. 15.

133 "when all the elements" Ibid., p. 13.

133 "displayed an ingenuous" Ibid., p. 16.

134 "atheists" Saint-Hilaire, quoted in Droit, *The Cult of Nothingness*, p. 158.

134 "materialists" Ibid.

134 "Regardless of the shortcomings" Ibid.

135 "if the religion of India" F. M. Müller, quoted in G. M. Müller, *The Life and Letters of the Right Honourable Friedrich Max Müller*, vol. 1, p. 362.

135 "I cannot resist" Ibid., vol. 1, p. 363.

135 "They start with a high" Ibid.

135 "there is this great" Ibid., vol. 2, p. 464.

136 "there is a Divine" Ibid., vol. 2, p. 349.

136 "And finally, if we may" F. M. Müller, "Buddhism," in *Chips from a German Workshop*, vol. 1, pp. 230–31.

137 "riddle which no one" F. M. Müller, "Buddhist Pilgrims," in *Chips from a German Workshop*, vol. 1, p. 243.

137 "We must distinguish" Ibid., p. 244.

137 "the attempt to produce" Collins, *Nirvana and Other Buddhist Felicities*, p. 101. The twentieth-century Japanese Buddhist scholar Hajime Nakamura explored the extreme limitations imposed on understanding by the Western fixation on the term "nirvana": "Many poetic terms are used [in Buddhism] to describe the state of the man who has been made perfect — the harbour of refuge, the cool cave, the island amidst the floods, the place of bliss, emancipation, liberation, safety, the supreme, the transcendental, the uncreated, the tranquil, the home of ease, the calm, the end of suffering, the medicine for all evil, the unshaken, the ambrosia, the nectar, the immortal, the immaterial, the imperishable, the abiding, the further shore, the unending, the bliss of effort, the supreme joy, the ineffable, the detachment, the holy city, and many others. Perhaps the most frequent term in the Pali texts is 'the state of him who is worthy' (arahatta, Arahatship). The term exclusively used in the West is Nirvana, which was translated as the 'dying out,' that is, the dying out in the heart of the fierce fire of the three cardinal sins — sensuality, ill-will, and stupidity. But the word Nirvana very often conveys a somewhat misleading impression. Contrary to the prevalent Western opinion about Nirvana, the craving for extinction in the sense of annihilation or non-existence (vibhava-tanha) was indeed expressly repudiated by the Buddha. Buddhists search not for cessation, but for the eternal, the immortal. He who has attained Nirvana is extolled as being afflicted neither by life nor by death" (Nakamura, *Buddhism in Comparative Light*, p. 55).

137 "celestial lubberland" Levi Gilbert (1852–1917), quoted in Collins, *Nirvana and Other Buddhist Felicities*, p. 100.

138 "It appeared to us" Dr. Edkins, quoted in F. M. Müller, "On Sanskrit Texts Discovered in Japan," in *Chips from a German Workshop*, vol. 5, p. 235.

138 "Is it not high time" F. M. Müller, "On Sanskrit Texts Discovered in Japan," pp. 236–37.

138 "It is only by serious" Saint-Hilaire, quoted in F. M. Müller, *Chips from a German Workshop*, vol. 2, pp. 368–69.

139 "There was a strange" T. W. Rhys Davids, quoted in Allen, *The Search for the Buddha*, p. 289.

139 "The choice of this term" T. W. Rhys Davids, quoted in Nakamura, *Buddhism in Comparative Light*, p. 56.

140 "Buddhist or not" T. W. Rhys Davids, quoted in Allen, *The Search for the Buddha*, p. 240.

140 "We can at least" T. W. Rhys Davids, *Lectures on the Origin and Growth of Religion*, p. 215.

140 "Had it not been" Thera, *Buddhism — A Living Message*, p. 67.

141 "Personally, I have no" Story, quoted in Peiris, *The Western Contribution to Buddhism*, pp. 35–36.

142 "Will ye, for love" Arnold, *The Light of Asia*, pp. 182–83. Arnold's was not the only epic poem of the period employing a Buddhist theme and composed by an eminent British subject. In Sir Richard Burton's pseudonymous *The Kasidah of Haji Abdu el-Yezdi* (first published in 1880), the life outlook of the spiritual pilgrim Haji Abdu, as Burton tells us in his "editorial" notes, is that of "the Sufi, with the usual dash of Buddhistic pessimism" (p. 103).

142 "More than a third" Arnold, *The Light of Asia*, pp. 5–6.

143 "the land of the Light" Arnold, quoted in Allen, *The Search for the Buddha*, p. 250.

143 "a representative committee" Ibid., p. 252.

Chapter Five

144 "purest humanity" Herder, quoted in Halbfass, *India and Europe*, p. 70.

144 "childlike Indians" Ibid.

144 "The Hindus are" Ibid., p. 71.

145 "the pinnacle of Romanticism" Schlegel, quoted in Halbfass, *India and Europe*, p. 75. Schlegel did give a small degree of attention to Buddhism, which he saw as a species of Indian Vedantic belief. Although he believed the heart of Buddhist teaching to be "that everything is nothing," Schlegel was able to see in nirvana not annihilation, but a quietistic joy: "Once this great disclosure has been made, and this all-encompassing, all-destroying, and yet so easy science and reason-wisdom that all is one has been discovered, then no further search or research is necessary; all that which others know or believe in other ways is simply error, deception, and weak-mindedness, just as all change and all life is mere illusion" (p. 77).

145 "Everything, yes, everything" Schlegel, quoted in J. J. Clarke, *Oriental Enlightenment*, p. 64.

146 "Hegel has been" Mehta, quoted in J. J. Clarke, *Oriental Enlightenment*, p. 66.

146 "nature religion" Hegel, quoted in J. J. Clarke, *Oriental Enlightenment*, p. 60.

146 "religion of being-in-itself" Ibid., p. 61.

146 "God is grasped" Hegel, *Lectures on the Philosophy of Religion*, p. 258.

147 "The image of Buddha" Ibid., p. 252.

147 "man must make" Hegel, quoted in J. J. Clarke, *Oriental Enlightenment*, p. 67.

147 "At first glance" Hegel, *Lectures on the Philosophy of Religion*, pp. 255–56.

148 "Buddha, Eckhart and I" Schopenhauer, quoted in Halbfass, *India and Europe*, p. 111. With these quotations from Hegel and Schopenhauer in mind, the validity of current-day scholarly judgments that D. T. Suzuki put forth — as Richard King has put it, "a Buddhification of the Christian thinker" (*Orientalism and Religion*, p. 157) — come into serious question. When three astute thinkers, from three quite distinct perspectives (Schopenhauer, for his part, reviled Hegel), point to the same similarity, it is tolerant to allow that the similarity may just exist. George Grimm (1868–1945), a German jurist and Theravada Buddhist, also argued, in his *Doctrine of the Buddha* (first published in 1915), for certain parallels between Buddhist thought and the writings of Eckhart. The German Protestant theologian Rudolf Otto (1869–1937), in his *Mysticism East and*

West, compared Sankara (whom Otto believed to be the greatest exemplar of Eastern mysticism, which included, for Otto, both Hinduism and Buddhism as essentially synonymous types) with Eckhart. Sarvepalli Radhakrishnan offered a similar analysis in his *Eastern Religions and Western Thought.*

148 "'The world is my representation'" Schopenhauer, *The World as Will and Representation,* vol. 1, p. 3.

150 "as a synonym" Willis, *On Knowing Reality,* p. 24.

150 "the Mongols adhered" Kant, *Religion Within the Limits of Reason Alone,* p. 99. Kant based his historical viewpoint here on the *Alphabetum Tibetanum* (1762) of Father Augustinus Antonius Georgius.

150 "Kant's *Critique*" Schopenhauer, *On the Fourfold Root,* p. 187.

151 "agreement" Schopenhauer, *The World as Will and Representation,* vol. 2, p. 169.

152 "up till 1818" Ibid., p. 169.

152 "I can really recommend" Schopenhauer, quoted in Nicholls, "The Influence of Eastern Thought on Schopenhauer's Doctrine of the Thing-in-Itself," p. 179.

152 "We must not even evade" Schopenhauer, *The World as Will and Representation,* vol. 1, pp. 411–12.

152 "this [nothing] is also" Ibid., p. 412.

153 "One may well marvel" Zimmer, *Philosophies of India,* p. 483.

153 "delight in declaring" Ibid.

154 "palingenesis" Schopenhauer, *The World as Will and Representation,* vol. 2, p. 502.

154 "we might say to the dying" Ibid., p. 501.

154 "Death is a refutation" Ibid., p. 601.

155 "true to the facts" Schopenhauer, "The Christian System," in *Essays,* p. 89.

155 "domestic worship" Schopenhauer, quoted in Droit, *The Cult of Nothingness,* p. 94.

156 "pilgrimage" Ibid.

156 "Both have that famous" Ibid.

156 "that these days even" Kalb, quoted in Droit, *The Cult of Nothingness,* p. 93.

156 "send to the Brahmins" Schopenhauer, *The World as Will and Representation,* vol. 1, pp. 356–57.

156 "Because of the doctrine" Schopenhauer, *On the Fourfold Root,* p. 187.

157 "the Christian faith" Schopenhauer, "The Christian System," p. 93.

157 "with all the Buddhas" Gobineau, quoted in Droit, *The Cult of Nothingness,* p. 110.

157 "excellence of Aryan blood" Ibid.

157 "by recruiting" Ibid.

157 "the vilest of the classes" Ibid.

157 "stagnated" Hartmann, quoted in Halbfass, *India and Europe,* p. 122.

157 "The development of religion" Ibid.

158 "movement from life" Mainländer, quoted in Halbfass, *India and Europe,* p. 492, n. 3.

158 "will to death" Ibid.

158 "will to life" Ibid.

158 "Nirvana principle" Freud, *Beyond the Pleasure Principle,* p. 49.

158 "to reduce" Ibid., p. 50.

158 "We have unwittingly" Ibid., pp. 43–44.

159 "This ego consciousness" Jung, *Nietzsche's Zarathustra,* vol. 1, p. 345.

160 "who is able to hold" Ibid., vol. 2, p. 1382.

160 "How sublime, how satisfying" Wagner, quoted in J. J. Clarke, *Oriental Enlightenment,* p. 77.

160 "perhaps the only real" Michael Edwardes, *East-West Passage: The Travel of Ideas, Arts and Inventions Between Asia and the Western World* (London: Cassell, 1971), quoted in J. J. Clarke, *Oriental Enlightenment*. p. 77.

161 "belong together" Nietzsche, *Twilight of the Idols and The Anti-Christ*, p. 129.

161 "The precondition for" Ibid., pp. 130–31.

162 "that profound physiologist" Nietzsche, *On the Genealogy of Morals and Ecce Homo*, pp. 230–31.

162 "a kind of *hygiene*" Ibid.

162 "*ressentiment*" Ibid.

162 "'Not by enmity'" Ibid., pp. 230–31.

162 "the lowest classes" Nietzsche, *Twilight of the Idols and The Anti-Christ*, p. 131.

162 "are considered unachievable" Ibid.

162 "Buddhism was making silent" Nietzsche, quoted in Halbfass, *India and Europe*, p. 127.

162 "opiatic" Ibid.

162 "a European Buddhism may prove indispensable" Ibid.

162 "could be the Buddha of Europe" Ibid., p. 128.

162 "to transvalue the values" Ibid.

163 "a final and purely practical" Spengler, *The Decline of the West*, p. 356.

163 "'You are mistaken'" Russell, *A History of Western Philosophy*, p. 772.

164 "I must say" Russell, *Why I Am Not a Christian*, pp. 18–19. It should be added that Russell was hardly an impartial judge in this regard, as he clashed with Christian institutions on a number of occasions during his lifetime, most notably with regard to his appointment to a chair of philosophy at the City College of New York. This appointment was blocked in part due to determined opposition by Episcopal and other Christian clergy. See the appendix to *Why I Am Not a Christian*.

164 "Interests (material and ideal)" Weber, quoted in Halbfass, *India and Europe*, pp. 142–43.

165 "All men's toil" Weber, *The Religion of India*, p. 211.

165 "complete Europeanization" Heidegger, quoted in Halbfass, *India and Europe*, p. 167.

166 "forgetfulness of being" Ibid.

166 "To say that philosophy" Ibid., p. 168.

166 "the inescapable dialogue" Ibid.

166 "beyond Occident and Orient" Ibid., p. 169.

166 "'Gelassenheit,' a serene" Halbfass, *India and Europe*, p. 170.

166 "The investigation concludes" May, *Heidegger's Hidden Sources*, p. xviii.

167 "the evidence from" Parkes, quoted ibid., p. x.

167 "In so far as Heidegger's" May, *Heidegger's Hidden Sources*, p. 63.

168 "the existential conception" Parkes, quoted ibid., p. 95.

168 "the question is whether" Ibid., p. 107.

168 "In order to gain" May, *Heidegger's Hidden Sources*, p. 57.

169 "a German friend" Barrett, "Zen for the West," introduction to D. T. Suzuki, *Zen Buddhism*, p. xi.

169 "nothingness is not 'nothing'" Heinrich Wiegand Petzet, quoted in May, *Heidegger's Hidden Sources*, p. 3.

169 "That is what" Ibid.

Chapter Six

171 "I have often been blamed" Müller, *Auld Lang Syne (Second Series)*, p. 166.

172 "Let us settle" Blavatsky, quoted ibid., p. 322.

173 "If Buddhism contained" Olcott, quoted in Prothero, *The White Buddhist*, p. 96.

173 "initiated Arhats retired" Blavatsky, *The Key to Theosophy*, p. 11.

173 "teach all that" Ibid.

173 "the truth has" Ibid.

174 "the doctrine of" Sinnett, *Esoteric Buddhism*, p. 3.

174 "been jealously guarded" Ibid.

174 "All my inquiries" Ibid., p. 9.

174 "a sublime state" Ibid., p. 197.

175 "The old Buddhists" Jennings, quoted in Deveney, *Paschal Beverly Randolph*, pp. 137–38.

176 "Once, when *en rapport*" Randolph, quoted in Deveney, *Paschal Beverly Randolph*, pp. 434–35, n. 21.

176 "What saved the situation" Blavatsky, quoted in Johnson, *The Masters Revealed*, p. 7.

178 "the Old Law" Kipling, *Kim*, p. 8.

178 "one of the works" Blavatsky, *The Voice of the Silence*, p. 5.

178 "Believe thou not" Ibid., pp. 48–49.

179 "all beings to enter" Panchen Lama, quoted in Cranston, *HPB*, p. 86. As to the judgment of D. T. Suzuki in this regard, Cranston provided the following account by Suzuki to a friend published in the *Buddhist News* (August 1965): "I saw *The Voice of the Silence* for the first time [in 1910] when at Oxford. I got a copy and sent it to Mrs. Suzuki (then Miss Beatrice Lane) at Columbia University, writing to her: 'Here is the real Mahayana Buddhism'" (p. 86). Suzuki also declared, in 1935, while visiting the Theosophist Boris de Zerkoff in Los Angeles and encountering a photograph of Blavatsky: "She was one who attained" (p. 85). This is according to the testimony of de Zerkoff, who may be suspected of bias given his allegiance to Blavatsky. Nonetheless, if these two accounts are given credibility, as they would seem to deserve, then Suzuki can be seen as something other than the habitual deprecator of Western capacity for Buddhist understanding that he is often portrayed to be by current Western scholars.

179 "had the pleasure" Fourteenth Dalai Lama, quoted in Cranston, *HPB*, p. 85.

179 "the first to introduce" Fourteenth Dalai Lama, blurb, Foster and Foster, *Forbidden Journey*, back cover.

179 "He was arrested" Hopkirk, *Trespassers on the Roof of the World*, p. 55.

180 "that both Christ and Buddha" Chesterton, *Orthodoxy*, pp. 241–42.

181 "the uneducated rabble" Blavatsky, *The Theosophical Glossary*, p. 312.

182 "was to stoop down" Olcott, quoted in Prothero, *The White Buddhist*, p. 74.

183 "There is no adequate proof" Ibid., pp. 82–83.

183 "is declared inviolable" Convention of 1815, British treaty on terms of rule in Ceylon, quoted in Prothero, *The White Buddhist*, p. 85.

184 "a religious pact" Olcott, quoted in Prothero, *The White Buddhist*, p. 127.

184 "encompassed an intriguing" Prothero, *The White Buddhist*, p. 128.

186 "Take my chair" James, quoted in Fields, *How the Swans Came to the Lake*, p. 135.

186 "This is the psychology" Ibid.

187 "nationalism, Buddhism" Tambiah, *Buddhism Betrayed?* p. 131, n. 5.

187 "Christian missionary" Ibid., pp. 5–7.

187 "From the day" *Sinhala Bauddhaya*, quoted ibid., p. 8.

187 "The Muhammadans" Dharmapala, quoted in Tambiah, *Buddism Betrayed?* p. 8.

188 "no doubt that" Gandhi, quoted in Allen, *The Search for the Buddha*, p. 254.

189 "all poet's invention" Lamb, quoted in Waddell, *Lhasa and Its Mysteries*, p. 12.

190 "Dirt, dirt, grease" Manning, quoted in Younghusband, *India and Tibet*, p. 34.

190 "Beautiful youth" Manning, quoted in Waddell, *Lhasa and Its Mysteries,* p. 13.

190 "No doubt my" Manning, quoted in Younghusband, *India and Tibet,* p. 38.

190 "Manning, the eccentric" Bell, *Tibet Past and Present,* p. 41.

191 "White Tsar" Dorzhiev, quoted in Meyer and Brysac, *Tournament of Shadows,* p. 269.

191 "Bodhisattva-tsar" Ibid.

192 "The morale of" Shakabpa, *Tibet: A Political History,* p. 214.

192 "The Chinese government" Bell, *Tibet Past and Present,* p. 68.

193 "He was full" Younghusband, *India and Tibet,* p. 325.

194 "As I now looked" Ibid., p. 326.

194 "Independence, indeed" Ibid., p. 438.

194 "Blessed are the pure" Tombstone of Younghusband, quoted in Bishop, *The Myths of Shangri-La,* p. 183.

195 "One of the few" Waddell, *Tibetan Buddhism,* p. viii.

195 "Realizing the rigid" Ibid., p. ix.

196 "Still, with all" Ibid., p. 573.

196 "Her closed doors" Waddell, *Lhasa and Its Mysteries,* p. 2. In this book, Waddell left a brief record of his encounter with a Tibetan oracle, or fortune-teller, who, as was common in Tibet, was also a member of the Buddhist clergy: "Before I left, the priest looked at me piercingly for an instant, and asked, 'What is your age?' On my replying, he promptly retorted, 'No! You are one year more; you are. . . .' Then I remembered that a few days before I had passed my birthday and had actually reached the exact age which he thus disclosed. With this oracular parting shot he vanished from our view into the gloom of his temple" (p. 386).

196 "in the University" Ibid., p. 448.

197 "The men who" Hopkirk, *Foreign Devils on the Silk Road,* p. 2.

198 "Oases that were" Baumer, *Southern Silk Road,* p. xi.

199 "robber of the Miran" Ibid., p. 118.

199 "With an agitated voice" Ibid.

200 "Chinese university circles" Ibid., pp. 104–6.

200 "devotion, genuine enough" Stein, quoted in Faure, *Chan Insights and Oversights,* p. 93, n. 1.

201 "My time for true relief" Ibid., p. 169.

Chapter Seven

202 "I trust that" Thoreau, *A Week on the Concord and Merrimack Rivers,* p. 60.

203 "I do not prefer" Thoreau, *The Journal of Henry David Thoreau,* vol. 1, p. 145.

203 "They reckon ill" Emerson, *Complete Essays,* p. 809. It is worth noting that Herman Melville (1819–1891), for a time an acquaintance of Emerson, penned late in his life a short poem titled "Buddha" that portrayed Buddhism — in a manner akin to Emerson — as a nihilistic escape from suffering. The poem reads:

> Swooning swim to less and less
> Aspirant to nothingness!
> Sobs of the worlds, and dole of kinds
> That dumb endurers be —
> Nirvana! absorb us in your skies,
> Annul us unto thee.

(Melville, *Selected Poems,* ed. Cohen, p. 144)

What is more surprising is that Melville left unfinished at his death a work of mixed poetry and prose titled "Rammon," in which, according to the American scholar Hennig Cohen, the title character, a son (invented by Melville) sired in the old age of King Solomon, "shows a familiarity with Buddhist ideas about death which are said to have reached the court of Solomon through the Queen of Sheba and commercial dealings with Hiram, King of Tyre" (Melville, *Selected Poems,* ed. Cohen, p. 253). In this speculation, Melville placed the arrival of Buddhism in Israel several centuries prior to the birth of the Buddha himself.

204 "The intuition of" Emerson, *The Complete Essays,* pp. 68–69.
204 "The Buddhist who" Ibid., p. 91.
204 "Nature will not" Ibid., p. 441.
205 "the Protestantism" J. F. Clarke, *Ten Great Religions,* vol. 1, p. 143.
205 "deeper and more essential" Ibid.
205 "The superiority of Christianity" Ibid., p. 169.
206 "The whole of Buddhism" Bucke, *Cosmic Consciousness,* p. 80.
206 "it may be that" Ibid., p. 192.
206 "when I was a young fellow" Whitman, quoted in Teller, ed. *Walt Whitman's Camden Conversations,* pp. 166–67.
207 "Magnifying and applying" Whitman, "Song of Myself," in *Leaves of Grass,* p. 64.
207 "so extraordinary for" Emerson, quoted in Fields, *How the Swans Came to the Lake,* p. 65.
208 "Emersonian optimism" James, *The Varieties of Religious Experience,* p. 44.
208 "Buddhistic pessimism" Ibid.
208 "I am ignorant" Ibid., pp. 404–5.
208 "the future union" Fenollosa, "East and West," quoted in Tweed, *The American Encounter with Buddhism,* p. 99.
209 "damn bhuddists" Pound, "Canto LIV," *The Cantos,* p. 285.
209 "In Tendai and Shingon" Bigelow, quoted in Tweed, *The American Encounter with Buddhism,* p. 74.
210 "His trips to China" E. F. Bleiler, introduction to Okakura, *The Book of Tea,* p. xi.
212 "Buddhism in some" Hearn, quoted in Murray, *A Fantastic Journey,* p. 84.
212 "The religion seized" Ibid., p. 125.
213 "When one has lived" Hearn, quoted in McWilliams, *Lafcadio Hearn,* pp. 350–51.
213 "Paradoxical as it" Yuzo Ota, "Lafcadio Hearn: Japan's Problematic Interpreter," in *Rediscovering Lafcadio Hearn,* ed. Hirakawa, p. 222.
214 "if it were possible" Hearn, quoted in Stevenson, *Lafcadio Hearn,* p. 238.
214 "The doctrine of" Hearn, *Gleanings in Buddha-Fields,* pp. 227–28.
214 "It would be up to" Kenneth Rexroth, introduction to Hearn, *The Buddhist Writings of Lafcadio Hearn,* p. xxvii.
215 "'Down with frivolous'" Anesaki, *History of Japanese Religion,* pp. 360–62.
215 "Buddhism usually has" Toshiaki, quoted in Keene, *The Japanese Discovery of Europe,* p. 83.
215 "chief among the important" Inoue, quoted in Pyle, *The New Generation in Meiji Japan,* p. 65.
215 "has been a stimulant" Pratt, *The Pilgrimage of Buddhism,* p. 728.
216 "'restoration of Christianity'" Anesaki, *History of Japanese Religion,* p. 374.
217 "I am, as it were" Carus, quoted in Tweed, *The American Encounter with Buddhism,* p. 101.
217 "The charges which" Ibid., p. 100.

218 "arrived in Yeddo Bay" Laury, *A History of Lutheran Missions,* p. 226.
220 "have purchased presses" Spence Hardy, *The Legends and Theories of the Buddhists,* p. viii.
220 "These are the characteristics" Ibid., p. 174.
221 "the now myriad-worshipped" Ibid.
221 "The time is very near" Thoburn, *The Christless Nations,* p. 14.
221 "Next to the Caucasian" E. Thomson, *Our Oriental Missions,* vol. 2, p. 7.
221 "Buddhism prevails in Ceylon" Ibid., p. 224.
221 "in order to support" Smith, quoted in Varg, *Missionaries, Chinese, and Diplomats,* p. 109.
222 "there may be virtuous" Ibid.
222 "You may go through" Taylor, quoted in Leitch and Leitch, *Seven Years in Ceylon,* p. 106.
222 "we don't want your opium" Leitch and Leitch, *Seven Years in Ceylon,* p. 106.
223 "Here, then, is the first" Monier-Williams, *Buddhism,* pp. 545, 563.
223 "'How much truth'" Caird, *The Evolution of Religion,* vol. 1, p. x.
223 "for the one" Ibid.
224 "The infinite pitifulness" Ibid., vol. 2, pp. 320–21.
224 "Buddhism had power" Ibid., vol. 1, pp. 361–62.
224 "As for Buddhism" Holmes, *Burton Holmes Travelogues,* vol. 9, pp. 183–85.
225 "One day after" Shih, quoted in Gih, *Into God's Family,* p. 23.
226 "If we considered" Tweed, *The American Encounter with Buddhism,* p. 46.
228 "California Senator James" Marty, *Modern American Religion,* p. 111.
229 "I would like" Imamura, quoted in Prebish, *Luminous Passage,* p. 128.
229 "the necessity of" Uchida, quoted in Marty, *Modern American Religion,* p. 111.

Chapter Eight
230 "This fellow was" Soyen [Sōen] Shaku, "A Short Autobiography," in Senzaki, *Like a Dream, Like a Fantasy,* p. 89.
231 "Buddhism in Japan" Kakichi, quoted in Victoria, *Zen at War,* p. 16.
231 "We may grant" Soyen [Sōen] Shaku, *Zen for Americans,* pp. 124–25. Arika Iriye offered an overview of Meiji military policies that forms a blunt counterpoint to Sōen's convictions: Japan "undertook military action in Korea and sought to entrench its power on the continent of Asia because it was politically and militarily equipped to do so and because national opinion firmly supported such action. [. . .] The years after the Sino-Japanese War, then, may be seen as a period in which imperialism came to occupy a central position in the politics, economy and culture of the Japanese state and in which tensions as well as convergence characterized national opinion" ("Japan's Drive to Great-Power Status," in *The Emergence of Meiji Japan,* ed. Jansen, p. 313).
232 "War is an evil" Soyen [Sōen] Shaku, *Zen for Americans,* pp. 201–2, 81.
232 "Were it not" Ibid., p. 203.
233 "the perversion of both" Tolstoy, "Bethink Yourselves!" in *Recollections and Essays,* p. 260. While Tolstoy was correct in his historical insistence on the Buddha's teaching of nonviolence, the Russian writer, who tacitly granted spiritual preeminence to the Christian outlook, shared the common Western conception of the time that Buddhism was a form of pessimism: "Simple paganism considers man to have a right to happiness, while Buddhism considers that the world ought to disappear because it produces suffering to the personality. Buddhism is negative paganism" (Tolstoy, "*On Life,*" p. 175, n. 1).
233 "Nor do the Japanese" Tolstoy, "Bethink Yourselves!" p. 261.
234 "What I firmly" Soyen [Sōen] Shaku, *Zen for Americans,* p. 81.

235 "some mystery surrounds" Eido Shimano Roshi, introduction to Senzaki, *Like a Dream, Like a Fantasy*, pp. 11–12.

235 "This may be better" Senzaki, quoted in Fields, *How the Swans Came to the Lake*, p. 172.

235 "He has to walk" Soyen [Sōen] Shaku, quoted in Senzaki, *Like a Dream, Like a Fantasy*, p. 127.

235 "For seventeen years, I have" Senzaki, *Like a Dream, Like a Fantasy*, p. 127.

236 "I was left in America" Ibid., p. 118.

236 "All Japanese faces will leave" Senzaki, quoted in Fields, *How the Swans Came to the Lake*, p. 193.

237 "to Nyogen Senzaki, 'homeless monk'" Reps, *Zen Flesh, Zen Bones*, p. xiv.

238 "He [Sokatsu] told" Sokei-an, *Holding the Lotus to the Rock*, pp. 88–89.

238 "I saw a dead" Ibid., p. 118.

239 "On February 22, 1936" Ibid., p. 155.

239 "I am often asked" Ibid., p. 148.

239 "monk-novice" Goddard, quoted in Fields, *How the Swans Came to the Lake*, p. 184.

240 "Coming under the influence" Ibid., p. 185.

240 "At this time" Sokei-an, *Holding the Lotus to the Rock*, p. 176.

241 "although in Asia" Watts, *In My Own Way*, p. 142. Monica Furlong, a biographer of Watts, offered this analysis of Watts's frustration with the koan method: "Ironically, in *The Spirit of Zen* he [Watts] had described this sort of discouragement as an essential stage in the student's development, the suffering described as an iron ball in the throat that could neither be swallowed down nor spat out. It was indeed precisely the experience of being driven 'out of one's mind' and thus onto another level of awareness altogether that the koan so uncomfortably existed to promote" (*Zen Effects*, p. 75). The fact that Watts could aptly describe a teaching method does not, of course, mean that he should have been able to thrive under that method. Books and their authors are often unalike, in great things and in small.

241 "contrary to my lone" Watts, *In My Own Way*, ibid.

241 "I decided, therefore" Ibid., p. 143.

241 "If I have stressed" Ibid., p. 146.

242 "I read it" D. T. Suzuki, *The Field of Zen*, pp. 2–3.

243 "[Joshu] was once asked" D. T. Suzuki, Fromm, and De Martino, *Zen Buddhism and Psychoanalysis*, p. 46.

243 "Up until then" D. T. Suzuki, *The Field of Zen*, p. 10. This account of his *samadhi* experience has been the subject of scholarly innuendo, on the implied grounds that, having been written by Suzuki at age ninety-four, it is perhaps a gilded account to enhance his reputation. Suzuki had refused on several earlier occasions in his life to speak on his personal Zen experiences. The fact that he did so only a year before his death more easily redounds to his credit than not. Further, if it is deemed unlikely that a person with the political views of Suzuki would be capable of *samadhi*, my own response would be that the history of Buddhism in particular, and of religious mysticism in general, does not readily serve to sanction any political point of view as innately related to or opposed to "higher truth." A further innuendo directed at Suzuki pertains to the fact that he was never ordained as a Zen priest. Given the lay emphasis of his teacher Sōen, and the displeasure of Sōen's Dharma heir Sokatsu when Sokei-an chose to be ordained, Suzuki's course seems understandable.

243 "The assumption that" Faure, *Chan Insights and Oversights*, pp. 57–58. As Faure discussed, the question of whether Zen experience should be viewed as ahistorical, or rather as

the product of complex historical factors, was the subject of a debate between D. T. Suzuki and the Chinese historian Hu Shih published in the journal *Philosophy East and West* in January 1953. The debate remains of great interest to scholars of Buddhism and comparative religion, as both men defended their positions with rhetorical vigor, in particular Suzuki, who argued, in an unfortunate tone, that "vis-à-vis Zen, there are at least two types of mentality: the one that can understand Zen and, therefore, has a right to say something about it, and another which is utterly unable to grasp what Zen is. The difference between the two types is one of quality and is beyond the possibility of mutual reconciliation. [. . .] Hu Shih, who represents the second type of mentality, is not properly qualified and equipped to discuss Zen as Zen apart from its various historical settings" (D. T. Suzuki, "Zen: A Reply to Hu Shih," p. 25).

245 "represented the total" Victoria, *Zen at War*, p. 79.

245 "Both before and after" D. T. Suzuki, quoted ibid., p. 150.

245 "Zen has no" D. T. Suzuki, *Zen and Japanese Culture*, p. 63. This book, published in 1959, was an expanded version of a prior work, *Zen Buddhism and Its Influence on Japanese Culture* (1938).

246 "Buddhism is not immune" Loori, quoted in Victoria, *Zen at War*, back cover.

246 "Looking at this period" Victoria, *Zen at War*, p. xi.

247 "In fifty years" Christmas Humphreys, obituary for D. T. Suzuki, *The Times*, July 13, 1966, reprinted in D. T. Suzuki, *The Field of Zen*, p. xvi.

248 "As a direct result of" Conze, introduction to D. T. Suzuki, *On Indian Mahayana Buddhism*, p. 1.

249 "suddenly realized" Kerouac, *Selected Letters, 1957–1969*, p. 165.

249 "For Mrs. Sasaki to say" Ibid., p. 186.

250 "The only thing" D. T. Suzuki, "An Interpretation of Zen-Experience," in *Philosophy — East and West*, ed. Moore, p. 129. Suzuki was not alone among the participants in the East-West Philosophers' Conference in employing glib dichotomies as to the mental capacities of the East and the West. F. S. C. Northrop, a professor of philosophy at Yale, expanded his contribution to that conference into *The Meeting of East and West: An Inquiry Concerning World Understanding*, an influential work of its era, which posed a Western culture governed since the time of the Greeks by rationality and the scientific method, and an Eastern culture in which intuitive observation, aesthetic appreciation, and empathy prevailed. The ultimate goal of world civilization was, of course, to combine the best of both approaches.

250 "The reception of Zen" Dumoulin, *Zen Buddhism in the 20th Century*, p. 87.

251 "The sutras, especially" D. T. Suzuki, "From Zen to the Gandavyuha," in *Essays in Zen Buddhism (Third Series)*, p. 25.

251 "When this liberation" D. T. Suzuki, Fromm, and De Martino, *Zen Buddhism and Psychoanalysis*, p. 20.

251 "that the superficial" D. T. Suzuki, *Mysticism: Christian and Buddhist*, dust jacket.

251 "as far as I can" Ibid., p. 4.

251 "Being combative" Ibid., p. 138.

252 "There are two" D. T. Suzuki, quoted in Merton, *Zen and the Birds of Appetite*, p. 133.

252 "Father Merton's emptiness" Ibid.

252 "It is clear" Merton, *Zen and the Birds of Appetite*, p. 135.

253 "Even to have" Shunryu Suzuki, *Zen Mind, Beginner's Mind*, pp. 127–28.

253 "there was little" D. Chadwick, *Crooked Cucumber*, pp. 97–98.

253 "During his twelve" Mel Weitsman, introduction to Shunryu Suzuki, *Branching Streams Flow in the Darkness*, p. 4.

254 "His wife, Mitsu-san" Ibid., p. 3.

254 "No, he's the big" Shunryu Suzuki, quoted in Chadwick, *Crooked Cucumber*, p. xiii.

254 "There's Page Street" Maezumi, quoted in Chadwick, *Crooked Cucumber*, p. 413.

Chapter Nine

255 "communications from mystic" David-Neel, *Magic and Mystery in Tibet*, p. 234.

255 "the most astonishing" Lawrence Durrell, foreword to Foster and Foster, *Forbidden Journey*, p. x.

256 "I had lost" David-Neel, quoted in Peter Hopkirk, new introduction to David-Neel, *My Journey to Lhasa*, p. xii.

257 "I don't like popes" David-Neel, quoted in Batchelor, *The Awakening of the West*, p. 311.

257 "foreign writers commonly" David-Neel, *Immortality and Reincarnation*, p. 60.

258 "What right had they" David-Neel, quoted in Hopkirk, new introduction, p. xiii.

258 "The first white woman" David-Neel, *My Journey to Lhasa*, p. 310.

259 "thumo reskiang practice" Ibid., p. 132.

259 "with great difficulties" Ibid.

259 "I saw some hermits" Ibid.

259 "On a night considered" Tenzin Gyatso [His Holiness the Fourteenth Dalai Lama], *MindScience*, p. 44.

260 "the more subtle aspects" Ibid., p. 48.

260 "Jokingly, I asked" Blofeld, quoted in Foster and Foster, *The Secret Lives of Alexandra David-Neel*, p. 274.

261 "Blakean imagery" Ginsberg, blurb, Foster and Foster, *Forbidden Journey*, back cover.

262 "I should have died" David-Neel, quoted in Foster and Foster, *Forbidden Journey*, p. 308.

262 "consciousness of existence" Evans-Wentz, quoted in Winkler, *Pilgrim of the Clear Light*, p. 7.

262 "I have been haunted" Ibid.

263 "I spent more than" Evans-Wentz, quoted in Leslie Shepard, foreword to Evans-Wentz, *The Fairy-Faith in Celtic Countries*, p. vii.

263 "English dictionary" Evans-Wentz, quoted in Winkler, *Pilgrim of the Clear Light*, p. 38.

263 "disciple" Ibid.

264 "The approach of comparing" Trungpa and Fremantle, *The Tibetan Book of the Dead*, p. 1. Francesca Fremantle, though sharing Trungpa's reservations, also acknowledged, "It is quite likely that if Evans-Wentz had introduced it to the Western world as *Great Liberation through Hearing during the Intermediate State* [the literal translation from the Tibetan], it would not have attracted so much interest" (*Luminous Emptiness*, p. 6). As for the extent of the interest it did attract, the judgment of Mircea Eliade in the concluding section of his three-volume *A History of Religious Ideas* is worth quoting: "The *Bardo Thodol* is certainly the best-known Tibetan religious text in the Western world. Translated and published in English in 1928, it has become, especially since 1960, a sort of bedside reading for numerous young people. Such a phenomenon is significant for the history of contemporary Western spirituality. It is a profound and difficult text, unequalled in any other religious literature. The interest which it arouses, not only among the psychologists, historians, and artists, but above all among the young, is symptomatic: it in-

dicates both the almost total desacralization of death in contemporary Western societies, and the restless inquiry and exasperated desire which seek to revalorize — religiously or philosophically — the act which terminates human existence" (p. 281).

264 "my constant companion" Carl Jung, "Psychological Commentary," in *The Tibetan Book of the Dead*, ed. Evans-Wentz, p. xxxvi.

264 "to it I owe" Ibid., p. 1.

265 "brings down these experiences" Govinda, book review, *Mahabodhi Society Journal* (August 1954), quoted in Winkler, *A Thousand Journeys*, p. 126.

266 "If the European" Jung, "Psychological Commentary," pp. lv–lvi.

268 "when the strong" Hilton, *Lost Horizon*, p. 116.

268 "entered the English language" Allen, *The Search for Shangri-La*, p. 37.

269 "When I was discussing" Lopez, *Prisoners of Shangri-La*, p. 112.

269 "In the 1960s, as a teenager" Chatsumarn Kabilsingh, "Nonviolence and Compassion in Action," in *Science, Spirituality and the Future*, ed. Mehrotra, p. 61.

269 "By that time I started" Ibid.

271 "Suddenly, there was" Rampa, *The Third Eye*, p. 100.

272 "Their opinions were" Frederick Warburg, publisher's foreword to Rampa, *The Third Eye*, p. 8.

272 "It comes near" *Times Literary Supplement*, quoted in Lopez, *Prisoners of Shangri-La*, p. 111.

273 "Flying saucers?" Rampa, *My Visit to Venus*, p. 31.

273 "because poor little cats" Ibid., p. 72. Rampa was devoted to cats; his *Living with the Lama* (1964) was written from the point of view of a feline narrator, Mrs. Fifi Greywhiskers, who conveyed the tale telepathically to Rampa, who served as scribe.

Chapter Ten

274 "One day, a party" Crowley, *Confessions*, p. 180.

274 "regarded the pleasures" Ibid.

275 "If you aspire to lighten" Metteyya, quoted in Harris, *Ananda Metteyya*, p. 34.

275 "It is the Wrong" Ibid., p. 46.

276 "as a Buddhist" Bax, quoted in Harris, *Ananda Metteyya*, p. 2. Harris, a biographer of Bennett/Metteyya, noted Metteyya's later desire to separate his Buddhist present from his magical past, which perhaps seemed to him to titillate what he regarded as the wrong sort of interest: "It is significant that several articles during his [Metteyya's] lifetime took pains to stress that he was not a man of 'mystery,' that he had rejected that part of his past. 'It is necessary to say this, since some attempts have been made to surround him with mystery. There is no more mystery surrounding the Bhikkhu Ananda Metteyya than any other person,' an editorial of 'The Buddhist Review' stated in 1909" (p. 17).

277 "The teaching of the Buddha" Nyanatiloka, "Essence of Buddhism," in *Fundamentals of Buddhism*, p. 8.

277 "What particularly touched me" Khema, *I Give You My Life*, p. 143.

278 "residence of unconditional love" Ibid., p. 205.

279 "dialogue is possible" Balthasar, quoted in Gawronski, *Word and Silence*, p. 220.

279 "natural mysticism" Ibid.

279 "world flight" Ibid., p. 221.

279 "Nothing" Ibid.

279 "We ought also" Toynbee, quoted in O. C. Thomas, *Attitudes Toward Other Religions*, pp. 160–61.

280 "the missionary attack" Tillich, quoted in O. C. Thomas, *Attitudes Toward Other Religions,* p. 179.

280 "In the depth of" Ibid., p. 189.

280 "ransacking the university library" Merton, *The Seven Storey Mountain,* pp. 187–88.

281 "In Christian terms" Merton, "Zen Buddhist Monasticism," in *Mystics and Zen Masters,* p. 228.

281 "I have said that" Merton, "Nhat Hanh Is My Brother," in *The Nonviolent Alternative,* p. 264.

282 "With all of them" Merton, *The School of Charity,* pp. 408–9.

282 "I have seldom met" Ibid., p. 410.

282 "Looking at these" Merton, *The Asian Journal,* pp. 233–35.

283 "He had the complete" Fourteenth Dalai Lama, quoted in Mitchell and Wiseman, *The Gethsemani Encounter,* p. 260. Since the 1996 encounter, continued collaboration between Christian and Buddhist clergy have led to at least two books of note — a dialogue by Asian and Western Buddhists on the monastic Rule of Saint Benedict, and a new translation of the psalms by a Jewish-born American Zen teacher and founder of the Everyday Zen Foundation, who was inspired in his translations by the chanting of the Abbey of Gethsemani monks. See Henry, *Benedict's Dharma,* and Fischer, *Opening to You.*

283 "Buddhism in its" Abbott, *The Documents of Vatican II,* p. 662.

284 "The Church therefore" Ibid., p. 663.

284 "Provided it be" Graham, *Zen Catholicism,* p. 21.

284 "Zen Meditation for Christians" Lassalle, "Zen Meditations for Christians," quoted in Dumoulin, *Zen Buddhism in the 20th Century,* p. 104.

284 "Those of us" Johnston, *The Mysticism of the Cloud of Unknowing,* pp. viii–ix.

285 "I know that I am" Hesse, *Siddhartha,* p. 149.

286 "'Prince of India'" Kazantzakis, *The Last Temptation of Christ,* p. 83.

286 "Could the Indian" Ibid., p. 85.

286 "Only now did I" Kazantzakis, *Report to Greco,* p. 348.

287 "'Come! Come!'" Kazantzakis, *Zorba the Greek,* p. 129.

287 "monasteries are" Nhat Hanh, quoted in Patricia Hunt-Perry and Lyn Fine, "All Buddhism Is Engaged: Thich Nhat Hanh and the Order of Interbeing," in *Engaged Buddhism in the West,* ed. Queen, p. 39. This anthology offers a particularly lucid series of essays on Engaged Buddhist practice.

288 "Our enemy is" Ibid., p. 38.

288 "Sometimes we had" Ibid.

289 "spiritual inspiration" Young, quoted in Hunt-Perry and Fine, "All Buddhism Is Engaged," p. 42.

289 "This gentle Buddhist" King, quoted in Hunt-Perry and Fine, "All Buddhism Is Engaged," p. 42.

289 "is the one" John Paul II, *Crossing the Threshold of Hope,* p. 43.

290 "does not seem" Nhat Hanh, *Living Buddha, Living Christ,* p. 193.

290 "Nearly 10,000 Italian Catholics" *Avvenire,* quoted in Kulananda, *Western Buddhism,* p. 184.

291 "The Buddha comes" Nhat Hanh, *Going Home,* pp. 197–98.

Chapter Eleven

292 "telling you off" Watts, quoted in Furlong, *Zen Effects,* p. 35.

292 "one's own self" Ibid.

293 "believed that witnesses" Horigan, "Christmas Humphreys: A Buddhist Judge in Twentieth-Century London," p. 15. As for Humphreys's temperament once he became an Old Bailey judge in 1968, Horigan noted that Humphreys "found sentencing to be an ordeal because it meant adding to the suffering of the criminal as well as making matters worse for the criminal's family, friends, and others. [. . .] Humphreys' lenient sentences would sometimes stir up prosecutors, but the most trouble came from the press. In June 1975, Humphreys passed a lenient sentence on a young black man who had pleaded guilty to rape. The man was eighteen years old and had actually raped two women at knifepoint. Humphreys sentenced him to a six months' suspended sentence. [. . .] Adding to the public outcry was Humphreys' sentencing a few days later of a man who had cheated his employer of 2,000 pounds. That man was jailed for eighteen months. The whole affair ended six months later when Humphreys was asked to resign. Humphreys' judicial career was thus over in 1976." One might speculate that in these two sentencings, patriarchal biases had as much to do with the outcomes as Buddhist-inspired compassion.

294 "He blazed out" Snyder, quoted in Furlong, Zen Effects, p. 216.

294 "too self-conscious" Watts, "Beat Zen, Square Zen, and Zen," in This Is It and Other Essays, p. 93.

294 "experience of awakening" Ibid., p. 106.

294 "I do not" Ibid., p. 80. This quote comes from a preface Watts appended to the original essay upon its inclusion in This Is It.

294 "synthesis between" Watts, Beyond Theology, p. xi.

295 "There is not" Ibid., p. xii.

295 "superior religion" Ibid., p. 224.

295 "an undeniably mystical" Watts, In My Own Way, pp. 344–47.

296 "having a perfectly" Kerouac, The Dharma Bums, p. 104.

296 "Dad, don't you" Mark Watts, quoted in Furlong, Zen Effects, p. 202.

296 "Yes, but it's" Alan Watts, quoted in Furlong, Zen Effects, p. 202.

297 "In that clear-aired" Suiter, Poets on the Peaks, p. 20.

298 "He must be" Sasaki, quoted ibid., p. 59.

298 "as a sort of sutra" Snyder, Mountains and Rivers Without End, p. 158.

299 "How did I" Snyder, Riprap, and Cold Mountain Poems, p. 42.

299 "an extremely subtle" Snyder, The Real Work, p. 98.

299 "to see the hearth-land" Snyder, Passage Through India, p. 83. A few years later, in Earth House Hold, Snyder assessed the value of LSD use among Americans of the decade and its benefit for Buddhist practice: "Those who do not have the money or time to go to India or Japan, but who think a great deal about the wisdom traditions, have remarkable results when they take LSD. [. . .] In several American cities traditional meditation halls of both Rinzai and Soto Zen are flourishing. Many of the newcomers turned to traditional meditation after initial acid experience. The two types of experience seem to inform each other" (pp. 108–9).

300 "The Dalai Lama is big" Snyder, Passage Through India, p. 83.

300 "Medical anthropologists" Huston Smith, preface to Badiner, Zig Zag Zen, p. 13.

302 "Was as calm" Kerouac, "239th Chorus," Mexico City Blues, p. 241. "Charley" is Kerouac's spelling.

302 "discovery and espousal" Kerouac, Some of the Dharma, p. ix.

302 "I dont really" Ibid., p. 221. "Dont" is Kerouac's spelling.

303 "We know what" Kerouac, The Scripture of the Golden Eternity, pp. 30–31.

303 "Nobody ever said" Snyder to Kerouac, March 10, 1959, quoted ibid., p. 245.

303 "Sexuality, the most" Kerouac, *Some of the Dharma*, p. 198.
304 "Myself, the dharma" Ibid., p. xii.
304 "waking up to" Cage, quoted in Westgeest, *Zen in the Fifties*, p. 47.
305 "Poetry can be" Allen Ginsberg, introduction to Kerouac, *Pomes All Sizes*, pp. ii–iii.
306 "in the wrathful" Trungpa, *Born in Tibet*, pp. 253–55.
306 "During my retreat" Ibid., pp. 253–55.
307 "an open, unguarded" Ibid., p. 253.
307 "a completely marvelous" Merton, *The Asian Journal*, p. 30.
307 "He has the same" Ibid., p. 31.
307 "When plunging completely" Trungpa, *Born in Tibet*, pp. 253–55.
308 "This loving is" Trungpa, "The Perfect Love Poem," in *Mudra*, p. 51.
308 "The time from" Mukpo and Gimian, "My Marriage to Chögyam Trungpa," p. 95.
309 "Suzuki had no relationship" Chadwick, *Crooked Cucumber*, pp. 374–75.
310 "That is why I respect" Shunryu Suzuki, quoted ibid., p. 375.
310 "Ego is able" Trungpa, *Cutting Through Spiritual Materialism*, p. 7.
310 "trying to live up to" Trungpa, *Crazy Wisdom*, p. 9.
310 "trying to live what you are" Ibid.
310 "The process is" Ibid., p. 10.
311 "You must offer" Trungpa, quoted in Clark, *The Great Naropa Poetry Wars*, p. 24.
311 "In the middle" Ginsberg, quoted in Clark, *The Great Naropa Poetry Wars*, p. 25.
312 "As time's gone on" Ginsberg, quoted in Schumacher, *Dharma Lion*, p. 646.
312 "I used to boast" Ibid., p. 649.
312 "founded on the sanity" Trungpa, *Shambhala*, p. 7.
313 "Passion has been" Trungpa, *Great Eastern Sun*, p. 119.
313 "Because we are living" Kongtrul, *The Treasury of Knowledge*, p. 52.
314 "Many Oriental advisors" Chögyam Trungpa, foreword to Tendzin, *Buddha in the Palm of Your Hand*, pp. xii–xiii.
315 "I asked" Fields, *How the Swans Came to the Lake*, p. 365.
315 "Fully aware of" Schumacher, *Dharma Lion*, pp. 550–51.
316 "whereas Trungpa" Simmer-Brown, *Dakini's Warm Breath*, p. xiii.
316 "Tibetan Buddhism" Ibid.
317 "To be part" Butterfield, *The Double Mirror*, p. 100.

Chapter Twelve
320 "The single most" Snyder, *The Real Work*, p. 106.
320 "Siddartha Gautama" Gross, *Buddhism After Patriarchy*, p. 17.
321 "Now you know" Fourteenth Dalai Lama, quoted in Sivaraksa, ed., *Buddhist Perception for Desirable Societies in the Future*, pp. 268–69.
322 "As a Buddhist" Ibid., pp. 270–71.
322 "I took this" Fourteenth Dalai Lama, quoted in John Zurbrzycki, "A Tibetan Tempest over Deity," *Christian Science Monitor*, May 18, 1998.
323 "The title itself" Fourteenth Dalai Lama, "Global View: A Conversation with the Dalai Lama," p. 36.
323 "There are compelling" Fourteenth Dalai Lama, *Ethics for the New Millennium*, p. 228.
323 "I have come" Ibid., p. 19.
324 "not so long ago" Fourteenth Dalai Lama, "The Dalai Lama on China," p. 28.
324 "Personally, I still" Fourteenth Dalai Lama, "The Controversial Dalai Lama," pp. 49–50.
324 "The purpose of" Dalai Lama, foreword to Epstein, *Thoughts Without a Thinker*, p. ix.

325 "To become fully" Fourteenth Dalai Lama, *The Kalachakra Tantra,* p. 163.
325 "What of it?" Blofeld, *The Wheel of Life,* p. 108.
326 "'You see,' the Abbot" Ibid., p. 109.
328 "pile of shit" Baker, quoted in Tworkov, *Zen in America,* p. 242.
328 "The two most" Ibid., p. 239.
329 "The accusation of" Ibid., p. 240.
329 "If I spent" Ibid., p. 236.
330 "inappropriate partner" Ashvaghosha, quoted in Coleman, *The New Buddhism,* p. 165.
331 "At first we'd" Dorsey, quoted in Schneider, *Street Zen,* pp. 128–29.
331 "Tears were" Glassman, quoted in Schneider, *Street Zen,* p. 117. These quotations appeared originally in *Nine-Headed Dragon River: Zen Journals 1969–1982* (1986) by the esteemed American novelist and nature writer Peter Matthiessen (Muryo Sensei), a student of Glassman who became his first Dharma heir.
332 "I couldn't stop" Ibid.
332 "That opening" Ibid.
332 "'Taste as much'" Bernie Glassman, foreword to Maezumi, *Appreciate Your Life,* p. xi.
333 "On the outside" Glassman, quoted in Tworkov, *Zen in America,* p. 122.
333 "If we didn't" Ibid., p. 116.
333 "As peacemakers" Glassman, *Bearing Witness,* p. 88.
333 "I don't know" Glassman, quoted in Christopher Queen, "Glassman Roshi and the Peacemaker Order," in *Engaged Buddhism in the West,* ed. Queen, p. 105.
334 "no one seems" Schumacher, quoted in P. De Silva, *The Search for Buddhist Economics,* p. 1.
335 "has expressed" Coleman, *The New Buddhism,* p. 144.
336 "First and foremost" Batchelor, *Buddhism Without Beliefs,* pp. 17–18.
336 "The Buddha" Ibid., p. 5.
337 "The Tibetan tradition" Batchelor, quoted in Mackenzie, *Why Buddhism?* p. 157.
337 "Shin failed" Amstutz, *Interpreting Amida,* pp. xi–xii.
338 "*Nam* represents" Jane Hurst, "Nichiren Shoshu and Soka Gakkai in America," in *The Faces of Buddhism in America,* ed. Prebis and Tanaka, p. 84.
339 "Racial diversity" David W. Chappell, "Racial Diversity in the Soka Gakkai," in *Engaged Buddhism in the West,* ed. Queen, pp. 206–7.
339 "They discovered" Johnson, *Turning the Wheel,* pp. 53–54.
340 "As a child" Willis, *Dreaming Me,* p. 300.
341 "He was chucking" Cindy Churchward, quoted in Jeanne Malmgren, "Florida Teen Identified as Reincarnated Buddhist Monk," *Minneapolis Star Tribune,* March 4, 2001, p. E9.
342 "They told me" Jack Churchward, quoted in Ibid.

SOURCES CONSULTED

❖

In all cases, the year of publication of the book listed is that of the edition I consulted and therefore not necessarily the year the book was first published. In certain instances, for the sake of clarity, the first publication year is listed as well.

Abbott, Walter M., ed. *The Documents of Vatican II*. New York: American Press, 1966.

Abe, Masao and Norman Waddell, trans. *The Heart of Dogen's Shobogenzo*. Albany: State University of New York Press, 2002.

Abe, Masao. *A Study of Dogen: His Religion and Philosophy*. Edited by Steven Heine. Albany: State University of New York Press, 1992.

———. *Zen and Western Thought*. Honolulu: University of Hawaii Press, 1986.

Abelson, Peter. "Schopenhauer and Buddhism." *Philosophy East and West* 43, no. 2 (April 1993):255–78.

Adams, Henry. *The Education of Henry Adams*. Boston: Houghton Mifflin, 1961.

Ahlstrom, Sydney E. *A Religious History of the American People*. New Haven: Yale University Press, 1974.

Aitken, Robert, and David Steindl-Rast. *The Ground We Share: Everyday Practice, Buddhist and Christian*. Boston: Shambhala, 1996.

Aiton, E. J. *Leibniz: A Biography*. Boston: Adam Hilger, 1985.

Akizuki, Ryomin. *New Mahayana: Buddhism for a Post-Modern World*. Berkeley, CA: Asian Humanities Press, 1990.

Allen, Charles. *The Search for the Buddha: The Men Who Discovered India's Lost Religion*. New York: Carroll & Graf, 2003.

———. *The Search for Shangri-La: A Journey into Tibetan History*. London: Little, Brown, 1999.

Almond, Philip C. *The British Discovery of Buddhism*. Cambridge: Cambridge University Press, 1988.

Amstutz, Galen. *Interpreting Amida: History and Orientalism in the Study of Pure Land Buddhism*. Albany: State University of New York Press, 1997.

Anesaki, Masaharu. *History of Japanese Religion, with Special Reference to the Social and Moral Life of the Nation*. Rutland, VT: Charles E. Tuttle, 1963.

Arberry, A. J. [Arthur John]. *Asiatic Jones: The Life and Influence of Sir William Jones (1746–1794), Pioneer of Indian Studies.* London: Longmans, Green, 1946.

Arnold, Sir Edwin. *The Light of Asia, Being the Life and Teaching of Gotama, Prince of India and Founder of Buddhism.* Chicago: Rand, McNally, 1890.

Arora, U. P., ed. *Graeco-Indica: India's Cultural Contacts with the Greek World.* New Delhi: Ramanand Vidya Bhawan, 1991.

Ascheim, Skip, ed. *Materials for the Open Classroom.* New York: Dell Publishing, 1973.

Avens, Roberts. *Imagination Is Reality: Western Nirvana in Jung, Hillman, Barfield and Cassirer.* Dallas: Spring Publications, 1980.

Badiner, Allan Hunt, ed. *Mindfulness in the Marketplace: Compassionate Responses to Consumerism.* Berkeley, CA: Parallax Press, 2002.

———, ed. *Zig Zag Zen: Buddhism and Psychedelics.* San Francisco: Chronicle Books, 2002.

Bair, Deirdre. *Jung: A Biography.* Boston: Little, Brown, 2003.

Baker, Archibald G., ed. *A Short History of Christianity.* Chicago: University of Chicago Press, 1965.

Bancroft, Anne. *Modern Mystics and Sages.* London: Paladin Books, 1978.

Banerjee, Anukul Chandra. *Sarvastivada Literature.* Calcutta, 1957.

Banerjee, Gauranga Nath. *Hellenism in Ancient India.* 1st rev. ed. New Delhi: Munshiram Manoharlal Publishers, 1981.

Baring-Gould, Sabine. *Curious Myths of the Middle Ages.* Edited by Edward Hardy. New York: Oxford University Press, 1978.

Barr, Pat. *Foreign Devils: Westerners in the Far East, the Sixteenth Century to the Present Day.* Harmondsworth: Penguin Books, 1970.

Batchelor, Stephen. *Alone with Others: An Existential Approach to Buddhism.* New York: Grove Press, 1983.

———. *The Awakening of the West: The Encounter of Buddhism and Western Culture.* Berkeley, CA: Parallax Press, 1994.

———. *Buddhism Without Beliefs: A Contemporary Guide to Awakening.* New York: Riverhead Books, 1997.

Baumer, Christoph. *Southern Silk Road: In the Footsteps of Sir Aurel Stein and Sven Hedin.* Bangkok: Orchid Press, 2000.

Beckwith, Christopher I. *The Tibetan Empire in Central Asia.* Princeton, NJ: Princeton University Press, 1993.

Bell, Sir Charles. *Tibet Past and Present.* London: Oxford University Press, 1927.

Benoit, Hubert. *The Supreme Doctrine: Psychological Studies in Zen Thought.* New York: Pantheon, 1955.

Berry, T. Sterling. *Christianity and Buddhism: a comparison and contrast.* New Delhi: Asian Educational Services, 1997.

Bhandarkar, D. R. *Asoka.* Calcutta: University of Calcutta, 1969.

Bishop, Peter. *The Myth of Shangri-La: Tibet, Travel Writing and the Western Creation of Sacred Landscape.* London: Athlone Press, 1989.

Blavatsky, Helena Petrovna. *Isis Unveiled: A Master-Key to the Mysteries of Ancient and Modern Science and Theology.* 1-vol. ed. Los Angeles: The Theosophy Company, 1982.

———. *The Key to Theosophy; Being a Clear Exposition, in the Form of Question and Answer, of the Ethics, Science, and Philosophy, for the Study of Which the Theosophical Society Has Been Founded.* London: The Theosophical Printing Society, 1893.

———. *The Secret Doctrine: The Synthesis of Science, Religion, and Philosophy.* 3rd rev. ed. 3 vols. London: Theosophical Publishing House, 1921.

————. *The Theosophical Glossary.* Los Angeles: The Theosophy Company, 1973.

————. *The Voice of the Silence and Other Chosen Fragments from the Book of the Golden Precepts, Translated and Annotated by H.P.B.* London: Theosophical Publishing Society, 1903.

Blofeld, John. *Bodhisattva of Compassion: The Mystical Tradition of Kuan Yin.* Boulder, CO: Shambhala, 1978.

————. *The Tantric Mysticism of Tibet.* New York: E. P. Dutton, 1970.

————. *The Wheel of Life: The Autobiography of a Western Buddhist.* Berkeley, CA: Shambala [later Shambhala], 1972.

Boldt, Laurence G. *Zen and the Art of Making a Living.* New York: Penguin Arkana, 1993.

Borg, Marcus, ed. *Jesus and Buddha: The Parallel Sayings.* Berkeley, CA: Ulysses Press, 1997.

Boucher, Sandy. *Turning the Wheel: American Women Creating the New Buddhism.* Boston: Beacon Press, 1993.

Boxer, C. R. *The Christian Century in Japan, 1549–1650.* Berkeley: University of California Press, 1951.

Branham, R. Bracht, and Marie-Odile Goulet-Caze, eds. *The Cynics: The Cynic Movement in Antiquity and Its Legacy.* Berkeley: University of California Press, 1996.

Broughton, Jeffrey L. *The Bodhidharma Anthology: The Earliest Records of Zen.* Berkeley: University of California Press, 1999.

Brown, Leslie. *The Indian Christians of St. Thomas: An Account of the Ancient Syrian Church of Malabar.* Rev. ed. Cambridge: Cambridge University Press, 1982.

Bucke, Richard Maurice. *Cosmic Consciousness: A Study in the Evolution of the Human Mind.* New York: Causeway Books, 1974.

Budge, E. A. Wallis. *The Monks of Kublai Khan, Emperor of China.* London: Religious Tract Society, 1928.

Bullis, Douglas, trans. *The Mahavamsa: The Great Chronicle of Sri Lanka Originally Written by Thera Mahanama-sthavira, 5th Century ACE.* Fremont, CA: Asian Humanities Press, 1999.

Burnouf, Eugène. *Legends of Indian Buddhism: Translated from "Introduction à l'Histoire du Bud-dhisme indien" of Eugène Burnouf.* Translated by Winifred Stephens. London: John Murray, 1911.

————, trans. *Le Lotus de la Bonne Loi.* 2 vols. Paris: Librairie Orientale et Américaine, 1925.

Burton, Richard [Haji Abdu el-Yezdi, pseud.]. *The Kasidah of Haji Abdu el-Yezdi.* Drexel Hill, PA: Bell Publishing, 1931.

Butterfield, Herbert. *Christianity and History.* London: Fontana Books, 1960.

Butterfield, Stephen T. *The Double Mirror: A Skeptical Journey into Buddhist Tantra.* Berkeley, CA: North Atlantic Books, 1994.

Cabezon, José Ignacio, ed. *Buddhism, Sexuality, and Gender.* Albany: State University of New York Press, 1992.

Caird, Edward. *The Evolution of Religion.* 2 vols. Glasgow: James MacLehose and Sons, 1899.

Cameron, Nigel. *Barbarians and Mandarins: Thirteen Centuries of Western Travellers in China.* 1970. Reprint, Hong Kong: Oxford University Press, 1997.

Candler, Edmund. *The Unveiling of Lhasa.* London: Edward Arnold, 1905.

Caraman, Philip. *Tibet: The Jesuit Century.* Saint Louis: Institute of Jesuit Sources, 1997.

Carpini, Giovanni di Plano [John of Plano Carpini]. *The Story of the Mongols Whom We Call the Tartars: Friar Giovanni di Plano Carpini's Account of His Embassy to the Court of the Mongol Khan.* Translated by Erik Hildinger. Boston: Branden Publishing, 1996.

Carus, Paul. *Buddhism and Its Christian Critics.* Chicago: Open Court, 1903.

————. *The Gospel of Buddha.* Chicago: Open Court, 1915.

Cashen, Richard Anthony. *Solitude in the Thought of Thomas Merton.* Kalamazoo, MI: Cistercian Publications, 1981.

Cassady, Neal. *Grace Beats Karma: Letters from Prison, 1958–60.* New York: Blast Books, 1993.

Cassirer, Ernst. *The Philosophy of the Enlightenment.* Boston: Beacon Press, 1960.

Chadwick, David. *Crooked Cucumber: The Life and Zen Teaching of Shunryu Suzuki.* New York: Broadway Books, 1999.

———. *Thank You and OK! An American Zen Failure in Japan.* New York: Penguin Arkana, 1994.

Chadwick, Henry. *Early Christian Thought and the Classical Tradition: Studies in Justin, Clement and Origen.* New York: Oxford University Press, 1966.

Chalmers, Robert. "The Parables of Barlaam and Joasaph." *Journal of the Royal Asiatic Society of Great Britain and Ireland* (1891):423–49.

Chandrakirti. *Introduction to the Middle Way: Chandrakirti's Madhyamakavatara.* Translated by Padmakara Translation Group. Boston: Shambhala, 2002.

Chatterji, Suniti Kumar. "Sir William Jones: 1746–1794." In *Sir William Jones, Bicentenary of His Birth: Commemoration Volume, 1746–1946.* Calcutta: Royal Asiatic Society of Bengal, 1948. Anonymously edited anthology of pieces, by an international range of writers, on Jones and India.

Chesterton, G. K. [Gilbert Keith]. *Orthodoxy.* New York: John Lane, 1909.

Clark, Tom. *The Great Narapa Poetry Wars.* Santa Barbara: Cadmus Editions, 1980.

Clarke, James Freeman. *Ten Great Religions: An Essay in Comparative Theology.* 2 vols. Boston: Houghton Mifflin, 1871, 1883.

Clarke, J. J. [John James]. *Oriental Enlightenment: The Encounter Between Asian and Western Thought.* London: Routledge, 1997.

Cleary, Thomas, ed. and trans. *Rational Zen: The Mind of Dogen Zenji.* Boston: Shambhala, 1993.

Clement of Alexandria. *The Writings of Clement of Alexandria.* Translated by Rev. William Wilson. 2 vols. Edinburgh: T. and T. Clark, 1868, 1869.

Cogan, Henry, trans. *The Voyages and Adventures of Ferdinand Mendez Pinto, the Portuguese.* London: T. Fisher Unwin, 1907.

Coleman, James William. *The New Buddhism: The Western Transformation of an Ancient Tradition.* New York: Oxford University Press, 2001.

Collins, Jeff. *Heidegger and the Nazis.* New York: Totem Books, 2000.

Collins, Steven. *Nirvana and Other Buddhist Felicities: Utopias of the Pali Imaginaire.* Cambridge: Cambridge University Press, 1998.

Collis, Maurice. *The Grand Peregrination: Being the Life and Adventures of Fernão Mendes Pinto.* London: Faber and Faber, 1951.

Conze, Edward. *Buddhist Thought in India.* Ann Arbor: University of Michigan Press, 1973.

———. *Further Buddhist Studies: Selected Essays.* Oxford: Bruno Cassirer, 1975.

Coomaraswamy, Ananda K. [Kentish]. *The Arts and Crafts of India and Ceylon.* New York: Noonday Press, 1964.

———. *Buddha and the Gospel of Buddhism.* New Hyde Park, NY: University Books, 1969.

———. *The Dance of Shiva: Fourteen Indian Essays.* New York: Noonday Press, 1957.

———. *Hinduism and Buddhism.* New York: Philosophical Library, n.d.

———. *Time and Eternity.* Berne: Artibus Asiae, 1947.

Cooper, Michael. *Rodrigues the Interpreter: An Early Jesuit in Japan and China.* 1974. Reprint, New York: Weatherhill, 1994.

Correia-Afonso, John. *The Ignatian Vision of India: A Historical Study.* Anand, India: Gujarat Sahitya Prakash, 1991.

Couliano, Ioan P. *The Tree of Gnosis: Gnostic Mythology from Early Christianity to Modern Nihilism.* New York: HarperCollins, 1992.

Covell, Ralph. *W. A. P. Martin: Pioneer of Progress in China.* Washington, DC: Christian University Press, 1978.

Craig, Mary. *Kundun: A Biography of the Family of the Dalai Lama.* Washington, DC: Counterpoint, 1997.

Cranston, Sylvia. *HPB: The Extraordinary Life and Influence of Helena Blavatsky, Founder of the Modern Theosophical Movement.* New York: G. P. Putnam's Sons, 1993.

Cronin, Vincent. *The Wise Man from the West.* 1955. Reprint, London: Harvill Press, 1999.

Crowley, Aleister. *The Confessions of Aleister Crowley.* Edited by John Symonds and Kenneth Grant. New York: Hill and Wang, 1969.

———. *Eight Lectures on Yoga.* New York: 93 Publishing, 1991.

———. "Science and Buddhism." In *The Works of Aleister Crowley.* Vol. 2. Foyers, UK: Society for the Propagation of Religious Truth, 1906.

Curuvila, Vadakekara George. *Apostolate and Martyrdom of St. Thomas.* Bombay: Society of St. Paul, 1969.

David-Neel, Alexandra. *Buddhism: Its Doctrines and Methods.* New York: Avon Books, 1979.

———. *Immortality and Reincarnation.* Rochester, VT: Inner Traditions, 1997.

———. *Initiations and Initiates in Tibet.* New York: University Books, 1959.

———. *Magic and Mystery in Tibet.* Baltimore: Penguin Books, 1971.

———. *My Journey to Lhasa.* Boston: Beacon Press, 1986.

David-Neel, Alexandra, with Lama Yongden. *The Power of Nothingness.* Boston: Houghton Mifflin, 1982.

———. *The Superhuman Life of Gesar of Ling.* Boston: Shambhala, 1987.

Davidson, Ronald M. *Indian Esoteric Buddhism: A Social History of the Tantric Movement.* New York: Columbia University Press, 2002.

Dawson, Christopher, ed. *Mission to Asia: Narratives and Letters of the Franciscan Missionaries in Mongolia and China in the Thirteenth and Fourteenth Centuries.* New York: Harper and Row, 1966.

Dawson, Raymond, ed. *The Legacy of China.* Oxford: Oxford University Press, 1971.

D'Cruz, F. A. *St. Thomas, the Apostle, in India.* Madras, India: Hoe, 1922.

De Korne, John C. *Chinese Altars to the Unknown God: An Account of the Religions of China and the Reactions to Them of Christian Missions.* Grand Rapids, MI: Smitter Book, 1926.

Demieville, Paul. "The First Philosophic Contacts Between Europe and China." *Diogenes* 58 (1967):91–93.

De Nicholas, Antonio T. *Powers of Imagining, Ignatius de Loyola: A Philosophical Hermeneutic of Imagining Through the Collected Works of Ignatius de Loyola, with a Translation of These Works.* Albany: State University of New York Press, 1986.

Desideri, Ippolito. *An Account of Tibet: The Travels of Ippolito Desideri of Pistoia, S.J., 1712–1727.* Edited by Filippo De Filippi. Rev. ed. London: George Routledge and Sons, 1937.

De Silva, Lynn A. *The Problem of the Self in Buddhism and Christianity.* New York: Harper and Row, 1979.

De Silva, Padmasiri. *Buddhist and Freudian Psychology.* Colombo, Sri Lanka: Lake House Investments, 1978.

———. *The Search for Buddhist Economics.* Kandy, Sri Lanka: Buddhist Publication Society, 1975.

Deveney, John Patrick. *Paschal Beverly Randolph: A Nineteenth-Century Black American Spiritualist, Rosicrucian, and Sex Magician.* Albany: State University of New York Press, 1997.

Dhamma, Dr. Rewata. *The First Discourse of the Buddha.* Boston: Wisdom Publications, 1997.

Dharmapal, Mahathera, ed. *Asoka 2300.* Calcutta: Bauddha Dharmankur Sabha, 1997.

Dharmasiri, Gunapala. *A Buddhist Critique of the Christian Concept of God.* Antioch, CA: Golden Leaves Publishing, 1988.

Dobbins, Frank S. *Story of the World's Worship: A Complete, Graphic and Comparative History of the Many Strange Beliefs, Superstitious Practices, Domestic Peculiarities, Sacred Writings, Systems of Philosophy, Legends and Traditions, Customs and Habits of Mankind Throughout the World, Ancient and Modern.* Chicago: Dominion, 1901.

Don Peter, W. L. A. *Francis Xavier, Teacher of Nations: The Educational Aspects of the Missionary Career of St. Francis Xavier.* Colombo, Sri Lanka: 1987.

Dorge, Rig'dzin. *Dangerous Friend: The Teacher-Student Relationship in Vajrayana Buddhism.* Boston: Shambhala, 2001.

Dow, Michael, and Elizabeth Cook, eds. *Annals of the Nyingma Lineage in America. Vol. 3, 1969–1985.* Berkeley, CA: Dharma Publishing, 1985.

Downing, Michael. *Shoes Outside the Door: Desire, Devotion, and Excess at San Francisco Zen Center.* Washington, DC: Counterpoint, 2001.

Dresser, Marianne, ed. *Buddhist Women on the Edge: Contemporary Perspectives from the Western Frontier.* Berkeley, CA: North Atlantic Books, 1996.

Droit, Roger-Pol. *The Cult of Nothingness: The Philosophers and the Buddha.* Chapel Hill: University of North Carolina Press, 2003.

Dumoulin, Heinrich. *A History of Zen Buddhism.* New York: McGraw-Hill, 1965.

———. *Zen Buddhism in the 20th Century.* New York: Weatherhill, 1995.

Durckheim, Karlfried Graf. *Zen and Us.* New York: E. P. Dutton, 1987.

Dutt, Nalinaksha. *Mahayana Buddhism.* Calcutta: Firma K. L. Mukhopadhyay, 1973.

Dwyer, Simon, ed. *Rapid Eye 2.* London: Creation Books, 1995.

Edgar, John Ware. *Report on a Visit to Sikhim and the Thibetan Frontier.* 1874. Reprint, New Delhi: Manjusri Publishing House, 1969.

Eliade, Mircea. *A History of Religious Ideas.* 3 vols. Chicago: University of Chicago Press, 1978, 1982, 1985.

———. *Yoga: Immortality and Freedom.* 2nd ed. Princeton, NJ: Princeton University Press, 1969.

Elison, George. *Deus Destroyed: The Image of Christianity in Early Modern Japan.* Cambridge, MA: Harvard University Press, 1988.

Emerson, Ralph Waldo. *The Complete Essays and Other Writings.* Edited by Brooks Atkinson. New York: Random House, 1950.

Epstein, Mark. *Thoughts Without a Thinker: Psychotherapy from a Buddhist Perspective.* New York: Basic Books, 1995.

Eusebius. *The History of the Church from Christ to Constantine.* Harmondsworth: Penguin Books, 1983.

Evans-Wentz, W. Y. *The Fairy-Faith in Celtic Countries.* New York: Citadel Press, 1990.

———, comp. and ed. *The Tibetan Book of the Dead; or, The After-Death Experiences on the Bardo Plane, According to Lama Kazi Dawa-Samdup's English Rendering.* 3rd. ed. 1927. Reprint, London: Oxford University Press, 1960.

———, comp. and ed. *The Tibetan Book of the Great Liberation; or, The Method of Realizing Nirvana Through Knowing the Mind, According to English Renderings by Sardar Bahadur S. W. Laden*

Lam and by the Lamas Karma Sumdhon Paul Lobzang Mingyur Dorje, and Kazi Dawa-Samdup. 1954. Reprint, London: Oxford University Press, 1971.

———, comp. and ed. *Tibetan Yoga and Secret Doctrines; or, Seven Books of Wisdom of the Great Path, According to the Late Lama Kazi Dawa-Samdup's English Rendering.* 2nd ed. 1935. Reprint, London: Oxford University Press, 1969.

Evola, Julius. *The Doctrine of Awakening.* Rochester, VT: Inner Traditions, 1996.

Faure, Bernard. *Chan Insights and Oversights: An Epistemological Critique of the Chan Tradition.* Princeton, NJ: Princeton University Press, 1993.

———. *The Red Thread: Buddhist Approaches to Sexuality.* Princeton, NJ: Princeton University Press, 1998.

———. *The Rhetoric of Immediacy: A Cultural Critique of Chan/Zen Buddhism.* Princeton, NJ: Princeton University Press, 1994.

Fenollosa, Ernest. *The Chinese Written Character as a Medium for Poetry.* Edited by Ezra Pound. San Francisco: City Lights, 1969.

Fields, Rick. *How the Swans Came to the Lake: A Narrative History of Buddhism in America.* 3rd ed. Boston: Shambhala, 1992.

———, ed. *Loka 2: A Journal from Naropa Institute.* New York: Doubleday, Anchor, 1976.

Figueira, Dorothy Matilda. *Translating the Orient: The Reception of Sakuntala in Nineteenth-Century Europe.* Albany: State University of New York Press, 1991.

Filoramo, Giovanni. *A History of Gnosticism.* Oxford: Blackwell, 1992.

Findlay, J. N. [John Niemeyer]. *Hegel: A Re-Examination.* New York: Collier Books, 1962.

Findly, Ellison Banks, ed. *Women's Buddhism, Buddhism's Women: Tradition, Revision, Renewal.* Boston: Wisdom Publications, 2000.

Fischer, Norman. *Opening to You: Zen-Inspired Translations of the Psalms.* New York: Viking Compass, 2002.

Foltz, Richard C. *Religions of the Silk Road: Overland Trade and Cultural Exchange from Antiquity to the Fifteenth Century.* New York: St. Martin's Griffin, 1999.

Foster, Barbara M., and Michael Foster. *Forbidden Journey: The Life of Alexandra David-Neel.* San Francisco: Harper and Row, 1987.

———. *The Secret Lives of Alexandra David-Neel: A Biography of the Explorer of Tibet and Its Forbidden Practices.* Woodstock, NY: Overlook Press, 1998.

Fowden, Garth. *Empire to Commonwealth: Consequences of Monotheism in Late Antiquity.* Princeton, NJ: Princeton University Press, 1993.

Franke, Wolfgang. *China and the West.* New York: Harper and Row, 1967.

Fremantle, Francesca. *Luminous Emptiness: Understanding the Tibetan Book of the Dead.* Boston: Shambhala, 2001.

Freud, Sigmund. *Beyond the Pleasure Principle.* New York: W. W. Norton, 1961.

Friedman, Lenore. *Meetings with Remarkable Women: Buddhist Teachers in America.* Boston: Shambhala, 2000.

Frothingham, Octavius Brooks. *Transcendentalism in New England: A History.* New York: Harper and Brothers, 1959.

Frye, Richard N. *The Heritage of Central Asia: From Antiquity to the Turkish Expansion.* Princeton, NJ: Markus Wiener Publishers, 1998.

Fulop-Miller, Rene. *The Power and Secret of the Jesuits.* New York: Viking Press, 1930.

Furlong, Monica. *Zen Effects: The Life of Alan Watts.* Boston: Houghton Mifflin, 1986.

Gallagher, Louis J., trans. *China in the Sixteenth Century: The Journals of Matthew Ricci, 1583–1610.* New York: Random House, 1953.

Gamage, Chamindaji. *Buddhism and Sensuality as Recorded in the Theravada Canon*. Colombo, Sri Lanka: Karunaratne and Sons, 1998.

Gawronski, Raymond. *Word and Silence: Hans Urs von Balthasar and the Spiritual Encounter Between East and West*. Grand Rapids, MI: Eerdmans Publishing, 1995.

Gay, Peter. *The Enlightenment: An Interpretation: The Rise of Modern Paganism*. New York: Vintage Books, 1968.

Gellner, David N. *The Anthropology of Buddhism and Hinduism: Weberian Themes*. New Delhi: Oxford University Press, 2001.

Getty, Alice. *The Gods of Northern Buddhism: Their History and Iconography*. New York: Dover Books, 1988.

Gielen, Martin. *St. Thomas: The Apostle of India*. Kottayam, India: Oriental Institute of Religious Studies, 1990.

Gih, Andrew. *Into God's Family*. London: Marshall, Morgan and Scott, 1955.

Gillman, Ian, and Hans-Joachim Klimkeit. *Christians in Asia Before 1500*. Ann Arbor: University of Michigan Press, 1999.

Ginsberg, Allen. *Deliberate Prose: Selected Essays, 1952–1995*. Edited by Bill Morgan. New York: HarperCollins, 2000.

———. *Indian Journals*. San Francisco: Dave Haselwood and City Lights, 1970.

———. *Spontaneous Mind: Selected Interviews, 1958–1996*. Edited by David Carter. New York: HarperCollins, 2001.

Glassman, Bernie [Bernard]. *Bearing Witness: A Zen Master's Lessons in Making Peace*. New York: Bell Tower, 1998.

Glassman, Bernie, with Rick Fields. *Instructions to the Cook: A Zen Master's Lessons in Living a Life That Matters*. New York: Bell Tower, 1996.

Godbey, Rev. J. E., and A. H. Godbey. *Light in Darkness; or, Missions and Missionary Heroes. An Illustrated History of the Missionary Work Now Carried On by All Protestant Denominations in Heathen Lands*. St. Louis: Vandawalker, 1893.

Goddard, Dwight, ed. *A Buddhist Bible*. Boston: Beacon Press, 1970.

Godwin, Joscelyn. *Athanasius Kircher: A Renaissance Man and the Quest for Lost Knowledge*. New York: Thames and Hudson, 1979.

———. *Mystery Religions in the Ancient World*. New York: Harper and Row, 1981.

———. *The Theosophical Enlightenment*. Albany: State University of New York Press, 1994.

Goettmann, Alphonse. *Dialogue on the Path of Initiation: An Introduction to the Life and Thought of Karlfried Graf Durckheim*. New York: Globe Press Books, 1991.

Gokhale, B. G. *Buddhism and Asoka*. Baroda, India: Padmaja Publications, 1948.

Goldstein, Melvyn C., and Matthew T. Kapstein, eds. *Buddhism in Contemporary Tibet: Religious Revival and Cultural Identity*. Berkeley: University of California Press, 1998.

Gomperz, Theodor. *The Greek Thinkers: A History of Ancient Philosophy*. 4 vols. London: John Murray, 1949.

Goodman, Michael Harris. *The Last Dalai Lama: A Biography*. Boston: Shambhala, 1987.

Goody, Jack. *The East in the West*. Cambridge: Cambridge University Press, 1996.

Govinda, Lama Anagarika. *Foundations of Tibetan Mysticism*. New York: Weiser, 1975.

———. *The Way of the White Clouds*. London: Hutchinson, 1969.

Graham, Dom Aelred. *Zen Catholicism*. New York: Harcourt, Brace and World, 1963.

Grant, G. M. *The Religions of the World*. New York: Anson D. F. Randolph, 1895.

Grimm, George. *The Doctrine of the Buddha: The Religion of Reason and Meditation*. Delhi: Motilal Banarsidass, 1965.

Gross, Rita M. *Buddhism After Patriarchy: A Feminist History, Analysis, and Reconstruction of Buddhism.* Albany: State University of New York Press, 1993.

———. *Soaring and Settling: Buddhist Perspectives on Contemporary Social and Religious Issues.* New York: Continuum, 1998.

Guignon, Charles, ed. *The Cambridge Companion to Heidegger.* Cambridge: Cambridge University Press, 1999.

Halbfass, Wilhelm. *India and Europe: An Essay in Understanding.* Albany: State University of New York Press, 1988.

Halifax, Joan. *A Buddhist Life in America: Simplicity in the Complex.* New York: Paulist Press, 1998.

Hamilton, Craig. "An Interview with Miranda Shaw." *What Is Enlightenment?* (Spring/Summer 1998).

Harney, Martin P. *The Jesuits in History: The Society of Jesus Through Four Centuries.* New York: American Press, 1941.

Harrer, Heinrich. *Seven Years in Tibet.* New York: Tarcher/Putnam, 1996.

Harris, Elizabeth J. *Ananda Metteyya: The First Buddhist Emissary of Buddhism.* Kandy, Sri Lanka: Buddhist Publication Society, 1998.

Harvey, Sir Paul, ed. *The Oxford Companion to Classical Literature.* London: Oxford University Press, 1969.

Hasegawa, Nyokzekan. *Japanese National Character.* Japan: Board of Tourist Industry, Japanese Government Railway, 1942.

Head, Joseph, and S. L. Cranston. *Reincarnation: The Phoenix Fire Mystery.* New York: Julian Press/Crown Publishers, 1977.

Hearn, Lafcadio. *The Buddhist Writings of Lafcadio Hearn.* Santa Barbara, CA: Ross-Erikson, 1977.

———. *Gleanings in Buddha-Fields: Studies of Hand and Soul in the Far East.* Rutland, VT: Charles E. Tuttle, 1987.

———. *Kokoro: Hints and Echoes of Japanese Inner Life.* Rutland, VT: Charles E. Tuttle, 1989.

Hegel, Georg Wilhelm Friedrich. *Hegel's Lectures on the Philosophy of History.* Translated by E. S. Haldane and Francis H. Simson. 3 vols. New York: Humanities Press, 1974.

———. *Lectures on the Philosophy of Religion: The Lectures of 1827.* Edited by Peter C. Hodgson. Berkeley: University of California Press, 1988.

Heidegger, Martin. *Being and Time.* Translated by John Macquarrie and Edward Robinson. New York: Harper and Row, 1962.

Heisig, James W., and John C. Maraldo, eds. *Rude Awakenings: Zen, the Kyoto School, and the Question of Nationalism.* Honolulu: University of Hawaii Press, 1995.

Hemacandra. *The Lives of the Jain Elders.* Translated by R. C. C. Fynes. Oxford: Oxford University Press, 1998.

Henderson, Harold. *Catalyst for Controversy: Paul Carus of Open Court.* Carbondale: Southern Illinois University Press, 1993.

Henry, Patrick, ed. *Benedict's Dharma: Buddhists Reflect on the Rule of St. Benedict.* New York: Riverhead Books, 2001.

Herrigel, Eugen. *The Method of Zen.* New York: Vintage Books, 1974.

———. *Zen in the Art of Archery.* New York: Vintage Books, 1989.

Hesse, Hermann. *The Journey to the East.* New York: Noonday Press, 1965.

———. *Siddhartha.* New York: New Directions, 1957.

Hilton, James. *Lost Horizon.* New York: Pocket Books, 1967.

Hirakawa, Sukehiro, ed. *Rediscovering Lafcadio Hearn: Japanese Legends, Life and Culture.* Folkestone, Eng.: Global Oriental, 1997.

Hirota, Dennis, ed. *Toward a Contemporary Understanding of Pure Land Buddhism: Creating a Shin Buddhist Theology in a Religiously Plural World.* Albany: State University of New York Press, 2000.

Hisamatsu, Shin'ichi. *Zen and the Fine Arts.* Palo Alto, CA: Kodansha International, 1971.

Hofstadter, Richard. *Anti-Intellectualism in American Life.* New York: Vintage Books, 1963.

Holmes, Burton. *Burton Holmes Travelogues: Down the Amur, Peking, the Forbidden City.* Vol. 9. Chicago: Travelogue Bureau, 1914.

Hopkirk, Peter. *Foreign Devils on the Silk Road.* Amherst: University of Massachusetts Press, 1984.

———. *The Great Game: The Struggle for Empire in Central Asia.* New York: Kodansha, 1994.

———. *Trespassers on the Roof of the World: The Secret Exploration of Tibet.* New York: Kodansha, 1995.

Horigan, Damien P. "Christmas Humphreys: A Buddhist Judge in Twentieth-Century London." *Korean Journal of Comparative Law* 24 (1996):1–16.

Hornblower, Simon, and Antony Spawforth, eds. *The Oxford Classical Dictionary,* 3rd ed. New York: Oxford University Press, 1996.

Huai-Chin, Nan. *The Story of Chinese Zen.* Translated by Thomas Cleary. Rutland, VT: Charles E. Tuttle, 1995.

Huc, M. L'Abbé. *Christianity in China, Tartary and Thibet.* 2 vols. New York: D. and J. Sadlier, 1873.

Hudson, G. F. *Europe and China: A Survey of Their Relations from the Earliest Times to 1800.* 1931. Reprint, Boston: Beacon Press, 1961.

Hume, David. *Dialogues Concerning Natural Religion.* New York: Hafner Publishing, 1960.

———. *Enquiries Concerning Human Understanding and Concerning the Principles of Morals.* Oxford: Oxford University Press, 2000.

———. *The Natural History of Religion.* Palo Alto, CA: Stanford University Press, 1972.

Hu Shih. "Ch'an (Zen) Buddhism in China: Its History and Method." *Philosophy East and West* 3, no. 1 (1953):3–24.

Hutchison, William R. *Errand to the World: American Protestant Thought and Foreign Missions.* Chicago: University of Chicago Press, 1987.

Ikeda, Daisaku. *Soka Education: A Buddhist Vision for Teachers, Students and Parents.* Santa Monica, CA: Middleway Press, 2001.

Ikeda, Daisaku, and Josef Derbolav. *Search for a New Humanity.* New York: Weatherhill, 1992.

Inge, William Ralph. *The Philosophy of Plotinus.* 2 vols. New York: Longmans, Green, 1929.

Isshu, Miura, and Ruth Fuller Sasaki. *The Zen Koan.* New York: Harcourt, Brace and World, 1965.

Jacobson, Nolan Pliny. "The Possibility of Oriental Influence in Hume's Philosophy." *Philosophy East and West* 19, no. 1 (1969):7–37.

James, William. *The Varieties of Religious Experience.* New York: Collier Books, 1970.

Janaway, Christopher, ed. *The Cambridge Companion to Schopenhauer.* Cambridge: Cambridge University Press, 1999.

Jansen, Marius B., ed. *The Emergence of Meiji Japan.* Cambridge: Cambridge University Press, 1995.

John Paul II. *Crossing the Threshold of Hope.* New York: Knopf, 1995.

Johnson, Charles. *Turning the Wheel: Essays on Buddhism and Writing.* New York: Scribner, 2003.

Johnson, K. Paul. *Initiates of Theosophical Masters.* Albany: State University of New York Press, 1995.

———. *The Masters Revealed: Madame Blavatsky and the Myth of the Great White Lodge.* Albany: State University of New York Press, 1994.

Johnston, William. *Christian Zen: A Way of Meditation.* New York: Harper and Row, 1979.

———, ed. *The Cloud of Unknowing and the Book of Privy Counselling.* New York: Doubleday Image, 1973.

———. *The Mysticism of the Cloud of Unknowing.* New York: Fordham University Press, 2000.

———. *The Still Point: Reflections on Zen and Christian Mysticism.* New York: Fordham University Press, 1970.

Jones, Ken. *The Social Face of Buddhism: An Approach to Political and Social Activism.* London: Wisdom Publications, 1989.

Jung, Carl Gustav. *Collected Works.* Vol. 11, *Psychology and Religion: West and East.* New York: Pantheon, 1963.

———. *Nietzsche's Zarathustra: Notes of the Seminar Given in 1934–1939.* Edited by James L. Jarrett. 2 vols. Princeton, NJ: Princeton University Press, 1988.

Kabat-Zinn, Jon. *Full Catastrophe Living: Using the Wisdom of Your Body and Mind to Face Stress, Pain, and Illness.* New York: Delta, 1991.

Kalu Rinpoche. *The Dharma That Illuminates All Beings Like the Light of the Sun and the Moon.* Albany: State University of New York Press, 1986.

———. *Secret Buddhism: Vajrayana Practices.* San Francisco: Clear Point Press, 1995.

Kamenetz, Rodger. *The Jew in the Lotus: A Poet's Rediscovery of Jewish Identity in Buddhist India.* New York: HarperCollins, 1995.

Kant, Immanuel. *Religion Within the Limits of Reason Alone.* Translated by Theodore M. Greene and Hoyt H. Hudson. Chicago: Open Court, 1934.

Kapleau, Philip. *The Three Pillars of Zen: Teaching, Practice, and Enlightenment.* Tokyo: Weatherhill, 1970.

Karunaratne, W. S. *The Theory of Causality in Early Buddhism.* Nugegoda, Sri Lanka: Indumati Karunaratne, 1988.

Kazantzakis, Nikos. *Buddha.* San Diego: Avant Books, 1983.

———. *Japan China: A Journal of Two Voyages to the Far East, 1935 and 1957.* New York: Simon and Schuster, 1963.

———. *The Last Temptation of Christ.* New York: Bantam Books, 1971.

———. *Report to Greco.* New York: Simon and Schuster, 1965.

———. *The Saviors of God: Spiritual Exercises.* New York: Simon and Schuster, 1960.

———. *Zorba the Greek.* New York: Ballantine, 1965.

Keene, Donald. *The Japanese Discovery of Europe, 1720–1830.* Palo Alto, CA: Stanford University Press, 1969.

Kennedy, J. "Buddhist Gnosticism, the System of Basilides." *Journal of the Royal Asiatic Society of Great Britain and Ireland* (1902):377–415.

Kennedy, Robert E. *Zen Spirit, Christian Spirit: The Place of Zen in Christian Life.* New York: Continuum, 1995.

Kent, Stephen A. "Valentinian Gnosticism and Classical Samkhya: A Thematic and Structural Comparison." *Philosophy East and West,* 30, no. 2 (1980):241–59.

Kerouac, Jack. *Book of Haikus.* Edited by Regina Weinrich. New York: Penguin, 2003.

———. *The Dharma Bums.* New York: Viking Press, 1958.

———. *Heaven and Other Poems.* Bolinas, CA: Grey Fox Press, 1977.

————. *Mexico City Blues.* New York: Grove Press, 1959.

————. *Old Angel Midnight.* San Francisco: Grey Fox Press, 1993.

————. *Pomes All Sizes.* San Francisco: City Lights, 1992.

————. *The Scripture of the Golden Eternity.* New York: Corinth Books, 1970.

————. *Selected Letters, 1940–1956.* Edited by Ann Charters. New York: Viking, 1995.

————. *Selected Letters, 1957–1969.* Edited by Ann Charters. New York: Viking, 1999.

————. *Some of the Dharma.* New York: Viking, 1997.

Khema, Ayya. *I Give You My Life: The Autobiography of a Western Buddhist Nun.* Boston: Shambhala, 1998.

Kimura, Ryukan. *A Historical Study of the Terms Hinayana and Mahayana and the Origin of Mahayana Buddhism.* Patna, India: Indological Book, 1978.

King, Richard. *Orientalism and Religion: Postcolonial Theory, India and "The Mystic East."* London: Routledge, 1999.

King, Robert H. *Thomas Merton and Thich Nhat Hanh: Engaged Spirituality in an Age of Globalization.* New York: Continuum, 2001.

King, Winston L. *Zen and the Way of the Sword: Arming the Samurai Psyche.* New York: Oxford University Press, 1993.

Kinsley, David. *The Goddesses' Mirror: Visions of the Divine from East and West.* Albany: State University of New York Press, 1989.

Kipling, Rudyard. *Kim.* New York: Bantam Books, 1983.

Kiriyama, Seiyu. *21st Century: The Age of Sophia: The Wisdom of Greek Philosophy and the Wisdom of the Buddha.* Tokyo: Hirakawa Shuppan, 2000.

Kirk, Kenneth E. *The Vision of God: The Christian Doctrine of the Summum Bonum.* 1931. Reprint, New York: Harper and Row, 1966.

Kitigawa, Joseph M. *On Understanding Japanese Religion.* Princeton, NJ: Princeton University Press, 1987.

Kitagawa, Joseph M., and Mark D. Cummings, eds. *Buddhism and Asian History.* New York: Macmillan, 1989.

Klimkeit, Hans-Joachim, trans. and ed. *Gnosis on the Silk Road: Gnostic Texts from Central Asia.* New York: HarperCollins, 1993.

Knox, Robert. *An Historical Relation of Ceylon Together with Somewhat Concerning Severall Remarkeable Passages of My Life That Have Hapnd Since My Deliverance Out of My Captivity.* Glasgow: James MacLehose and Sons, 1911.

————. *Robert Knox in the Kandyan Kingdom.* Edited by E. F. C. Ludowyk. London: Oxford University Press, 1948.

Kongtrul, Jamgon. *The Torch of Certainty.* Translated by Judith Hanson. Boston: Shambhala, 1986.

————. *The Treasury of Knowledge. Book Five, Buddhist Ethics.* Translated by Kalu Rinpoche Translation Group. Ithaca, NY: Snow Lion Publications, 2003.

Kraft, Kenneth, ed. *Zen Teaching, Zen Practice: Philip Kapleau and the Three Pillars of Zen.* New York: Weatherhill, 2000.

Kulananda. *Western Buddhism.* London: HarperCollins, 1997.

Kung, Hans. *On Being a Christian.* New York: Doubleday, 1976.

Lacouture, Jean. *Jesuits: A Multibiography.* Washington, DC: Counterpoint, 1995.

LaFleur, William R. *Liquid Life: Abortion and Buddhism in Japan.* Princeton, NJ: Princeton University Press, 1992.

Lancaster, Lewis R., and C. S. Yu, eds. *Introduction of Buddhism to Korea: New Cultural Patterns.* Berkeley, CA: Asian Humanities Press, 1989.

Lang, David Marshall, trans. *The Balavariani (Barlaam and Josaphat): A Tale from the Christian East Translated from the Old Georgian*. Berkeley: University of California Press, 1966.

Latourette, Kenneth Scott. *A History of Christian Missions in China*. New York: Macmillan, 1929.

Laury, Preston A. *A History of Lutheran Missions*. Reading, PA: Pilger Publishing House, 1899.

Layman, Emma McCloy. *Buddhism in America*. Chicago: Nelson-Hall, 1976.

Leary, Timothy, Ralph Metzner, and Richard Alpert. *The Psychedelic Experience: A Manual Based on the Tibetan Book of the Dead*. New York: Citadel Press, 1992.

Legge, Francis. *Forerunners and Rivals of Christianity: From 330 B.C. to 330 A.D.* 1915. Reprint, New Hyde Park, NY: University Books, 1965.

Leitch, Mary, and Margaret W. Leitch. *Seven Years in Ceylon: Stories of Missionary Life*. New York: American Tract Society, 1890.

Levi, Eliphas. *The History of Magic*. 1913. Reprint, London: Rider, 1986.

Ley, Charles David. *Portuguese Voyages, 1498–1663*. 1947. Reprint, London: Phoenix Press, 2000.

Lillie, Arthur. *India in Primitive Christianity*. London: Kegan Paul, Trench, Trubner, 1909.

Lopez, Donald S., Jr., ed. *Curators of the Buddha: The Study of Buddhism Under Colonialism*. Chicago: University of Chicago Press, 1995.

———. *Prisoners of Shangri-La: Tibetan Buddhism and the West*. Chicago: University of Chicago Press, 1998.

Loving, Jerome. *Walt Whitman: The Song of Himself*. Berkeley: University of California Press, 1999.

Macfie, A. L. [Alexander Lyon]. *Orientalism*. London: Longman, 2002.

Mackenzie, Vicki. *Reborn in the West: The Reincarnation Masters*. New York: Marlowe, 1996.

———. *Reincarnation: The Boy Lama*. Boston: Wisdom Publications, 1988.

———. *Why Buddhism? Westerners in Search of Wisdom*. London: Thorsons, 2003.

Maezumi, Taizan. *Appreciate Your Life*. Edited by Wendy Egyoku Nakao and Eve Myonen Marko. Boston: Shambhala, 2002.

Magee, Bryan. *The Philosophy of Schopenhauer*. Rev. ed. Oxford: Oxford University Press, 1997.

Magnus, Bernd, and Kathleen M. Higgins, eds. *The Cambridge Companion to Nietzsche*. Cambridge: Cambridge University Press, 1996.

Marlow, A. N. "Hinduism and Buddhism in Greek Philosophy." *Philosophy East and West* 4, no. 1 (1954):35–45.

Martin, Malachi. *The Jesuits: The Society of Jesus and the Betrayal of the Roman Catholic Church*. New York: Simon and Schuster, 1987.

Martin, Michelle. *Music in the Sky: The Life, Art and Teachings of the 17th Gyalwa Karmapa Ogyen Trinley Dorje*. Ithaca, NY: Snow Lion Publications, 2003.

Marty, Martin E. *Modern American Religion: The Irony of It All, 1893–1919*. Chicago: University of Chicago Press, 1986.

———. *Righteous Empire: The Protestant Experience in America*. New York: Harper and Row, 1977.

Matarasso, Pauline, ed. and trans. *The Cistercian World: Monastic Writings of the Twelfth Century*. New York: Penguin Books, 1993.

May, Reinhard. *Heidegger's Hidden Sources: East Asian Influences on His Work*. New York: Routledge, 1996.

McCrindle, John W., ed. and trans. *Ancient India as Described in Classical Literature*. London: Westminster, 1901. Reprint, New Delhi: Munshiram Manoharlal Publishers, 1979.

McEvilley, Thomas. "Early Greek Philosophy and Madhyamika." *Philosophy East and West* 31, no. 2 (April 1981):141–64.

McGiffert, Arthur Cushman. *A History of Christian Thought*. 2 vols. New York: Charles Scribner's Sons, 1954.

McKeon, Richard, ed. *The Basic Works of Aristotle*. New York: Random House, 1941.

McWilliams, Vera. *Lafcadio Hearn*. Boston: Houghton Mifflin, 1946.

Mehra, Parshotam. *The Younghusband Expedition: An Interpretation*. Bombay: Asia Publishing House, 1968.

Mehrotra, L. L. [Lakhan Lal], ed. *Science, Spirituality and the Future: A Vision for the Twenty-first Century, Essays in Honour of His Holiness the Fourteenth Dalai Lama, Tenzin Gyatso*. New Delhi: Mudrit, 1999.

Melville, Herman. *Selected Poems of Herman Melville*. Edited by Hennig Cohen. New York: Doubleday Anchor, 1964.

Menzies, Allan. *History of Religion: A Sketch of Primitive Religious Beliefs and Practices, and of the Origin and Character of the Great Systems*. Rev. ed. New York: Charles Scribner's Sons, 1909.

Merkur, Dan. *Gnosis: An Esoteric Tradition of Mystical Visions and Unions*. Albany: State University of New York Press, 1993.

Merton, Thomas. *The Asian Journal of Thomas Merton*. New York: New Directions, 1975.

———. *Mystics and Zen Masters*. New York: Farrar, Straus and Giroux, 2000.

———. *The Nonviolent Alternative*. New York: Farrar, Straus and Giroux, 1980.

———. *The School of Charity: The Letters of Thomas Merton on Religious Renewal and Spiritual Direction*. Edited by Brother Patrick Hart. New York: Farrar, Straus and Giroux, 1990.

———. *The Seven Storey Mountain*. New York: Harcourt Brace Jovanovich, 1976.

———. *Thoughts on the East*. New York: New Directions, 1995.

———. *Zen and the Birds of Appetite*. New York: New Directions, 1968.

Meyer, Karl, and Shareen Brysac. *Tournament of Shadows: The Great Game and the Race for Empire in Asia*. London: Abacus, 1999.

Mills, Edmund J. "The Buddhism in Heraclitus." *Buddhist Review* 11:1 (1910):269–79.

Mirsky, Jeannette. *Sir Aurel Stein: Archaeological Explorer*. Chicago: University of Chicago Press, 1977.

Mitchell, Donald W., ed. *Masao Abe: A Zen Life of Dialogue*. Boston: Charles E. Tuttle, 1998.

Mitchell, Donald W., and James Wiseman, eds. *The Gethsemani Encounter*. New York: Continuum, 1997.

Moffett, Samuel Hugh. *A History of Christianity in Asia*. Vol. 1, *Beginnings to 1500*. Maryknoll, NY: Orbis Books, 1998.

Mojumder, Md. Abu Taher. *Sir William Jones, the Romantics and the Victorians*. Bangladesh: University Press, 1976.

Monier-Williams [Sir Monier]. *Buddhism, in Its Connexion with Brahmanism and Hinduism, and in Its Contrast with Christianity*. London: John Murray, 1890.

Moore, Charles A., ed. *Philosophy — East and West*. Princeton, NJ: Princeton University Press, 1944.

Morgan, David. *The Mongols*. Oxford: Basil Blackwell, 1986.

Morris, Paul W. "*Siddhartha*, Hermann Hesse's Journey to the East," in *Tricycle: The Buddhist Review*, Fall 1999.

Morton, W. Scott. *Japan: Its History and Culture*. 3rd ed. New York: McGraw-Hill, 1994.

Moseley, C. W. R. D., trans. *The Travels of Sir John Mandeville*. Harmondsworth: Penguin Books, 1983.

Mott, Michael. *The Seven Mountains of Thomas Merton*. Boston: Houghton Mifflin, 1984.

Moule, A. C. *Nestorians in China.* London: China Society, 1940.

Mukpo, Diana J., with Carolyn R. Gimian. "My Marriage to Chögyam Trungpa." *Shambhala Sun,* September 2002.

Müller, Friedrich Max. *Auld Lang Syne.* New York: Charles Scribner's Sons, 1898.

———. *Auld Lang Syne (Second Series): My Indian Friends.* New York: Charles Scribner's Sons, 1899.

———. *Chips from a German Workshop.* 5 vols. New York: Charles Scribner's Sons, 1881.

———, trans. *The Dhammapada: A Collection of Verses, Being One of the Canonical Books of the Buddhists.* Sacred Books of the East, vol. 10. 1881. Reprint, London: Oxford University Press, 1924.

Müller, Georgina Max, ed. *The Life and Letters of the Right Honourable Friedrich Max Müller, Edited by His Wife.* 2 vols. London: Longmans, Green, 1902.

Mundanan, A. Mathias. *History of Christianity in India: From the Beginning Up to the Middle of the Sixteenth Century.* Bangalore: Theological Publications in India, 1984.

Mungello, David E. *Leibniz and Confucianism: The Search for Accord.* Honolulu: University of Hawaii Press, 1977.

Murcott, Susan. *The First Buddhist Women: Translations and Commentary on the Therigatha.* Berkeley, CA: Parallax Press, 1991.

Murphey, Rhoads. *East Asia: A New History.* New York: Longman, 1997.

Murray, Alexander, ed. *Sir William Jones, 1746–1794: A Commemoration.* Oxford: Oxford University Press, 1998.

Murray, Paul. *A Fantastic Journey: The Life and Literature of Lafcadio Hearn.* Ann Arbor: University of Michigan Press, 1997.

Murray-Aynsley, H. [Harriet]. *Symbolism of the East and West.* London: George Redway, 1900.

Nagarjuna. *Buddhist Advice for Living and Liberation: Nagarjuna's Precious Garland.* Translated by Jeffrey Hopkins. Ithaca, NY: Snow Lion Publications, 1998.

Nakamura, Hajime. *Buddhism in Comparative Light.* New Delhi: Islam and the Modern Age Society, 1975.

Ñanamoli, Bhikkhu, and Bhikkhu Bodhi, trans. *The Middle Length Discourses of the Buddha: A New Translation of the Majjhima Nikaya.* Boston: Wisdom Publications, 1995.

Narain, A. K. *The Indo-Greeks.* London: Oxford University Press, 1957.

Neill, Stephen. *A History of Christianity in India: The Beginnings to AD 1707.* Cambridge: Cambridge University Press, 1985.

———. *The Pelican History of the Church.* Vol. 6, *A History of Christian Missions.* Harmondsworth: Penguin Books, 1975.

Nhat Hanh, Thich. *Going Home: Jesus and Buddha as Brothers.* New York: Riverhead Books, 1999.

———. *Living Buddha, Living Christ.* New York: Riverhead Books, 1995.

———. *The Miracle of Being Awake.* Kandy, Sri Lanka: Buddhist Publication Society, 1976.

———. *Peace Is Every Step: The Path of Mindfulness in Everyday Life.* New York: Bantam Books, 1991.

———. *Present Moment, Wonderful Moment.* Berkeley, CA: Parallax Press, 1990.

Nicholls, Moira. "The Influences of Eastern Thought on Schopenhauer's Doctrine of the Thing-in-Itself." In *The Cambridge Companion to Schopenhauer,* edited by Christopher Janaway. Cambridge: Cambridge University Press, 1999.

Nietzsche, Friedrich. *The Birth of Tragedy and the Case of Wagner.* Translated by Walter Kaufmann. New York: Vintage Books, 1967.

———. *On the Genealogy of Morals and Ecce Homo.* New York: Vintage Books, 1969.

————. *Twilight of the Idols and The Anti-Christ*. Translated by R. J. Hollingdale. Baltimore: Penguin Books, 1969.

Northrop, F. S. C. *The Meeting of East and West: An Inquiry Concerning World Understanding*. New York: Macmillan, 1946.

Nyanaponika Thera. *The Worn-Out Skin: Contemplations on a Buddhist Poem "The Serpent Smile" Uraga Sutta of the Sutta Nipata*. Kandy, Sri Lanka: Buddhist Publication Society, 1957.

Nyantiloka. *Fundamentals of Buddhism: Four Lectures*. Colombo, Sri Lanka: Baudha Sahitya Sabha, 1956.

Odoric of Pordenone, Blessed. *The Travels of Friar Odoric*. Translated by Sir Henry Yule. Grand Rapids, MI: Eerdmans Publishing, 2002.

Okakura, Kakuzō. *The Book of Tea*. New York: Dover Publications, 1964.

————. *The Ideals of the East with Special Reference to the Art of Japan*. New York: ICG Muse, 2000.

Otto, Beatrice K. *Fools Are Everywhere: The Court Jester Around the World*. Chicago: University of Chicago Press, 2001.

Otto, Rudolf. *The Idea of the Holy*. New York: Oxford University Press, 1958.

————. *Mysticism East and West*. New York: Collier Books, 1962.

Oulton, John Ernest Leonard, and Henry Chadwick, trans. and eds. *Alexandrian Christianity: Selected Translations of Clement and Origen*. Philadelphia: Westminster Press, 1954.

Pagels, Elaine. *The Gnostic Gospels*. New York: Random House, 1979.

Pande, G. C. *Studies in Mahayana*. Sarnath, India: Central Institute of Higher Tibetan Studies, 1993.

Peiris, William. *The Western Contribution to Buddhism*. Delhi: Motilal Banarsidass, 1973.

Plato. *The Collected Dialogues*. Edited by Edith Hamilton and Huntington Cairns. Princeton: Princeton University Press, 1969.

Plotinus. *The Enneads*. Translated by Stephen MacKenna. Burdett, NY: Larson Publications, 1992.

Plutarch. *Lives of the Noble Greeks*. Edited by Edmund Fuller. New York: Dell, 1959.

Podipara, Placid J. *The Hierarchy of the Syro-Malabar Church*. Kerala, India: Prakasam Publications, 1976.

Pollak, Michael. *Mandarins, Jews and Missionaries: The Jewish Experience in the Chinese Empire*. New York: Weatherhill, 1998.

Polo, Marco. *The Travels of Marco Polo*. Edited by Milton Rugoff. New York: New American Library, 1961.

Pothan, S. G. *The Syrian Christians of Kerala*. Bombay: Asia Publishing House, 1963.

Pound, Ezra. *The Cantos*. New York: New Directions, 1971.

Poussin, Louis de la Vallée. *The Way to Nirvana, Six Lectures on Ancient Buddhism as a Discipline of Salvation*. Cambridge: Cambridge University Press, 1917.

Pratt, James B. *The Pilgrimage of Buddhism*. New York: Macmillan, 1928.

Prebish, Charles S. *Luminous Passage: The Practice and Study of Buddhism in America*. Berkeley: University of California Press, 1999.

Prebish, Charles S., with Martin Baumann, eds. *Westward Dharma: Buddhism Beyond Asia*. Berkeley: University of California Press, 2002.

Prebish, Charles S., with Kenneth K. Tanaka, eds. *The Faces of Buddhism in America*. Berkeley: University of California Press, 1998.

Prothero, Stephen. *The White Buddhist: The Asian Odyssey of Henry Steel Olcott*. Bloomington: Indiana University Press, 1996.

Pyle, Kenneth B. *The New Generation in Meiji Japan: Problems of Cultural Identity, 1885–1895.* Palo Alto, CA: Stanford University Press, 1969.

Queen, Christopher, ed. *Engaged Buddhism in the West.* Boston: Wisdom Publications, 2000.

Quinton, Anthony. *Hume.* New York: Routledge, 1999.

Radhakrishnan, S. [Sarvepalli]. *Eastern Religions and Western Thought.* 2nd ed. London: Oxford University Press, 1940.

Raju, P. T. *Idealistic Thought of India.* Cambridge: Harvard University Press, 1953.

Rampa, T. [Tuesday] Lobsang. *Doctor from Lhasa.* New York: Bantam, 1968.

———. *My Visit to Venus.* New Brunswick, NJ: Inner Light Publications, 1988.

———. *The Rampa Story.* New York: Bantam, 1968.

———. *The Third Eye.* London: Corgi Books, 1959.

———. *Wisdom of the Ancients.* New York: Award Books, 1970.

Rapaport, Al, comp. *Buddhism in America: Proceedings of the First Buddhism in America Conference.* Rutland, VT: Charles E. Tuttle, 1998.

Red Pine, trans. *The Zen Teaching of Bodhidharma.* San Francisco: North Point Press, 1989.

Ree, Jonathan. *Heidegger.* New York: Routledge, 1999.

Reichelt, Karl Ludvig. *Truth and Tradition in Chinese Buddhism: A Study of Chinese Mahayana Buddhism.* Shanghai: Commercial Press, 1927.

Reps, Paul, comp. *Zen Flesh, Zen Bones: A Collection of Zen and Pre-Zen Writings.* New York: Doubleday Anchor, 1961.

Revel, Jean-François, and Matthieu Ricard. *The Monk and the Philosopher: A Father and Son Discuss the Meaning of Life.* New York: Schocken Books, 1998.

Rhys Davids, Caroline A. F., ed. *Stories of the Buddha: Being Selections from the Jataka.* New York: Frederick A. Stokes, n.d.

Rhys Davids, T. W. [Thomas William]. *Lectures on the Origin and Growth of Religion as Illustrated by Some Points in the History of Indian Buddhism.* New York: G. P. Putnam's Sons, 1882.

Ricard, Matthieu, and Trinh Xuan Thuan. *The Quantum and the Lotus: A Journey to the Frontiers Where Science and Buddhism Meet.* New York: Crown, 2001.

Richardson, E. Allen. *East Comes West: Asian Religions and Cultures in North America.* New York: Pilgrim Press, 1985.

Robinson, James M., ed. *The Nag Hammadi Library in English.* Rev. ed. New York: Harper and Row, 1988.

Rooney, John M. H. M., ed. *St. Thomas and Taxila: A Symposium on St. Thomas.* Rawalpindi, Pakistan: Christian Study Centre, 1988.

Rowbotham, Arnold H. *Missionary and Mandarin: The Jesuits at the Court of China.* New York: Russell and Russell, 1966.

Rowland, Benjamin. *Art in Afghanistan: Objects from the Kabul Museum.* London: Allen Lane/Penguin Press, 1971.

Rudolph, Kurt. *Gnosis: The Nature and History of Gnosticism.* New York: Harper and Row, 1987.

Runciman, Steven. *The Medieval Manichee: A Study of the Christian Dualist Heresy.* New York: Viking Press, 1961.

Russell, Bertrand. *A History of Western Philosophy.* New York: Simon and Schuster, 1972.

———. *Selected Papers of Bertrand Russell.* New York: Modern Library, 1927.

———. *Why I Am Not a Christian, and Other Essays on Religion and Related Subjects.* New York: Simon and Schuster, 1964.

Said, Edward W. *Orientalism.* New York: Vintage Books, 1994.

Saint-Hilaire, Jules Barthélemy. *The Buddha and His Religion*. Varanasi, India: Bhartiya Publishing House, 1974.

Salomon, Richard. *Ancient Buddhist Scrolls from Gandhara: The British Library Karosthi Fragments*. Seattle: University of Washington Press, 1999.

Sanceau, Elaine. *The Land of Prester John: A Chronicle of Portuguese Exploration*. New York: Alfred A. Knopf, 1944.

Sangharakshita. *In the Sign of the Golden Wheel: Indian Memoirs of an English Buddhist*. Birmingham, Eng.: Windhorse Publications, 1996.

———. *The Rainbow Road: From Tooting Broadway to Kalimpong, Memoirs of an English Buddhist*. Birmingham, Eng.: Windhorse Publications, 1997.

Sansom, G. B. *The Western World and Japan: A Study in the Interaction of European and Asiatic Cultures*. Tokyo: Charles E. Tuttle, 1977.

Saunders, E. Dale. *Buddhism in Japan: With an Outline of Its Origins in India*. Tokyo: Charles E. Tuttle, 1972.

Schalow, Paul Gordon. "Kukai and the Tradition of Male Love in Japanese Buddhism." In *Buddhism, Sexuality, and Gender,* edited by José Ignacio Cabezon. Albany: State University of New York Press, 1992.

Schirokauer, Conrad. *A Brief History of Japanese Civilization*. New York: Harcourt Brace Jovanovich, 1993.

Schlipp, Paul Arthur, ed. *The Philosophy of Sarvepalli Radhakrishnan*. New York: Tudor Publishing, 1952.

Schneider, David. *Street Zen: The Life and Work of Issan Dorsey*. New York: Marlowe, 2000.

Schopenhauer, Arthur. *The Essays of Arthur Schopenhauer*. New York: Willey Book, n.d.

———. *On the Fourfold Root of the Principle of Sufficient Reason*. La Salle, IL: Open Court, 1997.

———. *The World as Will and Representation*. 2 vols. New York: Dover Publications, 1969.

Schumacher, E. F. *A Guide for the Perplexed*. New York: Harper and Row, 1978.

———. *Small Is Beautiful: A Study of Economics as if People Mattered*. New York: Harper and Row, 1973.

Schumacher, Michael. *Dharma Lion: A Biography of Allen Ginsberg*. New York: St. Martin's Press, 1994.

Schurhammer, Georg. *Francis Xavier: His Life and Times*. 4 vols. Rome: Jesuit Historical Institute, 1973, 1977, 1980, 1982.

Schwab, Raymond. *The Oriental Renaissance: Europe's Rediscovery of India and the East, 1680–1880*. New York: Columbia University Press, 1984.

Seager, Richard Hughes. *Buddhism in America*. New York: Columbia University Press, 1999.

Sen, Amulyachandra. *Asoka's Edicts*. Calcutta: Institute of Indology, 1956.

Senzaki, Nyogen. *Like a Dream, Like a Fantasy: The Zen Writings and Translations of Nyogen Senzaki*. Edited by Eido Shimano Roshi. San Francisco: Japan Publications, 1978.

Serrano, Miguel. *C. G. Jung and Hermann Hesse: A Record of Two Friendships*. New York: Schocken Books, 1966.

Shakabpa, Tsepon W. D. *Tibet: A Political History*. New Haven, CT: Yale University Press, 1967, 1973.

Shakur, M. A. *Gandhara Sculpture in Pakistan*. Bangkok: South-East Asia Treaty Organization (SEATO), 1963.

Shakya, Tsering. *The Dragon in the Land of Snows: A History of Modern Tibet Since 1947*. New York: Penguin Compass, 2000.

Shantideva. *A Guide to the Bodhisattva's Way of Life*. Translated by Stephen Batchelor. 1979. Reprint, Dharamsala: Library of Tibetan Works and Archives, 1992.

Sharan, Ishwar. *The Myth of St. Thomas and the Mylapore Shiva Temple*. 2nd rev. ed. New Delhi: Voice of India, 1995.

Sidor, Ellen S. *A Gathering of Spirit: Women Teaching in American Buddhism*. Cumberland, RI: Primary Point Press, 1987.

Simmer-Brown, Judith. *Dakini's Warm Breath: The Feminine Principle in Tibetan Buddhism*. Boston: Shambhala, 2001.

Singh, Sanghasen, ed. *Sarvastivada and Its Traditions*. Delhi: Dept. of Buddhist Studies, Delhi University, 1994.

Singh, Rev. Shree N. [Khyentse Trulku]. *Buddhism and Christianity — A Comparative Study and Other Selected Essays*. Delhi: Dr. Ambedkar Bodhi Kunja Foundation, 1995.

Sinnett, A. P. [Alfred Percy]. *Esoteric Buddhism*. 8th rev. ed. London: Theosophical Publishing Society, 1903.

Sir William Jones, Bicentenary of His Birth: Commemoration Volume, 1746–1946. Calcutta: Royal Asiatic Society of Bengal, 1948. Anonymously edited anthology of pieces, by an international range of writers, on Jones and India.

Sivaraksa, Sulak, ed. *Buddhist Perception for Desirable Societies in the Future: Papers Prepared for the United Nations University*. Bangkok: Thai Inter-Religious Commission for Development, 1993.

Smith, Bradwell L., ed. *Religion and Legitimation of Power in Sri Lanka*. Chambersburg, PA: Anima Books, 1978.

Snyder, Gary. *Earth House Hold: Technical Notes and Queries to Fellow Dharma Revolutionaries*. New York: New Directions, 1969.

———. "Highest and Driest for Philip Whalen's Poetic Drama/Dharma." *Shambhala Sun*, November 2002.

———. *Mountains and Rivers Without End*. Washington, DC: Counterpoint, 1996.

———. *Myths and Texts*. New York: Corinth Books, 1960.

———. *Passage Through India*. San Francisco: Grey Fox Press, 1992.

———. *The Real Work: Interviews and Talks, 1964–1979*. New York: New Directions, 1980.

———. *Riprap, and Cold Mountain Poems*. San Francisco: Four Seasons Foundation, 1977.

Sōen, Nakagawa. *Endless Vow: The Zen Path of Sōen Nakagawa*. Edited by Eido Tai Shimano. Boston: Shambhala, 1996.

Sokei-an [Sasaki Shigetsu]. *Holding the Lotus to the Rock: The Autobiography of Sokei-an, America's First Zen Master*. Edited by Michael Hotz. New York: Four Walls Eight Windows, 2002.

Soyen [Sōen], Shaku. *Zen for Americans*. Translated by D. T. Suzuki. Reissue title; original title *Sermons of a Buddhist Abbot*. New York: Barnes and Noble, 1993.

Spence, Jonathan D. *The Chan's Great Continent: China in Western Minds*. New York: W. W. Norton, 1998.

———. *Emperor of China: Self-Portrait of K'ang-hsi*. New York: Random House, 1975.

———. *The Gate of Heavenly Peace: The Chinese and Their Revolution, 1895–1980*. New York: Penguin Books, 1983.

———. *The Memory Palace of Matteo Ricci*. New York: Viking, 1984.

Spence Hardy, (Rev.) R. [Robert]. *The Legends and Theories of the Buddhists, Compared with History and Science*. London: Williams and Norgate, 1866.

———. *A Manual of Buddhism in Its Modern Development*. 2nd ed. 1857. Reprint, London: Williams and Norgate, 1880.

Spengler, Oswald. *The Decline of the West*. New York: Knopf, 1926.

Steinmetz, Andrew. *History of the Jesuits: From the Foundation of Their Society to Its Suppression by Pope Clement XIV; Their Missions Throughout the World; Their Educational System and Literature; with Their Revival and Present State*. 3 vols. London: Richard Bentley, 1848.

Stevens, John. *Lust for Enlightenment: Buddhism and Sex*. Boston: Shambhala, 1990.

Stevenson, Elizabeth. *Lafcadio Hearn*. New York: Macmillan, 1961.

Subhuti. *Bringing Buddhism to the West: A Life of Sangharakshita*. Birmingham, Eng.: Windhorse Publications, 1995.

———. *Women, Men, and Angels*. Birmingham, Eng.: Windhorse Publications, 1995.

Suiter, John. *Poets on the Peaks: Gary Snyder, Philip Whalen and Jack Kerouac in the North Cascades*. Washington, DC: Counterpoint, 2002.

Suzuki, Beatrice Lane. *Mahayana Buddhism*. London: David Marlowe, 1948.

Suzuki, D. T. [Daisetz Teitaro]. *Buddha of Infinite Light*. Boston: Shambhala, 1997.

———. *Essays in Zen Buddhism (First Series)*. New York: Grove Press, 1961.

———. *Essays in Zen Buddhism (Second Series)*. New York: Weiser, 1976.

———. *Essays in Zen Buddhism (Third Series)*. London: Rider, 1953.

———. *The Field of Zen*. New York: Harper and Row, 1970.

———. *An Introduction to Zen Buddhism, Including "A Manual of Zen Buddhism."* New York: Causeway Books, 1974.

———, trans. *The Lankavatara Sutra: A Mahayana Text*. Taipei: SMC Publishing, 1991.

———. *Mysticism: Christian and Buddhist*. New York: Harper and Brothers, 1957.

———. *On Indian Mahayana Buddhism*. Edited by Edward Conze. New York: Harper and Row, 1968.

———. "Zen: A Reply to Hu Shih." *Philosophy East and West*, vol. 3, no. 1 (1953):25–46.

———. *Zen and Japanese Culture*. Princeton, NJ: Princeton University Press, 1965.

———. *Zen Buddhism: Selected Writings of D. T. Suzuki*. Edited by William Barrett. New York: Doubleday Anchor, 1956.

———. *The Zen Doctrine of No Mind*. Edited by Christmas Humphreys. New York: Samuel Weiser, 1973.

Suzuki, D. T., with Erich Fromm and Richard De Martino. *Zen Buddhism and Psychoanalysis*. New York: Harper and Brothers, 1960.

Suzuki, Shunryu. *Branching Streams Flow in the Darkness: Zen Talks on the Sandokai*. Berkeley: University of California, 1999.

———. *Zen Mind, Beginner's Mind*. Edited by Trudy Dixon. New York: Weatherhill, 1973.

Tachibana, Shundo. *Ethics of Buddhism*. Richmond, Eng.: Curzon Books, 1994.

Tadgell, Christopher. *The History of Architecture in India*. London: Phaidon Press, 1994.

Takeuchi, Yoshinori. *The Heart of Buddhism*. New York: Crossroad, 1983.

Tambiah, Stanley Jeyaraja. *Buddhism Betrayed? Religion, Politics, and Violence in Sri Lanka*. Chicago: University of Chicago Press, 1992.

Tanahashi, Kazuaki. *Enlightenment Unfolds: The Essential Teachings of Zen Master Dogen*. Boston: Shambhala, 1999.

Tanaka, Kenneth K. *The Dawn of Chinese Pure Land Buddhist Doctrine: Ching-ying Hui-yuan's Commentary on the Visualization Sutra*. Albany: State University of New York Press, 1990.

Tanner, Michael. *Schopenhauer*. New York: Routledge, 1999.

Tarn, W. W. *The Greeks in Bactria and India*. Cambridge: Cambridge University Press, 1951.

Teller, Walter, ed. *Walt Whitman's Camden Conversations*. New Brunswick, NJ: Rutgers University Press, 1973.

Tendzin, Ösel [born Thomas Rich]. *Buddha in the Palm of Your Hand*. Boston: Shambhala, 1982.

Tenzin Gyatso [His Holiness the Fourteenth Dalai Lama]. *Aryasura's Aspiration and a Meditation on Compassion by His Holiness the XIV Dalai Lama*. Dharamsala: Library of Tibetan Works and Archives, 1981.

———. *Concerning the Kalachakra Initiation in America*. Madison, WI: Deer Park, 1981.

———. "The Controversial Dalai Lama." *Shambhala Sun,* March 1999.

———. *The Dalai Lama at Harvard: Lectures on the Buddhist Path to Peace*. Edited by Jeffrey Hopkins. Ithaca, NY: Snow Lion Publications, 1988.

———. "The Dalai Lama on China, Hatred, and Optimism." *Mother Jones,* November/December 1997.

———. *Ethics for the New Millennium*. New York: Riverhead Books, 1999.

———. *Freedom in Exile: The Autobiography of the Dalai Lama*. New York: Harper Perennial, 1991.

———. "Global View: A Conversation with the Dalai Lama." *Tricycle: The Buddhist Review,* Fall 1995.

———. *The Kalachakra Tantra: Rite of Initiation for the Stage of Generation*. Edited by Jeffrey Hopkins. London: Wisdom Publications, 1985.

———. *The Opening of the Wisdom-Eye and the History of the Advancement of Buddhadharma in Tibet*. Wheaton, IL: Quest Books, 1991.

Tenzin Gyatso et al. *Consciousness at the Crossroads: Conversations with the Dalai Lama on Brain Science and Buddhism*. Edited by Zara Houshmand, Robert B. Livingston, and B. Alan Wallace. Ithaca, NY: Snow Lion Publications, 1999.

———. *MindScience: An East-West Dialogue*. Edited by Daniel Goleman and Robert A. F. Thurman. Boston: Wisdom Publications, 1993.

Thapar, Romila. *Asoka and the Decline of the Mauryas*. Rev. ed. Delhi: Oxford University Press, 1997.

Thenayan, Paul. *The Missionary Consciousness of the St. Thomas Christians*. Cochin, India: Viani Publications, 1982.

Thera, Piyadassi. *Buddhism — A Living Message*. Kandy, Sri Lanka: Buddhist Publication Society, 1980.

Thoburn, (Bishop) J. M. *The Christless Nations*. New York: Hunt and Eaton, 1895.

Thomas, Edward J. *The History of Buddhist Thought*. 2nd ed. 1959. Reprint, Mineola, NY: Dover Publications, 2002.

Thomas, Owen C., ed. *Attitudes Toward Other Religions: Some Christian Interpretations*. New York: Harper and Row, 1969.

Thomas, Winburn T. *Protestant Beginnings in Japan: The First Three Decades, 1859–1889*. Rutland, VT: Charles E. Tuttle, 1959.

Thomson, (Bishop) Edward. *Our Oriental Missions*. 2 vols. Cincinnati: Hitchcock and Walden, 1871.

Thomson, James C., Peter W. Stanley, and John Curtis Perry. *Sentimental Imperialists: The American Experience in East Asia*. New York: Harper and Row, 1981.

Thondup, Tulku. *Buddhist Civilization in Tibet*. United States: Maha Siddha Nyingmapa Center, 1982.

Thoreau, Henry David. *Early Essays and Miscellanies*. Princeton, NJ: Princeton University Press, 1975.

———. *The Journal of Henry David Thoreau*. Edited by Bradford Torrey and Francis H. Allen. 2 vols. New York: Dover Publications, 1962.

———. *Walden; or, Life in the Woods*. New York: New American Library, 1949.

———. *A Week on the Concord and Merrimack Rivers*. London: M. Dent and Sons, 1932.

Thurman, Robert A. F. *The Tibetan Book of the Dead: The Great Book of Natural Liberation Through Understanding in the Between*. New York: Bantam Books, 1994.

Tolan, John V. *Saracens: Islam in the Medieval European Imagination*. New York: Columbia University Press, 2002.

Tolstoy, Leo. *"On Life" and Essays on Religion*. London: Oxford University Press, 1959.

———. *Recollections and Essays*. London: Oxford University Press, 1952.

Toms, Michael, ed. *Buddhism in the West: Spiritual Wisdom for the 21st Century*. Carlsbad, CA: Hay House, 1998.

Traubel, Horace, Richard Maurice Bucke, and Thomas B. Harned, eds. *In Re Walt Whitman: Edited by His Literary Executors*. Folcroft, PA: Folcroft Library Editions, 1973.

Trungpa, Chögyam. *Born in Tibet*. 4th ed. Boston: Shambhala, 2000.

———. *Crazy Wisdom*. Boston: Shambhala, 2001.

———. *Cutting Through Spiritual Materialism*. Boulder, CO: Shambhala, 1973.

———, ed. *Garuda IV*. Berkeley, CA: Shambhala, 1976.

———. *Great Eastern Sun: The Wisdom of Shambhala*. Edited by Carolyn Rose Gimian. Boston: Shambhala, 1999.

———. *Mudra*. Boston: Shambhala, 1987.

———. *Shambhala: The Sacred Path of the Warrior*. Edited by Carolyn Rose Gimian. New York: Bantam Books, 1986.

Trungpa, Chögyam, with Francesca Fremantle, trans. *The Tibetan Book of the Dead: The Great Liberation Through Hearing in the Bardo*. Berkeley, CA: Shambhala, 1975.

Trungpa, Chögyam, with Herbert V. Guenther. *The Dawn of Tantra*. Boston: Shambhala, 2001.

Tsomo, Karma Lekshe, ed. *Sakyadhita: Daughters of the Buddha*. Ithaca, NY: Snow Lion Publications, 1988.

Tucci, Giuseppe. *The Religions of Tibet*. Berkeley: University of California Press, 1988.

———. *Tibetan Painted Scrolls*. Rome: La Liberia Dello Strato, 1949.

Tuck, Andrew P. *Comparative Philosophy and the Philosophy of Scholarship: On the Western Interpretation of Nagarjuna*. New York: Oxford University Press, 1990.

Tulku, Tarthang. *Mind over Matter: Reflections on Buddhism in the West*. Berkeley, CA: Dharma Publishing, 2002.

Tweed, Thomas A. *The American Encounter with Buddhism, 1844–1912: Victorian Culture and the Limits of Dissent*. Chapel Hill: University of North Carolina Press, 2000.

Tworkov, Helen. *Zen in America: Profiles of Five Teachers*. San Francisco: North Point Press, 1989.

U Chan Htoon. *Buddhism and the Age of Science*. Kandy, Sri Lanka: Buddhist Publication Society, 1967.

Uhalley, Stephen, Jr., and Xiaoxin Wu, eds. *China and Christianity: Burdened Past, Hopeful Future*. London: M. E. Sharpe, 2001.

Vadakkekara, Benedict. *Origin of India's St. Thomas Christians*. Delhi: Media House, 1995.

Varela, Francisco J., ed. *Sleeping, Dreaming, and Dying: An Exploration of Consciousness with the Dalai Lama*. Boston: Wisdom Publications, 1997.

Varg, Paul A. *Missionaries, Chinese, and Diplomats: The American Protestant Missionary Movement in China, 1890–1952*. Princeton, NJ: Princeton University Press, 1958.

Vassiliades, Demetrios Th. *The Greeks in India: A Survey in Philosophical Understanding*. New Delhi: Munshiram Manoharlal Publishers, 2000.

Victoria, Brian. *Zen at War*. New York: Weatherhill, 1997.

Victoria, Brian, with Robert Aitken, Bernie Glassman, Bodhin Kjolhede, and Lawrence Shainberg. "Yasutani Roshi: The Hardest Koan." *Tricycle: The Buddhist Review*, Fall 1999.

Voltaire. *Candide, Zadig, and Selected Stories.* Translated by Donald M. Frame. New York: New American Library, 1961.

———. *Philosophical Dictionary.* Translated by Theodore Besterman. Harmondsworth: Penguin Books, 1983.

Waddell, L. [Laurence] Austine. *Lhasa and Its Mysteries: With a Record of the Expedition of 1903–1904.* London: Methuen, 1929.

———. *Tibetan Buddhism.* New York: Dover Books, 1972. Reprint of *The Buddhism of Tibet, or Lamaism.* London: W. H. Allen, 1895.

Walshe, Maurice, trans. *The Long Discourses of the Buddha: A Translation of the Digha Nikaya.* Boston: Wisdom Publications, 1995.

Watts, Alan. *Behold the Spirit.* New York: Pantheon, 1955.

———. *Beyond Theology: The Art of Godmanship.* New York: Pantheon, 1964.

———. *The Early Writings of Alan Watts.* Edited by John Snelling, Mark Watts, and Dennis Sibley. Berkeley, CA: Celestial Arts, 1987.

———. *In My Own Way: An Autobiography, 1915–1965.* New York: Pantheon, 1972.

———. *The Joyous Cosmology.* New York: Pantheon, 1962.

———. *Myth and Ritual in Christianity.* New York: Grove Press, 1960.

———. *Psychotherapy East and West.* New York: Ballantine, 1974.

———. *The Spirit of Zen.* New York: Grove Press, 1980.

———. *This Is It, and Other Essays on Zen and Spiritual Experience.* New York: Collier Books, 1970.

———. *The Way of Zen.* New York: Mentor Books, 1964.

Weber, Max. *The Religion of India.* New York: Free Press, 1968.

Weber, Renee. *Dialogues with Scientists and Sages: The Search for Unity.* London: Routledge and Kegan Paul, 1986.

Welch, Lew. *Ring of Bone: Collected Poems, 1950–1971.* Bolinas, CA: Grey Fox Press, 1973.

Weldon, David and Jane Casey Singer. *The Sculptural Heritage of Tibet.* London: Laurence King and Weatherhill, 1999.

Westgeest, Helen. *Zen in the Fifties: Interaction in Art Between East and West.* Zwolle, Netherlands: Waanders Publishers, 1996.

Whalen, Philip. *On Bear's Head.* New York: Harcourt, Brace and World and Coyote, 1969.

———. *Overtime: Selected Poems.* New York: Penguin, 1999.

———. "Poems and Zen Talks of Philip Whalen." *Shambhala Sun,* November 2002.

———. *Scenes of Life at the Capital.* Bolinas, CA: Grey Fox Press, 1971.

White unto Harvest in China: A Survey of the Lutheran United Mission, the China Mission of the N.L.C.A., 1890–1934, Written by the Missionaries. Minneapolis: Board of Foreign Missions, 1934.

Whitman, Walt. *Leaves of Grass, and Selected Prose.* New York: Holt, Rinehart and Winston, 1966.

Whitmyer, Claude, ed. *Mindfulness and Meaningful Works: Explorations in Right Livelihood.* Berkeley, CA: Parallax Press, 1994.

Wickramasinghe, Martin. *Buddhism and Art.* Colombo, Sri Lanka: Gunasena, 1971.

Williams, Angel Kyodo. *Being Black: Zen and the Art of Living with Fearlessness and Grace.* New York: Viking Compass, 2000.

Willis, Janice. *Dreaming Me: An African American Woman's Spiritual Journey.* New York: Riverhead Books, 2001.

———, trans. *On Knowing Reality: The Tattvartha Chapter of Asanga's Bodhisattvabhumi.* New York: Columbia University Press, 1979.

Wilson, Colin, ed. *Men of Mystery: A Celebration of the Occult*. London: Star Books, 1977.

Winkler, Ken. *Pilgrim of the Clear Light: The Biography of Dr. Walter Y. Evans-Wentz*. Berkeley, CA: Dawnfire Books, 1982.

———. *A Thousand Journeys: The Biography of Lama Anagarika Govinda*. Longmead, Eng.: Element Books, 1990.

Wise, Michael, Martin Abegg Jr., and Edward Cook. *The Dead Sea Scrolls: A New Translation*. New York: HarperCollins, 1996.

Wittgenstein, Ludwig. *Tractatus Logico-Philosophicus*. 1922. Reprint, New York: Routledge, 1922.

Wolin, Richard, ed. *The Heidegger Controversy: A Critical Reader*. Cambridge, MA: MIT Press, 1993.

Wollheim, Richard. *Sigmund Freud*. Cambridge: Cambridge University Press, 1990.

Woodcock, George. *The Greeks in India*. London: Faber and Faber, 1966.

Wriggins, Sally Hovey. *Xuanzang: A Buddhist Pilgrim on the Silk Road*. Boulder, CO: Westview Press, 1996.

Wright, Arthur F. *Buddhism in Chinese History*. Palo Alto, CA: Stanford University Press, 1959.

Yamasaki, Taiko. *Shingon: Japanese Esoteric Buddhism*. Boston: Shambhala, 1988.

Yokoi, Yuho with Daizen Victoria. *Zen Master Dogen: An Introduction with Selected Writings*. New York: Weatherhill, 1976.

Yongden, Lama. *Mipam, a Tibetan Novel*. San Francisco: Mudra, 1971.

Younghusband, Sir Francis. *India and Tibet: A History of the Relations Between the Two Countries from the Time of Warren Hastings to 1910; with a Particular Account of the Mission to Lhasa of 1904*. London: John Murray, 1910.

Zimmer, Heinrich. *Philosophies of India*. Edited by Joseph Campbell. 1951. Reprint, Princeton, NJ: Princeton University Press, 1971.

INDEX

❖